T0354712

The Black Maze

Charlotte Roberts

authorHOUSE®

AuthorHouse™
1663 Liberty Drive
Bloomington, IN 47403
www.authorhouse.com
Phone: 1 (800) 839-8640

Published by AuthorHouse 09/14/2017

ISBN: 978-1-5462-0808-2 (sc)
ISBN: 978-1-5462-0807-5 (e)

Print information available on the last page.

In loving memory of

Amy Fleming & April Stayner

We were not ready to lose you,
but God needed His angels.

Foreword

Though this forward is short and may seem a little dry, it is to provide a touch of background before the story begins. Keep in mind, I know God would never have put me through all of the terrible things in my life for no reason; I whole-heartedly believe my experiences, no matter how appalling, were lessons. My past is riddled with experiences I have worked hard to understand and share, so others may be guided through their own black mazes instead of being forced to face the challenge alone, as I did. Please keep in mind that some of the content of this book is not for the faint of heart and you may find yourself, at times, struggling to continue reading. Parents, if you allow your children to read this book they will be exposed to adult language as well as content and situations.

If I knew then, even half of what I know now, it seems I would have been better prepared to deal with life in general. A lot of alcohol, a little bit of pot, and a habit of smoking cigarettes, that began by the age of 12, seemed to define me. School was dreadful, friends were very few, and family seemed to be an active jury with no room to judge. Life may have been a great deal better had I been born to another family, but looking back now, I am glad for it all – for without my past I would not have become the person I am today.

Some people talk about their first memories and many

times, those memories are happy. In my case, however, one of my first memories was traumatic and involved being bitten by a dog that was half wolf. Apparently, my mother thought such an animal was appropriate to have in the house while raising a small child. It may not have been as bad, had some sort of attention been paid to the child, or even to the dog. Very little time was spent by my mother watching anything other than a beer can, an ashtray, and the various men who visited her regularly. In the years that followed that first memory, very few were happy. I remember having a pet raccoon in the house that I would play with for hours. Again, not exactly an intelligent pet choice since she was a wild animal, but I do not recall a hostile moment between the two of us. The last time I saw her, she was held up in the top of a tree, fighting with another raccoon. I'm not sure which animal championed over the other, but with her large size, I can at least imagine she survived to live a long life in the wild.

As a "white trash" family, options were few, and the acceptance of that made life seem a little easier for all of us. My brother and two sisters appeared to accept it as well, and went about their daily lives with the appearance of ease. Little did I know, they had already experienced some of the situations I would soon face, and many others of which I would not be aware for many years.

Examples of how bad it was could go on for countless pages, but highlighting a variety of the more prominent events, will compel my story just as well. If something happened once, it probably happened a hundred times. I hope, as you accompany me through my journey, you will be able to take something from it and apply it to your own life. If my story helps even one person through their own black maze, it will have all been worth it.

Please, read on.

Special Thanks To:

Patricia Halvorson

April Stayner

Monica True

Chapter One

$\mathcal{A}$va was a girl who many said would not amount to anything. She was born to Sonya, an alcoholic, drug-addicted individual, from a large family. Ava's father, Lars, was also an alcoholic and addicted to drugs. Before Ava turned eight months old, Lars left, never to return. Sonya already had three other children with another man, Simon, whom she had divorced before meeting Lars. The three other children, Lilli, Niles, and Emma, lived with Sonya and Lars as a family until he left shortly after Ava's birth.

Sonya had suffered from an illness in infancy that had not only threatened her life but left her mental processes unable to function normally. To complicate the situation further, her parents and siblings could not bring themselves to share the situation with others and seek help for her. It was likely, however, that even if the situation had been revealed and help was sought, treatment would not have been available due to the family's low income as well as the lack of medical knowledge of her condition. Ultimately, when there are so many children in a family, it becomes more complicated to pay attention to each child individually; even more so when none of those children were the boy who was always wanted by the father of the family.

Sonya was able to display herself, much of the time, as a

normally functioning individual simply because she did not seem mentally impaired. She quit school as soon as it was legally possible and left home, likely to avoid the rules her father had set for her and her sisters. She developed a drinking problem in her late teens and things got increasingly worse as she added drugs to the equation. After an abusive relationship with her first husband, Simon, Sonya met Lars and continued down the path she had always traveled, their interest in drugs and alcohol seemingly paralleled. She again found herself in an abusive relationship, one that included the abuse of her children, and as she crashed through her substance-ridden life, she also exposed her unborn child to the abuse.

Before Ava's birth in 1977, the events that occurred were all but happy and nurturing. Sonya and Lars' daily alcohol and drug abuse began to take a toll on their relationship and things quickly turned rocky. Lars would physically abuse Sonya and kept her in a submissive state that would not allow any retaliation, though he could never remove her capacity for manipulation. It became a normal occurrence for Sonya to stay locked in the house for days on end so her bruises and other wounds could heal in secrecy. Lilli, Emma, and Niles were also abused, but their injuries were written off as minor accidents and careless child's play.

About a year before Lars left, when Sonya was about four months pregnant with Ava, he convinced Sonya eleven-year-old Lilli was not a virgin and he would be able to determine the truth of the matter if he was allowed to have sex with girl.

Lars shouted, "That little slut isn't a virgin!"

"What are we guna do?" Sonya questioned, knowing it would be something horrible.

"If you hold her down, I'll fuck her and I'll know for sure if she's ever had it before," Lars snarled.

"If ya think that'll work then I'll help ya however I can!" Sonya said, willing to do whatever Lars asked.

Her eagerness to participate was rooted in her fear of the beating she was sure to receive if she did not cooperate, as well as her own twisted sense of reason.

"Maybe I'll just take her for a ride on the bike and while we're gone I'll find a place to nail her. If somethin' happens and I can't get it done, I'll bring her back here so ya can help me. I don't want anybody gettin' in the way!" he exclaimed.

The two continued to drink and construct their abysmal plan. They would force Lilli to go for a ride with Lars the next afternoon. If it turned out the plan was unsuccessful, they would isolate Lilli from the other children and take her to the living room so Lars had plenty of room to do what he felt needed to be done. The night wore on as Lars and Sonya continued to plot the horrible act that would reveal the truth about Lillie's assumed promiscuity. Though the girl had done nothing sexual in her young life, the drug and alcohol saturated thoughts which governed their lives seemed to demand proof of things that were simply formulations of the mind; specifically, the minds of two individuals who had virtually no grasp on reality.

It was October, 1976 and the leaves had only slightly begun to change. The sun still warmed the days and hints of fall were only evident on occasion when the temperature in the early morning hours was a little lower than it had been the day before. The night was warm as the little house Sonya and Lars lived in opened itself to the darkness. Soft light spilled across the grass outside, suggesting a poor but happy home. The house, with its peeling white paint, sagging roof, and overgrown lawn sat on a hard-surfaced country road atop a modest hill. Traffic zoomed by day after day, with no regard to the experiences of those inside the dwelling.

Emma, only six-years-old, was fast asleep in bed as Lilli and Niles hovered over the floor vent in their shared bedroom, directly above the kitchen, listening to a conversation as it took place in the room below them. Niles was only eight and Lilli a mere eleven, but they both knew what was going to happen. The two looked at each other and tears began to roll down Lilli's face as she shook with fear. Niles began to cry as well, knowing there was nothing he could do to stop it. Niles had witnessed, as well as experienced, the brutal beatings his mother and sisters received at the hands of Lars, always fearing if he tried to defend any of them, he would be beaten yet again.

At only eight-years-old, dread was already the dominating state that dwelt within his young mind. So much so that it was able to keep the youngster from trying anything heroic or even sharing information with others. The only stand he could ever muster involved ill-spoken words for which he was repeatedly kicked or beaten with a belt. Lilli was waiting to see what would transpire from the conversation taking place directly below them, between the two people she was forced to depend on. All she wanted to do was run away but the fear paralyzed her. No words were exchanged between Lilli and Niles as they crouched on the dirty, unforgiving floor of the bedroom. The silence between the two children was partially to avoid waking Emma but mostly because neither could find the words to speak. The cruelty of the pending situation, even for an adult, would have created feelings of horror. For the children, especially Lilli, that horror was enmeshed with confusion and anger. She knew there was nothing she could do to defend herself as Lars was too strong and her mother was planning to help. She did all she could to prepare her young mind for the terrible event that would occur, but no amount of preparation would ever be enough.

As the night turned into morning, the soft, warming glow of the sun slowly crept across Lilli's face as she slept on the cool, bare floor next to the vent. She had cried herself to sleep the night before and awoke with a feeling of peace as she realized the sun had come up. Her peaceful feeling ended abruptly as she realized the conversation she had witnessed the night before had actually taken place. She arose to find Emma and Niles already downstairs milling around the kitchen as they searched for breakfast. It was seven o'clock and quiet in the house except for the small noises made by the children. It would be hours before Sonya and Lars would awake due to their drunken state the night before. Lilli found some bread and butter and after pulling the moldy spots from the bread, made toast for the two younger children. She was far too upset to eat as her mind raced through the possible scenarios that may take place that very afternoon. She thought about running away but realized quickly, if she came up missing, Emma and Niles would likely receive the brunt of the anger Lars would surely spew. She did not want to be the reason the other children would be made to feel the pain meant for her. The three of them were like a litter of abandoned kittens; they would fend for themselves but when any of the three were treated badly, the hatred and fear toward the abusers grew inside of all three of them, collectively. Lilli decided to stay and do her best to figure out another way to avoid the motorcycle ride and the premeditated robbery of her innocence.

As the morning progressed into afternoon, all three of them played outside, busying themselves in the innocent ways of children. While Emma played with a fat, black cricket, Lilli did her best not to let her fear show. Niles had seemingly forgotten about the previous night's conversation as he happily chased a plump toad next to the dilapidated, junk-filled garage. Lilli simply sat in the grass, plucking it slowly and letting the blades float from her fingers in the gentle breeze. She seemed to remove herself from her own body as she tried to perfect the only defense mechanism she felt she had. She unconsciously reasoned that, if she could separate herself from the physical experience she would soon face, she may be able to endure the horrific act with little or no recollection.

Early in the afternoon Lars awoke and stepped outside onto the creaky porch. He was about six feet tall, thin, and considered by many, quite handsome. His short, black hair had been disheveled during his alcohol-induced sleep, from which he had just awoke. He was without a shirt or shoes, and his face showed the shadow of a beard that would not be shaved for at least another two days, presumably when he bathed. His faded blue jeans were just as unkempt with rips and holes in various places. Unexplained stains randomly tinted portions of the denim making the jeans seem as unclean as his body. As he stood on the porch gazing across the highway in front of him, he unzipped his pants and began to urinate off the side of the porch into the long grass. A lit cigarette hung carelessly from the side of his mouth. He puffed on it slowly as his eyes adjusted to the light of the afternoon. He looked around the yard and saw Emma and Niles playing. Tentatively looking around for Lilli, he spotted her as she sat alone in the tall grass. As he gazed at her the blue-grey smoke from the cigarette curled around his face. Their eyes met, hers full of fear and his full of lust. At that moment Lilli could feel the scream building in her throat and she was sure the time had come. Lars stood on the edge of the porch for several minutes, his penis hanging limply from his jeans, staring at her. She was paralyzed with fear, unable to move or even blink as she held her breath, unsure whether or not she could endure what was about to happen. Finally, Lars took the last drag from his cigarette and flipped it into the grass as he turned and walked back into the house. Lilli let out a small sigh of relief and looked quickly at Niles and Emma who were both completely unaware of Lars' presence. She slowly arose from the knee-deep grass and made her way cautiously to the side of the house, crouching to avoid detection by those inside.

The window to the living room was open, inviting the fresh breeze to flow through the small house. Lilli stood quietly next to it in order to listen as Lars and Sonya milled around the living room. Sounds of sex began to pierce the peaceful silence of the day as Lars moaned. Lilli covered her ears and squeezed her eyes shut to avoid witnessing any part of the act. After a few minutes, she ventured to find out whether or not Lars and Sonya were finished with the sickening act. The living room was quiet for a few seconds until she heard the unmistakable crack of a beer can and the flick of a lighter.

"Ya make that little bitch go with me today, Sonya," Lars snarled as he attempted to catch his breath.

"I will," Sonya said in a faint, breathless voice as she lay back on the couch with nothing on. "I'll make sure."

Lilli quickly returned to her place in the grass and tried to keep her mind occupied with thoughts of anything other than what might happen, but her efforts were in vein.

Lilli remained sitting soundlessly in the grass as the sun slowly moved across the sky. It was late afternoon and she knew the time was quickly approaching when she would have to accompany Lars on the motorcycle ride. Lars emerged from the house and made his way across the trash-strewn yard, toward the dilapidated motorcycle parked next to the garage. Sonya followed him out the door, stopping on the porch to take a long drink of her beer. She stood, wavering as her bloodshot eyes swept the yard in search of Lilli. As her eyes fell upon the girl, a flood of jealousy and hatred inundated her mind, just as it did every time she looked at the little girl. She hated Lilli and blamed her for all of the problems she and Simon had which lead to their divorce. Convinced Simon was more interested in Lilli from the day she was born, Sonya had vowed to herself she would pay the little girl back, some way, somehow. The day Sonya discovered she was pregnant with Lilli was the day she began to hate her. Sonya felt the little girl had stolen her youth and she had missed out on life because of her birth. She narrowed her eyes and glowered at Lilli.

Sonya's bra straps hung loosely around her thin arms under the vomit-stained tank top that stretched tightly over her swollen belly. She wore no pants; only underwear covered her from the waist down, her legs scraped, cut, and bruised from the many nights of careless drunken behavior and random abuse from Lars. Her long, dark, greasy hair fell over her shoulders, down her back, and had not been washed in days. She took a drag from her cigarette as she prepared to swallow the pills she held in her hand. She couldn't remember where she had gotten them or even what they were; she just wanted the high she was sure they would produce. She slowly put the pills on her tongue, swallowing them with a large gulp of beer as she stared at Lilli. She had only ventured outside to make sure Lars got his way. All at once, the motorcycle roared to life, backfiring and sputtering as Lars swung his leg over the seat.

"Lilli! Get over here! You're goin' with me!" he screamed as he removed the gas cap to make sure the bike had enough fuel for a few miles.

All of Lilli's muscles tightened the instant she heard the motorcycle roar to life. She froze, unable to move. Sonya stood watching as Lars screamed again, "Lilli! Ya li'l bitch, get your fuckin' ass over here now!"

Lilli remained in the grass, unable to do anything. Sonya threw her cigarette down and screamed at her, "Lilli! What the fuck is your problem? Get on that bike! It's not guna kill ya!"

Lilli still didn't move. Sonya angrily stepped off the porch, almost losing her balance, and headed for the little girl. Lilli wanted to run but was simply unable to move. Sonya quickly approached her and reached out menacingly. Grabbing a handful of Lilli's hair, she dragged the girl for a short distance before the child was able to clamor to her feet. Without letting go of Lilli's hair, Sonya forcefully escorted her across the yard to the side of the motorcycle. Lars smiled at Lilli and the gesture invoked nausea in the little girl. Knowing any further delay would result in a brutal beating, Lilli slowly climbed on the back of the motorcycle. Nothing more was said as Lars put the bike in first gear and clumsily started down the driveway.

Without looking to see if any cars were coming, Lars lurched the bike onto the highway, gaining speed quickly. At the first gravel road, he turned the bike sharply, almost losing control. Lilli did her best to keep from touching him but the reckless way he controlled the motorcycle forced her to grab for him in a desperate attempt to avoid being thrown from the torn seat. Lars regained control of the motorcycle, continuing down the gravel road more slowly than Lilli had expected. She knew why he had taken her for a ride and she did all she could to fill her mind so she would not have to think about what was about to happen. Lilli watched as the rocks on the road passed under the bald tires of the motorcycle; she examined the road closely, as if she could see each individual rock. After about a half mile, the motorcycle began to slow and Lilli looked up with a start.

This was it. It was time.

Tears were welling in her eyes as she tried to prepare herself. Just before the bike stopped, their speed began to increase again as a car drove slowly by them. As they continued down the road, Lilli watched the trees pass slowly by. She noticed that even though the day was warm and the trees were still green, a few of them wore yellow leaves on their bows, toward the bottom. She immersed herself in the freedom the landscape suggested, watching the birds fly over her and the grass in the ditches sway lazily in the breeze. The two made their way around a one mile section of farm land and returned to the house. Lilli's young mind was filled with confusion; she couldn't help but feel relief at the uneventfulness of the venture. As they pulled back into the driveway, Emma and Niles looked up from playing in the dirt to see who was coming. The motorcycle came to a stop and Lilli hastily climbed down from the seat, narrowly avoiding contact with the searing hot exhaust. Lars pushed the bike back into its original place, leaning it against the garage wall. Lilli stood motionless in the middle of the muddy driveway, unable to determine how the rape had been averted.

"That was a waste of fuckin' time," Lars hissed at Sonya as he walked toward the house. "Fuckin' worthless. I couldn't find any place to do it that people wouldn't see when they drove by."

"So what now?" Sonya questioned with disappointment.

"Fuck, I don't know, I want a beer," he replied.

Lars flung the screen door open and walked inside. Sonya followed him obediently, letting the wooden door slam shut behind her. Lilli knew, since Lars was unable to find a place during the motorcycle ride, the rape was then to take place in the living room. Lilli made her way to where Niles and Emma were playing and sat down next to them. Emma was completely unaware of the circumstances and Niles said nothing. Lilli decided to remain quiet about the entire thing with the fleeting hope it would all be forgotten somehow. The sun began to sink behind the trees and the three children continued to play. The red-orange sky gave way to the darkness that slowly crept over the land. A few gentle drops of rain began to fall as thunder boomed faintly in the distance.

Emma and Niles made their way to the house and went inside, hoping to find a meal waiting for them. As always, Lars and Sonya were drunk, and had no idea what the children were doing or even where they were. No meal awaited them so the children made their way upstairs to their bedroom. Emma and Niles had already settled into bed when Lilli finally made her way into the house and up the stairs. She crawled into bed with the other children and, as she drifted off to sleep, she was thankful the motorcycle ride had been dull and the rape forgotten, at least for today. The fear and horror that it might still happen, however, remained in her mind for a very long time.

Day after day it was the same thing with Sonya and Lars getting drunk and high, Lilli taking care of Emma and Niles, and none of the children looked after by either adult. The only attention paid to any of the children amounted to beatings and the occasional, attempted sexual intrusions that took place between Lars and the two girls. Though Lars' attempt to rape Lilli had been thwarted by both his inability to find a location to perform the act and the intoxication that had made him forget his intentions, the thought remained in his perverse mind for the rest of the time he spent with the small family. Sonya was close to delivering her baby and she was miserable as the pregnancy wore on. Lars would occasionally attempt sex with her but she repeatedly shut him down. Once again, because of her irresponsible ways, she was going to have yet another baby. The thought disgusted her and her anger toward her children, even the unborn baby, continued to grow. She vowed to herself she would never forgive any of her children for robbing her of her youth and freedom.

Finally, in the spring of 1977 the day arrived for the baby to be born. Lars and Sonya had just arose from sleeping off yet another drunken night. They sat quietly in the unkempt living room, watching television and drinking. It was early afternoon and the day was cold and dreary as a mixture of rain and snow fell from the grey sky. Sonya was already on her third beer when she set her burning cigarette in the ashtray and clumsily struggled to stand up.

"Where the hell ya think you're goin'?" Lars asked as he glared at her in disgust.

"I have to pee," Sonya answered as she gained her footing on the dirty, pea green carpet.

Lars scoffed and shook his head, mumbling a retort under his breath. Sonya walked slowly to the bathroom with her left hand on her belly. Her right hand helped to guide her as she made her way along the filthy, cracked wall to the doorway of the bathroom. As she stepped onto the yellow and green linoleum she felt a rush of warm liquid from between her legs. She stood still, confused about what was taking place; even though she had given birth three times before she had never been coherent enough to recall or consciously experience what actually happens when birth begins. She stepped toward the toilet, removed her soaked underwear and sat down. The liquid continued to flow for a short time and then she started to feel a great deal of pain. She suddenly realized she must be in labor. Without regard for who would be in the living room, she walked back to where Lars sat with nothing covering her from the waist down.

"I'm in labor, Lars," Sonya stated matter-of-factly with no emotion.

"Jesus Christ! I'm tryin' to watch T.V., what the hell do ya want me to do about it?" he sneered.

"Fuck you," she hissed. "You did this to me so get off your ass and take me to the hospital!"

Lars rose quickly from the couch, drew back his hand, and slapped her across the face hard enough for blood to begin trickling from her nose. Sonya retreated and lowered herself into the chair she had been sitting in, picked up her cigarette, and took the last drag from it. She crushed the cigarette out, wiped her face on her bare arm, finished her beer, and then made her way into their bedroom to find some clothes to wear to the hospital. Lars entered the bedroom swiftly and picked up a dirty T-shirt off the floor. As he put the shirt on he mumbled insults and complained about having to leave the house on such a dreary day.

"You're a fuckin' pain in the ass," he cussed at her.

Sonya said nothing and slowly finished dressing herself. She made her way through the dingy, dirty house to the door and stepped outside. Lilli, Niles, and Emma played in the slushy snow as the wintery mix drizzled down upon them.

"Lilli, watch the kids, we're goin' to town," Sonya said without looking at her.

The car sat in the driveway, a medium brown, rusty 1960 Dodge Polara station wagon with bald tires. As Sonya opened the passenger door rust fell to the ground and the hinges let out a tired creak. She got into the car and reached for the door handle to pull it shut. Lars had approached the car without Sonya noticing. As he walked around the front of the car Niles stood watching. Lars went out of his way to walk next to the little boy so he could kick him.

"You're fuckin' worthless you little piece of shit," Lars said with a growl.

Niles fell to the ground with his hands on the small of his back in the place where Lars' boot had made contact. He said nothing as tears slowly crept down his dirty, red cheeks.

"Where are ya goin'?" Emma squeaked.

"None of your fuckin' business ya little fuck," Lars screamed as he jerked the door of the station wagon open.

Lars plopped into the car and slammed the door. After two failed attempts the engine finally roared to life. Lars slammed the car in reverse and stomped on the accelerator, showering Niles with a storm of mud and rocks. Niles covered his face as

14

he turned away from the car. He secretly wished Lars would simply run him over so he would no longer have to endure the abusive treatment that befell him daily. Instead, Lars backed into the yard and slammed the car into drive. Once again he stomped the accelerator and the car's tires threw mud, this time peppering the front of house, beside which Emma and Lilli were standing. Both of the girls covered their faces and turned away to avoid the assault of rocks that flew at them. As the car sped down the driveway, the three children watched it go, hoping neither of the occupants would ever return.

Lars made no attempt to stop or even slow down as he reached the end of the muddy driveway and slid onto the highway. As the station wagon veered onto the road, the tires of an oncoming vehicle screeched as the driver attempted to stop short to avoid a collision. The oncoming car swerved into the other lane as the horn sounded an angry warning. Lars simply pressed harder on the accelerator with no regard for the other driver or what may have resulted from his careless driving.

"Where the hell are ya goin'?" Sonya exclaimed. "The hospital's the other way!"

"Shut the fuck up! We're not goin' to Ropschon, we're fuckin' going to Waterburn," Lars screamed.

"But that's further away!" Sonya yelled back at him. "What if the baby comes before we get there?"

"I hope it does!" he screeched. "Then we'll just throw it in the ditch and go home!"

Even though Sonya already hated her unborn child, she was not sure she would be able to simply dump it in a ditch. In reality, she knew she would do whatever Lars wanted her to do, and instantly realized, if the baby came before they reached the hospital, its fate was already determined. About thirty minutes after leaving their dilapidated house, the dented, rusty station wagon pulled into the parking lot of the hospital in Waterburn, spewing smoke from its rusty exhaust. Lars pulled into one of the many empty parking spaces and the car slid to a stop. He slammed the car into park and simply sat in the torn seat with the engine running.

"I'm guna get done with my smoke before I go in," Lars commented. "Since the fuckin' kid decided to make me drive all the way down here, you're guna wait until I'm damn good and ready to take ya in," he growled.

Sonya made no comment and simply sat still as the pains in her abdomen grew more severe. Her breathing was irregular and she did all she could not to utter a sound. Lars sat, seemingly pleased with himself and slowly smoked his cigarette. The smoke from the end of the cigarette curled around his face as he breathed it from his lungs, out through his nostrils. The two sat silently in the car until he finally turned to her with contempt in his eyes.

"Get the fuck out," he breathed.

Sonya opened the car door and stepped carefully out of the car. With each movement her pain increased and she struggled to stay on her feet. Lars slammed the driver's door shut and walked casually to Sonya's side. His stride was longer than hers and she quickly began to lag behind.

"Move your ass!" he barked.

Sonya did what she could to speed up her stride but was unsuccessful. By this time Lars was at least six steps in front of her. He spun around, clearly irritated, and walked back to Sonya grabbing her by the arm and jerking her forward. She lost her footing and fell forward, landing directly on her large, protruding belly. She let out a faint cry as Lars angrily reached down to drag her back to her feet.

"Ya clumsy bitch, come on!" he snapped.

Sonya struggled to get back to her feet as Lars yanked on her arm. Finally, she regained her footing and continued walking. The couple entered the hospital and were met with the bustle of busy people as they scurried through the reception area. Lars said nothing and walked with Sonya to the reception desk.

"I'm in labor," Sonya declared to the woman behind the desk.

"I'll get someone to help you, ma'am, please have a seat," the receptionist stated with concern.

Lars and Sonya made their way to the waiting area and sat down. Within minutes a nurse appeared with a wheelchair and helped Sonya into it. The nurse pushed the wheelchair down the hall with Lars following absentmindedly behind. They entered the birthing room and the nurse helped Sonya into bed.

Looking at Lars, the nurse inquired, "Are you the father?"

"Fuck, I don't know," he said flatly.

The nurse was surprised at his response but chose not to inquire any further about the couple's relationship.

"Will you be joining us in the delivery room?" she asked kindly.

"Nah, I'll wait outside," Lars answered indifferently.

The nurse was unsure of why Lars had chosen not to join Sonya in the delivery room, but it was against her training to question the details of the decisions of the patients and their families.

"I'll show you to the waiting area," the nurse replied politely.

After another nurse arrived to help prepare Sonya for the delivery, she walked from the room and down the hall to show Lars to the waiting area. Lars sat down in one of the chairs and attempted to watch television. He wanted a cigarette and a beer to calm his nerves as the other people in the waiting area were making him nervous. He sat for only a few minutes, deciding hastily to go to the car. Once he was there, he got inside and lit a cigarette. The beer he had taken from the house was sitting on the dash. He picked up the can and took a long drink. Without any further thought, he turned the key in the ignition and backed leisurely from the parking space. He put the car in drive and pulled away from the hospital, turning onto the street in front of the large building. Lars thoughtlessly made his way back to the house and pulled into the driveway. He felt relaxed now, and planned to kick off his boots and drink another beer.

Darkness had crept over the land as he drove home and by the time he reached the house headlights were necessary to complete the drive. The children were inside the house as the temperature had dropped outside and the soft glow of light spilled from the windows. The car came to a stop and he shifted it into park. As he sat motionless in the driver's seat his mind began to wander, thinking of the things he could do while Sonya was away. He thought he might go to Ropschon and pick up a hooker who would be willing to peddle her services for a good high instead of cash. It was already eight o'clock at night and he was feeling a little tired from the day's events. Instead of making the trip he decided to go inside and relax.

Lilli, Niles, and Emma were sitting in their bedroom on the second floor of the rundown house, playing on the filthy floor, giggling and laughing with one another. The unmistakable sound of the car's heavy door slamming shut interrupted their enjoyment of temporary happiness and freedom. They peered at one another with a mixture of dread and trepidation as they waited to hear the sound of the front door. The seconds clicked slowly by and then the sound of Lars entering the house finally came. They listened as he stomped through the kitchen to the refrigerator and opened a beer. Soon after, they heard his heavy footsteps coming up the stairs. They all froze and frightfully awaited whatever was about to take place. Their bedroom door flew open. Lars stood in the doorway piercing the children with his evil stare. No words were spoken and the silence became utterly deafening. Lars took another long drink of his beer, finishing it. He lowered the can from his lips and let out a loud belch. None of the children looked at him. They sat motionless with their hands in their laps, staring at the floor. All three children held different fears about what was about to happen. Lilli feared Lars would try to rape her and Niles and Emma feared they would be beaten. Lars walked slowly to the place where the children sat and looked down. The smell emulating from him was sour; a mixture of sweat, beer, cigarettes, and urine. The children did their best to hold their tongues so they might circumvent at least one motive for a beating.

"What are ya little fuckers doin'?" Lars sneered.

None of the three children uttered a word and continued to stare at the floor. Regardless of the answers they might offer, they knew Lars' response would be cruel and painful.

"What are ya, fuckin' stupid? I asked ya a question!" he yelled.

Still, none of the children responded. Lars' temper began to boil as he perceived the children's silence as a lack of respect for him. All at once Lars lunged at Niles and grabbed him by the back of the neck, ripping him from his modest seat on the hard floor. Niles let out a surprised cry and did all he could to stand quickly so the pressure on his small neck would decrease. Lars cocked his fist back and swung hard at Niles. Niles squeezed his eyes shut and braced himself for the blow. Lars' huge fist connected with Niles' face making a sound that could have been mistaken for a piece of celery breaking crisply in half. Pain surged through Niles' small face as the

Charlotte Roberts

skin around his right eye tore sharply. Blood trickled down his cheek and his eye instantly began to bruise and swell. The surface of Lars' fist was large enough to make contact with almost the entire side of Niles' small face. Blood began to trickle from his nose as well as the corner of his mouth and only a small whimper was heard as Lars threw him brutally to the floor. He landed in a crumpled pile and lay still, attempting to act as if he had expired. Lilli and Emma braced themselves for similar treatment but Lars was not yet done with Niles. He unbuckled his belt and pulled it from the loops of his jeans. The belt, passing through the denim loops, made an unambiguous sound, one with which Niles was quite familiar. On a regular basis, Niles was beaten severely at the hands of Lars with his leather belt. Lars doubled the belt over itself and snapped the paralleled pieces of leather against each other. The crack of leather upon leather made Niles jump and he knew what was coming next. With all his strength, Lars drew back his arm and swung it to the front with the belt flying in his fist. The belt struck Niles and made a very loud pop as it hit his tiny back. Niles coiled into a ball and remained on the floor, still crying, but only making slight noises for fear of invoking a continuance of the attack. Another pop sounded as the belt once again made contact with Niles' back, this time just above the last. A third pop seemed to satisfy Lars as he ceased the beating and stood above the small boy, panting as droplets of saliva dripped from his mouth and hung from the bedraggled hairs of his unshaven face. As his breathing slowed, he replaced his belt among the intact loops of his jeans. As he fastened the buckle of the belt, he looked down at Niles and smiled when he saw the small boy in a ball on the floor, shivering from fear, and crying quietly.

Lars turned to Lilli and took a step toward her. The girls both cringed since they had no way of knowing who was next.

Lars reached down and clutched a handful of Lilli's long, dark hair. She gasped from the pain that shot through her scalp and tried to stand up quickly with the hope he would let her go if she did what he wanted her to do. He held her small head steady as he drew back his hand and slapped her very hard across the face. She tried to pull away, but her attempt to protect herself proved to anger Lars even more. Once again, he drew back and swung his hand at her small face. Lilli's eyes squeezed shut as she prepared herself for the strike of his large, open hand. Another blow met her face with stinging pain, then a third, then a fourth. Lilli's right eye was beginning to swell shut and her nose was bleeding, the bruises materializing right away. Lars suddenly realized he had sufficiently dominated the young girl and wheeled his hand to strike once again. All at once he stopped himself, feeling he was satisfied with what he had accomplished so far, realizing he should save some of his energy for his next endeavor. With a disgust-filled grunt he pushed Lilli away and watched contently as her small body collided with the small bookshelf that held the few toys the children owned. She fell to the floor, holding her stomach where it had made contact with the unforgiving wood of the bookshelf. She curled into a ball and, like Niles, lay quietly crying. All of the children knew from experience, if they made noise while they cried, the beating would proceed until they were silent.

After standing for a brief moment admiring his work, Lars turned toward Emma, who had backed herself into a corner, cowering. Lars smiled malevolently as he slowly crept toward Emma. She was crying, her long, dark hair clinging to her face among the tears that had wet her cheeks. Her wide, terrified eyes moved up quickly as she looked Lars in the face. She saw cruelty in his eyes and quickly buried her head in her hands. She was afraid Lars would duplicate the treatment he had just displayed with Lilli and Niles. Emma trembled as she waited for the unknown. Lars stopped and turned back toward Lilli and Niles as they lay on the floor. Once again, Emma looked up as his pause was unexpected.

"Get in bed! Both of ya!" he screamed at Lilli and Niles.

In spite of the excruciating pain they still felt, the children moved quickly, scrambling to their feet, to run across the room to the bed they shared. Without looking back they hurled themselves into the bed, quickly burrowing under the blankets, and closing their eyes. Lars stood and watched, making sure they both obeyed him. Emma remained in the corner, afraid of what was about to happen. Lars reached down and grasped her small arm, pulling her to her feet. He forced her to walk beside him, as if she were a dog that had misbehaved. Pulling her small body along with him, he walked to the bedroom door, paused to turn off the light, and then slammed the door shut.

"Lilli, what do ya think is guna to happen to Emma?" Niles quietly questioned in the darkness.

"I don't know," Lilli shakily replied. "He'll probably beat her too."

"Why did he take her out of the room, Lilli?" Niles inquired in a voice that could not mask his tears.

"I don't know, Niles," Lilli said softly as she reached for her little brother to comfort him. "I don't know."

Lilli and Niles did their best to comfort one another as they lay in bed trying to fall asleep. Sleep finally came to them and they were once again able to escape reality for another night.

Lars dragged Emma beside him as he walked from the children's bedroom and made his way down the steep, narrow stairs of the old house. It was very difficult for Emma to keep her footing as she struggled to match his pace down the stairway. She fell a few times, scuffing her little legs on the rough wood of the bare stairs. Lars jerked on her little arm, lifting her off her feet to make her stay upright. The two of them made it to the bottom of the stairs; Lars dragged the little girl through the kitchen and sat her down hard on one of the metal kitchen chairs. The slick, yellow plastic of the chair's seat cover was cold on Emma's bare legs but she did not dare argue with him.

"Sit there," Lars growled.

Emma sat still, quietly wondering what was in store for her. Lars stomped to the refrigerator, pulling two beers from the shelf inside. He walked back to the kitchen table and set the cans down hard, all the while devilishly staring at Emma. She looked down at the grey-flecked, yellow metal kitchen table trying hard to concentrate on something other than her fear. Lars plopped down hard in the chair next to Emma and pulled the full ashtray over in front of him. As the ashtray slid across the table, some of the crushed butts spilled from it, scattering across the already dirty surface of the table. He continued to stare at Emma, looking her up and down as he made his plans for the next few hours. He reached into his shirt pocket and pulled out his pack of cigarettes. Nonchalantly, he flicked the top of the pack as he held it sideways and a cigarette partially sprang forth. He put the pack to his mouth and plucked the exposed cigarette with his rough lips. He raised his lighter and lit the cigarette, taking a long drag from it as it began to burn.

"Do ya know where your mom's at right now, Emma?" Lars sweetly asked.

"No," Emma humbly replied.

"She's in Waterburn at the hospital," he calmly stated. "She's havin' a baby. What do you think of that?"

Emma simply shrugged her shoulders and said nothing as her eyes searched the surface of the table.

"Ya know," Lars declared, seemingly in good humor, "Ya can look at me, I'm not guna bite ya."

Emma looked up sheepishly meeting his gaze only for a second. Her eyes shot back down, once again fixing on the surface of the table. Lars opened both of the beers in front of him and pushed one toward the seven-year-old girl.

"Ya want a beer?" he asked pleasantly.

Emma did not respond. Lars picked up the can in front of him and took a long drink.

"Beer doesn't sound good, huh?" he said. "How 'bout one of these?"

Lars reached into his pocket taking out a handful of assorted pills, placing them carefully on the table in front of Emma.

"It's candy," he said. "Do ya want some?"

Emma silently shook her head and continued to stare at the table. The pills intruded on her view of the table top so she looked at them. She knew the pills were not candy and refused to take any of them.

"Fuck ya, then. More for me," Lars proclaimed as he grabbed three of them and popped them into his mouth. He took a large gulp of beer to wash them down and let out a sigh to indicate his satisfaction.

"You're guna sleep with me tonight," he told Emma. "We're guna celebrate."

Emma did not know exactly what the comment implied but her instincts told her it would be terrible. Lars finished his beer and once again asked Emma if she would like some from the other can. Again, the little girl refused so he grabbed the can and held it to his lips, drinking thirstily. Only a few minutes went by and Lars set the second can, now empty, on the table with a sigh. The sound of the aluminum hitting the table made Emma jump and she quickly looked at Lars to see if he had noticed her movement. Lars was still staring at Emma; he had not taken his eyes off of her since he had turned away from the refrigerator. He continued to smoke his cigarette until the cherry reached the filter. Crushing it out, he blew the smoke from his lungs directly into the little girl's face.

"It's time for bed, girl," Lars declared in a devilish tone.

Emma was afraid to move as Lars walked behind her and placed his hands on her tiny shoulders.

"Mmmm," he breathed. "You feel great."

Emma closed her eyes and tried to think of something else. She was unable to fill her mind with anything other than fear and disgust. Lars gripped her little arms and lifted her out of the metal chair. He set her on her feet beside the chair and took her small hand. He led her into his and Sonya's bedroom and closed the door. She stood still with her feet together and her small hands clasped in front of her as she stared at the filthy carpet. Lars sat on the side of the bed and removed his boots. With a thump the first boot struck the floor and Emma jumped slightly. The second boot then struck the floor with a thump after he pried it from his foot. She jumped again, standing next to the dresser, trying desperately to wish herself away from the situation. Lars pulled his filthy T-shirt over his head and ran his hands across his hairy chest as he stretched his

25

back in a slight arch. He stood, unbuckled his belt, unbuttoned his jeans, and ran his zipper down. He pulled the jeans from his waist and, once again, sat on the edge of the bed letting out a grunt.

The room was dark and dingy, lit only by a small lamp with a maroon shade. The lamp's shade was lightly veiled with the silk of spider webs that had gathered dust over the years. Small specks of dust floated in the light above the shade, as if wafting playfully in an unnoticeable breeze, passing in and out of the illumination spilling from the top of the lamp. Emma remained steadfast next to the dresser as Lars attempted to coax her to him. She tried again to imagine herself somewhere else – anywhere else – as she closed her eyes.

Emma remained motionless, the seemingly enormous dresser next to her, hoping Lars would simply leave her alone and fall asleep. Lars sighed, realizing he would not be able to talk the little girl into coming to him. He stood and made his way across the cluttered bedroom to the place where Emma was frozen in place. Wrapping his hands around her small chest, he hoisted her up and swung her little body around in an attempt to play, but her dirty little face showed no signs of lightheartedness. He tossed her up, only a few feet playfully into the air, as a father playing with his child has been known to do. Lars tried to help Emma relax by offering a smile and a few noises suggesting she was flying.

"Whoosh," he said, each time he tossed her upward.

Instead of the jovial and playful impression Lars was attempting to communicate, Emma perceived an evil, frightening, and unwelcome feeling. To Emma, Lars' dirty, bearded face had come to resemble the image of an evil clown with long, sharp fangs and wicked eyes, similar to one that might decorate an especially frightening ride at a run-down carnival. On the third toss into the air, Emma felt the momentum of her body change as she flew backward instead of up. As her small frame connected with the mattress, she flailed about as if she were only a rag doll, bouncing a few times before coming to rest. She found herself lying on her back in only her pajamas, consisting of only a T-shirt and underwear. Emma squeezed her eyes closed once again as tears began to burn her eyes. She wanted to be in bed next to Lillie and Niles, the only sense of comfort and sanctuary she could think of. The smell of the rough, unwashed blankets surrounding her made her feel nauseous as the rancid smell forced its way into her nostrils. The odor seemed to resemble sour, stagnant water poisoned with the tragic death of someone never found and long forgotten by everyone.

Lars' fetid breath added to Emma's nausea, making her fight back the urge to vomit. The smell of old cigarettes, beer, and months of built-up food particles combined in his mouth to create a smell far worse than that of the blankets. The smells alone were enough to terrify her and she did her best to escape into her own imagination. She was enveloped with fear and paralyzed by the gravity of the situation, unable to move aside from the unintentional trembling that ran through her entire body.

Emma continued attempts to separate herself from the horrifying event that was unfolding, wishing herself into a magical world where she would never be exposed to Lars again. She was convinced death would be more pleasant than what was happening to her at that moment. Tears now streamed from her eyes as if they were rivers being fed by melting snow in the spring. The pain was excruciating but she was afraid to cry out. She wanted to scream but her voice had hidden from her. She felt as if her physical existence had been separated from her mind and she began to feel her entire body go numb. She tried to imagine playing in the sun with her dolls, the sweet smell of flowers and clean, fresh air surrounding her. She concentrated hard to replace the unspeakable noises filling her ears with the songs of birds and the rustle of the grass as a light breeze touched each blade.

After what seemed like an eternity, she felt Lars' weight shift and she no longer felt the incredible pressure forced upon her. She felt lighter than air but incredible pain surged throughout her body as her mind returned to the present moment, away from her imagination. She felt immense pain in her legs, hips, and back. It was if all of the bones had been broken. Her insides ached and she felt as if someone had beaten her ruthlessly from the waist down. As she moved slightly to escape the torture place she had been forced to inhabit, she felt a strange, sticky wetness beneath her. The wetness was cold as her warm skin touched it and it terrified her.

"Ya better be in this fuckin' bed when I wake up," Lars growled. "If ya ain't, you'll get what the other two got," he warned.

Feeling she had no choice, she reached for the blankets to cover herself up. Even though the smell of the blankets made her sick, she felt the warmth they might provide could help her feel at least a little comfort in a place devoid of safety. Her young mind wanted to put something between herself and the monster that lay next to her. As she rolled to her left side, she pulled her knees to her chest and tried, once again, to imagine herself somewhere else, playing happily. She desperately searched for sleep as tears continued to roll from her eyes and soak her mother's vomit-stained pillow. Finally, sleep overcame her and she was able to escape the horrible reality of what had just happened to her.

Lars quickly fell asleep, his naked body uncovered as he snored loudly. He had no remorse for the terrible act he had just performed, believing since he was too tired to go to Ropschon to find a hooker and Sonya was in the hospital it was his right to recruit anyone he felt would do. At the same time Emma's innocence was being viciously stolen from her, Ava was coming into the world, completely unaware of the life she would live and the environment to which she would be exposed.

When morning came, the light of day seemed to hold a different meaning for Emma. She awoke and found her small body had responded to Lars' intrusion with a bloody mess. She was afraid she would get into trouble for the mess Lars had made and was terrified to even move. Since Lars had not indulged in as much beer as he normally did the night before, he awoke much earlier than usual. The pills he had taken the night before had taken effect over the course of the night and he was high when he awoke. He rolled over and faced Emma as she lay awake with her eyes closed, pretending to be asleep with the hope he would overlook another opportunity to satisfy himself. He looked at Emma and assumed she was still asleep. He had even wondered if the little girl lying next to him was dead. He smiled at the thought and then sat up on the edge of the bed. He stretched and reached for his cigarettes. He lit one and breathed the smoke deep into his lungs. As he exhaled, he stood up and walked from the bedroom, heading for the kitchen. Emma stayed in bed and waited to hear the sound of a beer can opening. The unmistakable crack of the can sounded and Emma slowly rose from the bed, riddled with pain. She found her clothes, put them on, and made her way quickly to the bathroom to clean herself up. She washed herself carefully with a damp washcloth and proceeded to the kitchen door so she could make her way upstairs to her bedroom. Lars had turned toward the window and gazed outside while he drank his beer. Emma crept silently across the kitchen to the bottom of the stairs and began to climb them. Each stair creaked and Lars instantly knew it was Emma. He felt she was even more a piece of trash since she had allowed him to have sex with her. The fact she was only a child did not even enter into his twisted mind. He did not speak a word, keeping his back to her, therefore allowing her to climb the stairs with the belief he was unaware of her presence.

Emma made it to the top of the stairs and to the tattered door of the bedroom. She pushed the heavy wooden door open and looked around the room. Lilli and Niles were still in bed, their blood-stained pillows under their small heads. Emma made her way across the room and opened one of the drawers of the dresser shared by the three of them. She found a pair of pants and a sweater and put them on. She slipped her small feet into a mismatched pair of socks and made her way to the bed where Lilli and Niles lay sleeping. As she looked at them, she realized her life would never be the same. She wondered if Lilli had ever experienced what she experienced the night before and wondered how she coped with it all. She carefully climbed into the bed with the other two children and cuddled against Lilli's back. The three children lay close to one another and Emma attempted to find comfort in the company of her siblings. Once again, sleep came over her and she was able to escape the terrible pain still present in her tiny body.

Lars got dressed without a shower for the fifth day in a row and made his way to the car. After he got in and shut the driver's door, he opened his second beer of the day. He had six more in the passenger seat, just in case he had to wait. He drove down the driveway and onto the road as he began his second trip to Waterburn in two days. When he got to the hospital, he went in to ask the receptionist where he could find Sonya. The receptionist directed him to the correct location and he walked into the room. Sonya lay asleep in the hospital bed, clearly no longer pregnant. The baby had been born. He walked to her bedside and pushed on her arm to wake her. Sonya's eyes came open slowly and she realized Lars had come back to get her.

"I wasn't sure if you'd come back for me," Sonya said, her voice saturated with exhaustion from giving birth.

"I had to, I'm not takin' care of your brats," Lars responded with disgust.

The door opened and a nurse walked in, holding the baby. She handed the baby to Sonya while Lars watched from a short distance away. After the nurse left the room, Lars stepped back to the side of the bed.

"What is it?" he asked,

"It's a girl," Sonya stated flatly as she began to feed the baby.

"Worthless," Lars commented. "What are ya guna do with it?" he asked.

"Take it home, I guess," Sonya replied with disdain.

The night before, after the birth, Sonya lay in the hospital bed wondering what to do with the baby. She rationalized, if she kept the baby, Lars might be compelled to stay with her to raise it and maybe even marry her. She also realized having a baby with him was a good way to trap him. Little did she know, Lars would never in his life show any care for the baby.

"Is it mine?" Lars asked in a skeptical tone.

"Yeah," Sonya replied, clearly irritated.

"What are ya guna name it?" he asked.

"I don't know, I wanted to wait until ya came back to pick a name," she answered. "I wanted to make sure I didn't pick one of your whores' names."

Sonya had toyed with a few names and had a few choices in mind. Virginia was a name she had considered but, as it turned out, a woman by that name had been the first with whom Lars had cheated a few years ago. There had been many women during the time Lars and Sonya had been together. Some of the other names Sonya had considered matched the names of the women Lars had cheated on her with including; Elizabeth, Shannon, Crystal, and Sommer. Finally, after much deliberation, a name was settled upon; one which neither Sonya nor Lars was seemingly able to recall from any other person. The day after she was born, the baby was finally given the name, Ava Rose.

Chapter Two

After Ava's birth, Sonya kept up her normal behavior of drinking and doing drugs. In the midst of life, only seven months after Ava was born, Lars found another woman and left with no warning whatsoever. The blow to Sonya's emotional stability was brutal and she sunk even further into depression than she had ever been while her substance abuse seemed to reach its height. Lars did not consider how his actions, both past and present, would affect the children in the home, nor did he care. Whether Lars' abandonment was a blessing or a curse may never be determined, but it seems that Sonya may have been the lesser of the two evils.

A few weeks after Lars left, Sonya left the children with a neighbor, Jill, while she claimed to be going for groceries and a visit with her sister in Ropschon. Her real endeavor, however, was to find a new man to fill the gaping hole in her life. She believed if she could only find a man to take care of her she would finally find happiness. Little did she know, throughout her life and regardless of the situation, happiness would continue to elude her. She set out to make the short trip to Ropschon with a twelve pack of beer and a carton of cigarettes, purchased with part of the money remaining from her monthly welfare check. The car she drove was one she had borrowed from the neighbor with whom she had left her children.

As she drove into town she had no thoughts of getting groceries or supplies for her family. She made her way through a series of stop lights that led her to the bar she and Lars had frequented together. She finished the beer she had been holding between her legs and threw the can on the ground as she swung the car door open. She walked into the back door of the dirty little tavern and found a place to sit at the bar. There were many people in the establishment and many of them were men looking for a woman who had little or no expectations for a prosperous life.

By midnight Sonya had quite a few offers for sexual encounters, each including a financial component. She finally decided on the opportunity that offered the most financial gain for her, and she and the man left the bar together. Since the car she drove to town did not belong to her, she waited for him to lead her to his car to complete the transaction. After about an hour of sexual congress, the two exited the car and the man handed Sonya fifty dollars. With no conversation, Sonya turned and walked to the car she had driven to town. She opened the door and plopped into the driver's seat reaching for a beer. She opened the can and thirstily took a long drink. She lit a cigarette and took a long pull, inhaling the smoke deep into her lungs as she leaned back in the seat and closed her eyes. After relaxing for a few minutes, she decided to go pick up her children and go home. She left the tavern's parking lot and proceeded through town finally turning onto the highway that would lead her to the next traumatic event in her life.

As she drove down the dark, slushy highway, she paid little attention to the few cars she met. Her mind began to wander as she imagined what it would be like without children to take care of. She imagined driving by the neighbor's house, by her own house, and continuing on until she found a new place to live. As she approached the driveway of the neighbor's house where the kids were being taken care of, she unconsciously snapped out of her daydream and pulled into the driveway. She stumbled to the house and knocked on the door. There was no answer. Apparently, the neighbor had put the kids to bed and did not expect her to pick them up since it was so late. She decided she would come back the next day to pick up the children and return the car. Sonya got back in the car and slammed the door. She backed out of the driveway and aimed the car toward her house, only a few miles away. As she pulled onto the highway she saw an orange glow coming from somewhere over the next hill. She gave the glow little thought as she continued on. When she finally topped the hill just before her house the realization hit her; the orange glow she had noticed was the product of a very large fire. There were fire trucks and police cars everywhere and then she realized – her house was on fire! She attempted to pull into the driveway but was stopped by a police officer.

"I'm sorry, ma'am but I can't let you in here," the policeman stated.

"This is my house!" Sonya blurted. "What the hell is goin' on?"

"We aren't sure what caused the fire, ma'am," the officer answered. "At this time, we are just trying to get the fire under control. Is anyone in the house? Any pets?" he questioned.

"No," Sonya replied with a numb expression. "My kids are at the neighbor's house and we don't have no pets."

"I'm going to have to ask you to park your vehicle out of

the way so that emergency personnel can have access to the scene, ma'am," the officer stated.

"Where the fuck am I supposed to go?" Sonya yelled at the officer, as if everything were his fault.

"I understand you are upset, ma'am. Is it possible for you to go to your neighbor's house?" the policeman questioned.

With no response Sonya slammed the car in reverse and spun the tires as she attempted to leave the scene of the horrific fire. The car's tires dug into the soft earth and threw slush and mud from underneath. The flames that now engulfed the small house seemed to reach toward the sky like flickering orange fingers. The flashing reflections of red, blue, yellow, and white from the lights of the emergency vehicles, combined with the colors of the fire, seemed to portray a real-life abstract of a terrible, yet beautiful painting created by an artist who must be insane. Sonya pulled back onto the highway and returned to the neighbor's house. Since no one had answered the door in response to her knock before she decided to make her presence known, without a doubt. When she got to the front door she banged on it very hard with the expectation of creating a great deal of noise in her attempt to arouse those inside from their apparent slumber. As she waited under the dim, yellow light of the front porch she reflected on the evenings events, deciding she was very pleased with herself and her earnings. There were no thoughts of thankfulness she and her children were away from the house when the fire ignited nor of Jill's generosity in taking her children in for the evening. She only thought of herself. After what seemed like an hour, the door finally opened. Jill invited Sonya into her home reluctantly and listened to her recount the events of the night, real as well as fabricated.

"Our house is on fire," Sonya stated flatly to Jill.

"Oh Lord!" Jill replied with sincere concern. "What a blessing no one was home!"

"Ya, well now I gota find another place to fuckin' live," Sonya scowled as she sat down at the dining room table and lit a cigarette.

Jill and her husband, Ted, didn't smoke and usually did not allow smoking in their home. Jill said nothing to Sonya as she sat with her head in her hands, the cigarette burning as it rested between her fingers. Sonya had just finished a beer and the empty can sat in front of her. She flicked the ashes from the cigarette into the empty beer can and looked up at Jill.

"I don't know what the fuck I'm guna do," She said, irritated.

"I'm sure there are some homes in Ropschon or Nathia that are available," Jill offered in an attempt to be helpful and supportive.

The two women barely knew one another but it seemed Jill knew all she needed to know about Sonya as she gazed upon her, drenched in sweat from the night's sexual encounter and reeking of beer and cigarette smoke. She knew instantly the home in which the children lived was not one of structure, let alone virtue. In many ways Jill felt sorry for Sonya but her sympathy was contradicted by feelings of anger toward her for how the children were likely treated.

"You are welcome to sleep here tonight, Sonya," Jill offered sweetly. "I'll pull out the sofa and make it up for you. In the morning you can use the telephone to make arrangements for a new place to live."

"Fine," Sonya replied without looking up from the empty beer can. She offered no words of gratitude as Jill rose from the table.

Within a few weeks it was determined that faulty wiring had caused the fire, burning the small, dilapidated house on the hill to the ground. Though the family had little, what they did have was destroyed in its entirety. The small, fatherless family was forced to find another dwelling, one that would be affordable on a very modest welfare income. The small town of Nathia was less than ten miles from their destroyed home and determinably the easiest choice for finding a new place to live. With the help of a few of Sonya's drinking buddies, she was able to find an apartment located above the local television repair shop the day after the fire. After sealing the deal with a sexual encounter between Sonya and the owner of the apartment, the family moved in with hardly any belongings at all. Over time Sonya managed to gather a few beds and some rickety furniture that would otherwise be thrown out. The local food pantry served as the family's grocery store and blankets and clothing were donated by a few caring individuals from the small town.

By this time Ava was eight-months-old and had proven to be a large burden on Sonya and her ability to sexually exploit herself. Lilli was now twelve and fully responsible for Ava, Emma, and Niles. Sonya would disappear for days at a time with no word of her whereabouts. Lilli did the best she could to provide for the children with what little she knew and what was available to her. Niles, age nine, and Emma, age eight seemed to keep themselves occupied but Ava needed all of Lilli's energy and attention. Lilli's emotional and psychological health were being worn down, and the effects of the stress were becoming very evident in her actions.

One afternoon, Sonya sent Lilli, along with the other

children, to a friend's house to borrow money. The long walk to the friend's house was one Lilli would have normally enjoyed had she not been responsible for the others. As a twelve-year-old girl, Lilli simply wanted to be a kid, hang out with her friends, and have fun. Her life circumstances, however, would never allow anything of the sort.

The November air was crisp and quite cold but the sun provided a welcomed warming sensation as the children walked out of the shadows of the trees that loomed above. Lilli had made sure the younger children were dressed in clothes that would keep them warm, and Ava was wrapped in a warm blanket. Lilli held Ava close so the sharp air would not chill her and make her sick. After walking the two miles to the friend's house and asking for the money, the four began their journey back to the shoddy apartment where their mother waited impatiently. Within the last half mile before reaching the apartment, the group came to the river that snaked through the town. The bridge, old and rickety, creaked and rattled as the traffic crossed it. The sidewalk of the bridge, though protected from the traffic, seemed to be dangerous due to the diminutive guard rail on the water side. The bridge, constructed of steel and likely built sometime in the 1800s, loomed over the icy, rapidly flowing waters of the river below. As the tiny group began to cross the bridge Lilli's mind began to wander, wondering what it would be like to be without the responsibility of the three younger children. Niles and Emma scurried around her and ran ahead, making a game of crossing the old bridge. Lilli, still holding Ava close to her, reached the middle of the bridge where the water was at its deepest. She turned and faced the water looking down cautiously at the rushing water below her. She felt as if she were weightless except for the bundle she held in her arms. She stared at the moving water and began to feel the sensation the bridge was moving instead of the water. The sensation helped her to escape her dismal life for a few seconds but she snapped back to reality when Ava murmured a small cry. Lilli looked at the baby she held and began to wonder why she had to be responsible for her mother's child. She wished she could just be a typical twelve-year-old, expected only to go to school, hang out with friends, and get her homework done. She lifted Ava so she was eye-level with her and looked at the small, helpless child. She felt a twinge of anger directed at her mother and began to wonder what would happen if she held the child over the bridge rail, above the water. Ava's small face reacted to the chilly air by turning pink when the air made contact. Lilli knew the child was beginning to feel the cold but the thought was at the back of her mind. Lilli extended her arms and hung Ava over the side of the bridge. The baby had no idea what was happening and only looked at her sister with trusting eyes as she started to chew on her fingers happily.

The freezing water rushing under the bridge was peppered with large chunks of sharp, dirty ice. Though the water was muddy and murky all year, the cold weather had helped to clear it a little, but it was still impossible to see into the water any deeper than a few inches. The old bridge was anchored to the earth only about a hundred feet from a very large dam. The dam was as wide as the river and the water that rushed over it fell at least forty feet. The dam had once been the source of the small town's energy but had long since been abandoned. Over the years the falling water had cut a huge crater directly below the face of the dam itself. The soil had been carved away and only the jagged rocks remained, rocks so large their serrated points were only a small portion of the whole. The rocks were not visible but loomed only a few feet under the surface of the turbulent water as it swirled angrily at the bottom of the dam.

Lilli began to imagine letting go of the child. She held the baby tightly but could feel her small frame slipping from her hands. In her mind's eye she watched as the baby's small body fell to the water. She saw Ava go under the surface then pop back up for a few seconds. It was as if Lilli's mind was now somehow floating beside Ava as she struggled to find breath under the murky water. The water took her swiftly with it to the edge of the dam and then pulled her over the edge. Ava's shocked body fell quickly and hit the water below with more force than expected, due to the distance she had fallen. Her tiny body, already suffering from hypothermia was held under, trapped in the turbulence of the water falling from above. The baby had drowned at the bottom of the dam and her small frame was repeatedly bashed against the large, jagged rocks. Blood surrounded her limp body and eventually her corpse was washed down river and up on a bank, where the river began to calm, and a fisherman might find her in the spring.

After about twenty seconds, Lilli jerked the baby back to her chest and began to sob uncontrollably as she tucked the blanket back around Ava in order to keep her safe from the cold. The realization of what would happen to the child had shocked her back to reality and abruptly ended the horrible, imagined, events. She hugged Ava tightly and repeatedly apologized to the baby even though the baby had no idea what had just happened.

"I'm so sorry, Ava!" Lilli sobbed. "I'm so sorry! I love you and I'm so sorry for even thinking about that!"

Niles and Emma had not noticed what had happened and were already on the other side of the bridge throwing rocks into the river. Lilli's tears warmed her face only for a moment before turning icy cold.

"How could I have even thought about doing that?" Lilli thought to herself. "Nothing is this baby's fault!"

Lilli was relieved her grip on the baby had not, in reality, slipped while she held her over the rail of the bridge. Taking a last look at the fierce river below her, Lilli hugged Ava close once again and walked quickly to the other side of the bridge, as if attempting to flee from a dangerous threat.

That night, after Ava had been put to bed, Lilli reflected on what she had done. The thought of her actions terrified her as she pondered what she could have possibly been thinking. Though the thought of not being responsible for Ava was a desirable one, it horrified her to know she had actually held the baby over the water. The images of the event replayed in her memory; she felt the cold on her skin, heard the rushing water below her, and the speeding cars behind her. She could almost feel the weight of the baby pulling on her arms. Her heart raced as she once again realized the seriousness of the situation and imagined herself pulling the baby close to her again.

"What would have happened if I had dropped her?" Lilli wondered silently to herself. "Ma wouldn't have even noticed, I bet."

Lilli knew Ava was innocent and unaware of the situation. She knew her animosity should not be taken out on the small child. She felt trapped, as if she had no choice but to care for her brother and sisters. She thought of running away but could not bring herself to do it because of the other children. She decided to stop thinking about it for the night and assumed her duties, once again, as the replacement mother to Niles, Emma, and Ava while Sonya was away for yet another night.

It was time for Emma and Niles to go to bed and Lilli made sure they were tucked in tightly. At only twelve Lilli seemed to have the wherewithal of an adult woman and took very good care of her siblings. As usual Sonya was at the local bar and not expected home for hours. Once the children were in their beds and Lilli was confident they were asleep, she brushed her teeth and put on her own pajamas so she could settle into bed as well. Exhausted from the day's events and the cold, fresh air, Lilli was thankful to finally be crawling into bed. The apartment was very warm so she lay down in her bed on top of the blankets. She thought she might lay there for just a little while, until she cooled off, and then she would get under them. Within only a few minutes, however, she drifted off to sleep.

All at once Lilli felt a blinding pain in her head as she awoke to the sound of her mother screaming at her.

"Ya stupid little bitch! I told ya not to sleep on top of the covers!" Sonya screeched. "What the fuck is wrong with ya? Are ya fuckin' stupid?"

Lilli, torn from a deep sleep, had no idea what was going on. Natural instinct prompted her to cover her face to protect herself from another painful blow. Her face and pillow were wet and sticky from the blood that spilled from her nose as well as the gash between her eyes. Unable to speak, she quickly pulled the blankets back, without question, so she could crawl under them. Sonya stood over her, incredibly drunk and unrealistically enraged that the girl would dare sleep on top of her blankets. The lights in the room were bright but Lilli struggled to see her surroundings through her tears and the swelling of her face. Sonya stood over her, holding the baseball bat she had used to hit Lilli across the bridge of her nose as she slept. The blow was so hard the bat wore a smudge of Lilli's blood. Sonya looked at her with disgust as she dropped the bat slowly to the floor. Though Lilli tried to fight sleep the blow to her head had made her unable to remain conscious for very long and she drifted into a deep and dangerous sleep.

The next morning, Lilli awoke slowly, unable to lift her head from her pillow. The blood on her face and pillow had dried and turned a dark, reddish-brown color. She tried to remember the events of the previous night and finally recalled the image of her mother, standing over her holding a baseball bat. She wondered what would have possessed her mother to hit her while she slept.

"Did Niles or Emma tell her what I did with Ava?" she wondered silently.

The bat still lay on the floor next to the bed where Sonya had dropped it, the smudge of blood looking up at her like a terrible reminder of a nightmare turned to reality. Lilli's head was pounding and her face was very sore. She made her way to the bathroom and peered into the mirror at a person she did not recognize. Both of her eyes were a deep purple and swollen almost shut. The gash between her eyes still seeped a trickle of bright red blood and her nose was bruised and broken. Her face was covered in dried blood that had turned almost black throughout the night. She washed her face gingerly, trying to avoid the pain of touching her bruises. After all of the blood was washed away, she looked at herself in the mirror and wondered how she survived such a horrendous encounter. Since Sonya commonly had hangovers, headache medicine was one thing that could be found in the medicine cabinet in the apartment. Lilli took a few of the white tablets from the bottle and ventured to the kitchen for some water with which to swallow them. She took the pills and turned slowly to find Sonya, once again, passed out on the sofa in the living room. Not wanting to wake her, Lilli crept back to her bedroom and found some clothes to wear. She dressed and quietly left the apartment in an attempt to find solitude and escape the abuse of her mother.

Since Lars had gone away it seemed Sonya was even more angry and abusive. Lilli feared for Niles, Emma, and Ava and wondered what would happen if Sonya were no longer able to abuse her. Would she abuse the others? As Lilli walked along the sidewalk, the early morning air touched her skin and made her wounds tingle. She had no idea what she would tell others when they asked about her injuries. She knew if she said anything to anyone about what had really happened, her mother would make it even worse the next time. There was no way out for Lilli, and she was very aware of her imprisonment with Sonya. Repeatedly, school officials would question her about her bruises but she could not bring herself to disclose the events that caused them because of her fear of her mother. She simply told the officials she had fallen down the stairs, had been injured while playing a rough game with her siblings, or she had gotten into a fight with someone her own age. Silently, Lilli began to welcome death as her fear continued to consume her.

Over the years the abuse she endured had fostered an undeniable depression which seemed to control her. She found she cared little about herself or even whether she lived or died. In the attempt to make herself feel better Lilli did the things most girls her age did: visited with friends, went to school, and thought about boys. It seemed, however, no matter what she tried as she attempted to lift her own spirits, Sonya was always there to knock her back down. Sonya repeatedly demanded Lilli refrain from visiting with her friends so she was available to care for Ava at a moments notice. Sonya adamantly refused to allow Lilli the permission for sleepovers; partially because

Sonya enjoyed the ability to control another human being, partially because she wanted Lilli at her disposal, and partially because she simply did not want to see any part of Lilli's life enjoyable.

Sonya felt a deep resentment toward Lilli because she felt her birth ultimately robbed her of her youth and freedom. She hated Lilli, as well as the other children, though it was no fault of theirs they existed. Sonya believed her children were a punishment even though she believed she had never done anything wrong in her life. She felt her actions, attitudes, and virtually countless indiscretions were perfectly acceptable and if others did not agree with her beliefs and actions they were the ones who were mistaken.

The wounds on Lilli's face healed over time, accompanied by a battery of questions about what had happened. She wasn't sure if the story she told was believable but she ultimately did not care. With the New Year gone and spring just around the corner, Ava would soon be turning a year old. Lilli increasingly became more and more depressed as she continued to be the caregiver instead of Sonya. The depression was overflowing into her studies as well as into her social development. She tried hard to pay attention in class and complete the assignments she was given but struggled to stay focused. Her grades reflected the abusive situation at home but authority figures within the school seemed to assume it was only an indication of disinterest and laziness. Many times, Lilli was not able to complete her daily assignments for school simply because she was taking care of Niles, Emma, and Ava. Sonya's repeated absences from the home, though a blessing because of the lack of physical abuse, made things very tough on Lilli as she struggled to do her homework and care for the three children.

It was a Sunday night and Emma and Niles quietly played together on the floor of the living room while Lilli sat at the table feeding Ava. Sonya came stumbling into the apartment at only seven-thirty because the bar down the street had closed early. In her arms she griped a paper bag that held a twelve-pack of beer and four packs of cigarettes which would serve as refreshments for the night. Emma and Niles looked up briefly from their imaginary game but quickly lost interest when they found their mother had walked into the kitchen. Lilli did not even give her mother a glance but instead continued to spoon small amounts of baby food to Ava. This was a rare occasion, indeed, as Sonya had actually taken time away from drinking to venture to the local food pantry for provisions, at least for the baby. Sonya said nothing to Lilli as she passed through the kitchen and into the living room where she plopped heavily on the couch setting the paper bag on the cushion next to her.

"I want all of ya in bed by eight," Sonya ordered loudly. "I have company comin' over and I don't want him to know I have kids!"

"Why not, Mommy?" Emma questioned innocently.

"'Cause I can't get anything out of him if he thinks some little brats are here and he has to be quiet," Sonya screamed at Emma as she straightened her leg and kicked the little girl.

Emma immediately ran to her bedroom crying with Niles following close behind. It was already a quarter to eight. Lilli stood from her chair and began to clean up the small mess Ava had made while eating.

"Put that fuckin' high chair in your room and take Ava's crib too," Sonya yelled at Lilli. "Make sure ya keep that fuckin' kid quiet while my friend is here or you'll pay for it," she hissed.

Lilli said nothing as she walked to the living room to retrieve Ava's crib. She moved it into her bedroom then returned to the kitchen to get Ava and the high chair. As Lilli began to lift Ava from her high chair, it seemed Niles had found a small reserve of bravery and emerged from the bedroom he and Emma shared.

"Why won't ya get anything from him if he knows ya have kids, mamma?" Niles asked. "Is it bad to have kids?"

"Go to bed you worthless little fuck!" Sonya screamed. "If I hear another word out of any of ya tonight I'll beat all of ya 'til you're dead!"

Niles turned quickly and ran back to the bedroom, clearly terrified. Sonya seemed quite proud of herself for making Emma and Niles so upset. She sat smugly on the couch staring at Lilli. Lilli took Ava into her bedroom and placed her softly into her crib.

"Goodnight, little one," Lilli whispered.

Lilli then walked back into the kitchen and peered at her mother from the doorway.

"What the fuck are you lookin' at?" Sonya hissed.

Lilli looked down and tried to find the words. She knew, at this point, any words would likely earn her a beating but she mustered the courage to speak anyway.

"Why are ya so mean to us?" Lilli asked, matter-of-factly. "It's not our fault we're here."

Sonya rose clumsily from the couch and staggered toward Lilli with her hand raised high in the air. As Sonya brought her hand down she slapped Lilli so hard a large, red welt immediately began to form on her right cheek. Without turning away Lilli stood her ground. Sonya moved close to Lilli, almost touching her nose to her daughter's.

"I do what I want, when I want, and ya ain't guna stop

me," Sonya whispered. "If ya don't shut the fuck up and go to your room, I'll kill ya."

As Sonya hissed the words, Lilli could smell the horrid stench of beer and cigarettes. As Lilli gagged she began to turn but stopped. Sonya stood close to her, waiting for Lilli to walk away, so she could feel the triumph of prevailing over her daughter, yet again.

"How will I cover the mark on my face for school tomorrow?" Lilli softly asked without turning toward her mother.

"Ya won't," Sonya said as if there was nothing to worry about. "If anybody asks, ya fell."

"I thought maybe I could put makeup over it," Lilli suggested quietly.

"Oh really?" Sonya barked. "Ya wana put makeup on, huh? Forget it! You just wana pile on the makeup so ya can look like all your little whore friends!" Sonya exclaimed.

"No!" Lilli said with a start. "I won't wear it like my friends. I don't like how they wear it!"

"Forget it," Sonya said as she turned to walk back to the couch. "If I ever see ya with makeup on, ya know what's guna happen!"

Indeed, Lilli knew all too well what would happen. Though she wanted to talk with her mother about wearing makeup, she had not wanted to bring it up tonight. The opportunity, though bleak, seemed to present itself and Lilli did not think it through. Instead of attempting to discuss the matter further, Lilli simply walked to her bedroom and closed the door.

Emma and Niles were fast asleep by eight-fifteen, and by the time Lilli had made it back to her bedroom Ava was sleeping soundly as well. Lilli made sure to pull the covers back and slipped into bed without changing into her pajamas.

The events of the night had exhausted her and she quickly fell asleep.

The next morning, Lilli was up early to get ready for school. She hurried around the disheveled apartment as she helped Emma and Niles get ready for school first. Ava was simply playing on the floor with a few of her toys but Lilli was sure to keep an eye on her as she hurried about. After getting Emma and Niles ready, Lilli went into her room to dress and get herself ready. After dressing she went to the bathroom to finish her morning preparations. She peered at herself in the mirror and instantly noticed the large, red welt her mother had left on her cheek the night before. She thought about the threat Sonya had made but felt the need to cover the welt anyway. Another beating wouldn't be any worse than trying to lie to cover up her mother's abuse.

As Lilli began to apply the makeup to her face, her mind began to wander. She thought about her life and about the abuse she had endured at the hands of her mother as well as Lars, Ava's father. She thought about the words her mother spoke to her on a daily basis and struggled to dismiss the names her mother called her as mere words. She really was not sure when it had actually happened, but she realized, at some point, she had begun to believe the things her mother said about her. The list of harsh names seemed endless but the ones that stuck in Lilli's mind were: bitch, whore, worthless, and piece of shit. These were words her mother regularly used to describe her, not only to others but to Lilli as well. Unconsciously, Lilli had completed the application of her makeup and thoughtlessly left the bathroom to feed Ava and put her back in her crib to await Sonya's awakening. The three left the apartment and began their eight block journey to school. Sonya was asleep on the couch after yet another date with alcohol (and who knows which man) the night before. Though Sonya and her "friend" had been incredibly loud the night before, luckily none of the children had heard the sounds they made. The events that took place as the children slept were those of a woman with so little self-esteem she felt as if prostituting herself was the only way to make a living.

Lilli accompanied Emma and Niles to the elementary school and made sure they got to their classrooms. She promptly left the elementary school and headed for the junior high which was incorporated into the high school. The high school was only a block away from the elementary and she was able to cut her travel time in half by venturing through the playground and down a grass-covered alley. She had already started smoking, a habit she had picked up from her mother, and as she walked she enjoyed a cigarette. After walking only a few minutes she joined a few of her friends as they stood smoking just outside the cafeteria, a custom common to junior high and high school students. The girls commented on how pretty Lilli looked with her makeup on and she felt a rare feeling of joy and self acceptance. No one mentioned the welt. It was finally time to start the school day and as the bell rang the girls extinguished their cigarettes and headed to class.

The end of the school day arrived, seemingly too quickly for Lilli, as she dreaded going home every day. She quickly scampered into the bathroom to wash the makeup from her face before going home. She knew Niles and Emma would be waiting for her so she dutifully ventured to the street that ran along the side of the high school to meet them. The day was sunny and the slight warmth suggested summer was just around the corner. Lilli looked ahead and spotted Emma and Niles waiting obediently at the corner the three of them had designated as their meeting place. As she approached she signaled for them to cross the street and meet up with her so they could begin their short journey home. They had walked only a block when Lilli noticed Sonya was waiting for them in the light blue station wagon she had gotten from yet another "friend" who accepted payment in terms of sex rather than currency. The three children exchanged wary glances and slowly approached the car. Emma and Niles got in the back seat where Ava already sat babbling happily. Lilli opened the passenger door of the car and got in. Sonya sat in the driver's seat looking at Lilli with a smug, yet eerie grin on her face. She had purposefully put a great deal of makeup on before she had come to pick the children up that day. She wanted to make sure Lilli knew, without a doubt, she was in charge. Her face was painted with blush, eye shadow, eye liner, lipstick, and mascara as if she would be stepping onto a street corner to begin a night's work of prostitution. Her hair was sloppily done in an up-do but looked a great deal better than it usually did. Lilli looked at her mother with disbelief as rage began building inside of her. She knew she shouldn't say a word but she could not stop herself.

"Oh, so I can't wear makeup, but you can paint yourself up like a whore and that's OK?" Lilli questioned.

"Well," Sonya said with disdain, "I was guna to let ya wear a little makeup, but after that ya can just forget it!"

Sonya's statement made Lilli even more furious as her

young mind wondered if Sonya would have let her wear makeup if she had only kept quiet. Ultimately, however, Sonya knew she was lying and knew, whether or not Lilli had said a word, she would never have let her wear makeup. After all, wearing makeup was obviously something that would have brought some sort of happiness to the girl and Sonya could not allow her children to experience happiness. In her twisted mind, the children had robbed her of her happiness so she would rob them of theirs for the rest of their lives. Lilli said nothing else and stared at the road ahead of the car.

"We're goin' to see Ava's gramma and grampa," Sonya stated. "We're out of money."

Sonya put the car in gear and pulled onto the street as they began the hour drive to Oshen.

"If we're out of money, how are we guna get to Oshen?" Lilli flatly questioned.

"What the fuck do ya think I was doin' last night, dumbass?" Sonya blurted loudly, clearly irritated her daughter dared to question her. "I was gettin' money for today! That fucker wasn't good for any more than a hundred bucks though!" She sneered.

No words were spoken as the battered car made its way through the streets of Nathia. Lilli, Emma, and Niles were thinking similar thoughts as they noticed the houses with their freshly cut grass, small lawn ornaments, and tidy windows. Each began to wonder why they lived in a run-down apartment with virtually nothing to call their own. Though it may have occurred to each of them unconsciously before, it was at that moment all three, simultaneously, began to understand they were not as well off as others in the small town. That realization ultimately triggered one of many feelings that altered their perceptions of themselves; realizing they were, indeed, less important, less valuable, and ultimately beneath the other citizens in the town. They knew they were worthless but at that point Lilli was the only one who had any understanding of what it was to be worthless. Niles and Emma would not understand fully until they were older.

The trip seemed longer than it really was and when they got to Ava's grandparents' house Lilli, Emma, and Niles were made to stay in the car while Sonya took Ava in to visit. Though Sonya called it a visit, in reality it was no more than a begging session so Sonya could get money from them. After three hours, Sonya finally carried Ava to the car and they returned home. No words were spoken by any of them for the rest of the night. Apparently the trip was a success, because when the children returned home from school the next day, the cupboards were stocked and Sonya was already passed out on the couch while Ava played with a bottle of pills containing some unidentified drug, likely one of the very things responsible for Sonya's comatose state.

Lilli performed her normal duties after school: taking care of the children and trying desperately to concentrate on her studies. Though taking care of her brother and sisters was ultimately her mother's responsibility, Lilli had grown accustomed to making sure they were fed, bathed, and cared for. Lilli's mind wandered more and more as the days passed, struggling to understand her purpose for living. She wondered why she had been born. Was her existence ultimately to raise her siblings? Would life ever take a positive turn for her? The questions about life that flooded her mind overpowered her attempts to concentrate on her homework. She finally gave up and put her books aside as she sat on her bed and thought. Ava's crib was still in her room. Lilli figured it was just as well since she always took care of the baby anyway. She rose to check on the other two children and after making sure they were tucked into bed she returned to her room and closed the door.

"What if I really am worthless," Lilli silently pondered. "Is this all that life is going to be for me?"

She lay back on her bed and stared at the ceiling. Her thoughts began to gravitate around death as she wondered if she, and everyone else, would be better off if she was gone. She rationalized maybe Sonya would snap out of her terrible habits and be a mother to the other three children if she disappeared. She wondered if it would ever be possible to relive the times when her father was around. He always made her feel special and treated her with kindness. At this point, she thought about the situation, before Emma was even born, and remembered, when Sonya and Simon were together, Sonya treated Niles very well and Simon treated her very well. It was almost as if the two adults felt as if they were in competition with the child of the same sex. It seemed like Sonya hated Lilli and Simon hated Niles. She really wasn't sure why things were the way they were then, all she knew is she missed feeling like she mattered. Tears began to roll slowly down the sides of her face as she lay there feeling helpless and confused.

"Maybe I should just kill myself," Lilli thought. "Ma says I'm a worthless piece of shit. Maybe that's what worthless pieces of shit do."

Lilli's thoughts of suicide would ultimately stay with her throughout much of her life. These thoughts, ultimately a direct result of the treatment she suffered at the hands of her mother, would be a large part in determining the course of her adult life. Like Lilli, Niles, Emma, and Ava would also experience feelings of worthlessness and depression which would create thoughts of suicide for them as well.

The owner of the decrepit apartment was growing tired of the "transactions" with Sonya and began to demand money for rent instead of sexual gratification. Every month Sonya selfishly spent the family's welfare money on drugs, alcohol, and cigarettes so none was left over for rent. She was unable to solicit herself to the electric company for payment or to the utility company for water and waste services. She was forced to spend some of the money on that, at least, otherwise her children would be removed from her care and she would have to find work instead of continuing to collect government assistance, something she believed she was above. Each month residency in the apartment became more and more questionable.

It was February and Lilli, still responsible for the children, had gotten even more accustomed to her role as primary caregiver. It was cold that night and the children had gone in early from playing in the church yard a few blocks away with the other neighborhood kids. Niles and Emma were quite exhausted from all of the running and playing they had done that day and were in their room relaxing. Lilli was in the living room with Ava who was now able to move about quite well on her hands and knees, even pulling herself up when beside furniture. Lilli wondered if Ava was ready to start walking.

Lilli crossed the room to Ava, who was trying to stand next to the couch, and picked her up. Ava seemed to know Lilli as her mother and clung to her as if it were fact. Sonya was consistently absent from the apartment with no cares about the welfare of her children as she sat in the bar down the street night after night. Lilli lowered Ava to the floor and the baby's legs extended so her tiny feet met the carpet. Carefully, Lilli helped Ava balance, aided by the door frame, and encouraged the child to stand on her own. After a few clumsy attempts at standing, Ava finally stood on her own, quite well. Lilli then began to back away from Ava, short distances at first, and then further and further away so she would take steps on her own. Lilli had not realized how long she had been coaxing Ava to stand and walk. Emma and Niles had emerged from their tiny bedroom and stood, silently watching. Lilli helped Ava to her feet once again and stood her in the doorway. She backed up a few feet and put her arms out toward Ava. Ava's little face seemed to take on an expression of excitement and determination as she stretched her tiny arms toward her sister. She lifted her pudgy little leg and took a wobbly step toward Lilli. Lilli could not contain her smile and Niles and Emma felt their excitement grow as they looked on. Ava's other leg then moved forward as she took yet another step, then another, then another reaching Lilli's outstretched arms, giggling. Lilli grabbed her and hugged her as she laughed and praised the baby girl.

"Yey!" Lilli squealed. "You're walkin'!"

Emma and Niles ran to Lilli who was still crouched down, hugging Ava. Words of excitement, happiness, and congratulations filled the air as the once dismal apartment seemed to take on a joyous atmosphere.

"Let's go tell Ma!" Niles squealed with excitement.

"Ya!" Emma agreed.

"OK!" Lilli giggled as she scooped the baby up and headed for the door with Niles and Emma on her heels.

They ran down the stairs and across the street, Lilli carrying Ava in her arms. The bar was only a block away so it took no time at all for them to reach the front door. They burst through the door and immediately found Sonya sitting at the bar on her favorite bar stool. Even though they were interrupting her they had no doubt Sonya would be elated with the development.

"Ma!" Niles cried. "Guess what!"

"Ava walked!" Lilli gushed. "She walked to me in the living room!"

Sonya sat silently as the children continued to describe the news from their different perspectives. She turned back toward the bar and lifted her glass to her lips. After a long drink she set the glass back on the bar and lit a cigarette.

"Big fuckin' deal," Sonya retorted. "Now get the fuck outta here!"

Lilli, Niles, and Emma looked at one another in disbelief. With only a few words Sonya had managed to completely deflate them all. They stood motionless for a few seconds and looked at the floor.

"Get the fuck outta here now!" Sonya screamed at them.

Niles and Emma whirled around and ran for the door. Lilli stood holding Ava and looking at her mother. Sonya would not turn around. Lilli slowly turned and walked toward the front door, stopping to look at her mother once more. Her hatred for the vile woman continued to grow. She turned and pushed the door open, leaving the bar. They walked home silently and slowly climbed the rickety stairs. Upon entering the apartment Emma and Niles went to their room and Lilli took Ava to her room where the crib still resided. She lowered the baby into her crib and slowly made her way to her own bed. She lay down, closed her eyes, and drifted off to sleep.

The landlord had finally had enough and informed Sonya she must move out of the apartment. The June air was warm and Sonya wondered where she would go. As she sat in the bar that afternoon she struck up a conversation with a man next to her after he had asked to buy her a drink. As they talked Sonya purposely made no reference to her four children. After talking for some time she felt it was time to see what she could get out of the man. She began to talk of her imminent need to relocate and tactfully incorporated her manipulative indication of desperation. The man understood her immediately and offered to let her live in a house he owned, in the country, in exchange for an ongoing, no-strings-attached relationship with her. Sonya agreed happily as she knew sexual acts would be the only thing they would ultimately share. Throughout her nights in the bar Sonya had learned of yet another government assistance program that would ultimately pay most, if not all, of the rent for families with little or no income. She applied for the program and had only to find a dwelling. The necessary steps were taken and Sonya and the four children began to pack their belongings as they prepared for yet another move.

Sonya had asked some of her bar friends to help haul their things to the new house in the country and moving day finally arrived. Ava was walking on her own now, however unsteadily it was. Lilli, Niles, and Emma were busy taking things out of the apartment and loading them in the vehicles waiting on the street below. All three of the children were at the bottom of the stairs, dutifully turning to retreat up the stairs to fetch more items to load. Sonya had remained upstairs in the apartment, putting things into boxes from the kitchen, paying no attention to Ava. As the little girl sat playing happily alone she noticed the door was open. She took a few steps toward the door and plopped heavily to her knees, continuing her quest on all fours. She crawled to the open door and emerged into the sunlight of the warm, summer day. She had no idea what she was looking at as she peered over the edge of the platform at the top of the rusty stairs. Giggling, she turned her tiny head and noticed Lilli at the bottom. Ava squealed happily at the sight of her sister and began crawling toward the top of the stairs.

Lilli looked up when she heard Ava's voice but it was too late. Ava's little hand slipped over the edge of the top step and she fell. Her tiny body fell the entire length of the stairs, looking as limp as a ragdoll, as she flailed about. With each step a different part of her body collided with the rough metal and weathered, splintering wood. She made no sounds as she fell and the world seemed to fall completely silent. The only sounds Lilli could hear were the thumps the little girl's body made as it collided with the staircase. Though it only took a few seconds for the baby to reach the sidewalk, it seemed like an hour to Lilli. She rushed to the baby and picked her up holding her small head in her hand and hugging her close to her chest. Ava was silent, clearly shocked by the fall, and Lilli wondered if she was alive. Her little body was covered with scrapes, cuts, and gashes as bruises immediately begun to darken all over her. A few pedestrians who had seen Ava fall rushed to Lilli's side, curious about the injuries the baby had sustained. With tears in her eyes Lilli lowered Ava so she could look at her face. The baby's eyes were open but she made no sound. All at once the tiny girl was able to catch her breath and began to cry. It appeared the fall had knocked the breath out of her lungs. As Ava cried, Lilli pulled her close again and hugged her, thankful she had survived the fall.

From the apartment above, Sonya heard the commotion.

She was not sure what it was all about and really did not care. She turned slowly to look for Ava but could not see her. Irritated, Sonya walked to the open door of the apartment and looked down to where Lilli, Niles, and Emma stood with Ava. Sonya said nothing. Lilli looked up at her mother as she hugged the crying baby. Sonya only stood on the platform for a few seconds then turned and stepped back inside the apartment, seemingly unconcerned about the baby. Ultimately, Ava had only sustained minor injuries from the fall. The strangers who had stopped to help slowly departed, satisfied the baby would be alright. Lilli took Ava back up to the apartment to carefully clean the scrapes and check the rest of the little girl's body for any other injuries. Lilli was thankful Ava had not been hurt severely. She knew Sonya would not watch the baby, even now, so she moved the crib into the living room and placed the baby inside to keep her safe while she finished helping the other children load their belongings for the move. Lilli knew Sonya did not care about any of them and perceived Sonya's lack of concern for Ava as a lack of concern for all of them. Their mother did not care whether any of them lived or died.

A few weeks passed and Ava's injuries were still very apparent, though healing. As Lilli looked at the small child she felt a sense of helplessness. She reflected on the terrible fall Ava had taken and reasoned Sonya's negligence was ultimately a form of abuse that resulted in a similar end to the beatings she, Niles, and Emma regularly received. She wondered if her mother had purposely ignored Ava in the hope something terrible would happen. It seemed wrong to wonder such things about her own mother but after the horrible things she had experienced at the hands of Sonya she could not curb her negative thoughts.

The family had gotten settled in their new home and the children seemed to easily adjust to the move. The house was old but in much better condition than the last few places they had lived. The children would be able to continue their education in Nathia but would have to ride a bus every day. This meant, once the school year began, Ava would be home alone with Sonya even longer during the day. Ava was walking on her own now with a great deal of confidence and Lilli had begun potty training her. Ava seemed to be catching on quickly.

As the summer wore on, the four children spent a great deal of time outdoors exploring and playing. Niles had convinced Sonya to let him get a cat and she lived in the house with him. During one of their expeditions in the severely damaged barn the children found an owl. The owl was small and beautiful and would warily watch the children as they played but would not fly away. It was not tame enough for the children to touch it but it seemed comfortable enough with them in the barn it did not attack them.

The trees that grew on the west side of the property had, over the years, turned into a small grove where many different animals made their homes. The tree line extended all of the way to the ditch and the children would play for hours in the grove. One afternoon Emma and Niles ventured toward the gravel road during one of their explorations. They reached the end of the grove with a clear view of the road. Noticing a dark mass lying in the middle of the rocks, they approached curiously. Around the dark mass scurried six small creatures. The two climbed the steep ditch to the surface of the road and walked to the unidentified mass in the middle. It was a dead raccoon. The creatures scurrying about the dead animal were her babies. The baby raccoons were so small Niles and Emma knew they would surely die without their mother. They each scooped up three babies and headed straight to the barn.

Lilli was outside watching Ava play in the grass as Niles and Emma ran to the barn. Lilli wondered what they could be up to. She coaxed Ava to follow her and walked slowly with the child to the barn to investigate. Niles and Emma were very excited when they saw Lilli and Ava come through the door of the barn.

"Lilli!" Niles squealed, "We found some baby raccoons!"

"Their mommy is dead on the road," Emma said sadly.

Lilli looked at the tiny creatures feeling the same sense of hopelessness she felt when she looked at Ava. The babies had no one to care for them. She felt a strong tug in her heart telling her to take the animals in and care for them. The children gathered some milk and a washcloth and worked hard at feeding the baby raccoons. Sonya had no idea the animals were in the barn as she was virtually oblivious to what her children did every day.

As the weeks passed, the absence of the baby raccoons' mother began to take a toll on them. All of them, save for one female, died. During the following months the raccoon grew to full size and the children named her Babe. At some point, Sonya had learned of the raccoon but did not object. She had even decided to take in a few dogs, one of which, was part wolf. The dogs seemed tolerant of the children and the children were sure to keep Babe away from the dogs. Eventually, Babe was allowed to come into the house and she and Ava became good friends. The two played together every day.

After quite some time, Babe began to insist on going outside. Knowing they could not keep her in the house forever, they allowed her to come and go as she pleased. She was very large and the children were confident she could fend for herself. Babe regularly came to visit but as she roamed she became more and more the wild animal she was created to be.

Summer flew by and the school year was well under way. Ava had turned three and was quite independent. Lilli still looked after her brother and sisters but seemed to be needed less and less. Emma was now eleven and Niles, twelve. They were quite self-sufficient and even helped care for Ava.

Lilli longed more and more to spend time with her friends as her responsibility for Ava diminished. Sonya seldom allowed Lilli to visit her friends but was more receptive to her requests since Emma and Niles were getting older and able to help with Ava. Lilli's depression lingered and she thought more and more about suicide. Though her mother had begun to depend upon Emma and Niles to care for Ava while Lilli was away, she was sure to insult her even more than before. Lilli kept her home life to herself, not sharing anything with her friends. Her silence ultimately fostered her desire to escape her situation any way she could, even by death.

Lilli began to miss the days when Ava needed her, before the others could care for her. Raising Ava and caring for Niles and Emma was all Lilli had ever known. As her mother reformed the cruelty she regularly showed her, her freedom began to increase slightly. Maybe Sonya was somehow aware Lilli missed caring for Ava. Maybe she was just getting lazy in her strive to make Lilli's life hell. Ultimately, with every passing day, Lilli's suicidal thoughts became more and more tangible as she began to think of specific ways to end her own life. She spent hours at a time thinking about different ways to kill herself and what the implications of those methods would be. Could she jump off of a high building? Would that kill her? Could she shoot herself? Where would she find a gun? Questions like these seemed to flow smoothly through her mind with only fleeting interruptions. She wondered what would happen if she swallowed a bottle of pills. Would it kill her or just make her sick? She reasoned her options were limited and an overdose would be the most accessible way for her to take her own life. Now she had only to decide what type of pills to swallow. She wondered what was in the medicine cabinet in the bathroom. These thoughts continued to inundate her mind until it seemed as if the thoughts were second nature to her. She knew in her mind she would eventually kill herself but her heart seemed to occasionally interrupt her thoughts of death.

Chapter Three

As life proceeded, Sonya continued her abuse of alcohol and drugs as well as her mistreatment of the children. Little Ava, now almost four, had not yet begun to realize the abusive terrors Lilli, Niles, and Emma faced on a daily basis at their mother's hand. In her innocence, she was still able to live happily with virtually nothing upsetting in her life. Though she witnessed the beatings and harsh treatment of her brother and sisters by her mother, it was too soon for her young mind to store the memories or make sense of the reality. Eventually, Ava's memories would prove to be devastating and, even though she was unaware, she was learning behaviors that would impede her social development in the long run.

The day was cold as the February snow fell and the sharp wind blew through the trees. Ava was playing happily in the living room with Babe as Sonya sat at the table drinking a beer and smoking a cigarette. Niles was in his bedroom playing with his cat and Emma sat on her bed reading a book she had gotten from the school library. Lilli, alone in her own room, once again sat pondering her life and the reasons she and her siblings had to bear such mistreatment. Since Sonya no longer depended solely on her for Ava's care and had always abused Niles and Emma, nothing would change if she was gone. She rationalized Ava would eventually begin to experience the physical abuse as well and as soon as her cognitive abilities allowed it, the verbal, emotional, and mental abuse would take its toll on her too. Emma and Niles were already well on their way down the path of depression, just as Lilli had been at their age.

It was Thursday night and Lilli was looking forward to the slumber party she had been invited to the next night after school. Sonya had already given her permission so all she had to do now was wait for the time to come. Lilli stood up from her bed and ventured down the stairs to the kitchen to get a glass of water. She crossed the kitchen to the sink, passing by Sonya but saying nothing. She filled the glass about half way and began to drink as she stood in front of the sink.

"What the fuck are ya doin'?" Sonya hissed.

"Just get'n a drink of water," Lilli answered calmly.

"Did I say you could have a fuckin' drink of water?" Sonya sneered.

Lilli could feel the rage building within her. She had turned fifteen five months ago and her physical stature was equal to that of Sonya's but Lilli was thin while her mother was overweight. She put the glass down on the edge of the sink without emptying it and slowly turned to go back to her room.

"Wash that fuckin' glass!" Sonya exploded.

Lilli jumped slightly as she was not expecting the high volume of Sonya's voice. The sink and the countertop were both filled with dirty dishes, many of which wore dried, rotting food. Sonya hardly ever did any housework, which was evident, throughout the entire dwelling.

"While you're at it, wash the rest of the fuckin' dishes too!" Sonya barked.

"But it's Emma's turn," Lilli pleaded.

"I don't give a fuck whose turn it is! You're doin' the

fuckin' dishes or you're not goin' anyplace tomorrow night!" Sonya screamed.

Lilli turned and reached toward the sink. She knew she either had to do the dishes or she would get beaten, in addition to being kept from her outing. She stopped, her hand in mid-reach, and stood still. The adrenaline was pumping and her heart was pounding. The rage continued to grow and she brought her hand down hard on the edge of the sink as she cried, "No! I'm sick of this!"

"Excuse me?" Sonya growled as she slowly turned toward Lilli.

"You already told me I could go to Joyce's house for the sleepover! I'm tired of you always treatin' me like shit!" Lilli yelled.

Sonya shoved her chair away from the table and stood quickly. The sudden and unexpected outburst from Lilli seemed to fuel Sonya as she launched herself toward her daughter. Lilli moved quickly to the side and Sonya caught herself with her hands on the front of the sink, knocking the partial glass of water to the floor, shattering it.

"What the fuck did you just say?" Sonya screamed.

Lilli walked quickly across the kitchen to the bottom of the stairs. She knew even though Sonya had already given her permission to go to her friend's house she would never allow it now. She stopped at the bottom of the stairs and turned back toward her mother.

"I said, I'm sick of this!" Lilli screamed as she turned to take a step up.

Sonya, moving unexpectedly fast considering she was drunk, had already made her way to the bottom of the stairs. With one fluid motion Sonya took a swing at Lilli and made solid contact with her jaw. The shock of the blow left Lilli unprepared and widely exposed for Sonya's next attack. Lilli was now leaning against the door jam for support as the first blow had knocked her off balance. Sonya drew her hand back again and this time made contact with Lilli's left temple, dazing her. Lilli fell to her knees, all of her energy embezzled by the sudden attack. She lowered her head and rested it on her right arm on the bottom step as Sonya stood over her, panting.

"You little bitch!" Sonya hissed. "Ya ain't goin' anyplace now! Fuck you!"

Lilli remained motionless trying to regain the wherewithal to even stand. Sonya stomped away from her and back to the kitchen table, setting the chair she had shoved from the table back on its feet. She plopped heavily on the seat, took a long guzzle of her beer and lit a cigarette. She picked up the beer can again and sucked the remaining liquid from it. While still holding the empty can she glanced at Lilli, still at the bottom of the stairs. Sonya launched the can at Lilli and it connected with her head, bouncing off and rolling across the linoleum floor.

"Ya worthless little fuckin' whore!" Sonya roared with disgust. "You can forget goin' anywhere, ever! You'll be lucky if I let ya go to fuckin' school, ya little bitch!"

Though the can was empty, its trivial weight produced a crunching sound as it rolled across the filthy kitchen floor. The point at which the solid ring of the bottom of the can had made contact with Lilli's head began to swell a little and a small goose egg formed. Lilli slowly pulled herself up on her knees and crawled slowly up the stairs until she was able to stand up. Holding her face, she walked to her bedroom and shut the door softly. She lowered herself to the bed lying haphazardly on her stomach.

"I can't keep doin' this," she whispered softly to herself. "I don't wana be here anymore."

Tears began to seep from her eyes and she silently cried.

Her mind was racing and she was unable to make sense of all of her thoughts. All she really knew was that a life like hers was not worth living. The abuse she suffered at the hands of her mother for years had finally culminated. Something had to give. Lilli continued to lie motionless on the bed, crying as her mind began to slow down.

Sonya had finally calmed down from the confrontation with Lilli and decided to go to bed. She looked around the filthy kitchen and over to the place where Lilli had been sitting on the floor. She scoffed and blinked slowly, her vision blurred by the alcohol she had consumed. From the time she had plunged at Lilli, Ava had stopped playing with Babe and the two climbed on the couch, terrified by the loud voices. Sonya searched the doorway of the living room for the little girl but was unable to see her from where she was sitting. Sonya rose slowly from her chair, unable to balance herself without the help of the kitchen table. She took a few wobbly steps toward the living room doorway and found the wall to help her walk the rest of the way. As she stepped through the doorway she looked toward the couch to find Ava there. In the time it took for Sonya to calm down Ava had fallen asleep sitting up. Her small head and torso had lazily bent to the side until it rested upon the arm of the couch. Babe was curled up on Ava's lap, her large, furry body completely hiding Ava's tiny legs. She slept as well, comfortably trusting the little girl.

Babe sleepily opened her eyes when Sonya stepped into the room and watched her without moving. Sonya stumbled toward the couch and kicked Ava's foot to wake her up. Babe lifted her head swiftly, hissing and growling a warning at Sonya. Ava, groggy from sleeping, snapped awake and sat up quickly. Her little hands went directly to the raccoon and touched her thick fur, unconsciously grasping for comfort. Babe kept her keen eyes on Sonya and Ava sat completely still.

Another growl crept from Babe's throat and Sonya instantly knew the animal would attack her if she made another move toward Ava.

"Get the fuck up, Ava." Sonya said flatly. "It's time to go to bed."

Ava waited for Sonya to move toward her bedroom and then began to get off of the couch. Babe followed close to Ava as she climbed the stairs to the bedroom she shared with Lilli. Girl and raccoon entered the bedroom and made their way to Ava's disheveled bed, climbing in and falling almost immediately to sleep. Sonya had stumbled to her bedroom and passed out in her bed without undressing.

Lilli, still awake, heard Ava and Babe cross the floor of the room and knew they had both fallen asleep quickly. Lilli lifted herself from her bed and sat on the edge squinting in an effort to see across the room. Babe lifted her head and looked at Lilli but lowered it again after only a few seconds. Lilli's vision seemed to be blurred a little and her head was throbbing. A combination of stress, depression, and the blows to her head provided a generous basis for a migraine. She stood and walked to the door, turning to look once more at Ava. She left the room and descended the stairs, making her way to the bathroom to find something to help with her headache. As she opened the medicine cabinet she saw a bottle of aspirin containing only about four pills. She reached for the bottle but noticed a new bottle sitting a few inches away. Apparently, Sonya had restocked the aspirin supply when she received her monthly welfare check. Unconsciously, Lilli's reach adjusted and she picked up the new bottle of aspirin instead. She looked at the label of the generic medication and her mind started to wander.

"I wonder what would happen if I took all of these pills,"

she thought. "That might be a good way to kill myself, ya know, in my sleep."

She opened the bottle and broke the metallic seal across the top. The chalky, bitter smell of the aspirin filled her nostrils as she dumped a mound of pills into her hand. She closed the medicine cabinet and looked at herself in the mirror. Her eyes were red from crying and the skin around her left eye had swollen and begun to turn purple. Silently, she left the bathroom with the bottle of aspirin and merged to the kitchen to get a glass of water.

She noticed the shattered glass on the floor and her anger seemed to regenerate. She filled another glass with water and sat at the kitchen table with the bottle of aspirin in front of her and her hand still full of pills. Solemnly, Lilli tilted her head back and emptied the contents of her hand into her mouth. She picked up the glass of water and began to drink, swallowing all of the pills in her mouth. She continued swallowing handfuls of pills until the bottle of five hundred aspirin was empty. It took three glasses of water to wash them all down but eventually, she completed her task. She sat quietly and waited for something to happen. Everyone else in the house was asleep as it was one o'clock in the morning. She didn't worry about the school day slowly approaching, expecting to be dead before the bus arrived to take her to school. After about fifteen minutes, Lilli decided the aspirin were not going to do much of anything so, feeling a little tired, she made her way to the living room to watch some television.

Clicking the T.V. on, she backed toward the couch and sat down. Finding it strange that the sound on the television was so low, she walked back to the set and turned the volume up. Sitting back down, she realized she was still struggling to hear the voices of the people on the screen. At that time of the night, the only viewable program available was presented by the

Public Broadcasting Service, something about asteroids and dinosaurs. Lilli did not have a lot of interest in the program but it served the purpose of providing her with at least a little company. Dismissing the truncated audio as a malfunction of the machine, she decided not to do anything and simply sat down to watch.

Sonya awoke in her bed, fully dressed with her head pounding, to the sound of the television in the living room blaring. Instantly, her anger grew as she pushed herself from her bed and stomped into the living room.

"What the hell do ya think you're doin'?" she hissed.

Lilli offered no response, silently continuing to watch the program on the screen, as if simply ignoring Sonya. The only light in the room was the flicker of the images on the television screen so Lilli did not see Sonya standing in the dark.

"Dumbass!" Sonya yelled, "what the fuck are ya doin'? Go to bed!"

Still no answer as Lilli sat watching the program. Sonya stomped toward the couch and raised her hand. Bringing her hand down, she slapped Lilli's face. Lilli jumped, surprised by the blow as well as her mother's presence in the room. Looking up at Sonya with fear filling her eyes, she said nothing. Sonya was glaring at Lilli with wide, angry eyes.

"What the fuck do ya think you're doin'?" Sonya screamed once again.

Lilli, looking at Sonya, realized she couldn't hear anything. That was the reason for the television's volume seeming so low. She realized, when she turned the television up, the sound of the program must have awakened her mother. Still saying nothing, Lilli rose from the couch and took a step toward the stairway. Sonya had no idea Lilli was unable to hear her, nor was she aware of what Lilli had done. Lilli continued to the stairway slowly, finding it difficult to balance herself as she moved.

"Ya better nota drank all my beer!" Sonya growled. "Get upstairs and sleep it off! You're goin to school tomorrow, ya little bitch!"

Again, Lilli heard none of the words Sonya had spewed at her. The overdose of aspirin was beginning to affect her, first robbing her of her ability to hear. Her body felt heavy and she realized she was suddenly very, very tired. With no acknowledgement Sonya had said a word, Lilli slowly climbed the stairs to her bedroom. Climbing in bed she covered herself, feeling cold, as if the room's temperature had dropped twenty degrees. Across the room, Ava and Babe slept with no idea Lilli's health was being compromised. As she lay still under her blankets, her breathing began to quicken and her heart raced. She felt afraid of what would happen to her but she welcomed the thought of never waking up, once she was able to fall asleep. As she drifted further and further toward sleep, her thoughts began to mesh together, no longer making any sense. She surrendered herself to sleep with a feeling of triumph; no longer would she be subjected to her mother's brutal beatings and every day abuse. Consciousness faded from her tired mind and she drifted off into a peaceful sleep.

"Get you're ass up!" Sonya screamed as she tore the blankets from Lilli's body. "If ya miss the bus you're walkin' to school!"

Lilli lay motionless in her bed, unaware Sonya was standing beside her. Sonya reached over her daughter, slapping her face several times, very hard.

"Get your lazy ass up!" she shrieked. "Ya gota make sure the other kids get to school too, ya know! It's not all about you!"

Lilli's eyes fluttered faintly as she began to re-enter consciousness. Her hearing had not recovered, but she was able to make out most of what Sonya was screaming at her. She tried to move her arms and legs but their weight was remarkable. Feeling as if she weighed seven hundred pounds, she struggled to pull herself into a sitting position. Sonya stormed from the room and down the stairs, satisfied she had roused her daughter from sleep. Rubbing her face with both hands, Lilli tried hard to focus on the floor in front of her. She was disappointed she was still alive, deciding the overdose of aspirin just wasn't enough. Her stomach cramped and she felt very nauseous. She attempted to change her clothes so she could catch the bus but was unable to determine what to wear or even where her clothes were located. Giving up, she left the bedroom and crept slowly down the stairs. The bus pulled up by the driveway and Niles and Emma ran out the door. Ava was not yet old enough to go to school but was awake, regardless. Lilli walked by the little girl and tousled her hair in a loving gesture. She closed the door behind her and boarded the bus.

The morning was typical and Lilli made her way to her first class in a daze. The hallways seemed more crowded than usual and she found it difficult to navigate through the flow of people rushing around her. It almost seemed as if everyone around her were in fast-forward and she in slow-motion. Finally, reaching her class and sitting at her desk, she felt even more tired than she did the night before when she had finally gone to bed. Her nausea increased and she was sweating heavily, still unable to hear.

"Lilli, are you alright?" her teacher, Mr. Jordan, asked as he stepped close to the front of her desk.

Lilli, surprised at his proximity, looked at him. Her face looked very pale and her hair was soaked with sweat. She murmured a faint sound, attempting to indicate she was alright so Mr. Jordan would walk away.

"Are you feeling sick, Lilli?" Mr. Jordan asked, growing increasingly concerned.

Lilli's eyes began to roll back in her head as her body went limp. She fell slowly to the floor, seemingly melting from the chair she sat in.

"Amy, go to the office and tell someone to call an ambulance!" Mr. Jordan said to another student standing nearby, with urgency in his voice. "Hurry!"

Amy rushed from the room as Mr. Jordan crouched by Lilli, doing his best to comfort her. Lilli was unable to hear her teacher's voice or any of the other noises in the room. Her eyes rolled back to the front and tears began to fall slowly down her face as she lay on the floor, uncertain about whether or not she would survive, but hoping whole-heartedly she would be able to drift out of consciousness again, and then to death.

As the emergency medical personnel rushed Lilli into the emergency room at the Ropschon hospital, she was unable to discern what was happening around her. She did not remember the ambulance ride from Nathia at all. The medical personnel fussed around her busily as they connected her to the hospital's monitoring equipment. She lay panting in the hospital bed, unable to control her extremely shallow breathing. The nausea seemed to be getting worse and her head was pounding.

"Lilli, can you hear me?" one of the nurses loudly asked. "If you can hear me squeeze my finger."

Lilli squeezed the nurse's finger but the effort was almost nonexistent. Her hearing seemed to have returned slightly and even though the pressure from Lilli's hand was slight, the nurse was able to feel it and report the tiny triumph to the doctor who had just come rushing in. Lilli opened her eyes slightly, the blinding lights above her making it very difficult to see anything. She groaned quietly and the nurse immediately turned back to her.

"Lilli, are you doing alright?" the nurse questioned, ultimately trying to keep Lilli engaged in communication.

Lilli struggled to nod her head but to no avail. Though she tried hard, she was simply unable to move.

"Do you know what happened to you, Lilli?" the nurse questioned. "If you know what happened, squeeze my finger."

Lilli squeezed the nurse's finger once more, indicating she was aware of what had happened to her.

The medical team had already begun to run tests on Lilli's blood and knew the incident had nothing to do with alcohol.

"Do you use drugs, Lilli?" the nurse inquired. "If you use drugs, squeeze my finger once, if you don't, squeeze my finger twice, OK?"

Lilli struggled but was able to squeeze the nurse's finger twice. The only drug Lilli had ever indulged in was nicotine.

"Did you do this to yourself, Lilli?" the nurse asked. "If you did, squeeze my finger once, if you didn't, squeeze it twice, OK?"

Lilli squeezed the nurse's finger once, indicating she had done this to herself.

"Did you take something, Lilli?" the nurse questioned. "If you did, squeeze my finger, OK?"

Lilli squeezed the nurse's finger. The nurse reported what she had learned from Lilli to the doctor and he immediately ordered Lilli's stomach pumped. The nurse began to feed the tube into Lilli's mouth. As the tube passed the back of Lilli's throat she began to heave as if she would throw up. The nurse stopped and removed the tube at once. Lilli heaved a few more times and, turning her head to the side, began to vomit. At first, only stomach acid spewed forth but then a white, foamy substance began to drain out of the corner of her mouth. She heaved again, this time producing a mushy, white mass. Then another. The aspirin had collected in the bottom of her stomach and created a soft, chalky ball. Lilli continued to wretch, the remaining dissolved aspirin creating an opaque, white liquid. She turned her head back toward the ceiling and tried to catch her breath.

"What did you take, Lilli?" the nurse questioned. "If you can, tell me what you took."

Lilli attempted to find her voice but it continued to elude her. She mouthed the word "aspirin" but no sounds came from her throat. She tried again to say the word but still failed.

"You took aspirin?" the nurse attempted to confirm. "Squeeze my finger if you took aspirin." the nurse said.

Lilli squeezed the nurse's finger slightly and closed her eyes as the tears began to flow.

"How many aspirin did you take, Lilli?" the nurse questioned.

Lilli clumsily mouthed the words "five hundred."

"Five?" the nurse asked.

Lilli again attempted to speak the number. Her mouth formed the word "five hundred" but again, she was unable to produce any noise.

"Five hundred?" the nurse asked. "Squeeze my finger if you said five hundred."

Lilli slightly squeezed the nurse's finger to indicate she had gotten the number correct. The nurse immediately reported her findings to the doctor. Lilli began to fade out of consciousness once again. She felt so tired. Her eyes fluttered, then closed as she slipped into unconsciousness.

She awoke several hours later in a dimly lit room. The back of her hand was sore where a needle had been inserted and taped to her skin. Her throat felt raw and her head felt as if it would explode at any moment. She tried to recall the events that lead her to this place but was unable to remember more than a few fleeting events. She lay quietly in her hospital bed, unable to believe she was still alive.

A nurse walked into the room and noticed Lilli was finally awake.

"Hello there, Lilli!" the nurse said in a hushed but excited voice.

Lilli did her best to show a smile as the nurse approached the bed to check her vital signs.

"How are you feeling?" the nurse asked.

"Alright," Lilli said in a crackly voice.

"Do you think you might be able to drink some water?" the nurse questioned.

"Maybe," Lilli answered.

"Doctor wants you to drink as much water as you can, OK?" the nurse stated. "There is a vomit container here on your table if you get sick."

"OK," Lilli said.

The nurse left the room and Lilli was left alone with her thoughts. The day had been a blur but she was well aware of what had ultimately brought her to be in this hospital bed. She had tried to kill herself but had failed.

The next day Lilli awoke to the sun peeking through the blinds of the large window in her hospital room. She wondered what the next few days would bring and dreaded returning to her mother's house.

A woman, dressed professionally, entered the room with a briefcase. She noticed Lilli was awake and smiled at her sweetly.

"Hi Lilli," the woman said softly. "How are you feeling?"

"I'm OK," Lilli said softly.

"Are you up to a visit?" the woman asked.

"OK." Lilli said.

"I'm Donna and I'm a social worker for the state," the woman said. "I would like to visit with you about what happened. Would that be alright?"

"Yeah, I guess." Lilli agreed in a hushed voice.

Lilli felt relief that a social worker had come to speak with her. Though she felt pangs of failure from the botched suicide attempt, she seemed to feel as if she may be able to not only help herself, but help her siblings as well. Lilli and Donna discussed the events of the previous few days in detail so Donna could get a clear picture of what had caused the suicide attempt. Lilli described the abuse she and the others endured and by the end of the conversation Donna seemed to be speechless. It was decided immediately Lilli would not return to the home after her recovery, but instead, be sent to a foster home.

As the days passed, Lilli spoke often with Donna about the situations she and the other three children had experienced, Sonya's drug and alcohol use, and the brutal beatings she,

Niles, and Emma had received throughout the years. She spoke of the motorcycle ride and the failed rape attempt by Lars, Ava falling down the stairs of the apartment, and the many, many sexual encounters and reckless behavior Sonya engaged in. Donna understood the type of environment Lilli and the other children were in and felt a strong devotion to helping all of them.

A few weeks after Lilli's attempted to take her own life, Sonya, Niles, Emma, and Ava came for a visit. Lilli had heard nothing from her mother before the visit and luckily, Donna was in Lilli's room when they arrived. At once Donna intercepted Sonya and asked who she was.

"Can I help you?" Donna questioned as she stood and walked toward Sonya.

"I'm Lilli's mom," Sonya said flatly.

Niles, Emma, and Ava stood obediently behind Sonya, looking down at the floor as she spoke, a telling detail Donna noticed immediately.

"I'm Donna, Lilli's case worker," Donna said as she extended her hand for a formal handshake.

Sonya made no effort to shake the woman's hand and only stood glaring at her.

"Lilli's fine and needs to come home," Sonya said sternly.

"I'm sorry, Sonya, but that is not possible at this time," Donna explained. "She has experienced severe trauma to both her physical and psychological state and must be monitored."

"Bullshit!" Sonya retorted. "She's just tryin' to get attention!"

As Lilli listened to the conversation, tears streamed down her face. She had always been well aware her mother did not care about her and the two weeks it took her to even make an effort to visit was proof of that. Donna had informed Lilli her mother had been notified the day she was brought to the hospital so she knew she had simply decided not to come.

"It's been two weeks and I'm here to take her home," Sonya said as she began to take a step toward Lilli.

"Ma'am, please, wait out in the hallway while I speak with Lilli alone," Donna said with a tone of force in her voice.

Sonya looked at Donna, seemingly deciding whether or not the woman would take any physical action toward her.

"Ya don't need to talk to her alone," Sonya said. "I'm her mother and whatever ya need to say to her ya can say in front of me, right Lilli?" Sonya continued with an unnatural sweetness in her voice.

Donna turned and quickly looked at Lilli in the attempt to discern whether or not she wanted her mother in the room.

"Ma'am, if you do not leave the room I will be forced to call hospital security to remove you," Donna stated.

Sonya scoffed and turned around to exit the room. She and the three children stepped into the hallway and Donna quietly closed the door.

"Lilli, do you want your mother here?" Donna questioned.

"I wana see Niles, Emma, and Ava," Lilli said sadly.

"Alright, that's OK," Donna said.

Donna walked across the room and opened the door, stepping out into the hallway. She closed the door behind her, leaving Lilli in the room alone.

"Sonya, Lilli would like to see the children, however, I feel your presence will upset her," Donna said. "The children can go in for a visit, but I would like to speak with you out here," she continued.

"Fine, whatever," Sonya said, rolling her eyes.

Donna opened the door and invited the children inside. Niles, Emma, and Ava were clearly happy to see Lilli and as soon as Sonya was out of view all three of the children seemed to come out of their shells. Donna made sure everything seemed alright and returned to the hallway.

"Sonya, may I ask you a few questions?" Donna inquired.

"I guess," Sonya answered, irritated.

"First, why did it take you two weeks to visit your daughter here in the hospital?" Donna questioned.

"I was busy," Sonya said, clearly upset by the situation.

"OK," Donna said in disbelief. "Do your children experience any kind of abuse in the home?"

"Fuck no!" Sonya said loudly, clearly offended.

After only two questions, Donna was certain the information Lilli had given her was true. She knew a detailed investigation would have to take place but knew it could not happen at that time. Sonya was clearly irritated and angry and Donna felt uncertain about how she would react to any more questions.

"At this time, I am going to ask you to wait in the waiting area down the hall," Donna said. "I'll bring the kids to you when their visit is over.

Sonya said nothing and simply turned and walked away. Her normal ability to manipulate and demand seemed to be failing and her anger grew. She couldn't wait to get Lilli home so she could punish her for being so disrespectful. Sonya had no idea what would transpire as a result of Lilli's desperate attempt to escape her. Donna watched Sonya walk down the hallway and turn into the waiting area. She was uncertain whether or not Sonya would even wait.

Donna returned to Lilli's room and observed the interactions of the four siblings. They were all clearly happy to see one another and obviously bonded tightly. Lilli and Ava seemed especially close, confirming the things Lilli had told her during their conversations over the past few weeks. Donna knew she had to do all she could to remove all of the children from the home. After about twenty minutes the visit came to an end and Donna led the children back to Sonya. Donna returned to Lilli's room and discussed with her the joy she felt from seeing her brother and sisters.

Lilli's hospital stay ultimately lasted for seventy-nine days. In February of 1981 she was finally released to her foster family. In the time Lilli spent in the hospital, Donna tried to get the other three children removed from Sonya's care as well, but to no avail. She repeatedly attempted to get Niles and Emma to indicate abuse, recount events, and connect with her. Ava, though confidently developing her language skills, was still too young to indicate much detail. Sadly, the three children were still very much under the spell of their mother and would not disclose any information warranting their removal from the home. It almost seemed as if Sonya may have promised them the abuse would stop if they would just keep the secret and ultimately, they did.

Lilli received counseling during her stay in the hospital and looked forward to joining her foster family in their home. The family lived in Korin and even though Lilli had some reservations about starting a new school, ultimately she welcomed the change. She was allowed to visit Sonya's home every other weekend. At first, the visits were monitored by Donna and eventually, as Lilli's self esteem, will, and confidence grew, the visits were no longer monitored. On the weekends Lilli came to visit she would bring gifts for the children, however, as soon as she left Sonya would take the gifts from them. Niles and Emma told Lilli of the continuing abuse but, when questioned by others, would deny it. Ava had not started to experience the physical abuse at the time but the verbal, emotional, and mental abuse was spilling over onto her and the seeds of depression were being abundantly planted.

As the days went by Ava found herself playing alone often. In order to create fun and excitement for herself she found different things to play with and different imaginary situations to deal with. During one particularly hot day, she decided to play with the two dogs her mother had taken in. One of Sonya's drinking buddies had come for a visit so Ava was told to play outside. Niles and Emma were out in the grove, as usual, and told Ava she was too young to join them since she was only four-years-old. The car Sonya's friend had driven to their house sat unlocked in the driveway so Ava decided to play inside it. She pretended to drive, climbed in and out, and opened and closed the doors for no apparent reason. The dogs, clearly very hot, lay in the shade of an enormous tree in the front yard. Ava thought it would be fun to pretend she and her dogs were going for a drive. She found a piece of twine in the barn and tied it to the first dog's collar. His name was Blackie, a black mutt with very thick fur and a curly tail. She led the dog across the yard and to the car. She opened the driver's side rear door and urged the dog to jump inside. Blackie, a relaxed dog with a calm disposition, hopped in the car and lay down, panting. Ava untied the twine, shut the car door, and ventured back to the shady place in the yard where the other dog was lying. This dog, named Blackie II was a mix as well, however, his mix was more distinguishable. His fur was a dark, reddish-brown and very thick. His tail curled into a crescent but not enough to touch his back. His mix had been explained to Sonya before she took him in but in spite of the possible dangers to her children and the inability to feed either dog, she took him in as well. The previous owners explained the dog was a mix of Labrador retriever, Irish setter, and wolf.

Blackie II was not as laid back as Blackie but still very tolerant. He was used to Ava petting and touching him and when he was tired of the attention he would simply go on his way with no problems. This time, however, Ava tied the twine to his collar and urged him across the yard to the car. She opened the rear passenger side door and urged the dog to jump inside. He balked at the request and attempted to escape his constraints. In her determination to get both of dogs in the car, her attention turned completely toward Blackie II. With the car door still open, the other dog jumped out of the car and went to the barn. Ava lost her grip on the twine and Blackie II made his way to the porch to lie down. Ava followed the dog to the porch and once again got a grip on the twine still tied to the dog's collar. She urged him to his feet and tried to lead him down the stairs but the dog had run out of patience. He growled but Ava was not aware the noise was a warning. She continued to try to urge the dog down the stairs but he wouldn't budge. The growl coming from deep in his throat got louder and more urgent. He nipped at the hand that held the twine and Ava dropped it, surprised. After only a few seconds she reached for the loose end of the twine once again but he wouldn't allow it. He lunged at her, teeth bared and mouth open, knocking her to the floor of the porch. She had no time to even attempt to avoid the dog's advance and within seconds the dog's teeth dug into the flesh around her right eye. Ava shrieked from a combination of surprise and pain but the dog held tight, growling, with his jaws locked. Niles and Emma had ventured back to the yard and rounded the corner of the house only a few seconds after the dog had taken ahold of Ava's face.

"Hey!" Niles yelled.

The sudden, loud noise of Niles' voice surprised the dog and he released his grip on Ava. With the twine still tied to his collar he ran to the barn and disappeared. Ava lay on the bare, weathered wood of the porch floor crying from the pain the dog's bite had caused. Niles picked Ava up and carried her into the house as Emma held the door open. As the three children entered the house Emma called for Sonya but her bedroom door was closed tight and she was unable, or unwilling, to acknowledge the address. Niles took Ava into the bathroom and cleaned the wound on Ava's little face. The bite had broken the skin and the tissue around her eye was quickly swelling as the bruise darkened. After Ava calmed down, Niles was able to coax her into lying down and taking a nap. Sonya, busy with her friend in the bedroom, had no idea Ava had been bitten. Her drunken state prevented her from noticing the wound for three days after it had happened. Blackie II did not return to the house or the yard after he had bitten Ava. Niles, Emma, and Ava would never know what happened to him and Sonya claimed the dog must have run away.

Within the year Lilli was sent to live with a foster family, Sonya once again had to move. This time the situation was warranted by the sale of the house she was renting. She was once again able to secure a place to live in Nathia through a deal made with a bar mate. That summer the move was made to an apartment above a small restaurant located directly across the street from the town's high school. Once again, Sonya had recruited help from the bar and their belongings were packed and loaded. As the last of their belongings were loaded, Ava played in the yard. Even though she was very young she understood she would not be able to take Babe with her to the new apartment. She searched for raccoon but was not able to find her before Sonya ordered her to get into the car. With no regard for Ava's safety Sonya set her on her lap in the passenger seat of the car that would take them to their new home in Nathia. Ava searched the yard for Babe but she could not find her. Her little eyes followed the trunk of the big tree in the front yard all the way to the branches high above. She saw Babe, in the tree with another raccoon. The other raccoon was smaller than Babe and the two animals faced each other. Ava decided Babe had made a new friend and would be alright on her own. In reality, Babe was fighting with the other raccoon, high in the tree. Whether the two animals were fighting over territory or food or something else will never be known. Ava never knew whether Babe survived but in her mind her very first best friend would live on forever.

Ava had turned four in March and would be starting pre-school in the fall. Sonya realized she would finally be able to have some peace and quiet from her children as they would all be in school, at least part of the week. The move was also a positive thing, since living in Nathia meant she could frequent the bar once again with little effort.

As Sonya aged and the children grew, the physical abuse dwindled. Niles had turned thirteen and Emma was twelve. Both had grown a lot and their stature made Sonya question her ability to overpower them. Regardless of their size, however, Sonya knew she could still emotionally and mentally manipulate them.

Ava, now five-years-old, had no recollection of Lilli. The time Lilli spent taking care of her before she was sent away took place before Ava's conscious memories were able to be recalled completely. Ava was aware she had another sister and wondered about her often but never asked. Since Ava was still very young, she was still a victim of the physical abuse once aimed toward the three older children, however, Sonya was sure to keep it a secret from Emma and Niles. Ava was old enough to understand many of the things that transpired around her. Virtually every night she was forced to fall asleep in the booths of the local tavern until closing time finally rolled around. More times than not Sonya would stagger to the door with no thought of taking her child with her. The bartender would remind her and she would scoff at him as she stumbled to the booth to get her, waking her with a slap across the face or the back of the head. Ava would walk slowly beside her intoxicated mother the four blocks to their home. Upon arrival, she would sleepily climb into her bed and fall fast asleep unaware of the appalling events that would soon plague her life.

Not more than a year after the move to the apartment above the restaurant, Sonya found a house for rent just on the other side of the block. The search was prompted by yet another situation involving the sale of the structure in which she and the children lived. The restaurant was being sold and the apartment above it would serve as the new owner's dwelling. The house came open immediately and Sonya and the children moved in. Niles and Emma were old enough to venture out on their own and had their own groups of friends they spent time with.

Niles began to turn the tables on Sonya and seemingly became the household authority. At fourteen-years-old he began to refuse to do his homework and ordered Sonya to do it for him. His attitude had developed in a very negative way and he seemed to hate everything. For a brief time Sonya refused to do his homework for him and he began to fail his classes. His concern for his own future and Sonya's inability to provide structure produced an incredibly reckless way of life for Niles. Sonya began to do his homework for him, a practice that would continue until he graduated high school. As a product of the abuse he had endured, Niles had developed a hatred of most people, as well as Narcissistic tendencies. In his mind he simply felt he was above doing the work that would eventually produce his high school diploma. He felt as if he was better than everyone else in the house and was not afraid to express his feelings of superiority. He came and went as he pleased and in a very short amount of time Sonya realized she would never be able to control him again. He hated her with every fiber of his being and made that fact completely clear to her.

In spite of the closeness once shared between Niles and Emma, Niles had become incredibly mean to Emma. He hated her almost as much as he hated Sonya and felt, it was his right as a man, to judge both of them. In so many different ways Niles would do all he could to make Emma feel terrible about herself. He seemed to follow in Sonya's footsteps with the way he treated others but still felt he was better than everyone else. Emma tried to simply do her own thing but Niles would repeatedly intrude, calling her names, telling her she looked like a whore, and even cutting up her clothes and burying them in the back yard. However, if Sonya, Emma, or Ava dared to set foot in his bedroom or touch anything that belonged to him he would make it clear no one was to touch anything he owned, his warnings accompanied by threats. Niles conveyed this message vocally as well as physically. He began to physically abuse Emma and Ava sporadically, when he would disagree with the things they said or did. On occasion he would even use physical aggression against Sonya, though not often due to the almost constant company of her drinking buddies. Typically, the time she spent alone was used to recover from being drunk, sleeping until she was sober, sometimes for two and three days at a time. Since Niles had learned the physical and verbal abuse in tandem, he would unconsciously only assault others if both tactics were effective. Ultimately, if the person he was planning to attack could not hear him, he would hold his aggression inside and let it build up for the next time.

Emma, now thirteen, was expected to care for Ava due to Sonya's continued inability to do so. She felt Ava cramped her style and would regularly leave without her. Emma had made some friends at school and felt as if Ava was interfering in her social time. One of Emma's friends, John, had come to be a welcome addition to the group as he hung around a great deal and was usually up for anything. He was a tall, thin boy who was a few years older than Emma but chose to hang around just the same. He always seemed to have money and this was very interesting to Sonya. At this point Sonya was thirty-eight but had no reservations about intimacy with an adolescent. She threw herself at the sixteen-year-old boy and he greedily accepted her offers. He happily paid small amounts of money to have sex with Sonya and she happily continued the invitations. Emma had no romantic interest in John so the very inappropriate relationship between the two did not upset her. He seemed to be a permanent fixture of the house and no one thought anything of it.

The lack of structure in the home had led to many unfortunate things throughout the years, virtually too many to recall. For Emma, it seemed, appropriate boundaries had not been established. Her insecurities along with her very low self-esteem prompted her to seek relationships with others in order to feel as though she mattered. Her father's absence likely contributed to her tendency to share relationships with men, though nothing was ever clinically declared. Emma struggled with depression and strived to escape her mother's home. Emma's anger, unlike Niles', remained inside of her, eroding her self-confidence and plunging her further into herself. She desperately searched for the affection and acceptance which had eluded her throughout her life. She developed romantic relationships with various men but was still unable to find what she was looking for.

Lilli had turned seventeen and was doing very well with her foster family, though she still felt a void within herself. This void, the unmistakable product of the abuse she had endured, haunted her. She developed a relationship with Shane, a married man who was fifteen years older than her. Shane had three children with his wife and during their affair Lilli became pregnant with twins. Shane, afraid he would be discovered, forced Lilli to abort the twins she carried, further damaging her already fragile psyche. The relationship continued and Shane divorced his wife. Just after Lilli finished high school in Korin, she and Shane moved in together, a few miles outside of Nathia.

Though Ava did not recall Lilli's visits, nor did she recall the time during which Lilli took care of her, Lilli strived to have a relationship with her. Before she graduated, Lilli invited Ava to spend Easter weekend with her in her foster home.

Ava knew very little about Lilli (because of a child's typical inability to recall memories at a very young age) and was very intrigued by her.

They arrived at Lilli's foster home after what seemed like an eternity of driving. Ava, only five-years-old, had fallen asleep in the back seat of Shane's car after she started to feel sick from the ride. The house was very nice and Ava wondered why this house was so clean but her house was not. There were nice things on the walls, the floors were clean, and it felt cozy, warm, and welcoming. Ava tried to stay close to Lilli because, even though she did not know her well, Lilli was the closest thing to familiar that existed in the new surroundings. Over the weekend Ava and Lilli spent time together, colored Easter eggs, and had egg hunts in the house as it was too cold and wet to hide and hunt eggs outside. Ava felt an automatic and deep connection with Lilli which she would not fully understand for many years. Though the weekend seem to end quickly, the memory of that time with Lilli would stay with Ava throughout her life.

The time Ava and Lilli spent together after that was random but seemed to increase. Ava was always excited to see Lilli but at the same time was timid around her. Ava, like the others, had developed depression as well as other residual effects of the abuse she was still experiencing, and would experience, for many years. Ava had turned inward on herself and was quiet around people she wasn't used to. Even at the tender age of five she was already experiencing low self-esteem, self hatred, and feelings of inferiority. She wanted to spend time with Lilli but her fear always seemed to get in the way.

Chapter Four

After Ava's visit with Lilli in the foster home the days seemed to fly by. She soon began to lose touch with the bond she and Lilli had shared for so long as spent her days simply trying to avoid provoking Sonya's temper.

Just after Ava's sixth birthday, Sonya propositioned John to be Ava's babysitter. John eagerly accepted the position with no expectation of payment. The first time Sonya left Ava with John, Niles was already out of the house for the afternoon and was not expected to return until the next day. Emma had claimed to be going to a friend's house and was not expected to be home the entire night. Sixteen-year-old John and six-year-old Ava were alone in the house. They played "Go Fish" with a deck of regular poker cards for a while and then John invited Ava to sit on the couch with him to watch television. She happily and innocently accepted his invitation, not knowing what was about to happen. His continued and regular presence in the house had established a situation void of trepidation for the little girl. She was used to him being there and trusted him as much as she trusted anyone else. The two of them sat on the couch, first with a cushion between them, as the sitcom on the television screen continued. A few minutes later, John began to inch toward Ava as she continued to watch the show.

In only a few minutes, he had moved right next to Ava and

put his arm around her in a seemingly unthreatening gesture. She immediately felt an inherent sense of fear and discomfort, but at the same time, a strange warmth grew inside of her as she felt a sense of affection. Since affection was not something easily found in her home or family, she was unsure about the positive feelings she was experiencing in the moment. She had no earthly idea what healthy affection was and starved for any type of warmth or connection with another person.

It seemed as if John could sense Ava's welcome of his closeness and began to relax himself. A flood of confusion quickly entered Ava's mind as her basic need for connection and her conscious mind battled viciously in a warzone that would plague her for many years after. Quickly, she sorted out the confusion in her mind and understood the situation was not right. The comfort she had first felt quickly melted away to create an ocean of trauma waiting to tragically drown her. As the overwhelming feeling of discomfort returned, fleeting memories of slaps across the face as a result of objection flooded her mind and her heart began to race. She was unable to oppose anything taking place, paralyzed by fear, and unable to make even the slightest move to contest anything.

An intense storm began to rage inside Ava's mind and she was in immediate danger of being devoured by it. The upholstery of the dirty, gold-colored couch felt rough to her, and the sensation gained intensity as she was unwillingly moved about. She tried to remove herself from the horrendous events that were unfolding, separating her conscious mind from the present, and mentally placing herself into a different situation. The clouds of rage moved into her mind, black and menacing, as the wind accompanying them began to howl deafeningly. She tried to ignore what was happening and immerse herself in the television show flickering on the screen in front of her. The sounds from the television only faded from her consciousness and transformed into the sounds of the storm she was imagining. She could see herself, trapped in a tiny boat on the water's surface, unable to save herself. She desperately hoped, if she did not respond and behaved as if she didn't notice anything, he would abandon his efforts and it would all go away.

She was unable to move or muster the courage to stop him and felt her body stiffen as pain shot into her abdomen. It was as if she had lost all ability to control her own movements as John physically positioned her as he wished while her mind screamed out in terror. She could see herself, there in the tiny boat, afloat on the surface of the water as the storm continued to build and the wakes grew. She realized she could not hear her own voice, even in her mind, though she could clearly see an image of herself, screaming desperately. Sounds from the present moments were being transformed into the noises of the storm, all of them growing louder by the second. She began to feel the drops of rain on her face and the turbulence of the wakes as they turned to waves, tossing her about freely in the tiny boat. More pain surged through her body and she wanted to vomit. Thunder boomed in her imagination and her head began to pound as the storm became even more forceful, still drowning her cries for help. She felt herself being exposed as never before, completely and unequivocally vulnerable to the heinous intentions of a wicked individual.

Her eyes burned with tears and she wanted to escape. Paralyzed by fear and disgust, her muscles were incapacitated and simply would not obey her mind's commands to move. She knew her cries for help were in vein and no one could hear her. Ava could summon no words and simply shook her head in an effort to remove the heinous act from her mind. John arose from her and tucked himself back into his jeans. Ava remained lying on the couch, now with her legs crossed and squeezed tightly together. The blanket beneath her now wore a stain of blood in remembrance of her innocence. After John had finished getting himself dressed, he took the blood-stained blanket from under her and drew it across her stomach, wiping away the warm liquid puddled there. He picked up her underwear and shorts and tossed them at her.

"This is our little secret," he whispered with a tone of sick triumph in his voice. "If you tell anybody, you'll be in deep shit."

"Get dressed before anybody gets back," he demanded. "We don't wana get in trouble now, do we?" he questioned in a sickly-sweet tone.

Ava shook her head again and slowly reached for her clothes. As she sat up she pulled her shirt back down. She then put her underwear and shorts on and sat there, unable to move.

He sat next to her again, putting his right arm around her as if nothing happened, and resumed watching television. Ava still wanted to run away – she wanted to scream to the world something wasn't right. Her young mind was unable to grasp the situation and she was left to deal with it completely on her own.

The incident had exhausted her and she unwillingly drifted into a very troubled sleep. She awoke in the night to find John had fallen asleep, leaning to his left, away from her on the couch. Sonya was still not home, undoubtedly pursuing her own sexual adventures with a random man from the bar. She carefully got up from the couch and quietly retreated to her bedroom, closing the door softly behind her. After lying down in her bed she pulled her tattered, dirty blankets over her head and sobbed. Her tears did not stop until after the sun had come up and by then she was again exhausted. She fell asleep once again and this time her dreams were inundated with images of the previous night's horrific event. When she awoke her pillow was soaked with tears and she went to find her mother.

Sonya sat at the dining room table, a six pack of beer already down and an assortment of different colored pills scattered on the table. As Ava entered the room, Sonya barked her usual insults.

"'Bout time ya get up ya lazy li'l bitch!" she snarled. "Who the fuck do ya think ya are? What makes ya so fuckin' special ya think ya geta sleep all fuckin' day?" Sonya prodded, having only been up for an hour herself.

A few of Sonya's friends sat at the table with her, laughing at the comments she made to Ava. Ava stood next to the wall, leaning on it for support because her inner thighs were bruised and sore. Her stomach was turning and she felt a trickle of something running down her right leg. She slowly made her way to the bathroom and sat down on the toilet. She felt as if she had to urinate but nothing happened. She sat on the toilet for what seemed like an eternity before she felt it was safe to give up. She looked for some toilet paper, though there was rarely any to be found. Realizing her mother had again chosen to spend her modest welfare check on other things, Ava found a dirty washcloth to clean herself. After wiping herself she looked at the washcloth, now smeared with blood. She felt fear wash over her. She wanted so much to tell her mother what had happened the night before but knew if she did she would undoubtedly be the one getting into trouble. She walked carefully back through the dining room, on her way to her bedroom to change her clothes. Sonya and her friends were engrossed in their social drunkenness as Ava passed through the room, none of them noticing her presence. She changed her clothes and climbed back into her bed. Her little body hurt so much and there were no comforting words to be offered from anyone. As the silent tears rolled from her eyes she began to realize the feeling fear was likely to result in pain.

Unconsciously, her fledgling mind began to transform its reaction to fear in an effort to protect itself and the small being in which it existed. Ava's reaction to fear would ultimately change from innocently seeking protection to blinding, virtually uncontrollable anger. She cried herself to sleep once again, this time able to escape the terrible event and the nightmares which had plagued her the night before. Finally, her tiny body was able to relax and she slept peacefully throughout the night.

Regularly, John was asked to babysit Ava, and regularly the events of the first night reoccurred. Ava's young age and John's convincing words were enough to keep her silent for just over a year. John was able to convince the little girl he was the only one who cared about her. With Niles gone all of the time and Emma away from home a great deal, Ava was left with only Sonya as her hope for love and protection, only to find nothing but beatings and incredible verbal and emotional abuse. This type of home life supported John's claims and Ava was too young to rationalize the situation any differently. During the year of repeated rape, Ava never willingly did anything with John sexually, hoping each time would be the last. Every time it would occur she was only able to close her eyes and cry. As time went on, during the sexual acts, she became disconnected from herself imagining she was somewhere else. She rationalized sex must be necessary to feel any type of love from anyone. She concluded the attention and affection gained through sexually activity, even if unwelcome, was better than constantly feeling alone. John had even asked Ava to marry him and even though she had little idea about what the question meant, she felt as if he cared for her and would protect her. She began to feel as if there might be some hope and she may, at one point, be able to feel like a whole person, deserving of love and appreciation.

Shortly after Ava's seventh birthday, Sonya borrowed a friend's car in exchange for the usual sexual favors. Emma was helping Ava deliver papers for John while he worked at a local convenience store.

"Why are ya doin' John's paper route, Ava?" Emma taunted with a jealous tone.

"'Cuz he asked me to, duh," Ava stated matter-of-factly from the back seat.

"Ya know, he's just using ya to deliver papers so he don't have to do it," Emma sneered.

"Nuh-uh, he loves me. He told me so!" Ava jeered back in an attempt to confirm she was not being taken advantage of.

"What do ya mean, he loves you?" Sonya questioned, her voice immediately filled with jealous rage.

Ava realized she had slipped and now feared the worst. She sunk into the torn back seat of the borrowed car as her mother swiftly jerked the car to the side of the road, screeching to a stop. Sonya and Emma turned around to look at Ava as she began to sob uncontrollably.

"What do ya mean, he loves you?" Sonya screamed again, anger and disbelief saturating her voice, displaying the enraged jealousy she felt toward her seven-year-old daughter.

"I don't know." Ava squeaked, as she cringed and covered her face to hinder the anticipated blow usually following such a tone from her mother.

Surprisingly, Sonya made no effort to strike Ava and nothing more was said as the car slowly made its way back to the dilapidated house and pulled into the overgrown driveway. Sonya and Emma got out of the car, slamming their doors as they made comments about what they assumed had happened. Sonya was filled with jealousy and disgust, that John could even think of being interested in anyone besides her, without giving a thought to the physical and psychological damage her youngest daughter had endured for so long. Emma felt raging anger toward John because of what he had done to her baby sister but she was unable to convey her sorrow and empathy to Ava; partially because of the psychological damage Lars had imposed on her, and partially because of Sonya's inability to instruct her children about sincere conveyance of care for the wellbeing of others. Ava sat in the back seat of the car until her mother opened the door and threatened her.

"You get outta that fuckin' car and spill it!" she screamed. "I wana know what happened and why you're sayin' John loves ya! Why would he ever love you? You're just a spoiled little bitch that don't know shit!" she hissed.

Ava crept from the back seat, crouched low, as if any minute Sonya would assault her with a terrible blow. Sonya threw the door of the car shut so hard the entire car swayed under the force. She grabbed Ava's upper arm with a firm and painful grasp and forced her to move quickly into the run-down house. Ava, in an attempt to keep up with her mother, stumbled repeatedly, scrapping her hands and knees on the rough, dry ground. As her mother climbed the stairs, dragging Ava along, Ava simply gave up trying to walk and her body went limp as she hoped for death at that very moment. Still gripping her arm tightly, Sonya bent down and with a partially closed fist, hit Ava on the side of her head. As the blow connected, Ava's sight was altered for a moment as everything gained a lightened effect and small points of bright, white light flickered throughout her vision. Ava tried to rise but the fear and pain she felt overtook her and she was simply unable.

"Fine. Ya don't wana get up, I'll fuckin' drag ya! Doesn't make a damned bit a difference to me!" Sonya yelled. "Ya lazy little fuckin' whore!"

Sonya kept her grip on Ava's arm with her right hand and threw her half-empty beer can into the front yard. Her cigarettes and lighter were already in the brown leather cigarette case, safe and sound, so she put the case between her teeth and grabbed a handful of Ava's long, brown hair. The grip she had on the little girl's arm and the handful of hair were perfect handles to drag her up the stairs and into the house. Emma was already inside and saw nothing that had taken place. When Sonya reached the door, she let go of Ava's hair, long enough to swing it open, then resumed her grip and dragged the girl through the opening. The splintered wood and jagged metal of the threshold dug into the soft, tender skin on the back of Ava's legs, instantly drawing blood and leaving deep scratches and cuts. As Sonya dragged Ava through the breezeway toward the second door, Ava began to black out, the stress of the situation proving to be too much for her young, traumatized mind. All at once, Sonya rifled the little girl's limp body toward the middle of the couch. As she felt her entire body hit the back of the couch she began to gain consciousness once again. She found herself in a rumpled pile on the torn, imitation velvet of the gold-colored couch that sat in the filthy living room. Ava's face was wet with tears, her left upper arm already showing large, dark bruises. Her hands and legs bloody from the wounds to her soft flesh.

"What the fuck is goin' on!" Sonya screamed at Ava, only inches away from the little girl's face.

Emma sat quietly at the table, in sight of Ava, but behind Sonya. Ava's entire body shook as she was faced with revealing everything that had happened to her over the last year involving John. Her grey-green eyes were downcast and her tiny hands clenched one another as she tried to think of a way to undo what she had done and take back what she had said.

"Spill it!" Sonya screamed. "I wana know everything that went on and why the hell ya think ya deserve a man ya little bitch!"

Ava simply sat quietly and still, unable to describe anything or share her thoughts. Her mind had gone blank and the only thing she could think about was escaping the terrible situation.

Emma sat quietly, still peering at Ava from across the room. She felt so much pain and sorrow for the little girl but was unable to utter a word. She escaped the situation by imagining what life would be like when she could finally quit school and move in with the man she had been seeing for quite some time. He was much older than her and the relationship was kept secret from Sonya. Without a doubt, Sonya would react in a similar way, had she known of Emma's secret rapport. Emma's mind wandered as she thought about things in her life. Things had changed so much since Lilli had been sent away. Niles and Emma seemed to hate one another and Lilli's name was rarely mentioned. Ava was never able to experience the closeness to her siblings Lilli, Niles, and Emma had once shared. Emma's attention did not return to what was happening in front of her. It was much more comforting to daydream and think of other things.

"Ya better start fuckin' talkin' ya little fuckin' whore!" Sonya screamed. "I'm not guna wait all fuckin' day! Spill it, bitch!"

Ava took a deep breath and slowly raised her eyes to her mother's chin. She was unable to look her in the eyes with the knowledge she could not trust or depend on her.

"I don't know." Ava whispered as fresh, hot tears streamed from her eyes.

"Ya don't know. How fuckin' convenient. We're guna talk to the cops and then maybe you'll be able to remember. They'll make ya fuckin' talk, ya sick little whore." Sonya threatened.

Sonya, Niles, Emma, and Ava had moved to the dilapidated, weathered house that sat only a few blocks from Main Street in the small, Midwest town of Nathia after their house in the country had been destroyed by fire. The Nathia house had no carpet, its paint was chipped and worn, the doors sagged, and the roof leaked. Sonya spent the majority of her monthly welfare money on cigarettes, beer, and drugs so she had little left for luxuries such as a telephone. This meant the three must venture out once again and make their way to the local police station.

"Ya guna get off your ass and get back in the fuckin' car?" Sonya questioned Ava.

Ava rose slowly from the couch and began to make her way toward the door silently in an effort to avoid being drug again.

"If they ask why ya look shitty tell 'em you were playin' outside, got it?" Sonya commanded.

Ava nodded her small head to indicate she understood her orders and silently continued out of the house with Sonya, Emma following closely behind. Ava's mind began to wander in an attempt to rationalize all that had happened.

She concluded, although not consciously, she would not speak unless spoken to if she did not trust the people she was around. At that moment it seemed the psychological pressure from within her began to manifest into an introverted personality which would hinder her future in so many different ways. Silently, the three got into the car. Sonya gulped a beer and lit a cigarette to help relax her nerves and give her courage. The car backed out of the uneven, bumpy driveway and set off for the police department. When they arrived, Sonya threw her cigarette out the car window and without turning, instructed Emma and Ava to wait in the car.

"I'll be right back. You two stay here and don't fuckin' touch anything," she hissed.

Sonya got out of the car and slammed the door shut. She walked toward the stairs leading to the police department and climbed them, her anger and jealously driving her forward. As she entered the office, she saw only one woman sitting behind a desk. Sonya walked up to the secretary and, without being prompted, began to speak.

"I need a cop." Sonya rudely stated.

"Alright, please have a seat," the secretary hesitantly responded as she looked up at Sonya. "I will call the on-duty officer."

Sonya sighed loudly to communicate her disgust in having to wait and turned toward the chairs lined up on the opposite side of the room. She sat down and crossed her arms, sighing loudly again to purposely show her impatience and disgust at having to wait. She was nervous and wanted to smoke so she lit up while she waited. She hated being in police stations. Being in a police station made her terribly uncomfortable and her mind was automatically filled with thoughts of all the illegal things she had done and still continued to do.

"Fuck, if these idiots knew about all of the shit I do I'd be put in jail and they'd throw away the key," Sonya thought to herself as she smiled deviantly. Her thoughts drifted to a night when she and Lars had stolen an American flag and a state flag from a very tall flag pole in a rural cemetery. She closed her eyes, remembering how some of the headstones had been damaged as Lars drove through the grounds toward the flag pole. She recalled the beer cans they had tossed to the ground during the escapade and all the fun they had that night. She smiled again when she remembered, even now, the state flag hung on the wall in Niles' bedroom.

Sonya was torn from her daydream as an officer emerged through the front door of the station and approached Sonya.

"Can I help you?" the officer inquired.

"My daughter was raped," Sonya blurted in a tone suggesting nervousness and anger.

"Oh, alright," the officer said. "A matter such as this requires attention from the sheriff's office. I'll call it in and have an officer visit with you as soon as possible," he reassured.

"When will that be?" Sonya barked. "How long is it guna take?" she demanded.

"A deputy should be able to visit with you yet today, ma'am," the officer replied. "Please wait here and I'll contact them."

Sonya once again plopped down in the same chair letting out yet another loud sigh. The officer walked into the only office in the police station and closed the door. He picked up the receiver and dialed the number to the sheriff's office and patiently waited for someone to answer.

"Corral County Sheriff's Office, how may I help you?" the voice at the other end of the line said.

"Hi Evelyn," the officer said. "It's Jim. I have a woman here at the station claiming her daughter has been raped. Can you send Baker to talk with her?"

"Sure Jim, I'll call him on the radio if you want to hold on for a minute," Evelyn replied.

"Sure, thanks Evelyn," Jim said.

The line went silent as Evelyn put Jim on hold while she called Officer Baker. Jim's thoughts began to wander as he waited and he wondered if the woman's claims were true and if so, who could have committed such a horrendous act. He believed it was likely the event had taken place largely due to the woman's inattention to her children, if in fact, it was true.

"Jim? You still there?" Evelyn asked.

"Yep," Jim replied. "What did you find out?"

"Don is heading your way now so he should make it to Nathia in about fifteen minutes," Evelyn said.

"Great, thanks Evelyn. I think it will be best if we both go talk with this family," Jim stated. "Just have Don meet me at the station and we'll go together, okay?"

"Sure Jim, I'll let him know," Evelyn replied.

"Thanks, Evelyn," Jim said

"No problem, Jim," Evelyn said as the call ended.

Jim hung up the phone and made his way back to the waiting area to find Sonya smoking a cigarette and looking very uncomfortable and out of place.

"A deputy is on his way now, ma'am," Jim stated. "I need your address so we can proceed with an interview in the home," he added.

Sonya repositioned herself in the hard chair and proceeded to give the officer her address.

"When are ya guna get there?" Sonya questioned impatiently.

"Someone should be there in about a half hour to speak with your family, ma'am," Jim replied.

"Fine, whatever," Sonya retorted as she stood from the chair and began walking toward the front door.

Sonya walked down the front steps of the police station, letting the heavy door slam behind her. Her nerves seemed to instantly calm as she exited the building and her only thought was she wanted a beer and another cigarette. She made her way to the car where the girls waited and got in.

"The cops are comin' to talk to ya so ya better tell 'em everything," Sonya said to Ava without looking at her.

Nothing more was said as the car's engine roared to life and carried them back to the house. All three got out of the car and went into the house silently. Ava went straight to her room and closed the door while Emma began to watch television. Sonya went directly to the filthy kitchen and found a beer in the refrigerator. She opened it and took a long drink. She belched loudly and made her way to the dining room table, sitting down as she lit a cigarette. As Ava hid in her bedroom, Sonya and Emma sat quietly, immersed in their own thoughts. It seemed as if nothing had happened.

About twenty minutes passed and suddenly there was a knock on the door. Emma immediately rose to peer out the small window overlooking the front porch to see who was waiting outside.

"It's the cops," Emma said with no emotion in her voice as she turned and walked away from the window.

"Come in!" Sonya shouted angrily.

Emma returned to her seat on the couch and resumed her interest in the television show on the screen. Sonya was seated at the dining room table drinking a beer and smoking a cigarette. The house smelled of stale cigarettes and old beer; an aroma that escaped Emma and Ava, simply because the two were exposed to it on a continuous basis. The only member of the household who seemed to notice the stench was Niles as he was away from the house much of the time.

Jim, the officer Sonya had talked to at the police station,

and Don, the sheriff's deputy, stood on the concrete porch of the old, unkempt house. They noticed the untidy way the home's exterior was kept and both knew the inside would be just as bad, if not worse. The old concrete porch seemed to be molded, as if made up by one large piece. To the left of the porch's landing a flower bed had been built and looked just as old as the porch itself. No flowers grew in the flower bed but empty beer cans and cigarette butts littered the dirt among the weeds. Jim knocked on the door of the house and heard someone yell from inside. Both officers waited, their training governing their decision not to enter.

Sonya, annoyed and angry, finally rose from the table and stomped across the living room to the door. She threw the door open and saw the two officers standing outside the wooden screen door.

"She's in her room," Sonya said to the officers, as if they were familiar with the layout of the house.

Sonya turned and walked swiftly across the living room, in spite of the buzz she already had from drinking all morning.

"Ava, get out here!" Sonya screeched.

Ava heard her mother's command but was unable to move. She wanted to scream for help and run to the officers so they could take her away. Sonya screamed the command again but was unable to wait for a response. The jealousy, anger, and curiosity she felt fueled her to seek out the little girl and force her to speak. She stepped inside the room and found Ava under the bed, curled up in a ball.

"Get out here, now!" Sonya ordered.

Ava couldn't move. A barrage of emotions assaulted her and she could not think straight. In the back of her mind she knew her mother would beat her for not coming out from under the bed but the anger, shame, embarrassment, fear, and sadness that enveloped her simply would not allow her to move. Sonya lowered herself to one knee and peered under the bed.

"You get your ass out here right now!" Sonya hissed.

Both officers had approached the bedroom and were alarmed by Sonya's tone of voice as she spoke to Ava. They exchanged a glance and knew it was time to act.

"Ma'am," Don said, politely, "maybe I can get her to come out."

Surprised, Sonya looked up at the deputy and reluctantly surrendered her place on the filthy floor next to the bed. She stood closely by so she would not miss anything that was said.

"Hi, Ava," Don said gently. "How are you doing?"

Ava held her position under the bed and could not even bring herself to look at the officer. Though her fear consumed her, his gentle voice seemed to help calm her. In spite of the lessons she had inadvertently been taught by her mother, Ava somehow felt a little safer, knowing the officers were there, but remained under the bed like a filthy, unwanted dog.

"Ava, do you think you can come out and talk to me?" Don asked gently.

Ava merely shook her head to indicate she could not come out from under the bed. She wanted to tell the officer everything but was filled with fear. She knew if her mother heard even one detail, the beating sure to come would be monumental.

"Do you think you can talk to me if you stay under the bed?" Don asked sweetly.

Ava nodded her small head and seemed to feel an immediate relief. Finally, she could tell someone what had happened to her. She wondered if the terrible things John did to her would finally stop if she told someone.

"What happened, Ava?" Don asked.

Ava simply buried her face in her hands and began to cry. She couldn't even speak the words.

"Did someone hurt you?" Don questioned.

"Yes," Ava squeaked, barely making a sound.

"Who hurt you?" Don asked.

"John," Ava answered quietly.

A sudden and angered scoff came from Sonya as she rolled her eyes. Jim, still standing quietly in the bedroom doorway looked at Sonya with curiosity.

"Ma'am," Jim said, "please step out of the room. I have a few questions to ask you."

Sonya looked at Jim with contempt as she reluctantly stepped past Don, who was still on one knee. She hated Jim would ask her to leave the room. She wanted to hear what had happened and how Ava had seduced John, stealing him from her. In Sonya's mind, she was the most wonderful thing that had ever happened to John and she felt he owed her because she had allowed him to have sex with her. She could not wrap her twisted, sick mind around the idea John would want Ava. The hatred she felt for the little girl grew exponentially since she had learned of the affair between John and Ava. Sonya saw Ava merely as another reason she couldn't be happy and not as the delicate child she actually was. Instead of being concerned for Ava, Sonya only felt jealousy toward her because she felt Ava had stolen John from her. In reality, the little girl had been a victim of a teenaged boy who felt no remorse for what he had done.

After Sonya left the tiny bedroom, Don continued to talk to Ava, eventually coaxing her from under the bed. Ava could not look at the officer as she revealed the heinous events of the past year, tears flowing from her eyes. She told the officer about the terrible sexual acts John had involved her in, at least three times a week, over the past year. It was so difficult for Ava to talk about what had happened because she truly believed she would, indeed, get into trouble. She had already experienced the physical assault of her mother, prompted by the initial shock of the situation. Ava knew she was in for so much more and her relationship with her mother would change forever.

While Don continued to talk with Ava, Jim questioned Sonya about her knowledge of the events.

"Ma'am, when did this start?" Jim questioned.

"Fuck, I don't know!" Sonya exclaimed, defensively. "I just found out about it today and she won't tell me a fuckin' thing!"

"Have you noticed any behavior from Ava that may have been due to the alleged abuse?" Jim asked.

"Nope," Sonya stated, matter-of-factly as she plopped down in one of the chairs next to the dining room table.

Sonya reached for her cigarettes and pulled one from the pack. She lit the cigarette, leaned back in the chair, and crossed her arms. Jim didn't have any proof, but he had a feeling Ava's behavior had changed, the changes going completely unnoticed. Of course, Sonya had noticed nothing as her virtually continuous drunken state prevented her from noticing much of anything. Jim continued to question Sonya but was unable to discover anything other than the fact Sonya cared little for her children and likely had a sexual relationship with the sixteen-year-old boy the little girl was accusing.

Don talked with Ava for about an hour in an attempt to find out the whole story. Though Ava disclosed much of what had happened, she was only a child and unable to convey her thoughts in a way that offered an abundance of details. Don emerged from the bedroom and addressed Sonya.

"I think it would be best for you to get a lawyer," Don said, looking at Sonya.

"How the hell am I guna pay for that?" Sonya snapped.

Don was not prepared for Sonya's reaction and looked at her in disbelief.

"If you're unable to afford a lawyer on your own, it is possible the state will assist you, given the circumstances, ma'am," Don stated. "If what your daughter says is true, something needs to be done immediately."

"Aren't you guys guna do somethin' about it?" Sonya asked, noticeably irritated.

"At this point, there's nothing we can do, other than speak with John," Don answered. "Without physical proof we will only be able to take legal action if he admits it."

"What a fuckin' joke!" Sonya blurted. "That son-of-a-bitch has been fuckin' my daughter and all you're guna do is talk to him?"

Sonya's anger and jealousy had provoked her to use the situation against John. She knew she could use the situation to get her revenge on him. If she could appear to care about her daughter's welfare, she may be able to manipulate the officers into doing something more than talking to him.

The officers offered no more information or advice and left the house. They talked about the situation briefly and then proceeded to contact John for questioning. Of course, John denied everything and was left alone. Don knew something terrible had happened and believed what the child had told him to be truth.

"Little kids don't make shit like that up, Jim," Don stated after a long silence.

"I know, Don, but what are we going to do?" Jim answered.

"Nothing we can do, I guess," Don replied, feeling he had let the situation escape him.

He wanted to help but felt the family had no hope of being anything more than white trash. The conversation stopped and the officers began to talk of other things.

Ava remained in her bedroom for the rest of the night, unable to bring herself to move from the bed she and Emma usually shared. She cried herself to sleep that night while Sonya proceeded to get drunk with a few of her friends. Sonya made no effort to comfort Ava but acted as if things were the same as they had always been. Emma had gone to a friend's house and was not expected home until sometime the next afternoon. Niles was nowhere to be found and no one knew where he was or when he would return. Sonya, having fun with her friends, felt as if she had no responsibilities at all and she loved it.

The next morning, Ava awoke with a feeling of wretchedness that seemed to consume her. She felt relieved she had finally been able to tell someone about the terrible things John had done to her and somehow knew it would finally stop. At the same time, however, she felt even more alone than before. She longed for affection from her mother and a feeling of closeness to her family. Even though John had done so many disturbing things to her, she couldn't help but feel a sense of acceptance when she was with him. She knew she would no longer be able to feel that acceptance since her mother knew about what had happened. She mourned the death of the only affection she had ever known and knew, from that point on, she would be utterly alone. She began to close herself off from everyone else in the world and the feeling of loneliness grew more and more every day.

Ava emerged from the bedroom and looked around the large room her mother used as both a living room and dining room. The table was stacked with empty beer cans and her mother was passed out on the pull-out sofa with two men. Ava went to the bathroom and then returned to her bedroom. She climbed back into the bed and covered herself. She gazed out the window at the house across the street and imagined how it would be to belong to a happy and caring family. She closed her eyes and drifted off to sleep in an effort to escape her wretched feelings.

Over the course of the next few days Sonya informed Niles about what had happened and he was furious. Even though he seemed to have narcissistic tendencies, he understood the wrongs that had been done and seemed to care for his little sister, at that point, instead of only himself. Niles looked at the situation differently than Sonya and vowed to get revenge on John. Since Niles was free to do whatever he wished at any point of every day, he made roaming the small town at night a regular activity, if for no other reason than to escape the situations that existed at home. Niles and his friends committed many misdemeanors, none of which they were ever caught and punished for. Niles' past had molded him into a hate-filled individual who displayed many symptoms of bipolar disorder and narcissism. He was incredibly mean to Emma and Ava and treated Sonya with contempt on a regular basis. During one of his efforts to entertain himself, he gathered all of Emma's school clothes, shredded them with scissors, and buried them in the back yard. Sonya half-heartedly attempted to correct his behavior by yelling at him but her attempt was short-lived. Niles barked back at Sonya and she cowered in fear. Her only son had grown into an abusive individual of whom she was now terrified. Emma and Ava were terrified of Niles as well and he never missed an opportunity to exercise the control he had over all of them.

Ava, only seven-years-old, had known Niles as the only male authority figure in her life since Lars had left long ago and never returned. Niles' ability to continually overtake Sonya at every opportunity showed Ava men would likely attempt to rule her life as well. This display also showed Ava Sonya may not be someone to be afraid of, though she would not embrace this lesson completely for several years.

Life went on as usual and the summer wore on. Ava played alone much of the time, occasionally venturing to a friend's house. At only seven, Ava had already seen a great deal of the world and the horrors that lurk in the shadows of life. Her introverted personality continued to develop and her emotional state continued to worsen. The little girl began to harden toward things most girls her age would embrace. She began spending time with a few friends who were a little older than she and began to take lessons from them about how to behave and how to do things. She continued to disconnect herself from Sonya more and more and Emma's presence became scarce in the dilapidated home. Niles continued to roam the streets at night and finally caught up with John outside the local grocery store.

"Hey ya fuckin' piece of shit!" Niles exclaimed.

John felt a twinge of fear as he turned to meet Niles' icy stare. John was unable to speak and knew Niles meant to hurt him for what he had done to Ava.

"Ya think it's okay to do sick shit to little girls?" Niles sneered.

John looked down and silently shook his head. It was unclear if the gesture was meant as an answer to Niles' question or the premature response to what he knew was about to happen. Niles rushed upon John grabbing him by the front of the shirt, his rage erupting. Niles swung his fist hard at John's face, connecting solidly. John's right eye immediately began to swell and blood trickled down the side of his face. Niles had hit John so hard his vision faltered for a second as he stumbled backward. Niles grabbed John again, this time by the back of the shirt and the back of his pants. Niles forced John to bend forward and with all the strength he could muster, slammed John's head into the face of a soda machine. The front of the soda machine, made of very thick plastic, shattered as the top of John's head made contact, his head continuing through the broken plastic, creating a gapping hole in the front. The force of the blow was so hard John's head bounced off of the inner mechanisms of the machine, forcing his body to rebound. John fell to the ground in a heap, blood draining from each of the numerous cuts on his head, face, and neck. Niles stood over John, watching him as he laid on the sidewalk, bleeding. Niles' rage was still at its peek and he began to kick John repeatedly in the stomach and back. John, barely conscious, moaned in pain as he attempted to crawl away from Niles' repeated blows. Niles' fury began to dissipate and he stopped kicking John. Panting heavily, he lowered himself in order to be almost face to face with John.

"Ya fuckin' piece of shit! Don't ever let me catch you near Ava again!" Niles hissed.

John, still lying on the sidewalk curled into a ball on his side, began to sob uncontrollably.

Niles spit in John's face and then stood up. Niles walked away from the scene of the terrible beating, making it only a block when he heard a car drive up behind him. The unmistakable sound of a police siren blipped twice and Niles turned to look at the car as if he was unsure of why the officer would want to talk to him. Niles recognized the face of one of the town's officers through the driver's side window of the police car.

"Niles, what did you do?" the officer asked as he shook his head slightly.

"I beat that worthless fuck, Tim," Niles replied, matter-of-factly.

"I know, Niles. Someone watched the whole thing from the apartments and called us," Tim answered with a tone of sorrow in his voice.

"He raped my little sister, Tim," Niles said. "He fuckin' had it comin'."

Tim looked around, as if to assure himself no one was listening, and in a quiet voice said, "I know what he did to Ava. He deserved what he got but you should've made sure no one was watching. Now I have to take you in, damn it."

Niles smiled, as if the officer had told a weak joke, turned, and continued to walk down the sidewalk. The police car continued slowly down the street, keeping pace with Niles.

"Niles, come on," the officer said from the slowly moving car. "I gota take you in."

Niles stopped walking and stood motionless on the sidewalk looking down at his bloody knuckles. He sighed, then said, "Not tonight, Tim," and continued walking.

Tim stopped the car and decided the next day, with some backup, he would catch up with Niles. Niles walked home, pleased with what he had done to John, and went to bed. The next day Niles got up around the usual time and was listening to music in his bedroom. There was a soft knock on the door.

"What," Niles stated loudly.

"The cops are here and wana talk to ya," Sonya answered in a playful tone from the other side of the door.

Niles had hoped Tim would just let it go. Taking his time, Niles turned off his music, put on a pair of sweat pants, a T-shirt, and his shoes. He looked out his window and thought of climbing out and running. The thought passed quickly and he decided to go talk to the officer. Niles opened the door to find Tim and a deputy standing in the living room. Niles let out an ironic chuckle and shook his head.

"You're under arrest, Niles," Tim stated.

"For what?" Niles questioned, chuckling sadistically.

"Assault," the deputy answered authoritatively.

Niles chuckled and shook his head again. Sonya sat at the dining room table and watched in silence. She was happy Niles had beaten John. Silently she hoped John had learned his lesson and she would be able to continue her relationship with him. In Sonya's mind, John had deserved the beating for stepping out on their relationship but in reality the beating was intended to make John suffer for what he had done to Ava. Niles left with the officers and went to the sheriff's office for questioning.

Though Niles had attempted to settle the score with John on Ava's behalf, Ava knew nothing about what had happened until a few days later. Ava had been at a friend's house for the afternoon and upon returning home, found Sonya in her usual drunken state.

"Where the fuck have ya been?" Sonya prodded as Ava walked into the house.

Immediately, Ava's eyes began to well with tears. "I was at Emily's," Ava answered meekly.

"Ya little fuckin' bitch," Sonya sneered as she sat glaring at Ava. "Because ya couldn't keep your legs closed, Niles is in trouble."

Ava did not understand what Sonya meant and dared to ask her to clarify. "What?" she questioned.

"Ya little whore, you know what," Sonya retorted.

Ava's tears continued to flow and she dared to inquire once again. "No, I don't know," Ava responded.

"Well, since ya saw fit to steal John from me and say he raped you, Niles got all pissed off and beat the shit out of him. Somebody saw it and the cops took Niles to jail," Sonya explained with little emotion.

Ava could not believe what she was hearing. She was crushed at the thought of her mother blaming everything on her. She chose to say nothing and went to her room.

"That's right ya little bitch, run and hide 'cause ya know ya fucked up!" Sonya screeched as Ava walked by her.

Ava closed her bedroom door and threw herself onto her bed. She cried into her pillow in an effort to hide the pain her mother had caused her. While she lay alone in her room, she decided she would not let her mother hurt her again. It was time to turn off the longing for acceptance and take care of herself. She somehow knew it would be difficult, and may not happen all at once, but she vowed to overcome the guilt she felt as a result of the entire situation. As Ava stared at the ceiling, her seven-year-old mind began to think about what it would be like if she escaped her own life. She wanted to run away but knew she had nowhere to go. She wanted to hide but knew someone would find her. With no other conceivable solution to her torment, she began to think about taking her own life. Little did she know, the thought of suicide would plague her for many years to come.

Chapter Five

Within the weeks following the disclosure of the events that had taken place over the previous year, Sonya was able to find and contact a lawyer in Nathia. In an effort to tug at the heartstrings of the lawyer, she took Ava along to her first appointment. Sonya rationalized, if the lawyer could see Ava, he may take the case and possibly at no charge.

Niles had faced the charges against him and was sentenced to complete community service as punishment for the beating he had given John. He spent even more time away from home and would seldom return, spending most of his time staying with friends. Sonya did not ask him about anything when she saw him, hoping he would continue to stay away. She felt she was in control when he was not around and she liked it that way.

Ava had taken to playing alone outside the house much of the time. Ava, not a typical little girl, enjoyed playing with cars and trucks in the dirt. She constructed roads in the bare spots in the lawn, pretending she was part of a family who enjoyed driving in the country and looking at the scenery. She sat in the overgrown back yard, pushing the small, metal cars through the dirt. Her clothes were filthy and the exposed skin on her body had taken on a greyish hue from the dust and dirt in which she played.

"Ava," Sonya stated, with no emotion. "C'mon, we gota go."

Ava looked up from her cars, somewhat surprised at the lack of an angry tone in her mother's voice.

"Where?" Ava innocently questioned.

"Move it!" Sonya stated with a hint of annoyance settling in her voice.

Ava rose to her feet and left the cars and trucks where they were. The toys seemed to represent a small, lonely, dry town people had abandoned a long time ago. She walked cautiously toward her mother, who stood at the corner of the garage, waiting. It was very seldom Ava would raise her eyes from the ground as she walked. She had become so accustomed to feeling ashamed and her eyes seemed to remain downcast, regardless of what she was doing.

Sonya waited a few seconds to ensure Ava would continue approaching the house, then turned and walked back inside. Ava climbed the stairs to the front door and went into the house, curious about where her mother would be taking her. Sonya gulped down the last of her beer and lit a cigarette as Ava crossed the threshold into the living room. Ava said nothing, completely aware of her mother's likely response if she questioned their destination any further. Ava stood quietly by the door, waiting for her mother's next instructions.

Sonya picked up her cigarette case as she turned away from the dining room table. She walked toward Ava with the intention of walking out the front door. Secretly, Ava glanced up at Sonya as she approached. She noticed Sonya must have bathed. Her hair was put up off her neck and she was dressed in a pair of pink slacks she had made herself. Her sleeveless shirt was made of a delicate fabric and tinted a light brown. Ava looked down at her own outfit and felt a tinge of embarrassment. She wore a pair of green shorts and an orange T-shirt, both of which were filthy from the day of play. As Sonya walked by, Ava's eyes shot back to the floor. Sonya passed Ava, as if she were not there, and walked out the front door.

"Let's go," Sonya stated as the screen door slammed shut behind her.

Ava followed her mother obediently, still unaware of their intended destination. She followed close behind Sonya as she made her way to the corner and proceeded down the transverse road toward Main Street. The day was beautiful and Ava enjoyed walking and looking at the things around her. She could smell the fresh-cut grass from one of the neighbor's lawns and wondered why Sonya never mowed theirs. As they made their way to the sidewalk on Main Street, Ava tried hard to pay attention to what she was doing and where she was going. She had been corrected many times in the past by her mother for dawdling and aimlessly wandering without keeping up. Before Ava knew it, her mother slowed her gait and stopped at one of the doors facing Main Street. Ava did not recognize the business and had never noticed it before. Sonya pushed the heavy glass door open and entered the dark hallway. Ava felt instantly on edge and followed closely as Sonya approached the only door in sight. Sonya turned the gold-colored knob on the door, opening it to find a large office. A young woman, sitting behind a large, dark brown desk, looked up at Sonya and smiled.

"Hello, may I help you?" the young woman inquired happily.

"I need to see the lawyer," Sonya stated, nervously.

"Do you have an appointment?" the young woman asked sweetly.

"Yeah, at two," Sonya responded.

"Okay, please have a seat," the young woman said as she

gestured toward the row of chairs against the wall opposite her desk.

Sonya turned to find a chair, grabbing Ava's upper arm much too hard in an effort to force her to follow. Ava walked quickly behind Sonya as the pressure on her upper arm sent a burning sensation through her shoulder. As Sonya sat down, she let out an irritated sigh. She hated being in places like this, especially when she had to have Ava with her. To Sonya, Ava was an embarrassment. The little girl was always dirty and didn't have the slightest idea how to behave. Sonya sat quietly, watching Ava out of the corner of her eye.

"This little bitch isn't guna help me at all," Sonya thought to herself as she made a weak attempt at adjusting her shirt. "I gota make that fuckin' John pay for what he did to me."

Sonya's anger and jealously began to grow toward John and Ava, once again, fueling her to do all she could to hurt him because of what she perceived he did to her - not giving any thought to what he did to Ava.

The young woman behind the desk had telephoned the lawyer in the next office to let him know his appointment had arrived. The door to the neighboring office swung open and the lawyer stepped through. Ava looked at him as he approached Sonya to shake her hand. He was a heavy man, about six feet tall, with thinning dark hair. He was dressed in a very nice black suit, accented with a white shirt and bright blue tie. Ava, once again, felt uncomfortable as she compared her messy appearance with his.

"Hello," the lawyer said in a strong but peaceful voice. "I'm Gary Winter," he continued as he stretched out his hand to shake Sonya's.

"I'm Sonya Bauer," Sonya answered, clearly intimidated.

"It's nice to meet you, Sonya," Gary said with a polite

smile. "And what is your name?" he asked as he knelt down on one knee to address Ava.

Ava, taken by surprise, and very untrusting of everyone, said nothing and stepped behind her mother to hide from his inquisitive stare.

"She don't talk much," Sonya said, clearly embarrassed by Ava's behavior.

"That's alright," Gary said as he stood, once more offering a friendly smile to Ava. "Please, come in," he continued.

Sonya followed Mr. Winter into the office as Ava tried desperately to cling to the only familiar thing in the room – Sonya.

Mr. Winter walked behind the huge desk in the middle of the room and gestured for Sonya to seat herself. Sonya took a chair on the opposite side of the large desk, facing him. Ava chose to sit on the floor in front of Sonya's feet in order to avoid any eye contact with the lawyer. From her seat on the forest green carpet, Ava could see the walls were paneled in a dark, maple brown wood, giving the room a cozy feel. The carpet upon which she sat was soft but not thick and she wondered how it stayed so very clean. The chair in which her mother sat was made of dark brown wood as well, the cushions apparently made of light brown leather. Ava sat quietly and continued to look around the parts of the room she could see as she listened to the conversation taking place.

"So, what can I help you with today, Sonya?" Mr. Winter inquired.

"I need to know what I can do to this guy that raped my daughter," Sonya said with a tone of distrust in her voice.

"Okay," Mr. Winter said with obvious surprise, both in his voice and on his face. "Is this something that happened recently?" Mr. Winter asked.

"Yeah, well, over the last year. I just found out a few weeks ago," Sonya answered as she nervously fingered her cigarette case.

"Oh, okay," Mr. Winter replied. "How old was your daughter when the rape occurred?" he asked.

"Six." Sonya stated flatly. "She said it's been goin' on for a little over a year but I don't know for sure. She's seven now, so…" Sonya continued, trailing off.

Mr. Winter was clearly taken aback by the statement and fumbled for his words. "Uh, well, okay," Mr. Winter stumbled. "Is this…" he began to ask as he gestured toward the place he thought Ava was sitting.

"Yeah," Sonya answered, understanding his gesture and glaring toward Ava.

"Oh, okay," Mr. Winter responded, still clearly trying to keep his composure. "What would you like to do?"

"I don't know what I can do," Sonya said, frustration and irritation beginning to overtake her tone.

Sonya's apparent discomfort was evident to Mr. Winter and he thought it best to suggest a few possibilities to her.

"Well, you have a few options," Gary began. "You could take him to court in an effort to send him to jail for the crimes he has committed, sue him for court costs, and for damages," he continued.

"How much money would that get me?" Sonya asked matter-of-factly.

Mr. Winter was surprised by Sonya's question but was able to conceal his shock. His mind was immediately inundated with wonder about why Sonya would be asking such a question.

"I'm not sure," Mr. Winter answered, pausing more than he should between his words. "You could also sue him in an effort to force him to pay for any type of treatment your daughter needs," he added.

"I'm not worried about that, I just wana know how much

I can sue him for," Sonya retorted, noticeably irritated with the lawyer's concern for Ava. "I got bills to pay."

"Um, okay," Mr. Winter said, unsure of how to proceed. He realized he may be stepping outside his boundaries but chose to inquire anyway. "Has your daughter received any treatment?" he asked.

"She talked to the cops. They wouldn't tell me what she said and she won't either," Sonya answered with disdain in her voice.

Though Gary did not know Sonya, and was not familiar with their economic situation, her choice of answers, grammar, ill-placed concerns, and the physical condition of the little girl told him all he needed to know about the situation. He dared to press the matter even further, concerned Ava had not had an opportunity for counseling or medical treatment.

"So she has not spoken with a counselor or been seen by a doctor concerning the rape?" he inquired.

"Rapes," Sonya corrected. "And no, she's fine," Sonya stated, glaring at the lawyer. "If she won't tell me she ain't guna tell anyone else either," Sonya rationalized.

"Okay," Mr. Winter replied. "Who are you alleging committed the rape?"

"I ain't *alleging* anybody committed the rape," Sonya said, purposefully enunciating the word "alleging" to drive her point. "I *know* John Timmer did it and he needs to pay," Sonya continued, this time enunciating the word "know".

"Alright," Mr. Winter responded evenly in an effort to calm Sonya's obvious defensive attitude. "I do know the family and I know they don't have much," he continued.

"So you're sayin' I can't get nothin' from him?" Sonya asked in a rough tone.

"If you would get anything, considering the girl has not seen a doctor or counselor, it would likely be only enough to cover the cost of any type of treatment deemed necessary, being paid directly to the caregivers," Mr. Winter informed.

"That's bullshit," Sonya scoffed as she slumped in her chair, letting out a large, loud sigh.

"It would be beneficial to the girl if you were to seek treatment for her, especially psychological care," Mr. Winter advised with a concerned tone.

Sonya said nothing and simply stared at the little girl sitting on the floor in front of her. She was in disbelief John would only have to pay for something for Ava.

"Like he hasn't done enough for the little bitch already," Sonya thought to herself.

"Whatever," Sonya said after several minutes of silence. "Guess ya can't get blood out of a turnip, right?" she said, attempting a joke at the lawyer's expense.

"Yeah, I guess," Mr. Winter answered, unclear about whether or not Sonya was interested in pursuing punishment of the young man, even though it would not likely produce a monetary reward for her.

"Well, I guess if ya can't get anything out of him there's no reason to talk about it anymore," Sonya said flatly as she stood to leave, kicking Ava out of her way.

"Okay," Mr. Winter said as he stood to thank Sonya for coming in.

Sonya ignored Gary's gesture of politeness and professionalism and made her way to the door silently.

"Let's go," Sonya blurted at Ava as she swung the door open.

Ava had already stood and was close behind Sonya before she had even barked the order.

"Thanks for nothin'," Sonya snapped as she walked out of the office.

Mr. Winter sat quietly behind his desk for several minutes,

now able to show his disbelief in the meeting which had just occurred. The young receptionist, having heard Sonya's last retort, made her way to the lawyer's adjoining office.

"What was that about, Gary?" the receptionist asked as she sat in the chair Sonya had just abandoned.

"I'm really not sure, Carol," Gary answered. "It seems the little girl was raped and the mom just wanted to know if she could get money out of the guy who did it. She didn't seem the least bit concerned for the little girl," he continued.

"Really?" Carol said in disbelief. "Do you believe it really happened?" she asked.

"I don't know," Gary replied, clearly uncertain. "I can see how it might have happened, given that woman's personality and the character of the guy she blamed, but I don't know," he said.

"Well, there's not a lot you can do about it, Gary," Carol offered with a slight smile in an effort to help him stop worrying about it.

"Yeah, I know," he said, offering a trivial smile back.

"Your next appointment isn't until three," she said as she rose from the chair and walked to the door.

"Okay, thanks," he answered as the door closed behind Carol.

Gary knew he could do little, if anything, for the little girl but was determined to try to do something. After collecting his thoughts he picked up the phone to call the sheriff's office in Corral County. He reached the Sheriff and proceeded to describe his meeting with Sonya, inquiring if the little girl had, indeed, talked to an officer. Gary wondered if the rape had really happened or if Sonya was simply attempting to involve her daughter in a lie for financial gain. The Sheriff informed Gary about the encounter his deputies had with Sonya and Ava and there was, indeed, reason to believe the little girl had been raped, numerous times, over the course of about a year. Gary shared his concerns with the Sheriff and stressed he truly believed the little girl was not well cared for. The Sheriff agreed, and divulged the Nathia police had been instructed to watch the family closely, in case anything else came up. Gary hung up the telephone and devoted only a few more minutes of thought to the situation before moving on to the next thing. His hands were tied and he clearly understood, if he spent too much energy worrying about all of his client's problems, he would not have any energy for the ones he could actually help.

Within the next few months, Ava tried hard to do all she could to win her mother's approval. She attempted to tidy up the incredibly dirty house, hoping her mother would be appreciative of her efforts, only to be met with insults and accusations of attempted thievery. Her mother repeatedly blamed Ava for stealing things she had misplaced while she was drunk. When Ava would attempt to deny any wrongdoing, she was met with a hard slap to the face. In the event Ava happened to know where a lost item was, she would offer the information freely in the hope Sonya would be grateful. Ava's knowledge of the lost item would ultimately only confirm Sonya's suspicions and accusations Ava had stolen the item in the first place and Ava was still beaten. Ava tried hard to come up with something that would bring Sonya closer to her, dreaming of a day her mother would love her and the abuse would stop.

Night after night, for the rest of the summer, Ava would fall asleep wherever Sonya was, as if she was an obedient dog. Many of the nights when the weather was warm, Sonya and her friends would drink outside in the front yard. Ava would inevitably appear next to Sonya in an effort to fall asleep by her mother.

In the fall, the school year began, but the nights were still warm. Sonya, without a job, was free to do what she liked. After the first week of school, Friday finally came and Ava was again free to join her mother as she drank to excess in the front yard of their decrepit home. Though Sonya would never admit it, she felt a certain triumph in Ava's actions, as if she had finally trained the little girl and broken her will. Sonya regularly celebrated the accomplishment and seemed to know the little girl would do anything to serve her. As Sonya sat on the weathered concrete porch, she drank and laughed with her friends, paying little attention to Ava. Once again, in an effort to be close to her mother, Ava dragged a pillow and blanket out on the front porch to fall asleep. Sonya, along with three men, continued to laugh and have fun, behaving and speaking as if there were no children present. Ava, used to the dialogue, ignored most of it as she tried to drift off to sleep. Since Sonya allowed Ava to be in the vicinity, at some level, Ava felt as if Sonya may be accepting her. As her only source for solace, Ava clung to the thought and tried to feel comforted.

Ava had fallen asleep, out of the way of Sonya and her friends, and the night air began to chill her. The clock had reached four a.m. and it seemed the party was finally ending.

"Get up," Sonya blurted at Ava as she kicked at the little girl, missing because the alcohol had affected her aim.

Ava slowly came to consciousness and began to stir.

"What a cute little kid," one of the men observed as he finally noticed Ava in the corner of the porch.

The man had been drinking with Sonya at the house for the last five hours but his intoxication had not allowed him to notice the little girl.

"Ya look so tired," he said, slurring his words as he tried to sound nice. "Don't get up, I'll carry ya," he continued as he stumbled toward the porch.

Ava seemed to awaken fully in a split second as the drunken man staggered toward her. Fear immediately rushed through her mind and she wanted to run into the house, away from him.

"Then carry her," Sonya said to the man as she giggled and turned to walk toward another man.

The man, trying hard to walk straight and struggled to climb the four stairs leading to the top of the weather-beaten porch. He made it up the first step but tripped on the second, falling forward and catching himself with his hands in front of him. He continued up the stairs, stabilizing himself with his hands outstretched in front of himself, as if he knew he would fall again. Triumphantly, he reached the landing of the porch and used the side of the house to bring himself to a standing position. Laughing hysterically for no apparent reason, he turned to face the others, thrusting his hands above his head as if he had just won a race. The small group, now all standing next to one of the cars in the driveway, laughed and cheered for him. Ava, in an effort to escape the man, stood from her makeshift bed on the hard porch, and reached for the screen door.

"You let him carry ya!" Sonya barked as she noticed what Ava was attempting.

Ava froze, her small hand still on the door lever, and obeyed her mother. The man, now wavering as he stood next to Ava, reached down and swooped her up in his arms. She lay across his forearms, his left under her knees and his right behind her back. He stood straight up and attempted to take a step with his right foot toward the wooden storm door, its dark green paint, chipped and peeling. At first, the step forward seemed to be successful, until the man lost his balance. He began to fall to the right and in an effort to correct himself he put his weight instead on his right foot while attempting to move his left, falling hard against the side of the house, next to the door. Ava was still in his arms and she could feel his balance escaping him again. As his back hit the side of the house, he shifted Ava's weight to the right. The miscalculation of the small amount of weight Ava's body added, caused him to pitch further to the right than he had anticipated. She could feel herself slipping from his grip and her natural reaction was to grab for his neck to keep from falling. Ava felt his arms slip from under her and she fell toward the empty flower bed looming about four feet below the landing of the small porch. The flower bed had been constructed, years ago, with cinder blocks. The surface of the dirt in the flower bed was five inches or so below the top of the cinderblock wall that created its perimeter. Ava fell hard on the dirt, the back of her head striking the high concrete foundation of the house. The days had been dry and a cloud of dust exploded around her small body as she made contact. Instantly, the base of her skull began to throb and a terrible pain shot up her back and down her legs as her tail bone made contact with the parched, rock-hard dirt. Within a fraction of a second, the full weight of the man who had tried to carry her crashed down on top of her, the bulk of his weight connecting just below her left knee cap. Instantly, Ava felt a blinding pain in her left leg, accompanied by what seemed to be a deafening cracking sound. The man lay motionless for a few seconds then hoisted himself up and out of the flower bed. Ava looked down at her left leg, now bent at the knee, in the wrong direction. When Ava had landed, her left foot had landed on top of the cinderblock wall that created the outside of the flower bed while the rest of her small body was on the surface of the dirt. When the man's body weight had made contact with Ava's tiny knee, the bone directly below the knee cap had split in two from the force and the uneven plane. Ava immediately screamed in pain. After the man had lowered himself to the ground, he instantly started to panic, turning to Sonya and begging for her forgiveness.

"She'll be alright," Sonya said sweetly to the man as he walked toward her.

Sonya looked at Ava and glared, as if Ava had made the man fall on top of her on purpose. Sonya took her time as she said farewell to two of the men she had been drinking with. The third man walked toward Ava and picked her up in his arms the same way the first man had. In an attempt to find comfort, Ava unknowingly wrapped her arms around the man's neck and cried loudly as the pain in her leg worsened with the movement. The man made no effort to keep Ava's leg from moving as he lifted her small body from the dirt. The leg bent limply at the knee and the man stumbled up the stairs to the landing of the porch and opened the door to the house. He carried Ava to the couch in the living room, clumsily dropping her there, then walked back outside. Ava screamed in pain and groped for her knee.

"Ya really know how to fuck up a party, don't ya?" Sonya sneered as she walked into the house.

Emma had been asleep in the room she and Ava shared and all of the commotion had awakened her. She came out of the bedroom with a start to find Ava lying on the couch screaming.

"What happened?" Emma exclaimed as Sonya walked away from the couch.

"She fuckin' fell, the little klutz," Sonya remarked, slurring her words and grinning without looking at Emma.

Emma knew Sonya was incredibly drunk and without a second thought went to the couch to ask Ava what had happened. Ava was unable to speak clearly as she wailed in pain from the broken bone.

"Is it your leg?" Emma asked in a loud voice so Ava could hear her over her own cries of pain.

Ava nodded her head, indicating it was her leg. Emma reached for Ava's right leg and watched as the little girl continued to cry. With no differing reaction, Emma then reached for Ava's left leg. The instant Emma touched the leg she saw Ava's face twist in pain, tears still streaming from her eyes.

"Okay, okay," Emma said soothingly in an attempt to calm Ava. "It'll be okay."

Emma covered Ava with some blankets but did not dare move the little girl. The way Ava had been dropped on the couch allowed Ava's left leg to bend at a 45 degree angle, her left foot trapped under her right leg. Ava lay as still as she could, trying hard not to move. Her small body began to shake and she was unable to relax. She felt so cold and the pain from her head, tailbone, and leg consumed her. Emma sat on the floor in front of the couch in an effort to help Ava feel comfortable, though there was nothing she could really do.

Sonya had retreated to the bathroom to throw up. After crying hard for about thirty minutes, the pain began to overtake Ava and her small body began to numb itself. Through Ava's tears, she watched as the man who had fallen on her walked back into the house. Ava hoped Sonya would tell him to leave and defend her. Instead, Ava watched as her mother lead the man to the tiny kitchen and talked to him. Ava could hear Sonya repeatedly telling the man not to worry about what had happened.

"Shouldn't we take her to the hospital or call the ambulance?" the man questioned, clearly upset by the situation.

"I don't know about you but I'm drunk," Sonya said, her voice laced with a small laugh. "We'd be in deep shit if anybody found out this happened while we were drunk," she continued. "Plus, if anybody finds out you're the one that dropped her you'll be in deep shit too."

"Oh, shit," the man said. "What can I do to help? I can't have any more charges."

Sonya leaned close to the man and whispered something. Ava was unable to hear what she had said but it became obvious as Sonya began to passionately kiss the man. Ava's tears refreshed themselves as she once again realized she meant very little to Sonya.

"Are we guna to take Ava to the hospital?" Emma asked Sonya, disgust filling her voice.

Sonya pulled herself away from the man slightly and said, "Maybe tomorrow," immediately resuming her make-out session.

Ava squeezed her eyes tightly closed, and tried to will herself away from the horrible feeling. Though the pain throughout her body was incredible, the pain she felt from Sonya's indifference seemed to surmount it. She slowly calmed herself and began to try to simply deal with the pain. Sonya and the man disappeared into the basement and Ava and Emma knew exactly what was happening. In her anger, Emma rose from her place in front of the couch and returned to the bedroom to cry herself to sleep. She wanted to help Ava but simply did not know how.

At some point Ava had lost consciousness, either from the blow to the head, from the exhaustion caused by the incredible pain, or a combination of both. When she finally awoke her small body was still filled with excruciating pain and she was still unable to move her left leg, regardless of how hard she tried. To Ava's surprise, Sonya walked into the house from the front door accompanied by a neighbor. The neighbor was an old man but was still able to pick Ava up from the couch and carry her to his waiting car.

"What happened?" the neighbor asked Sonya.

"She was fuckin' around last night and fell," Sonya explained.

The neighbor said nothing more and continued to the car, placing Ava in the back seat so she could lie down. Ava's tears once again began to flow as the pain seemed to refresh itself. Ava tried hard to keep her cries to herself as the car backed from the driveway and headed toward the hospital in Ropschon. As the car moved toward the next town, Ava slipped in and out of consciousness, lying limply on the black, imitation leather seat of the car. She could smell the scent of old booze in the air, coming from Sonya, who still had a great deal of alcohol in her system. The car drove into the parking lot of the same hospital in which Lilli had spent so much time, and Ava lost consciousness once again.

When she awoke she was lying on a gurney in the emergency room while a doctor checked her leg. Sonya informed a woman on staff the family had no insurance but were covered by state funded medical aid. As the doctor and nurses hurried around her, Ava was unable to keep their conversations straight. X-rays were taken and her leg was set in a cast extending from the top of her thigh to her toes in order to immobilize the entire leg and allow healing. Sonya was questioned by the doctor and the smell of alcohol prompted hospital staff to notify the authorities. Sonya was questioned by the Ropschon police but the officers failed to question Ava, believing she would be unable to coherently answer any questions due to the sedation the emergency room staff had given her to dull her pain. Sonya did not mention Ava's blow to the head, nor did she mention the impact the little girl's tail bone had endured. Her silence was not due to her usual cruelty, but instead, to the fact she had no idea of the additional injuries. Ultimately, she could not remember what had happened for sure and had not taken the time to even attempt to talk with Ava about the incident. During the drive home from the hospital no one spoke. Ava slept comfortably in the back seat and Sonya recalled the threat the Ropschon officer had made involving losing custody of Ava. Of course, this disturbed Sonya, but not because she would miss her daughter. Ultimately, Sonya hated the thought of losing her welfare and the thought of being forced to get a job seemed to sicken her.

The car pulled in the driveway and the neighbor carried Ava back into the house. The hospital had provided Ava with a small pair of crutches, which she would be required to use for the following ten to twelve weeks, as the bone in her leg healed. She was placed carefully on the couch, her leg propped up by several pillows, in order to keep the swelling down. Once again, she drifted off to sleep, finally able to escape the incredible pain in her body with the help of the sedation she had received.

Ava's leg healed slowly over the next several weeks and in order to keep her welfare, Sonya seemed to slow her drinking a little. Ava still remembered the vision of her mother in the arms of the man who had hurt her. Even though the man had not hurt her on purpose, she felt as if Sonya would not protect her, regardless of the situation. Sonya continued to go to the bar on a regular basis and Ava was forced to tag along, even before her leg was healed. Ava was unable to take the swimming lessons offered through the school due to her broken leg and seemed to be resentful of Sonya for it, among many other things. The relationship between Ava and Sonya clearly became even more strained than before and Ava gave up trying to capture Sonya's affection. It seemed the events throughout her young life had fostered her will to pull away from everyone. She sunk deeper into her loneliness and drifted further toward the unwillingness to trust anyone.

As the school year continued, Ava seemed to develop normally in academics, though she was unable to be socially open with her peers. Sonya continued to take Ava to the bar with her, and Ava attempted to occupy her time by busying herself with the various games offered to the patrons of the establishment by the vending company. Sonya was willing to provide quarters for Ava to play games, as long as Ava left her alone. Ava had become accustomed to the drill and kept herself occupied. One Saturday night, as Ava stood playing a video game, she was able to listen to a conversation taking place directly behind her. Though the music was incredibly loud in the back of the bar, Sonya and the man she was conversing with were both drunk and talking much louder than necessary. Ava continued to play the video game but her attention was focused on her mother's conversation.

"That your daughter?" the man asked Sonya, gesturing toward Ava.

"Yeah, why?" Sonya responded in an inquisitive tone.

"She's cute," the man said. "I'd like to take her out to my car for a while."

Sonya did not answer right away and Ava wondered if her mother had walked away. Ava knew better than to turn around. If Sonya knew she was listening her punishment would be sever, to say the least.

"So, what do ya think?" the man asked.

"How much ya give me?" Sonya answered perversely in happy tone.

"How much ya want?" the man inquired.

"A hundred bucks," Sonya said, trying to get all she could.

Ava was in disbelief. Her mother was trying to get money from a man and she was going to make her go to his car with him. She couldn't think straight. Ava, only eight-years-old, was undoubtedly sure of what it would mean to go to the man's car and knew it would be sexual. She froze, unable to continue playing her game or even pay attention to what was on the gaming screen. She listened closely, waiting to hear the conclusion of the conversation.

"I can't afford a hundred bucks," the man argued. "But she *is* cute.

Ava could see the man's reflection in the glass of the video game. She watched as he looked her up and down, as if she were a twenty-five-year-old woman. She felt a disgusted shudder start between her shoulder blades and tried to control it.

"How 'bout eighty?" Sonya asked.

"Do I get both of ya?" he inquired, smiling deviantly.

"No, I already got plans," Sonya answered as she gestured toward a man across the room with whom she had already sealed a deal.

"Forty," the man offered, anxiously awaiting Sonya's reply.

"Fifty," Sonya countered and waited for his response.

"How long do I get to keep her?" the man questioned as he thought seriously about Sonya's offer.

"Half hour," Sonya answered with a crooked smile.

"That's barely worth the money!" the man debated. "I won't be able to get a lot done. How about an hour and a half?" he suggested.

"Hour and a half?" Sonya mocked with a giggle. "Mine don't even last an hour and a half! I'd rather save ya for myself!" she said as she stepped closer to him.

It was becoming very clear to Ava Sonya was negotiating what the man would pay for sex with her and when he would have to have her home. She was terrified. She remained in front of the video game, stone still, and continued to listen. She wanted to run away but again, she simply could not move. She hated the fact fear made her freeze. Even if she could make her muscles move, she would never be able to get out of the bar fast enough. There were too many people. She waited in disgust and terror to hear what her fate would be.

"Okay, an hour," the man said.

"An hour will cost you eighty," Sonya said as she began to understand the man was more interested in Ava than in her.

"Guess we can't make a deal," the man said. "Too bad," he continued as he once again looked Ava up and down.

"Guess not," Sonya said with a crooked grin, attempting to call his bluff.

The man started to walk away from Sonya and she let him take a few steps past her.

"Wait," Sonya said, grabbing his arm. "Okay, you can have her for an hour for fifty."

"I better not," the man replied. "My wife will wonder where the money went."

"Fine," Sonya said with a bitter tone, clearly upset she had lost the deal.

She turned away from the man and leaned close to the back of Ava's head.

"Let's go," Sonya ordered loudly.

Ava closed her eyes, thankful the man had changed his mind. She was surprised at Sonya's order to follow her, thinking Sonya would lower the price even further. She turned from the video game and followed her mother through the sea of people in the bar. It was closing time and people streamed out of both exits. Of course, Sonya and the man she would be with that night, hung back and ordered another drink to go. Ava stood by the front door waiting for her mother. As the people filtered past her and out the door, a man paused to look at her. She looked at his face quickly and thought his was the reflection she had seen in the glass of the video game. She looked at the floor and waited for him to walk away. He stepped toward her and paused again.

"Hey dude, let's go!" Another man's voice barked playfully.

Ava quickly looked up to see another man talking to the man who had been staring at her. He looked at her again, this time briefly, then turned to walk out the door with his friend. Ava again felt a wave of relief and quietly waited by the door until she saw her mother stumbling toward her.

"Let's go!" Sonya barked happily as she walked through the door and stepped onto the sidewalk.

Ava followed obediently. She stood, waiting for an indication from the man to reveal which car was his. Ava watched as the man walked toward a very large motorcycle and climbed on. Sonya happily followed him and climbed on to the back of the motorcycle. Ava paused, unsure about where she would even sit.

"Get on," Sonya ordered, gesturing to the very small space in front of her and behind the man.

Ava didn't move. She could feel fear starting to take hold of her again.

"Get on!" Sonya ordered again, this time with angry authority.

Ava didn't know what was happening. She started to shake. Her fear consumed her. Before she knew what she was doing, she had turned and started walking away from Sonya and the man on the motorcycle.

"Ava!" Sonya screamed. "Get you're fuckin' ass on this bike!"

"No!" Ava screamed back at her mother as she started to run.

Ava's fear seemingly melted as she was consumed with anger. She did not know if she was angry because of the conversation she overheard, because her mother would risk her life riding on a motorcycle with a drunk man, or whether it had anything to do with the night at all. The anger flooded through her and she refused to get on the motorcycle. She ran toward home, listening as Sonya and the man followed her on the motorcycle. She could hear Sonya screaming at her but paid little attention to the words she actually spoke. She ran about a block then turned to look behind her. She watched as the drunk man struggled to keep the huge motorcycle from tipping over. Ava turned and continued down the sidewalk, fully intending on going home. She began to run again, and soon lost sight of the motorcycle. She ran the three remaining blocks to the broken down house and went inside. She couldn't seem to calm down. She walked back outside and sat on the top step of the tiny porch to watch for her mother. The man Sonya was with lived close to them and she could see the front of his house from where she sat. Within about twenty minutes Ava watched as the motorcycle sloppily pulled into the man's driveway. Sonya climbed off of the motorcycle, followed by the man. She continued to watch as Sonya followed the man into his house. Ava was completely aware Sonya had no idea if she had run home or gone somewhere else.

"She doesn't even know where I'm at," Ava thought to herself. "She doesn't fuckin' care."

Ava sat on the porch for the next two hours, wondering how long it would be before Sonya would find her way home and what she would do the next day when the beating was upon her. Finally, tired of waiting and struggling to keep her eyes open any longer, she stood and walked into the house, realizing she no longer cared about her mother.

Ava learned an important lesson that night at the bar. She learned, when she felt fear she was unable to move, but when she felt anger she could defend herself. Though it was not a conscious decision, from then on, Ava became more and more proficient at replacing fear with anger. The replacement of fear with anger would prove to be yet another scar which would plague her for many, many years.

Throughout the rest of the year Ava experienced constant pain in her legs and lower back. At times, the pain was so bad she was unable to walk. Sonya, in an effort to display superficial care for the girl, took her to the local doctor's office to find out what was wrong. Once in the examination room, the doctor prompted Ava to lie flat on her back. The pain from lying flat on her back was excruciating, but she endured the pain silently with the hope the doctor would be able to reveal the cause. The doctor asked Ava to relax and physically picked up her legs, one at a time, to move them. After the very brief examination, the doctor invited Ava into the hallway to get a piece of candy. He returned to the examination room where Sonya waited and explained his findings.

"It's all in her head," the doctor explained.

"What?" Sonya replied, clearly surprised and immediately angry.

Sonya had never known Ava to be dishonest or complain if she was not really in pain or sick.

"I don't think there's anything wrong with her," the doctor continued, shrugging his shoulders.

"So, she's fakin' it?" Sonya asked.

"I think so," the doctor answered, nodding his head slightly. "She's making it up so she doesn't have to go to school."

Sonya thanked the doctor and guided Ava out of the doctor's office. She said nothing to Ava about what the doctor had said.

"Do your legs still hurt?" Sonya questioned Ava.

"Yeah," Ava answered.

"Bullshit. It's all in your fuckin' head," Sonya retorted. "The doctor says there ain't a damned thing wrong with ya."

Ava began to feel fear but anger immediately blocked it out. She said nothing, concluding Sonya would not listen to her, regardless of the situation. Sonya made no attempt to converse any further, feeling quite proud of herself for catching Ava in a lie.

In reality, the pain in Ava's legs was due to a birth defect in her lower back caused by the drugs and alcohol Sonya had consumed while she was carrying Ava. The two lowest discs in her spine had not fully developed and the pain she felt at such a young age was the result of that fact. Ava endured the pain and did what she could, refusing to say anything more to Sonya about it. Even though her pain was very real, the true source of the pain would not be discovered until she was in her mid-twenties, then again in her early thirties. Eventually, the pain Ava felt in her legs, and later in her back, would force her to have back surgery at only thirty-six years old. It will never be fully understood whether or not the blow to her tail bone initiated the pain, but it is certain Ava would have suffered with it at some point, regardless.

Chapter Six

In the midst of the dreadful things Ava was forced to face in her life it had become painfully obvious she had no one to turn to. Sonya was so enthralled in her revolting way of life she felt as if she were above any type of authority or religion. It was as if her very way of thinking kept her from the doors of any sanctuary, like a clear glass window keeps a fly confused and unable to find a way around it. Ava found herself wondering about God from time to time, but with no exposure to His teachings the thoughts were fleeting, at best. Some of the children in her classes during the school year spoke of religion classes, Sunday school, and religious-based retreats. She wondered what it would be like to be a part of those things but ultimately concluded religious matters were reserved for those who led better lives than hers. As Ava sat alone in her room thinking of the various ways she could end her life, her mind wandered to a memory from a few years before. The memory was one which seemed to leave a bitter feeling in her heart and brought her back, again and again, to the resentment she felt toward her mother. She closed her eyes and allowed her thoughts to be consumed by the memory, replaying it in her mind as if she were watching it play out in front of her on a screen.

The memory flooded into Ava's mind, giving way to the

sunny day and a first-time meeting with another little girl. Emily, a girl only a year older than Ava, lived about six blocks away and seemed to be just as lonely. The two girls spent a great deal of time together and had fun when neither of them were forced to deal with their families. Ava, only six-years-old and Emily, only seven-years-old, seemed to have many things in common. Emily's family, though not engulfed in religion, had encouraged her to attend Sunday school at a tiny church only a block from Ava's home. A few weeks after the girls had become friends she invited Ava to accompany her to Sunday school, as the day had been deemed "bring a friend" day. Ava was excited about the new venture and attending with Emily would help to ease any apprehension she might feel about attending such a new place. She rushed home to ask permission to go with Emily. As she scurried home she could not think of any reason her mother would not allow her to attend the class with her friend. She walked into the house and immediately spotted Sonya sitting in her usual place at the dining room table, drinking a beer and smoking a cigarette. Sonya looked up when she heard Ava pass through the doorway.

"Where the fuck have ya been?" Sonya probed angrily.

Ava stopped in her tracks and her eyes shot to the dirty floor in front of her. Suddenly, all of the positive feelings Emily's invitation had produced drained away and Ava was afraid to speak.

"Well?" Sonya screeched. "Where the fuck were ya?"

"At Emily's," Ava answered in a voice barely louder than a whisper.

Sonya said nothing and raised the beer can to her lips, taking a long drink. Ava stood frozen for a few minutes then found a single thread of courage to help her speak.

"Emily wants to know if I can go to Sunday school with

her tomorrow," Ava said cautiously, still looking at the filthy floor directly in front of her.

Sonya looked hard at Ava, as if trying to stare a hole through her. When Ava was finally able to lift her eyes to meet her mother's, an evil glare had taken hold of Sonya's face, one Ava had never seen before. Ava's eyes shot back to the floor, unwilling and afraid to see the next transformation of Sonya's expression.

"Why the fuck would ya wana do that?" Sonya barked.

Ava shrugged her shoulders slightly and found herself unable to think of a reason. It seemed Sonya was able to paralyze Ava's mind by merely speaking to her. She continued to stare at the floor for several minutes without offering a response to Sonya's question.

"What, ya think you're better'n me?" Sonya tested. "Ya think Sunday school will help ya do anything? It's a waste of fuckin' time."

Ava was unable to answer and simply stood before her mother, stone still. Sonya continued to glare at Ava, even as she continued to drink her beer. The house was quiet and Ava felt terribly uncomfortable. The silence seemed to last for hours and she jumped when Sonya finally decided to speak.

"Do whatever the fuck ya want, ya little bitch," Sonya barked. "Won't matter anyway. You'll always be a piece of shit!"

Ava had become accustomed to the insults her mother constantly fired at her and seemed to be unaffected. Ultimately, every insult Sonya shot at Ava only added another brick to the wall being built around her. Ava finally turned and walked out of the house to return to Emily's to deliver the good news. Ava and Emily made plans and it was happily determined Emily would stop and get Ava on her way to the church. Ava accompanied Emily to the Sunday school session and enjoyed herself a great deal. Though Ava felt a warm and calming feeling while in the church, she never attended again as she was too afraid to approach her mother on the subject, even one more time.

The memory faded and Ava blinked her eyes as tears ran silently down her face. The thought of church wafted from her mind, as if blown away by a gentle breeze, leaving feelings of sadness automatically transforming into anger.

In the months following Ava's discovery of how anger could free her it seemed as if things changed little. The abuse she endured at the hands of her mother continued and Ava became even more disconnected from her family. She spent more and more time away from home, much of the time roaming the streets of the small town at night, in the same way Niles had. Ava, now nine-years-old, was spending a great deal of time with her friends, the majority of whom were at least twelve-years-old. Sonya began to understand even more she was losing her twisted grip on Ava but made no changes to better herself or cease her extracurricular activities.

For those who knew Ava's family, a downtrodden perspective had been forming for years. Sonya was a well known drunk in the small town and most knew her as the freelance prostitute of Nathia. She had been with so many men, for so many different reasons, she struggled to remember even half their names. Most of the time, during her sexual escapades, she was so intoxicated she barely remembered who she had been with at all. Ava learned quickly her mother was the type of individual who traded sex for favors, money, or even food and even though she was still too young to understand things in depth, she was ashamed of her mother.

As another school year ended, Ava wondered how she would spend her time. Ultimately, she knew she wanted to spend as little time at home as she could. She joined up with one of the small town's deviant groups, seemingly welcomed with open arms. All together the small group only had about eight members, the rest coming and going randomly as they felt the need to connect with people less fortunate than themselves. Though Ava felt more accepted by the ruffian group than she had ever felt in her own family, she still felt as though she didn't completely belong. As the summer wore on, she participated in many illegal acts along with the rest of the members of the group. She struggled to feel as if she belonged and began to try harder to fit in. She dated a few of the boys in the group, each of which tried to convince her she should have sex with them. Each time the subject came up, she would feel a twinge deep within her screaming warnings against it. She repeatedly refused to let her relationships turn sexual, and each time, the relationship would end because of her refusal. At only nine-years-old and already dating, Ava was taught yet another lesson involving sex; it had become clear to her – if she was not willing to have sex no one would ever care about her. She was left with this realization and dared not ask her mother for any clarification. The other girls in the group had already been sexually active for at least two years and made their relationships sound glamorous to Ava. She longed for the kind of closeness the other girls referenced in their relationships.

One of Sonya's drinking buddies, Carl, had taken to hanging out with the kids in Ava's group, especially the girls. Ava had joined the group initially because of her friend Emily. Emily spent a great deal of time at Carl's house in the country and naturally, Ava followed suit and began to spend as much time with Carl as Emily did. There was no doubt Carl had a mental disability as his mannerisms, rational, speech, and social behaviors conveyed the fact clearly. In his late forties, he felt more at home with kids from the age of nine to sixteen. Carl behaved as if he was slightly retarded, having been kicked in the head by a cow at a very young age. He freely bought alcohol and cigarettes for the teens and invited them to stay with him at their leisure, for any reason they chose. After spending more than half of the summer with Emily, much of the time at Carl's, Ava had adopted many of Emily's mannerisms and ideals.

Emma was no longer at home, after getting pregnant and dropping out of school in the eleventh grade. The man she was now with, Lee, was one who drank a great deal and, seemed to Ava, to be very abusive. Niles had joined the National Guard and his presence was scarce, to say the least. It seemed to Ava even though she knew Emma and Niles were her siblings, they would soon fade away the same way Lilli did. She felt incredibly alone and searched for any closeness she could find.

In the heat of one late August night, Ava and Emily made their way to Carl's house on foot, about a two mile walk. When they arrived, Carl was not home but Emily knew where Carl kept the key to his house. She retrieved it and the two girls went inside, immediately looking in the refrigerator for alcohol. As usual, the refrigerator was stocked and the girls helped themselves. To Ava, Carl's house had become like a second home, only without the beatings. Carl was always nice to her and offered to buy her anything she wanted, though she rarely accepted anything from him aside from alcohol. As the girls settled into the living room, Emily was the first to speak.

"Carl's gonna be home late, but he knows we're here," she said to Ava.

Ava nodded her head as she took a long drink of her beer. "Cool," she replied. "Where is he?"

"Don't know," Emily answered. "Doin' something for his dad, I think."

Ava responded with only a facial gesture indicating she understood and settled on the couch to get comfortable. It was not yet dark outside but early evening had crept upon them and the hot summer days wore on for what seemed like forever. Ava peered out the window from her seat on the couch and wondered what it would be like to live in such a nice house. Ava's fleeting thoughts were disrupted by the ringing of the door bell. The two girls looked at one another, puzzled, both wondering who could possibly be ringing the bell. Emily rose from her chair and made her way to the door. Ava could hear Emily talking to someone but could not make out the muffled words. Within a few seconds, Emily returned to the living room, leading the way for a handsome young man of about twenty-one whom Ava had never seen before.

"Hi," the young man said to Ava with a sweet smile as he entered the room.

He was about six-feet-tall, thin, and built very well. His dirty-blond hair was short and a little messy, making him seem as if he was clean-cut but secretly a little bit of a bad boy. Ava was caught by surprise and was only able to smile back at him as her cheeks took on a rose-colored hue. Emily and Ava looked at each other and smiled, both girls silently agreeing the young man was very handsome. Emily playfully plopped on the couch next to Ava and the girls giggled quietly. The young man proceeded with the reason for his visit, standing alone in the middle of the living room in front of them.

"Thank you for lending me some of your time, ladies," he

began. "My name is Rick and I hope to help you decide on your next vacuum cleaner purchase."

Emily and Ava did not care at all about the vacuum cleaner Rick was trying to sell them. Neither of them had a penny to their name and neither offered any information about who actually lived in the house. Rick proceeded with his speech about the vacuum cleaner and reiterated how wonderful the cleaning machine really was. The girls sat gazing at Rick as he spoke, both thinking of things having absolutely nothing to do with cleaning. After Rick had gone through his entire speech, Ava decided to speak, something very uncharacteristic for her.

"Um, we don't live here," she said, smiling as she let out a small laugh.

Rick looked at Ava, unmistakably embarrassed and smiled, his face turning very red. Emily giggled loudly and Ava joined her.

"You don't have to leave though," Ava continued. "We really like listening to you talk 'n' well, watching you."

Ava could not believe her courage as the words flowed from her mouth. She could not believe she felt comfortable enough to talk to a complete stranger in such a way, the effects of the alcohol she had consumed never entering her mind.

Rick smiled wide and set down the parts of the vacuum cleaner he was holding, obviously flattered, and without a doubt unsure of what to do next.

"Thanks," Rick said sheepishly as he made eye contact with Ava.

Ava quickly looked away and she and Emily giggled again.

"You want a beer?" Emily asked as if she had known Rick for years.

Rick thought for a second before accepting, knowing he would not be selling a vacuum cleaner at this house. Emily went to the kitchen to get a beer for Rick and returned quickly.

He popped the top and took a drink. He stood in the middle of the living room, as if on display, in front of the two girls.

"Can I talk to you, Ava?" Emily inquired, having walked to the door of the kitchen after handing the beer to Rick.

Surprised, Ava followed Emily into the kitchen.

"I think he likes you!" Emily exclaimed in an excited whisper as she attempted to muffle her voice with her hands.

Ava didn't know what to say. She had never been the center of anyone's attention in a positive way like this. She smiled and felt the excitement building inside of her. The two girls leaned toward one another, whispering and giggling. Ava got another beer from the refrigerator and gulped it down quickly. Her head began to feel tingly as she walked back to the living room.

With the excitement of the situation along with the way the alcohol was affecting her, she felt as if everything in her past had disappeared into a fog. It felt great! She felt as if she were the bravest woman in the world. Emily patiently waited in the kitchen for Ava to make her move. To the girls' surprise, Rick made his move before Ava could make hers. He walked toward Ava as she reluctantly stood her ground. He gently put his arms around her, resting his hands on the small of her back. She felt as if she would explode. Emily, watching the events take place, decided it was okay to walk back into the living room without the fear of interrupting the moment. Ava didn't know what to do. She many feelings rushed through her at the same time, none of which she had ever felt before. She felt warm, relaxed, and wanted. Rick's lips gently pressed against hers for a brief second before his tongue slipped into her mouth. Ava wrapped her arms around his neck and kissed him back. The kiss ended abruptly when the phone suddenly rang. Rick, completely consumed in what was happening, ignored Emily as she walked to the phone to answer it. Ava, however, spared a small bit of her attention to monitor what was being said as she looked at Rick's chest, watching it heave slightly as he breathed.

"Hello," Emily said into the receiver. "Yeah. Okay. Yup," she said, then hung up the phone.

"That was your mom. She wants ya to get home," Emily relayed flatly, clearly disappointed.

Ava tried hard to ignore what Emily had just told her. She knew, however, if she did ignore the information she would not leave the comfort of Rick's arms and ultimately face a horrendous beating when she finally got home.

"I gota go," Ava said quietly. "Fuck."

"I can give ya a ride, where do ya live?" Rick said, noticeably eager to spend more time with her.

"In town. You don't have to. I'll just walk," Ava answered as she slowly pulled her body away from his.

Rick insisted on giving Ava a ride home and she finally accepted. She said goodbye to Emily then she and Rick left Carl's house.

"This sucks," Ava stated matter-of-factly as she slipped into the passenger seat of Rick's car.

"Yeah," Rick said. "Too bad you can't come back out later. I'd wait for ya."

With a new determination Ava declared, "Oh, I'll be able to come back out. My bitch mother isn't guna fuck my life up any more."

Rick offered no response for several minutes then asked, "What time ya think you'll get out again?"

"Not sure," Ava answered. "Prob'ly have to sneak out after she passes out."

He said nothing and drove the car the rest of the way to Ava's house. Before she could get out of the car, he leaned over to kiss her once more.

"I'll catch ya later," Rick said with a sexy smile.

"Yeah," Ava answered, returning a sheepish smile as she got out of the car.

Sonya peered through the filthy window pane as a small car pulled in the driveway. She wondered who it was and if it was someone bringing Ava home since she did not recognize the car. She watched as Rick leaned over and kissed Ava, an unexplained rage beginning to build within her. She had no idea who the person in the car was, nor did she care. Her feelings of rage were compelled by the jealousy she harbored for her nine-year-old daughter. She felt inferior next to Ava but would never reveal that fact to anyone. She immediately knew she had to find a way to ruin Ava's life the same way Ava had ruined hers by being born. She watched as Ava exited the car, closed the door, and began to make her way to the front door.

"Who the fuck is that?" Sonya barked as soon as she saw the door open.

"Rick," Ava stated flatly.

"Well lah-di-dah!" Sonya remarked. "Where the fuck did ya meet him?"

"Carl's," Ava said with no emotion in her voice.

"Oh, bullshit," Sonya retorted. "What do ya think you're doin' with him?" Sonya questioned, clearly jealous.

"Nothin'," Ava responded as she walked toward her bedroom.

Ava heard a beer can open as she closed her door behind her. Sonya had been surprised by Ava's lack of fear when she confronted her. Sonya felt the first pang of uncertainty as she realized Ava was no longer the same meek and timid girl she used to be. Sonya sat alone at the dining room table, drinking beer and watching television. As the beer began to affect her she allowed her mind to wander and once again the jealousy living inside her managed to take control.

Ava sat on her bed, reflecting on what had happened. She couldn't believe someone really liked her. She knew if her mother had not called she would have had sex with Rick. She smiled and threw herself backward on her bed, still thinking about the events of the night and the feelings she had experienced. She didn't want the feelings to go away – ever. For the first time in her life she was able to think about something other than escaping the terrible situation she was in. She didn't feel scared at all and the feelings seemed to empower her. With all of the abuse she had endured, Ava did not consider any inappropriateness regarding a romantic relationship between a nine-year-old girl and a twenty-one-year-old man. That fact alone was tragic.

After about an hour, Ava felt it would be safe to go to the bathroom. She stood up and crossed the tiny room. As she began to turn the knob she heard the sound of voices from the other side of the door. She recognized the tone of voice her mother usually used when she would talk badly about someone. Ava listened closely to hear what her mother was talking about before she opened the door. As Ava listened, she heard Sonya reminiscing with an unknown person about how she had tried to convince Lee to be with her instead of Emma. Ava, wanting to know more, stayed quietly in her room next to the door. She thought about a few nights, before Emma had gotten pregnant, when she had overheard Sonya talking about Lee and how he was in love with her. Sonya had reiterated she could not understand how a man would want Emma when Sonya was right in front of him.

"Must be a fuckin' idiot," Ava heard Sonya remark to the unknown person.

Ava decided she could no longer wait for the conversation to develop and opened the bedroom door.

"What the fuck are ya doin'?" Sonya screeched at Ava.

Ava made no attempt to answer and walked purposefully to the bathroom, stepping inside and closing the door behind her. While Ava was in the bathroom, she could hear muffled conversation and loud laughter, though she could not make out what was being said. Opening the door, she switched off the light and walked back toward her bedroom.

"Hey!" Sonya yelled at Ava.

She turned slowly to face her mother, unable to look at her.

"Ya little bitch," Sonya began in a voice so filled with hatred even Ava was surprised. "I don't know who the fuck ya think ya are but I think you're a piece of fuckin' shit!" she continued as a maniacal laugh began to build in her throat.

Ava quickly glanced at the other person sitting at the dining room table but did not recognize him. The man, clearly drunk, joined in Sonya's laughter. She said nothing and slipped into her bedroom, closing the door quickly behind her. Normally, Sonya's insults would destroy Ava's day but this time it was different. It seemed as if nothing could take away the wonderful feeling Rick had left her with. She lay on her bed and thought about what she would do later that night, in order to see him again.

Little did Ava know, Sonya was rethinking the beatings she had delivered to Ava on a regular basis. The difference in the way Ava had responded to her made her very uncomfortable and she knew she must find another way to control the girl. The night wore on and Ava listened intently for her opportunity to escape the house. Sonya had turned the television off around midnight, since nothing was on after that time of the night. The sounds of the usual actions filled the air and Ava was unable to make out any conversation between Sonya and the mystery man.

The years of exposure to her mother's promiscuous behavior and the influence of repeated rape had affected Ava's understanding of what was appropriate for a girl her age. Even though she was only nine-years-old she seemed to have the mental maturity of a sixteen-year-old girl and seemed to be at the point where she could confidently behave as if she were sixteen, unable to forget about Rick.

Sonya and the mystery man seemed to forget about Ava and enveloped themselves in Sonya's usual sexual exploits. Ava could hear the explicit noises coming from the other side of her closed bedroom door and did all she could to ignore them. As she sat on her bed waiting for her opportunity, she let her mind drift back to the earlier events of the evening. She relived the brief encounter and seemed to be able to feel all the same feelings that had been invoked by the actual event. She couldn't wait to see Rick again. After what seemed like an eternity, she noticed the noises from the living room had finally stopped and she could hear someone snoring. She rose from her bed and quietly opened the door, only a few inches at first, to see if her opportunity to sneak out had finally arrived. She saw the man lying on the couch and Sonya in front of him, both naked and barely covered by a thin blanket. The radio was on and Ava could tell her mother was also asleep. With only a lamp offering light to the large room, Ava knew she would be able to slip by unnoticed. Quietly, she made her way across the room and to the door, slipping through without a sound. As she stepped off the front porch she felt exhilarated, as if nothing could stop her, and she began the two mile walk back to Carl's house.

When Ava finally arrived at Carl's house, her heart sank as she realized Rick's car was not in the driveway. She walked into the house and found Emily watching television in the living room.

"Hey," Emily said with a small smile.

"Hey," Ava answered. "Where's Rick?"

"He had to take off," Emily answered sleepily as she stretched her arms above her head. "He left something for you though," she continued as she rose from the couch, her arms dropping to her sides.

"Really?" Ava asked, somewhat confused.

Emily did not answer but walked to the dark kitchen and turned the light on. On the back of one of the kitchen chairs Ava noticed a very colorful leather jacket. Emily picked the jacket up with both hands and handed it to Ava.

"He left this for ya," Emily said as she extended the jacket toward Ava.

She took the jacket carefully and examined it. It was the nicest coat she had ever seen. The majority of the coat was soft, black leather and it was heavy. Brightly colored, various shaped patches were sewn on the elbows, the upper chest area, and the back. Smiling widely Ava slipped the large jacket on and it dwarfed her small frame. She searched the pockets, not

163

knowing what she was looking for. Inside the jacket was a hidden pocket, inside which she found a folded piece of paper. Excitedly she pulled the paper from the pocket and unfolded it. She read the message on the paper to herself as Emily stood closely by, ready to burst with curiosity. Ava looked up at Emily and squealed with excitement.

"What's it say?" Emily squealed in return.

"It says he wants to come back to town tomorrow and see me," Ava replied excitedly. "He left the coat for me so I would know he was serious about me!"

"That is so awesome!" Emily giggled, obviously happy for Ava.

"I can't wait!" Ava squealed with excitement. "His number is on here too!"

"Are you guna just have him come to your house?" Emily asked.

"I don't know. It says he'll be back in town around six and wants me to call him and let him know where I wana meet him," Ava answered with a wondrous look in her eyes.

She hugged the paper close to her chest then refolded it, replacing the letter in the hidden pocket. It was three o'clock in the morning and she knew she should be getting home. Since Rick was not there she had no reason to stay out and press her luck. Wearing the multicolored jacket, in spite of the warm weather, she set out on the walk home feeling as if she were floating. When she arrived at home she quietly slipped into the house and to her room. Sonya had no idea she had even been gone. Once inside her bedroom she carefully took off the jacket and hid it beneath her mattress. She knew if Sonya saw it she would take it. Ava slipped into bed and fell asleep almost immediately. Even though she was bursting with excitement, the night's events had exhausted her and she would not have been able to stay awake even if she had wanted to.

Since Ava had been up so late the night before, she slept quite late into the day. When she awoke it was already past noon and the day was sunny and hot. She got out of bed and went to the bathroom to get ready for the day ahead of her. Sonya was still passed out and the mystery man was gone. Ava took a bath and dressed in her nicest summer clothes. Without waking Sonya, she found some change in the front pocket of her mother's jeans, and left the house making her way to the pay phone a few blocks away. She dialed the number and Rick answered the phone.

"Hello?" Rick said when he picked up the receiver.

"Hi," Ava said sheepishly. "It's Ava."

"Ava! Hi!" Rick replied, clearly excited to hear from her. "I was beginning to wonder if you would call."

"I don't have a phone so I had to find some change and use the pay phone," she explained, embarrassment lacing her words.

"That's okay," Rick said. "Where do you want me to meet you?"

"How about at the fairgrounds?" Ava suggested. "There's nothing going on there."

"Okay, sounds good," Rick answered. "See ya there at six?"

"Yeah," Ava answered. "I'll be by the front entrance.

"Cool," Rick said. "Can't wait."

"Okay, bye," Ava said.

"Bye," Rick responded.

Ava hung up the phone. She still felt like she was floating even though she carried the heavy jacket. She couldn't wait until six o'clock. Instead of going home, she decided to make her way to the fairgrounds. She walked slowly, knowing she had plenty of time to get there. The fairgrounds was a few miles away and Ava took her time enjoying the peace and quiet of the walk.

When she finally arrived at the front gate of the grounds, she walked through it and found a bench in the shade behind the gate building. She sat and waited, hardly able to contain her excitement. She watched every car intently as it passed by, each time feeling a spark of excitement as she anticipated Rick's arrival. Finally, his car drove in and found a place in the shade to park. She sat quietly on the bench waiting for Rick to get out of the car. The door opened and he stepped out as Ava suddenly realized she was extremely nervous. The courage she felt the night before had faded and she began to feel very uncomfortable. Even though she knew she would have had sex with Rick the night before, today seemed to be a completely different story. She watched as he walked toward her, his smile seeming to penetrate her very soul. Without hesitation he knelt in front of her, taking both of her hands in his as he lowered his head to her lap. The excitement she felt consumed her and she found herself unable to speak. After only a few seconds, he rose to sit on the bench beside her, putting his arm around her. She felt so safe and leaned into his chest.

"How was your night?" he asked quietly.

"Okay, I guess," she replied softly without looking up.

She felt as his finger slipped under her chin, coaxing her to lift her face to his. She surrendered herself to his prompt and lifted her face, her eyes already closed. A surge of warmth filled her as she felt a sense of acceptance and closeness with him. They remained close to one another, eagerly continuing to slip closer to the irretrievable loss of Ava's self worth and confidence. As if she could read his mind, she matched his guiding touch and moved precisely in response. She felt as if she was doing what she should be doing, making Rick happy, and in return she would feel loved. It never occurred to Ava she was too young to be in such a situation, nor did it occur to her Rick was much too old for her.

Exhilaration filled her and her heart pounded as her inner voice of reason attempted to stop her from going any further. She knew, if she stopped now, she would lose the closeness and love he would likely give to her. She made no effort to stop him, wanting desperately to give in and let him do whatever he wanted to, even though she knew in her heart she should not. Her thoughts were those of a girl almost twice her age and she didn't feel at all like she was nine-years-old.

"We should go somewhere more private," he breathed.

"Where?" she asked, almost unable to speak the words.

"Hang on to me," he said as he wrapped his arms around her.

Before walking away from the bench he picked up the jacket with one hand and then turned toward his car, carrying Ava in front of him. With the heavy jacket in one hand and Ava held securely to his chest, he opened the back door of the car. Carefully leaning into the back, he placed her softly on the seat then handed the jacket to her.

"I'll pull the car somewhere out of sight," her whispered in her ear. "You wait here and as soon as I get the car parked I'll join ya."

Rick rose from Ava and she pushed herself further into the back seat of the car to allow him to close the door. He got into the driver's seat and started the car. Backing up, he turned the car to go further into the fairgrounds, to find a place the car would not likely be easily noticed. Finding a place virtually undetectable from either of the streets skirting the grounds, he backed in and shut off the engine. The sun had begun to sink toward the horizon but a few hours of daylight still remained. Ava sat in the back seat feeling both apprehensive and energized. Rick climbed over the back of the bench seat and settled next to her.

"Now, where were we?" Rick said, still slightly out of breath.

The two resumed the unmistakably wicked performance between them, as Ava continued to doubt her ability to actually go through with it. She chose not to speak but responded to him by letting her head slowly fall back in a gesture of welcome invitation. She wanted so much to give him what he wanted, the fear of losing him buried deep in her mind. Continuing to follow his suggestive movements, she obediently performed the actions he silently requested of her. Still fully clothed, Ava's very young mind struggled to make rational sense of what was happening. She was simply unable to stop herself and she felt as if she was watching herself from outside of her own mind. Though it did not consciously occur to her, the influences in her life were the very things driving her forward in what she was doing. Because of the things she had experienced, the events unfolding seemed to make confusing sense to her and she did not realize the incredible inappropriateness of the entire situation. The fact Ava had not yet physically entered puberty had no apparent affect on her responses to Rick, and the twelve years between the two of them did not have any influence over the situation, as he did not seem to see anything wrong with what was happening either.

Ava looked at Rick's face, his eyes closed, seemingly far away from the place in the car where the two of them sat. She wondered what he was thinking and if her actions in that moment would help him to love her if she ever disappointed him. Though her hands were small, she was able to help him reach a level of excitement and pleasure she was previously unaware existed.

"You are so beautiful," he said softly as he slowly opened his eyes and gently touched her cheek.

Ava was still unable to speak and had stopped moving her hands. Now still, she waited for something unknown to happen. She had never performed any type of sexual act willingly and the feelings rushing through her were both wonderful and terrifying. She tried to build up the courage to look at him, and after a few seconds, she finally did. She lifted her eyes to meet his as he gazed at her with a warm and loving look. They stared into one another's eyes for only a few seconds then Rick leaned forward to kiss her. While they kissed, he guided her hands toward his T-shirt, indicating she could wipe her hands on it. After she wiped the once warm liquid from her hands, he pulled the shirt over to clean himself. Picking up a different shirt from the floorboard of the back of the car, he pulled it over his head and then pulled his jeans back up around his waist. Ava sat next to him with her knees bent and her feet pulled up beside her. He reached for her and put his arms around her.

For the first time in her life it seemed as if she had done something right. She had participated, made another person happy, and had not been yelled at or beaten. The hug afterward seemed to confirm the warm feeling of acceptance. She wanted to stay in the car with Rick forever, never letting the feeling leave her.

Rick dozed off for a few minutes but awoke with a start when Ava repositioned herself.

"I should probably get going," he said softly. "It's getting late.

Ava did not argue and simply nodded her head to indicate her agreement. Rick got out of the car and adjusted himself before fastening his pants. She exited the back seat of the car and closed the door.

"Ya want a ride home?" Rick asked.

"Okay," Ava said as she opened the passenger door and got in. She did not care about what Sonya would say to her, nor did she fear any of the questions she was sure would come.

Rick drove Ava to her house slowly, holding her hand the entire way. He pulled the car into the driveway and shifted it into park.

"When can I see you again?" He asked sweetly as he turned toward her and smiled.

"I don't know," she answered bashfully.

"How about tomorrow?" He suggested.

"Okay," she agreed. "Do you want to just come here and we can hang out?"

"Yeah," Rick answered, clearly happy about the invitation.

He leaned toward her and kissed her gently. She got out of the car and closed the door then walked up on the porch and waved to him as he pulled out of the driveway.

Sonya heard a car door shut but did not look out the window. She had already been drinking for the last few hours and felt the tingle of alcohol in her head. She lit a cigarette and smoked it slowly as she waited for Ava to enter the house. Before Ava was in the house far enough for Sonya to see her face she started yelling.

"Where the fuck have ya been?" Sonya screeched.

Ava walked through the open doorway into the large living room. She looked at Sonya to find the usual circumstances; a lit cigarette, an open beer, numerous empty beer cans, and Sonya sitting at the table.

"Out," Ava replied flatly.

"Out where?" Sonya questioned with an angry and irritated tone.

"Just out." Ava answered.

"Was that the same guy as before or did ya find a new one?" Sonya badgered.

Ava chose not to answer and walked past Sonya on her way to her bedroom. She opened her bedroom door and walked inside, closing the door behind her. She knew she needed to change her clothes, at least her underwear and shorts, due to the wetness caused by the arousing encounter she had just experienced. She pulled her shorts and underwear off and found dry ones to put back on. After changing she lay on her bed with her eyes closed reliving the entire encounter.

"Who the fuck do ya think ya are?" Sonya screeched as she threw Ava's bedroom door open.

Ava did not move, lying still on her bed, not letting Sonya know she had startled her.

"Hey!" Sonya yelled at Ava, now only inches from her ear.

Ava opened her eyes and turned her head toward Sonya. "What?" Ava calmly and quietly asked.

"Who the fuck is this guy?" Sonya yelled. "What, do ya think you're guna do, move in with him? What makes ya think he even cares about ya?"

Once again, Ava chose to stay silent, automatically letting her fear of Sonya convert into anger. Ava turned her head away from Sonya and closed her eyes once again in an effort to ignore her mother's comments. When Ava turned her head away Sonya felt the rage build even more within her. She wanted to hurt Ava in an effort to make her pay attention. She lifted her right foot high off of the floor, bringing her heel down hard in the center of Ava's abdomen. Ava let out a cry as the force of the blow made the air rush from her lungs. Her natural instinct was to curl in a ball to protect her abdomen from any further attack. Tears streamed from Ava's eyes as the pain enveloped her midsection. Her arms automatically hugged her stomach and she lay on her side trying hard not to vomit.

"There!" Sonya screamed. "If ya were pregnant, now ya ain't!"

Ava had no idea why her mother would have thought she was pregnant. She had only seen Rick twice and had never actually had sex with him. Little did Ava know, Sonya automatically assumed Ava was doing the same things she did, regardless of her age. It seemed deep within Sonya's twisted mind she knew she had taught the girl all of the wrong things.

"When's he comin' back?" Sonya yelled at Ava.

Ava said nothing and continued to lie in the fetal position.

"When?" Sonya yelled louder.

"Tomorrow," Ava said, clearly struggling to speak clearly.

"Oh? And where are ya goin' to fuck him? Ya ain't doin' it here!" Sonya screeched.

Ava remained silent, still holding her stomach. Sonya, seemingly satisfied she had made Ava cry, turned and stormed out of the small bedroom. Ava remained in the same position, unable to move due to the physical pain her mother had inflicted. She was furious with herself that she had, once again, allowed Sonya to make her cry. The anger within her continued to build and she once again made the promise to herself, one day, her mother would not be able to hurt her anymore.

Ava turned her thoughts to the time she had spent with Rick that day. She recreated every detail in her mind, unaware of the indecency of the entire situation. She had become accustomed to sexual activity in so many aspects of her life she didn't realize how wrong it was for someone her age to engage in any act of a sexual nature. To her, promiscuity was the norm and she had done nothing wrong. She learned, however, she must do what she could to avoid becoming pregnant, no matter what happened. Sonya had returned to the kitchen table and a few of her drinking buddies had arrived with a fresh supply of beer and random pills. The party thrived in the next room and Ava drifted into a disturbed sleep.

Ava awoke to the sun shining through the window and the house incredibly quiet. She had no idea what time Rick planned to stop by so she got up to get ready for his visit. Sonya was asleep on the couch, for once, alone. After Ava cleaned herself up and put on clean clothes she quietly went outside to wait for Rick. It was about ten o'clock in the morning and she assumed it would be afternoon before he would arrive.

While Ava sat on the porch waiting for Rick, Sonya woke and went to the bathroom. She remembered Ava had said her boyfriend would be stopping by so she took extra special care in cleaning herself up and getting ready to meet him. She knew physically beating Ava had lost much of its affect and had devised a better way to hurt the girl.

After Ava had waited only about an hour, she looked up, surprised to see Rick's car pulling in the driveway. Ava had no idea Sonya had prepared herself to meet him. She sat quietly on the front steps as Rick turned the engine of the car off and got out. From inside the dilapidated house, Sonya heard the car door close. She moved toward the small window above the porch and secretly watched as Rick moved toward Ava. Rick approached Ava wearing the same sweet smile he always did. Looking at him, Ava couldn't help but smile back. Rick reached for Ava's hand and she accepted, allowing him to guide her into a standing position. Rick stood on the landing and Ava on the step above as the two embraced. He pulled away slightly and kissed her tenderly. It seemed as if nothing could hurt her when she was with him.

"C'mon," Rick said as he pulled on Ava's hand, encouraging her to follow him.

Ava willingly followed, curious about where he wanted to go. To her surprise, he only took a few steps before turning back toward her. He reached into his pocket, retrieving a small object. Before she had time to wonder what it was, he dropped to one knee and looked up into the nine-year-old girl's innocent face.

"Will you marry me?" Rick asked as he produced a thin golden band and held it out to her.

Ava did not answer. She looked at the gold band and struggled to wrap her mind around what was happening. She had only known Rick for two days, but it seemed like life would be so much better with him than with her mother. Without saying yes or no, Ava reached for the ring and slipped it on her finger. The band was at least two sizes too big for her ring finger so with a giggle she slipped it on her thumb. While still on one knee, he hugged her small body close and buried his face in her chest. Sonya had seen everything and decided the best way to hurt Ava would be to take Rick from her.

Sonya walked out the door of the house and onto the porch. She was dressed as if she were twenty-years-old, even though she was much older. Rick noticed as Sonya emerged from the house and stood to meet her. Once again, Ava had no idea anything taking place was inappropriate. Rick kissed Ava on the cheek, then walked toward Sonya with his hand stretched out in front of him, indicating a handshake.

"I'm Rick," he said as he climbed the stairs toward Sonya.

Sonya took his hand, shaking it as a lady might. "I'm Sonya," she said sweetly, offering a smile suggesting acceptance.

Ava was startled by her mother's kind tone and failed to remember the last time she had heard it. Sonya invited Rick into the house and Ava followed with skepticism as hundreds of abusive events flooded her mind. Sonya sat down at the table, kindly offering Rick a chair. She behaved as if she and Rick were the only two people in the house, though Ava took a chair at the table as well. Sonya politely questioned Rick about his last name, where he lived, and how he made a living. Rick conversed with Sonya, apparently trying to win her trust for the sake of his relationship with Ava. Throughout the conversation, as Ava listened, Sonya displayed a side of herself Ava had never seen before. After about an hour and a half, the conversation began to die and Sonya began to busy herself with other things, pretending to be a caring and nurturing person. Rick turned to Ava and noticed the skepticism in her eyes.

"What's wrong?" he whispered to Ava as Sonya pretended to be busy in the kitchen.

"Nothin'," Ava answered quietly. She was unable to process the abrupt and radical change in her mother's behavior and felt uncomfortable trying to explain her confusion.

Ava suddenly felt a twinge of hope, as if it might be possible her mother had really started to change. She rose from her place at the table and meekly made her way to the kitchen where her mother appeared to be stacking dishes in preparation for washing.

"Is it okay if me and Rick go to my room to talk?" Ava asked with downcast eyes.

"Sure!" Sonya answered with a seemingly happy tone.

Still skeptical of her mother's newly developed kindness,

Ava chose to end the conversation abruptly and return to Rick at the table.

"C'mon," Ava said to Rick as she took his hand and led him to her room.

At first, the two sat on the edge of Ava's bed as if they had never before touched one another. Ava felt a strange shame in her heart, the reason eluding her. After a few minutes, Rick put his arm around Ava and kissed the top of her head. Without offering an explanation, she pulled away from him and lay down on top of the blankets. Without question, Rick lay down next to her and held her hand. Silently, the two of them lay side by side on the bed holding hands. After only a few minutes Ava heard the front door slam shut and recognized the sound of footsteps walking across the small porch and down the stairs. She knew Sonya had at least walked outside and maybe even left for some unknown destination.

Rick told Ava about awards he had won during his years in high school and talked about how he felt he had found his soul mate in her. She listened quietly, offering no response. He seemed to be content with talking and she simply let him continue. She was very impressed with the things he told her, not even considering the possibility some, if not all of it, may be a lie. Rick repositioned himself so Ava's head could lie comfortably on his shoulder and she fell asleep quickly. Not long after, he fell asleep as well.

When Ava awoke Rick was gone and Sonya sat at the dining room table with a beer and a cigarette. Ava walked sleepily out of her room, rubbing her eyes as she tried to wake up.

"Where's Rick?" Ava asked quietly, not yet fully alert.

"Gone," Sonya replied flatly, her familiar mannerisms seemingly back in place.

Ava wondered why Rick hadn't let her know he was

leaving. She felt a feeling in the pit of her stomach, a feeling of emptiness and dread.

"He won't be comin' back either," Sonya added. "I don't want ya seein' him ever again."

Ava knew better than to argue and simply turned to go back to her bed.

"I want the ring he gave ya," Sonya said with a growl.

"But it's mine," Ava retorted in an emotionless tone.

"No, it's mine," Sonya corrected, her voice flooding with irritation.

Ava did not understand what Sonya meant and simply stood in the doorway, motionless, with her back to her mother.

"He said I could have it before he left," Sonya continued, as if Ava had asked.

Ava pulled the ring from her thumb and held it out behind her. Sonya did not move, expecting Ava to bring it to her. Since Sonya did not move to take the ring, Ava simply dropped it on the floor and closed the door behind her. The gold band struck the floor and bounced before it rolled solemnly across the filthy, uncarpeted floor. Slowly falling to the side as it loses momentum, it rolls in tight circles until if finally comes to rest, as if symbolizing the final fall of Ava's hopes to feel love and acceptance from her mother. She sat down on her bed and cried silently, realizing physical pain was not the worst type of pain her mother could inflict on her.

Little did Ava know, Sonya had initially invited Rick to sit with her at the table so she could find out some information about him. Though Ava sat at the table and listened to every word of the conversation, Sonya knew she would not catch on. She knew the girl would be confused by her kind behavior and used it to her advantage. Sonya found out all she needed to know about Rick and then pretended to be busy in the kitchen. When Ava asked if she and Rick could go to her bedroom, Sonya happily agreed. She wasn't concerned about what would happen to Ava, she only wanted to find a way to hurt her. Sonya knew Rick was quite a bit older than Ava and once she knew his age for sure she had all she needed. When Ava and Rick went to Ava's bedroom, Sonya went to the neighbor's house to use the phone. She found the phone book and looked for the names of Rick's parents, which he had happily shared with her. Sonya called Rick's parents and informed them he had asked Ava, a nine-year-old girl, to marry him. Rick's parents then informed Sonya Rick had dated girls his own age before but had pursued a few girls who were way too young for him in the past. Sonya threatened them with a lawsuit and they readily agreed to forbid Rick to see Ava again. Sonya happily returned home and quietly walked into Ava's room to wake Rick up.

"Rick," Sonya said quietly as she shook his arm.

Rick's eyes fluttered open and he looked up at Sonya.

"We need to talk," Sonya said in an irritated voice. Then indicated she wanted Ava to stay asleep.

Rick slowly slid his arm out from under Ava as she slept, carefully moving so she would not wake up. Ava had rolled over in her sleep and removing his arm from under her head was surprisingly easy. She did not wake up and Rick stepped out of her room. Sonya quietly closed the door and indicated to Rick she wanted him to follow her outside.

"You're done seein' Ava," Sonya informed him in a stern but low voice.

Rick looked at Sonya with confusion. After the conversation

earlier in the day he thought Sonya had accepted him as Ava's boyfriend. He had planned to wait for a few months before telling Sonya he had proposed to Ava.

"I talked to your dad," Sonya began. "He said ya take advantage of little girls," she continued.

Rick began to object then remembered the conversations he and his parents had had in the past, including the threats of institutionalization that had been made concerning his attraction to prepubescent girls.

"You're guna leave here today and not come back, got it?" Sonya ordered.

Rick looked down and said nothing.

"If ya leave and never come back I won't call the cops," Sonya added clearly angry.

Rick looked at Sonya briefly and simply nodded his head to indicate he understood her demand. He turned slowly and walked to his car. Sadly, he got in and started the engine. The car backed out of the driveway and made its way to the stop sign at the end of the block. Sonya watched as the car turned the corner and disappeared, never to return.

Though it was a good thing Sonya had stopped the relationship, she had done it for all the wrong reasons. Her daughter's welfare had never once entered her mind. She only wanted to get rid of Rick to hurt Ava, and that is exactly what she did. Sonya had planned the moment when she would inform Ava of Rick's departure and planned to take the ring as a trophy for herself. After all, she rationalized Ava did not deserve such a treasure. When Ava finally awoke Sonya informed her of what had happened with a tone of contempt and irritation in her voice. Ava argued very little and simply gave up the ring confirming Sonya's assumption Ava could be controlled in more ways than one. Sonya was happy with herself and slipped the ring on her finger after picking it up off of the floor. She returned to her chair at the table and took a long drink of the beer she had just opened. She lit a cigarette, breathing the smoke deep into her lungs and as she lowered her hand back to the table she smiled smugly to celebrate her triumph over the nine-year-old girl.

Ava never told a soul about what had happened at the fairgrounds with Rick. Sonya failed to tell Ava the whole story about why Rick had left and Ava was left to believe Rick had simply left her, giving the ring to her mother instead. Ava never tried to contact Rick nor did he attempt to contact her. With that, yet another solid layer of bricks were firmly secured around Ava's heart.

Chapter Seven

For the next few years Ava began to develop a personality and style all her own. Having barely graduated high school, Niles had gone on to join the Navy, finally escaping Nathia and his mother. News eventually traveled home about his decision to change his name and embrace atheism. He wanted no connection to his parents and legally became Able Hahn, in an ironic effort to poke fun at the Christian faith. His first choice, Arion Hahn, had been denied by the government due to the perceived satanic ring of the name.

Emma quit school during her junior year, having gotten pregnant by Lee. She married him in the summer of 1987 and moved to a very small town called Bonwhall, about fifty miles from Nathia. In spite of the resentment Emma carried in her heart toward her mother, regular invitations were extended to Sonya to stay the weekends with Emma and her new family. Of course, Ava went along for each visit as Sonya was unwilling to leave her alone at home for fear she would lose her welfare.

Lilli was still a stranger to Ava but the two had finally begun to slowly reconnect. Lilli had married Shane during the summer of 1989 had already had two children by the time the reconnection began. She lived close to Nathia and hoped to rediscover her relationship with Ava.

Ava had turned twelve in the spring of 1989 but felt as

if she were at least eighteen. She had adopted a style of dress unique to those who were known to be delinquent in the small town. Her hair had grown long and the majority of the time it hung loosely over her right eye. She wore ripped jeans and a leather jacket almost every day. The eye liner she wore formed a thick, black line around her eyes, creating the illusion her lashes were much longer than they actually were. She spoke to very few people and most of her classmates were afraid of her, avoiding contact with her as much as possible. It seemed as if the previous few years had changed her in a way no one had ever expected. Sonya had continued to abuse Ava in every possible way, regularly adding more bricks to the wall around Ava's heart. Over time Ava had begun to feel only numbness concerning her mother and her reaction to the abuse continued to slowly transform into uncontrollable anger.

The way Ava presented herself, along with the company she kept, helped most people assume she was a tough girl who would stand up for herself. Day by day her new personality seemed to give her courage even though her self-esteem was still less than nothing. The boys who attended her school chose not to talk to her and she pretended she was fine with the arrangement. On the inside, however, she really only wanted to be accepted but she would never admit that fact to anyone. Ava rationalized to herself, at least people would leave her alone, which was a big change from the usual peer torment she had grown used to throughout the years. Most of her peers had made fun of her for being poor and relentlessly teased her about virtually everything. To Ava, isolation seemed to be so much better than social unacceptance so she clung to her new identity and nurtured it. There were three other girls in her class who seemed to be outcasts as well and the four of them seemed to gravitate toward one another. When the school year ended they continued to spend as much time together as possible.

Ava still spent time with Emily as well but never together with her friends from school. Ava and Emily regularly ventured to Ropschon to go cruising or attend parties with whomever would take them. Ava began to learn about life quickly and Emily seemed to be an effective teacher.

Another school year had finally ended and Ava spent a great deal of time with her friends. When she was with Emily, they spent time with Carl, either drinking at his house, drinking at parties, or cruising in Ropschon. A few weeks after the end of the school year Emily invited Ava to go to a party in Ropschon and Ava happily accepted. She felt as if she needed excitement of some kind to offset the numbness created by the years of abuse. Carl drove the girls to the party and dropped them off at a house Ava had never been to before. Emily claimed a few of her friends lived in the house so Ava did not question anything and blindly followed her friend.

The house was large and had two stories, covered in a deep maroon-colored slate siding with windows that wore black shutters on both sides, perceivably stylish and appealing at the time the house was built. At first glance, the house seemed quite nice, however, a closer look revealed a different perspective. A few of the shutters had begun to detach from the house and hung loosely from their original places. Three of the individual panes in the large windows were cracked and strips of duct tape covered the wounds in the glass. The roof looked shabby, with bare spots giving way to shingles that had come loose, and the majority of the remaining shingles had begun to curl under from age and wear. The boards on the old, grey, wooden porch were loose and a few of them groaned as the girls walked across them to the door.

Without knocking, Emily opened the door and walked into the house with Ava right behind her. A few women and several men had arrived before the girls, each with a beer in one hand and a cigarette burning in the other. The living room was very large and the walls were decorated with what seemed to be antique wallpaper. The wallpaper, printed with dark green and beige stripes was tattooed with small, intermittent designs that provoked the impression of royalty. Immediately and without question, Emily and Ava were offered a beer, and both happily accepted. Emily lit a cigarette and popped her beer can open. The warmth of the welcome extended by the people in the house made Ava feel as if she had been there all day. She drank her beer and tried to relax as she continued to look around the room wondering what it would be like to be in a wonderful environment like this all the time. Everyone in the room seemed to be happy and joking with no intention of being cruel to anyone. Each person wore a smile and Ava heard laughter flutter through the air randomly. Her eyes continued to sweep the room as she absentmindedly listened to the conversation taking place between Emily and one of the women. She noticed the room was not clouded with smoke in spite of the number of people smoking. She rationalized the fan was the reason for the displaced smoke as she noticed it spinning and wobbling slightly in its permanent seat on the ceiling. Then she saw him. He had dark hair that fell to his shoulders and Ava thought he might be a little older than her. He was thin and not much taller than Ava and seemed to be very confident. She lost all track of the conversation she had been listening to and seemed to be enveloped in watching the boy across the room.

"Ava," Emily said, glancing quickly at the woman she had been talking to.

Ava did not hear Emily as she stared at the boy across the room.

"Ava!" Emily said again, this time a little louder and with a giggle.

Ava snapped her head back toward Emily and began to blush.

"Huh?" Ava said as she attempted to speak.

"What are ya lookin' at?" Emily questioned with a smile as she turned in the direction Ava had been gazing.

Emily's eyes came to rest on the boy and then slowly moved back to Ava as a wide grin spread across her face.

"Ya wana meet him?" Emily asked, giggling.

Ava simply nodded her head to indicate she wanted to meet the boy and glanced back toward him with a shy smile on her face. A split second after Ava's eyes had come to rest on him again she watched as his eyes lifted to look at her. Immediately, her eyes darted back to Emily's and then down to the floor. She could feel her face turning red. Emily turned toward the boy and motioned for him to join them where they stood. He rose from his makeshift seat on the arm of a large, light brown sectional and walked toward them confidently, as if he were afraid of nothing.

"What's up?" the boy said with a smile as he approached.

The boy's voice filled Ava's ears and she loved the sound of it. All she could think about was how much she liked him, even though she had never met him before and knew absolutely nothing about him.

"Jeff, this is Ava," Emily said as she lightly touched Ava's arm.

Ava looked up sheepishly and made brief eye contact with him.

"Hi," he said to Ava sweetly as he smiled.

"Hi," Ava responded, unable to keep from smiling and blushing as she looked back toward the floor.

"Maybe we can have a beer later?" Jeff said to Ava as he stepped close to her and touched the small of her back.

"Sure," Ava answered softly as she felt his touch.

Jeff walked back to his original place in the living room as Emily and the woman she had been talking to smiled at each other. Ava suddenly felt lighter than air and felt as if she were free as a bird. She tipped her beer can up and took a long drink. Throughout the night Ava continued to drink, and as often as she could, tried to catch glances of Jeff as he spoke to others in the room. People continued to walk into the house by twos and threes for the next hour and before she realized it the living room was full of people. The music had been turned up loud and she was beginning to feel the affects of the alcohol. Even though she was only twelve she seemed to be able to handle her alcohol, not a surprising development, considering she had already been drinking regularly for two years. She talked to a few guys as they approached her but she tried hard to keep Jeff in her sights. Emily had wandered off somewhere and Ava slowly circulated through the room in an attempt to find her. The music blared and the sound of multiple conversations filled the air. Ava had lost sight of Jeff and had no idea where Emily had gone.

A man who had been sitting on the large, light brown couch stood and stepped in front of Ava, handing her another beer. Ava took the beer and smiled as she popped it open and took a drink. As Ava approached the doorway of what seemed to be the kitchen, Jeff suddenly stepped out in front of her. He smiled sweetly at her and she smiled back. He extended his hand toward her and she took it as a thousand feelings rushed through her body and mind at the same time. With no words, Jeff gently led her into the kitchen. The room was dimly lit, with only a small light burning over the sink. He looked into her eyes and took the beer from her hand. She let him take the can and stared back into his eyes. He set the beer can on the table then guided her so her back was against the wall. He stepped close to her and kissed her gently. Ava closed her eyes and surrendered herself to him openly. The kiss lasted for several minutes before Emily stepped into the kitchen to find them together.

"Ya ready?" Emily yelled over the music.

Ava turned her head toward Emily and smiled, clearly not ready to leave.

"Carl's here to get us," Emily shouted with an apologetic look in her eyes.

Again, with no words, Ava looked back at Jeff and kissed him again. She pulled away from him and took a step toward Emily. He reached out and took her hand once again, as if asking her not to leave. She turned back toward him as he placed a small piece of paper in her hand. She took the paper and looked at it, reading the telephone number he had written on it. She looked back at him and smiled as she shoved the paper into her pocket. They stood for a few seconds holding hands before he leaned toward her for one more kiss.

"C'mon!" Emily shouted over the loud music, giggling and clearly amused by Ava and Jeff's behavior.

She turned from Jeff and followed Emily out of the kitchen, across the living room, and to the front door. They exited the house and immediately noticed Carl's car waiting at the curb. Though it didn't seem like it, the girls had been at the house for more than four hours and it was already going on one o'clock in the morning. Ava's mind soared and she felt so wonderful. She did all she could to relive the feelings Jeff's kisses had created as she climbed in the front seat of the car. Carl pressed on the gas pedal and the car began its journey toward Nathia, taking Ava back to her terrible life. She wished she could stay at the house in Ropschon forever but knew it was not possible. The realization Sonya would attack her in some way when she got home wafted around her mind but she was unable to pay much attention to it.

Ava had consumed several beers and even though it was enough to impair her thinking and coordination she felt as if she hadn't had anything to drink at all. After the fifteen minute drive from Ropschon to Nathia, Carl's small car pulled into Sonya's driveway to drop Ava off.

"See ya," Ava said to Emily and Carl with a smile as she exited the car.

"Later," Emily answered from the back seat, winking at Ava and smiling.

She swung the car door shut and turned toward the house. The living room light was on and she knew she would have to face her mother.

Sonya had been sitting at the table, as always, drinking beer and smoking cigarettes. As Ava walked through the door she looked around the room to find Sonya staring at her with a hateful glare.

"Where the fuck have ya been?" Sonya growled.

"With Emily," Ava responded flatly.

Sonya was clearly drunk and Ava knew the interaction

would not turn out well. She could feel the anger building within her, igniting as her mother began to speak.

"S'pose ya been trampin' around and gettin' fucked, haven't ya, ya little whore?" Sonya fired at Ava loudly.

Ava said nothing and stood still in the middle of the room. Her eyes lifted from the dirty floor and met her mother's glare. Sonya had seen her daughter's eyes before but this time Ava held her gaze, without looking away at all. She began to feel uncomfortable and knew she had to do something to make her daughter cower.

"So who'd ya fuck?" Sonya questioned deviantly as she broke eye contact with Ava to look at her beer can as she raised it to her lips.

Ava remained in the middle of the room, offering no response as she felt her body begin to tremble slightly. Sonya took the last drink from her beer and slammed the can down on the surface of the table. The connection between the table top and the aluminum can created a loud crack but Ava didn't move. Sonya had slammed the can down in order to make her respond, even if the response was involuntary, but the sound had no effect whatsoever. She didn't jump or even blink. Sonya's aggravation grew within her and she slowly rose from her chair. Without understanding the reason, she felt she must make Ava respond in some way. Ava continued to stare at her mother, the initial seed of fear having given way to a blossom of anger unlike any she had ever felt before. Her whole body was now trembling and even though she hadn't realized it her hands had contracted to form tight fists. Her breathing had changed into a slight pant as her anger continued to build. She had finally had enough of her mother's insults and abuse. Sonya slowly walked around the table toward Ava keeping her gaze fixed on her daughter's face. She noticed Ava's face looked different but was only slightly concerned about the reason why, having become enveloped in her endeavor to break the girl once more.

"You little bitch," Sonya hissed as she slowly moved toward Ava. "Looks like I gota teach ya a fuckin' lesson."

Ava's body tensed as she prepared for her mother to rush at her. It seemed as if Ava was taking the poise of a vicious guard dog as she slightly dropped her head without breaking her gaze. She continued to stare at her mother from under her brow, and was ready to fight back. In a blur of movement Sonya rushed at Ava, her hands in front of her in an attempt to grab her daughter's hands. Ava responded to the quick burst of movement by bringing her hands up in front of her. She was quicker than Sonya and before Sonya could object, she found both of her forearms trapped in Ava's grip. Sonya tried to retreat but Ava's hold was too strong. Ava's head was still tilted downward as she began to speak.

"If you touch me again I will fucking kill you," Ava growled at Sonya in a clear and even voice, enunciating each word as she glared at her hatefully.

Sonya had not looked away from Ava throughout the confrontation but it seemed as if she was really seeing her daughter for the first time. The girl she saw in front of her was no longer the little girl she had always been able to control. Sonya searched Ava's eyes for a hint of weakness and found none. Sonya's face began to change in reaction to the situation in which she found herself. She somehow knew, if she attempted to hit Ava again, Ava's promise of death would likely turn into reality. Sonya's arms went limp and would have fallen to her sides if Ava had not been holding them in place. Sonya's rage began to drain from her mind and was quickly replaced with fear. Ava's gaze seemed to be as hard as stone and had not faltered. Sonya was the first to look away, casting her eyes downward to indicate defeat. Ava slowly released the grip she had on her mother's forearms and deliberately lowered her hands to her sides. Neither of them spoke for several minutes as they stood facing each other. Sonya now wore deep red marks completely encircling her forearms where Ava's hands had ruthlessly gripped them. Ava's breathing began to even out but her body remained rigid and continued to tremble. Sonya took a breath in preparation to speak but before she could say anything Ava interrupted her.

"No!" Ava barked loudly.

Sonya's head snapped up, forcing her eyes to meet Ava's. She glared at her daughter with contempt in her eyes as her fear subsided.

"I'm done with this," Ava hissed at her mother. "I promise you, if you ever hit me again, I will kill you."

Sonya was unable to speak, somehow understanding the seriousness of the situation. Sonya, now unable to meet Ava's gaze, turned to walk back toward her seat at the table.

"You're only twelve, little girl," Sonya began once she was out of Ava's reach. "Ya wouldn't know how to get it done."

Sonya sat back down at the table and lit a cigarette, unable to completely hide the uncertainty she felt as a result of Ava's threat. Her hands shook as she attempted to make the flame of the lighter ignite the end of the cigarette. Even though she had just been threatened and clearly defeated by her daughter, she was still able to hold a smug attitude, as if she had won. Ava once again raised her head to look at her mother normally.

"Try me," Ava growled. "I beg you - fuckin' try me."

Sonya looked down at the ashtray as she rolled her cigarette on the inside of it, pretending to knock the ashes off. She was unable to respond as the realization of the situation inundated her with fear once more. Ava stood in place for another few minutes then walked slowly toward her bedroom. Sonya offered no words as Ava closed the door quietly behind her.

Ava sat on the edge of her bed and thought about the events of the night. She tried hard to take herself back to the encounter she and Jeff had shared but the adrenaline coursing through her from the confrontation with her mother wouldn't allow it. Silently, tears began to well in her eyes as she thought about what had just occurred. She hated she had to take such a stand against her mother. She wondered why Sonya could not simply love her and behave in a nurturing way. She hated the anger that welled up inside of her but she knew she would not survive without it. She lay back on her bed and cried silent tears, mourning the loss of the hope she had had in her heart for so long. She knew her mother would never change and the realization seemed to devastate her as her childhood anticipation of her mother's love dissolved into nothing. She would never again hope for her mother's love. She was exhausted from so many years of longing and simply could no longer bring herself to care.

Sonya retrieved another beer from the refrigerator and returned to her seat at the table. The confrontation she had just had with Ava had upset everything she thought she knew. She reflected on all four of her children and the things she perceived had happened. She thought about Lilli and the lies she told in order to get sent away. She wondered what Lilli had thought was so terrible about living at home. She was still convinced Lilli had not tried to commit suicide and simply did not want to follow the rules at home.

"Li'l bitch just didn't wana do what she was told," Sonya thought to herself as she stared into space and shook her head slightly in anger.

Sonya's thoughts then turned to Niles and how mean he had become before he had left for the Navy. She concluded his father's personality must have been handed to him at birth since she believed nothing had happened to him that would make him turn out that way.

"Niles was just as much of a son-of-a-bitch as his dad," Sonya thought. "He made me do his homework just so he could fuckin' graduate." Sonya's gaze continued to focus on nothing and her eyes narrowed into a glare.

She thought then of Emma and wondered how she could have let herself get pregnant by Lee. She recalled how Lee had tried to fool around with her before he had expressed an interest in Emma and wondered how Emma could have stolen Lee from her.

"Lee wanted me, not Emma," Sonya thought. "Why the fuck would he dump me for her? Li'l bitch." Sonya absent mindedly took another long drink from her beer can and set the can back on the table without looking.

Finally, her thoughts turned to Ava and the drastic changes that had taken place in the last few years. Sonya rationalized she was trying to teach Ava the ways of the world so she would be prepared when she grew up. She knew Ava's threat on her life had been real and she resolved to never physically beat the girl again. Still, she had to find a way to control her and decided sympathy would be her next powerful tool. If she could make Ava feel sorry for her she knew she could still control her.

"Fuckin' li'l whore," Sonya thought to herself. "She'll fuckin' learn life ain't all fun and games. I'll make sure of it." Sonya finally focused her eyes on a photo hanging on the wall and pulled her mind away from her thoughts.

As Sonya's thoughts moved through her mind she had no idea how mistaken her memories really were. It seemed she had always remembered things the way she wanted to remember them and made herself into the victim in each situation. Lilli would have obviously rather died than continue living with her mother, the suicide attempt ultimately saving her life, as it was the definitive cause of her relocation to a foster home. Niles had turned out the way he had, partly because of the abuse he had endured at the hands of Simon, Sonya, and Lars and partly because of the mental issues he had been born with, which were never diagnosed. Further, Sonya had been the one trying to fool around with Lee and Emma had done what she could to escape her mother's control by getting pregnant and moving away, even if she had done it without conscious thought.

A few days later Ava called Jeff and a relationship began to form. She did everything she could to spend as much time as possible with him and finally felt as if she had connected with another person. It turned out Jeff was only two years older than Ava so they seemed to have a great deal in common. Little did Ava know, however, Jeff was a heavy drug user and spent a great deal of time with a man who supplied drugs to several young adults in Ropschon. Ava and Jeff dated for over three months before Sonya was aware of the relationship and the two of them had been sexually active numerous times. Since Ava had finally reached puberty, and the issue of pregnancy had become a real threat, Sonya insisted Ava start taking birth control pills. Ava and Jeff dated exclusively, or so Ava thought, for a little more than two years before the relationship began to fail. Ava had discovered, through a mutual friend, Jeff had been seeing other girls. Ava had also discovered Jeff's drug use and begged him to stop, her pleading falling on deaf ears. Several of the members of her group regularly reported sightings of Jeff with at least three other girls to Ava. She tried to ignore the rumors about Jeff's relationships with other girls but, after quite some time, was simply unable to discount the tales any longer.

Finally, the day came when Ava felt she could no longer deal with the situation and decided to end her relationship with Jeff. She confronted him about the other girls and he quickly admitted his guilt. Ava felt a surge of pain as the realization washed over her and she proceeded to end the relationship. The pain she felt as a result of the failed relationship seemed to automatically transform into anger. It took Ava several months to get over Jeff as he had been the first boy for whom she had ever felt love. As the days passed her anger dwindled but for many years she would feel a specific loathing for him. It seemed she was better able to deal with hating him than missing him.

After Ava broke up with Jeff she continued to spend time with her friends from school as her relationship with Emily seemed to weaken. Their relationship began to deteriorate due to the choices Emily had made, all of which seemed to take her further and further away from Nathia. The time they spent together continued to decrease and after a while Emily seemed to disappear all together. Even though Ava had added her own touches to the personality Emily had helped to create, Ava's social involvement at school changed little.

Ava turned fourteen in the spring of 1991, her social group now consisting of only a few girls who were in her grade. Since Ava had stood up to her mother, Sonya had not physically abused her, however, she had found a way to make Ava feel like a horrible person on a daily basis by continuing to call her names and constantly reminding her of her failures and shortcomings, whether they were real or not. When Ava would reflect on the physical and verbal abuse she would compare it to the emotional and mental abuse she was now enduring. She often thought she would rather be physically beaten than made to feel emotionally worthless, rationalizing at least she was able to see a physical injury as it healed, whereas an emotional injury seemed to last forever. Ava seemed to somehow know her life would be a struggle and her thoughts of suicide increased. She thought about ending her own life, at least once each day, usually at night as she tried to fall asleep.

At fourteen Ava had begun to blossom into a young woman but portrayed herself as a tom-boy. Her frame was small and at only 5'2" she weighed about 98 pounds. Her hair had grown even longer than before, now hanging below her waist, but she had finally decided to cut her bangs so both of her eyes were visible. Ava's small group of school friends included three other girls besides herself, all four girls growing closer by the day. Eliza was the same height as Ava but was heavier. Her hair was a little lighter than Ava's, not as long, and she wore it in a ponytail every day, classifying herself as a tom-boy also. Rachel was the same height as Ava and Eliza but was even heavier than Eliza. Her hair was much darker than Ava's and she wore it short most of the time. Julia was taller than the other three girls and seemed to have a thicker frame. She was neither fat nor thin but her hips were wide. Her hair was as dark as Rachel's and also short. The four girls had a great deal in common, however, their tom-boy images were unique to themselves. Ava seemed to be the leader of the group, always ready to fight and never backing down. Eliza and Julia were both farm girls, each having horses and spending a great deal of time outside, but Julia still tried to be feminine much of the time whereas Eliza did not. Rachel lived in the country but had no livestock, her tom-boy image resonating from her love of softball and racing.

Julia lived closer to town than Eliza and Rachel so she was able to spend more time with Ava. It was summer again and Ava and Julia were doing what they could to stay cool. The two girls had decided to spend the weekend together, camping out in Ava's backyard. The afternoon was warm, but not unbearable, as the girls sat in the shade of a tree enjoying the slight breeze that moved the air.

"Ya wana go with me?" Julia asked Ava, breaking the silence.

"Okay," Ava said without looking at Julia. "Where?"

"There's this guy, Alex," Julia said. "I haven't seen him in a while. Might be fun."

"Sure," Ava agreed.

The two girls rose from their seats in the grass and made their way across the yard, toward the street. Ava did not bother to tell her mother where she was going, afraid she would say something hurtful. Julia chattered about the end of the school year and how she was having trouble with her father. Ava tried to listen but struggled to pay attention. They made their way through the streets of the small town and arrived at a house only six blocks from Ava's. Ava followed Julia as she led the way to the front door and knocked loudly. The door opened and a man of about twenty years of age stood in the doorway. He was about 5'10" tall, slender, and muscular. His hair was cut very short and tinted a reddish-brown. Julia exchanged a brief greeting with him before he invited the girls into the house. Ava said nothing as she followed Julia through the kitchen and into the living room.

"Whatcha been up to?" Alex inquired as he hugged Julia.

"Not much," Julia answered as she pulled away from him and looked around the room.

"This is Ava," Julia offered as she gestured in Ava's direction.

"Hi," Alex said to Ava, smiling widely.

"Hi," Ava answered softly, offering a half-hearted smile in return.

The three sat down as Julia and Alex continued to converse. Ava did not try to involve herself in the conversation but simply sat quietly while her friend visited. After about thirty minutes, the conversation drifted toward a country singer who was one of Julia's favorites. Alex offered Julia a magazine containing a photo of the singer and Julia's excitement was obvious. While Julia gazed at the photo, Alex attempted to make conversation with Ava. His attempt at conversation was not as successful as he would have liked and after a few minutes he seemed to give up.

"Ya wana come hang out with us?" Julia asked Alex.

"Sure!" Alex replied excitedly. "Where we goin'?"

"I don't care," Julia responded as she looked at Ava.

Ava shrugged her shoulders, clearly indifferent about their plans for the rest of the day.

"Let's go for a walk," Alex suggested, smiling at both of the girls.

"Let's go!" Julia said as she stood from her seat on the couch.

Ava stood as well and waited for Alex and Julia to make their way to the door. The three of them set out, with no particular destination, wandering the streets of the small town. It was early summer and the school year had just ended only a few weeks before. As Ava became more comfortable with Alex she was able to participate in the conversations that developed and began to have fun as time passed. After walking for over an hour the trio found themselves entering the larger of the town's two parks. With no sidewalk to use, the three walked along the road with Ava close to the grass, Alex in the middle, and Julia walking on the street side. A pickup truck slowed down and stopped next to Julia.

"What the hell ya think you're doin'?" A man barked angrily from the driver's window of the truck.

Julia quickly walked to the driver's side of the truck to speak with the man. Ava and Alex exchanged a brief glance and waited for Julia to return. The man in the truck was Julia's father and had apparently spent the day searching for her as she failed to tell either of her parents where she would be. Ava and Alex could hear the heated argument between Julia and her father but could not make out most of the words. Julia had started to cry and was yelling at her father through the window of the truck as he yelled back at her. All at once, with no explanation, Julia swiftly walked to the passenger side of the truck and got in. Before she could shut the door, her father had shifted the truck into drive and the tires barked as it sped away. Ava and Alex stood together, awkwardly for a few seconds, before either of them spoke.

"Wonder what that was all about," Alex said thoughtfully.

"No idea," Ava replied. "So, what now?"

"No reason me and you can't hang out, is there?" Alex inquired, smiling sweetly.

"Guess not," Ava answered flatly as she shrugged her shoulders slightly.

The two continued to walk into the park and found a

picnic table next to the lake upon which to sit. The sun had begun to set, though it would still be light for quite some time. There were campers in a different area of the park, leaving Ava and Alex virtually alone. Ava had taken up smoking cigarettes during one of her visits with Emma two years before so she pulled her cigarettes from her pocket and lit one. Alex pulled a pack of cigarettes from his pocket and lit one as well. For the first few minutes, neither of them spoke as they quietly sat, staring out across the lake. Alex seemed to try very hard to converse with Ava even though it seemed she was uninterested. In reality, Ava was very interested in everything about Alex. He had a quiet mystery about him which drew her unconsciously toward him. She had already felt a great deal of pain as a result of relationships, first with Rick and then with Jeff, and combined with the abuse she had been forced to deal with throughout her life she was afraid another heartbreak would be more than she could deal with.

"You look tense," Alex stated in a warm tone.

"I'm alright," Ava said, shrugging her shoulders slightly and looking down at the ground in front of her.

Alex rose from his seat next to Ava on the bench of the picnic table and repositioned himself on the table top directly behind her with one leg on each side of her. Ava's defenses immediately went up and she felt tense, yet exhilarated. She sat quietly as Alex began to rub her shoulders, massaging as if his touch would take away all of her troubles. His touch was exciting but Ava remained guarded.

"Maybe this will help you relax," Alex said as he leaned close to Ava's ear.

Ava said nothing and felt herself being captivated by his touch. She closed her eyes and began to relax slightly.

"Does that feel good?" Alex asked, almost in a whisper.

Ava nodded her head and relaxed even more. Alex

continued to massage her shoulders and then began to work his way down her arms. His hands were strong but did not cause pain as he rubbed her muscles. Simultaneously, his hands worked down her arms toward her hands. As he reached her hands he slipped his fingers among hers, locking their hands together as if they were puzzle pieces. He leaned close to her left ear and breathed softly on her neck. Immediately, Ava began to feel herself being consumed by Alex and the fresh lake air. The light of the day had begun to fade and darkness settled around them. Alex's hands released Ava's and began to softly move back up her arms, barely touching her skin. He began to massage her shoulders again, this time with a different touch. Ava felt the spark as it ignited a small fire between them but she was still trying to remain shielded from any emotional threat. His hands softly caressed her neck, moving her hair away from her skin. She could feel him lean closer and an excited shiver ran through her as he began to kiss her neck gently. His hands softly worked their way down to her waist then up the front of her shirt, only advancing upward to just below her breasts. Ava did nothing to stop him. She loved the feeling of being wanted and loved. Her initial attempt at shielding herself from any more pain melted away and she seemed to forget all the pain she had ever felt. Alex gently guided her to stand and turned her around so she was facing him. His movements were fluid as he slipped from his seat on the table top and stood in front of her. With one hand on each side of her face he gently pulled her toward him and kissed her passionately. She could no longer fight the feelings Alex was invoking and slipped her arms around his neck as she gave in and kissed him back. His hands explored her body as they continued their kiss and she was completely unable to intervene. For quite some time the two remained in a passionate embrace seemingly communicating only through touch. Alex finally pulled himself away for a moment.

"When do ya have to be home?" He asked, panting slightly.

"I should probably go," Ava answered in a whisper.

"Okay," Alex replied quietly. "I'll walk you home."

They kissed again, this time only for a moment, then turned to walk out of the park as they made their way to Ava's house. They walked together for only a few feet before Alex reached out and took Ava's hand. Once again he slipped his fingers between hers and it seemed as if their hands were made to fit together. Neither of them spoke as they made their way through the streets toward their destination. When they finally arrived at Ava's house they stood facing one another in the yard beside the garage. The shadows in which they stood were pitch black and just beyond them a pool of light was being cast across the driveway and grass from the porch light. Alex held both of Ava's hands and slowly leaned down to kiss her again. It seemed to feel so right to Ava, as if Alex had single handedly erased all of her terrible memories.

"Can I see ya tomorrow?" Alex asked sweetly.

Ava nodded her head shyly and smiled slightly.

"Maybe I could stop by after work?" Alex suggested.

"Sure," Ava answered, feeling as if she would burst with joy.

Alex smiled and bent to kiss her once more.

"See ya tomorrow," Alex whispered softly, making Ava shiver slightly.

He walked across the yard and stepped onto the street, turning to wave at Ava. She returned the wave and smiled. She watched him as he walked up the street until he disappeared into the darkness. Once he was out of sight, she turned and walked toward the front porch, feeling as if she were floating. It seemed, once again, she had been unconsciously overtaken by the curious feelings which led her to yet another relationship. Though she had no idea of what was in store for her, she chose to ignore the threats of heartbreak and immerse herself in the promise of happiness.

The following day Alex went to Ava's house as planned. When he arrived Sonya was at the bar and not expected home for several hours. Ava felt a surge of embarrassment when Alex entered the ramshackle home, feeling as if he must have come from a much nicer one. Alex seemed not to notice the scuffled mess that existed throughout the house, fixing his attention completely on Ava. The two of them went outside and sat on the front porch to enjoy the evening air. Their conversation seemed to grow from nothing, each seeking to find out as much as they could about the other. Laughter filled the air and they continued to talk until well beyond sunset. It was Saturday and Ava was happy Alex did not have to leave early in order to get up for work the next day. During the hours they spent getting to know one another, they seemed to grow very close. Ava, though still a little hesitant, allowed herself to be persuaded to sit in front of Alex, between his legs, on the step below the one upon which he sat so he could put his arms around her and hold her. Being with him seemed to free Ava, as if she had no worries at all. It seemed as if time flew by quickly and before they knew it Sonya appeared out of the darkness as she walked clumsily across the uncut front lawn. Immediately Ava stiffened and braced herself for a barrage of ugly words. Sonya was clearly surprised by Alex's presence and paused briefly to look at him. Seconds later Alex noticed Sonya and stood to introduce himself.

"Hi, I'm Alex," he said with an innocent smile.

A devious smile spread across Sonya's face, quickly transforming into a sweet-looking mask as she continued to approach the porch.

"Hi," Sonya answered, matching his smile.

Immediately, Sonya knew exactly how she could put Ava in her place.

"This'll be so easy," Sonya thought to herself as she walked boldly up to Alex. Pushing Ava out of the way Sonya wrapped her arms around Alex's neck and started to giggle playfully. Ava stood a short distance away, watching intently for Alex's response to the situation. Clearly confused, Alex pulled himself away from Sonya, at the same time trying to help her to continue to stand. He let out a nervous laugh and stepped away from her, toward Ava. Ava's anger began to build but she was able to hide it, at least for the moment. Sonya, in an attempt to appear sober, tried to sit on the steps of the porch gracefully, though her drunken state would not allow it. She clumsily plopped on the top step then tried to appear as if she had meant to sit down forcefully. Ava watched her mother closely, understanding completely what she was planning to do. She felt her heart sink a little, but immediately remembered how only moments before, Alex had stepped away from Sonya.

"So, you're my li'l girl's man, huh?" Sonya asked Alex, her speech slurred from drinking.

"Uh, well, I don't know," Alex answered with a nervous laugh as he looked at Ava. "Am I?" He asked, now clearly speaking to Ava.

Ava smiled and looked at him with wonder as she nodded her head, "yes."

Alex smiled and returned his attention to Sonya. She had

no idea Alex had just asked Ava to be his girlfriend right in front of her. He knew Sonya was drunk and was well aware she likely did not catch on to the development.

"Yep," Alex answered again with a smile.

Sonya looked at Alex for several seconds before speaking again, clearly looking him up and down as if deciding whether or not she was interested in him.

"Isn't that fuckin' sweet," Sonya said, rolling her eyes.

Alex was unprepared for the encounter with Sonya and was clearly at a loss for what to do next. He stepped toward Ava and put his arm around her, pulling her close to him as he kissed the top of her head. Ava had never experienced anything like this and had no idea what to expect next.

Sonya struggled to stand, using her hands to help stabilize herself as she tried to gain her footing. Unable to stand on her own in the middle of the porch she crawled a few feet to the door and pulled herself up with a sloppy grip on the rusted metal handle of the door. After gaining her footing, she turned only partially back toward Alex and Ava, as if they weren't worth the effort of turning all of the way around.

"I'll deal with ya tomorrow," Sonya slurred, her eyes only half open. She continued to mumble as she entered the house, stumbling. Ava could not make out all of the words but she clearly heard Sonya refer to her as a little whore.

Ava's eyes found the ground in front of her and immediately felt her face turning red. Alex turned Ava toward his chest and hugged her softly, resting his cheek on top of her head. Ava wrapped her arms around him and closed her eyes. She felt so safe with him and hated the idea he would probably be leaving soon.

"Alcohol makes people do silly things, huh?" Alex said softly to no one in particular.

Ava nodded her head in agreement as she felt hot tears sting her eyes.

"You guna be okay?" he asked softly.

Once again, Ava nodded her head, afraid to admit she was really not sure. She feared, if he found out how her mother really was, he would run away as fast as he could.

"Okay," he said. "I'll see ya tomorrow?"

"Yeah," Ava said, confused about why he would ever want to come back but elated he was willing to return to see her.

Alex gently pulled Ava's face up toward his own and kissed her softly.

"G'night," he whispered.

"G'night," she responded softly.

Alex slowly pulled himself away from Ava and set out across the yard into the darkness. She stood motionless for a few minutes, as if trying to think of another place to go besides into the house. Finally, she turned slowly and climbed the steps to the door.

As she entered the house she could already hear her mother snoring loudly. She knew she would likely find the same thing she had found countless nights before, her mother passed out on the torn, gold-colored couch in the living room. Sure enough, the picture was the same and Ava was allowed to pass through the living room, into her bedroom, without further confrontation with her mother. She closed her bedroom door softly behind her and lay down on her bed. The sound of the box fan in the window seemed to help drown her thoughts about how badly things could have gone earlier in the evening when Sonya had met Alex. She drifted off to sleep, playing back the time she and Alex had spent together in her mind. Even the thought of him seemed to calm her heart but the thought of ending her life still found its way into her thoughts, even if only for a fleeting moment.

The next morning Ava awoke to bright sunlight and the sound of the box fan still humming in the window. The consistent breeze from the fan on Ava's face felt good and seemed to comfort her. She lay motionless on her bed for several minutes, her mind completely absorbed in the memories of Alex, from the previous few days. She smiled to herself and hoped she would see him again soon. She rolled from her bed and winced as pain surged through her back and into her legs. The pain had become a normal part of her life and she was usually able to overcome it. She opened her bedroom door and stepped into the living room. Sonya was sitting at the dining room table smoking a cigarette and had already opened a beer. Ava barely paid attention to her mother as she walked toward the bathroom and Sonya said nothing. Ava stepped into the bathroom and closed the door so she could perform her morning ritual involving brushing her teeth, taking a bath, and the like.

Sonya watched as Ava silently passed through the room and her eyes automatically narrowed into a glare, just as they did every time she looked at her daughter. She barely remembered the night before and the brief encounter she had with Alex. She refused to admit to anyone she was unable to remember the details of most of her life and decided to patiently wait until Alex returned. She knew the person she had met was a boy interested in Ava and, that alone, seemed to be enough for her to begin formulating a plan to carry out her promise of teaching Ava another lesson. She planned to wait until Ava was out of the room and then extend an offer to the boy he wouldn't be able to refuse. She had a very high opinion of herself and believed she was virtually irresistible to all men. Silently, a deceitful smile spread across her lips as she lifted the beer can for a drink.

Ava stepped from the bathroom and walked toward her bedroom to get dressed. After her door had closed Sonya heard a soft knock on the front door.

"Come in!" Sonya barked.

She watched the empty doorway to see who would appear. Listening as the door opened slowly, Sonya seemed to know it was Ava's boyfriend. Alex stepped into the open door way of the living room and offered a friendly smile.

"Is Ava here?" Alex asked politely.

"Yeah," Sonya answered. "Come on in and have a seat," she continued as she offered a sweet smile.

Alex walked across the living room and took a seat across the table from Sonya.

"So where ya from?" Sonya questioned with a politeness incredibly unnatural for her.

"I live here in Nathia," Alex answered politely.

"How nice," Sonya replied. "How long have ya been seeing my little girl?" She asked, in an effort to convince him she cared for her daughter.

"We've only known each other a few days," Alex explained.

Sonya smiled again and stood from her chair. She walked toward Alex and stepped behind his chair. She brought her hands to rest on each of his shoulders and leaned down next to him to whisper in his ear.

"You're built," she said in a soft voice. "Ya know ya could have a woman instead of a girl, all ya gota do is say the word," she continued.

Alex was taken by surprise and immediately stood up from his chair to face Sonya. His reaction obviously surprised her, the look on her face clearly showing her shock. Alex laughed nervously and took a step backward, away from her. She knew she would have to get to know Alex a little more before making another move. She also knew she had to be quick about it, before Alex grew fonder of Ava. Sonya's look of disbelief at Alex's rejection faded from her face quickly and was replaced with a seductive smile.

"Too bad," Sonya said softly. "I would have taken ya 'round the fuckin' world."

Alex did not know what to say and again let out a nervous laugh. He couldn't believe what was happening and wished Ava would appear.

"So, Ava's here?" he asked again in a shaky, nervous voice.

"She's in her room," Sonya answered. "She doesn't even know you're here. Why waste the opportunity?"

Alex glanced behind him toward the closed door. Ava had given him a quick tour of the house the day before so he knew where her room was. He backed toward the closed door until his back was against the jam, keeping a close eye on Sonya as he knocked softly.

Ava was dressed and sitting quietly on her bed reading a book as she waited for him to arrive. She heard a soft knock on her door and knew it must be him, since her mother would have simply thrown the door open and burst in. Ava stood and crossed the small room to the door. Opening it, she found Alex standing with his back against the door jam and looking at Sonya who was standing behind one of the dining room chairs.

"Hi," Ava said softly with a smile.

"Hi," Alex answered, sounding somewhat nervous.

He quickly stepped into the bedroom and immediately hugged Ava. She hugged him back and ignored the nervousness she thought she had noticed in his voice only a few seconds before. His muscular arms wrapped around her seemed to melt all of her worries into nothing and she loved it.

"Whatcha wana do today?" He asked her playfully.

"I don't know, you?" She responded.

"Let's go outside and sit for a while. Maybe we can come up with somethin'," he said with a smile.

Alex took Ava's hand and led her through the living room toward the door. As they passed Sonya, Alex quickly glanced at her and offered a tense and confused smile. Sonya watched them walk quickly by and chose to remain silent. She was confident she would be able to get him into bed without much effort and could not wait to tell Ava after the fact. She knew the news would destroy the girl and she looked forward to the triumph.

Alex and Ava sat on the steps of the porch, once again, Ava in front of Alex and between his legs. She felt comfortable with him and the way he held her created the feeling nothing could hurt her. After a few hours Sonya walked out of the house and pushed her way past them down the stairs.

"Be back later," Sonya said flatly over her shoulder as she walked across the yard toward the street.

Ava said nothing to her mother and felt relieved she would be gone for a while.

"Ya wana go inside?" Alex asked.

"Okay," Ava answered.

They went into the house and made their way to Ava's bedroom. They sat beside one another on the bed, not bothering to close the door. Throughout the course of the day they talked, laughed, hugged, and kissed. Eventually they found themselves sitting cross-legged, facing one another. Sonya had been gone all day and the light had begun to fade from the sky. No lights had been turned on in the house and the lack of illumination seemed to cast a romantic mood over Alex and Ava. Neither gave a thought to Sonya's return and both were captivated by each other's company.

Alex leaned toward Ava and kissed the end of her nose gently. They had explored forbidden actions many times before but this time felt different to Ava. Without worry, she immediately surrendered herself to him and anything that was about to happen. He rose slightly from his place on the bed and guided Ava to lie back. She responding to his physical suggestions as if he were speaking clearly to her. Her mind was completely enveloped in Alex and everything about him. No thoughts of consequences entered her mind at all and she was swept away by his words, his touch, and his attention. The fears that had flooded her mind at six-years-old were now nowhere to be found as she willingly chased the feelings of connection she so desperately longed for. When everything was finished, they remained close to one another in a tangle of affection, their conversation fleeting, at best. The emotions and sensations they had just experienced together seemed to rob them of their ability to return to the present moment. Ava felt so complete with Alex, so safe, and so happy. He lightly kissed her again then whispered the words that would change her life forever.

"I love you," he said quietly.

Ava was unsure about how to respond at first but as the words fell upon her ears she felt as if she had transformed into a different person. A person worth loving and worth existing. She felt excitement and happiness, well within her heart, something she had never felt before.

"I love you too," Ava breathed as she closed her eyes and kissed him.

They continued to lie next to each other in elated silence for several minutes. Suddenly, they were torn from their euphoria by the sound of the front door creaking as it opened. Alex shot to his feet and swiftly pulled his pants on. Ava was on her feet in a flash and dressed quickly as well. Alex slipped his shoes on quickly and, as he pulled his shirt on over his head, caught a glimpse of Sonya standing in the living room. He looked at her for a few seconds in an effort to decipher her reaction but she displayed no indication of her perception. Alex and Ava exited the bedroom and walked slowly through the living room toward the front door. Sonya glared at both of them as they approached her.

"Ya li'l fuckin' whore," Sonya hissed. "Ya knew I wanted him so ya just had to fuck him."

Ava stopped in her tracks and looked at her mother in disbelief. Alex stopped as well and stood beside Ava, his eyes downcast. Slowly, Ava turned to look at Alex, her eyes filled with pain and anger. Alex looked at her and simply shook his head to indicate he had not wanted anything to do with Sonya. Ava returned her gaze to Sonya in an effort to find any indication of deceit in her mother's face. For the first time in her life she was able to see through her mother's mask, to grasp the tangible intent behind her words. Instead of searching her mind for a retaliation Ava simply walked past her mother and out the door. Without speaking, Alex stepped past Sonya as well and followed Ava outside. Sonya smiled to herself, believing she had put a wedge between the new couple.

"That'll teach ya, ya li'l fuckin' bitch," Sonya thought to herself as she walked to the refrigerator to get a beer.

She carried the beer to the table and sat down. She was sure a comment like that would destroy whatever superficial feelings the two had for one another by creating a question in Ava's mind. What she did not know was Ava had chosen long ago to distance herself from her mother and in only three days Alex had shown Ava more care and love than Sonya had in throughout her life.

Ava walked quickly to the middle of the front yard as the tears began to fall. Within a fraction of a second Alex was standing closely behind her with a hand on each of her arms to comfort her. She immediately turned and buried her face in his chest. He wrapped his arms around her and she felt as if she were safe once more.

"Why would she say that?" Ava randomly asked, not really expecting an answer.

"I don't know but she hit on me when I got here today," Alex answered, wanting to be honest with her.

Ava quickly pulled away from Alex and looked into his eyes.

"What?" Ava hissed. "Why didn't you tell me?"

"I wasn't even sure if she was serious," Alex said. "And I figured, if she was serious, I wasn't interested anyway so why upset you?"

Ava considered his answer for a few seconds before she was able to find a response.

"She has been out to fuck up my life since day one," Ava said as she stared at the front door of the dilapidated house.

Alex stepped toward Ava and once again wrapped his arms around her.

"I'm sorry I didn't tell you," he said softly. "Don't worry though, I don't want anything to do with her. I love you."

Ava stood with her arms at her sides for a few seconds then decided to accept his apology and trust him. She wrapped her arms around him and they stood motionless in the grass for quite some time.

"I gota go," Alex finally said quietly. "I gota get up early for work tomorrow."

Ava said nothing and stepped away from Alex.

"Are you okay?" He asked as he crouched a little to meet her gaze.

Ava nodded and attempted a half-hearted smile. Alex

leaned down and kissed her gently, satisfied she trusted what he had said.

"See ya tomorrow," he said as he turned to walk away.

"'Kay," Ava said as she watched him walk away.

Ava sat on the porch, unwilling to go inside and face her mother right away. Sonya had displayed a new tactic she had never seen before. She struggled to wrap her mind around it but was simply unable to do so. She finally wiped the tears from her face and walked into the house with her eyes cast downward. Without looking at her mother she walked slowly to her bedroom and closed the door behind her.

Sonya watched as Ava walked slowly through the living room and felt confident she had ruined the relationship. She chose to say nothing to Ava in order to let the girl simmer in the pain she assumed she had created. Ava closed her bedroom door behind her and Sonya decided to compose the next step of her plan to destroy the young girl.

Chapter Eight

Over the next few weeks Alex and Ava spent every possible moment together. The virtual world their relationship created for Ava seemed to lift her above the torment her mother provided on a daily basis. Sonya relentlessly attempted to create doubt about Alex in Ava's mind as she simultaneously continued her sexual advances toward him. Alex persistently denied Sonya which allowed her anger and jealousy to continuously grow.

Ava learned, the house in which Alex lived, did not actually belong to him. His sister and her husband owned the house and allowed him to stay there with some guidelines in place. The time for Ava to attend driver's education was quickly approaching and her excitement grew more by the day. Sonya began to realize her attempts to break the young couple apart were ultimately unsuccessful so she resolved to approach things from yet another angle.

It was Friday, late afternoon, as Ava and Alex sat together in Sonya's living room, holding hands and watching television. Sonya sat at the table drinking a beer as she usually did, silently attempting to decide upon just the right time to launch her next attack.

"Fuckin' li'l bitch," Sonya thought to herself as she silently glared at Ava.

Her anger seemed to reach its peak as Ava leaned closer to Alex and rested her head on his shoulder.

"Ya fuckin' think ya deserve to be happy?" Sonya thought as she continued to watch her daughter with disgust.

From out of nowhere, as if provoked by some invisible enemy, Sonya suddenly began to verbally attack Ava.

"Get offa him ya li'l whore!" Sonya screeched without moving from her seat at the table.

Ava and Alex were both startled, slightly jumping at the volume of Sonya's voice. Ava's head lifted from Alex's shoulder like a shot and her eyes snapped toward Sonya to meet her hate-filled gaze. Ava was unable to speak as she stared back at her mother. Immediately, Ava could feel the anger within her begin to grow, innately preparing her for yet another confrontation with Sonya.

"This shit's gone on long enough ya li'l bitch!" Sonya squawked.

In an attempt to defuse the situation Alex rose from his place next to Ava and began to speak.

"What's goin' on?" he said calmly to Sonya, clearly confused.

"I told both of ya I don't like this shit but ya don't give a fuck!" Sonya yelled at Alex.

Ava stood from her seat and stepped into place next to Alex, both of them now facing Sonya.

"Ya don't like what?" Alex questioned, still speaking calmly.

"Whatever the fuck the two of ya got goin' on!" Sonya blurted as she waved her right hand in the air adding emphasis to her words.

"We were just watchin' TV," Ava said, her voice slightly quivering.

"Oh bullshit," Sonya screamed. "Both of ya are always all over each other and it's fuckin' sickening!"

Sonya turned her gaze toward her beer and lifted the can to her lips. She took a long drink then set the can back on the table with a loud crack. She reached for her cigarettes and lit one, then tossed her lighter to the surface of the table. As the lighter hit the table top it made a loud noise and bounced a few times. The bouncing of the lighter across the table seemed to anger Sonya even more as she made a scoffing sound and clumsily stood to grab the lighter and slam it down on the table next to her cigarette pack. Alex and Ava looked at each other, neither of them able to determine the cause of Sonya's eruption. Ava knew, nothing either of them could say, would help Sonya to calm down and silently they decided to simply turn and walk out of the house. After only a few steps toward the door Sonya resumed her attack.

"Where the fuck ya think you're goin'?" Sonya screamed.

"Outside," Ava answered flatly as she continued to walk toward the door.

"Well, don't think you're guna go take driver's ed next week," Sonya blurted.

Ava stopped in her tracks and turned to look at her mother.

"What?" Ava said in disbelief.

"You're not takin' driver's ed. Fuck ya. Ya don't wana do what I tell ya, ya don't geta do what ya want!" Sonya rambled loudly.

The anger inside Ava suddenly erupted and she could no longer hold her tongue.

"What the fuck are you talkin' about?" Ava shouted back at Sonya.

Alex put his arm around Ava in an attempt to calm her, though his effort seemed to go completely unnoticed.

"You're pissed 'cause I hold hands with my boyfriend

so you're sayin' I can't take driver's ed?" Ava screamed, simultaneously making a statement and asking a question.

Sonya looked at Ava and smiled malevolently.

"If ya think you're goin' to driver's ed ya got another think comin'!" Sonya barked.

A look of complete confusion, combined with insurmountable anger and frustration, washed over Ava's face as she tried to understand why her mother would try to punish her in such a way and what had caused her explosion of anger. A few seconds later Ava watched as a look of determination formed on Sonya's face and her eyes narrowed once more into a glare.

"Fuck you ya li'l whore! Get the fuck out!" Sonya screamed, standing from her chair while she held onto the table to stabilize herself.

"Get out?" Ava asked, a new level of confusion leaking into her voice.

"Get the fuck out!" Sonya repeated with a growl. "Go find somebody else to support your fuckin' ass!"

Ava's anger continued to consume her and her mother's order seemed to open a proverbial door that had not occurred to her before.

"Fine," Ava growled back at her mother. "Fuck you too!"

Ava turned and stormed out of the house, needing to get away from Sonya. Alex followed quickly behind her, catching up with her in the front yard.

"What the fuck just happened?" Alex said to Ava, his voice saturated with confusion and nervousness, not really expecting an answer.

Ava stood in the yard and covered her face with both hands as the tears started to fall. Alex wrapped his arms around her and simply let her cry for a few minutes. He looked back at the house, expecting Sonya to appear in the doorway at any moment. Ava's tears didn't last long before she regained her composure and raised her eyes to meet Alex's.

"Will you take me to Lilli's?" Ava asked softly.

"Yeah," Alex replied as he hugged her.

Ava and Lilli had spent some time together in the last month, mostly when Alex was at work. There were a few times they had gone to visit Lilli together and things between the sisters seemed to be great. They climbed into Alex's pickup and left the house. Alex steered the truck through the streets of the small town and finally turned onto the gravel road that would lead them to Lilli's farm. As they drove into the driveway Ava spotted Lilli working in one of the flower beds she loved so much. Lilli looked up from her work and raised her hand in a wave as she recognized the truck. Ava and Alex got out of the truck and made their way slowly across Lilli's fresh-cut lawn, toward her. Lilli stood, and made a feeble attempt to brush the dirt from her jeans, though dark spots remained.

"Hi guys!" Lilli said with a smile.

Ava and Alex remained silent as they continued to approach Lilli. As they drew closer to her, she was able to see Ava had been crying and Alex wore a look of great concern on his face.

"What's wrong?" Lilli asked, suddenly very concerned.

"Ma kicked me outa the house," Ava answered solemnly.

"What? Why? What happened?" Lilli said as she tried to make quick sense of Ava's statement.

"She basically said she doesn't like Alex and me together and said I couldn't take driver's ed," Ava said, trying to captivate the strange message Sonya had screamed at her only a short time before.

"What?" Lilli said, clearly confused as well.

Ava shrugged her shoulders and looked down at the ground. Lilli looked at Alex, searching for some further explanation. Alex shrugged his shoulders and held his hands out indicating he was unable to understand the situation any more than anyone else.

"I'm not sure what happened," Alex said to Lilli as she stepped forward and hugged Ava. "We were watchin' TV then Sonya just started yellin' at us," he continued.

"Well, what the hell?" Lilli said in a soft voice, indicating she was unable to grasp the concept of what was happening.

"Can I stay with you?" Ava sheepishly asked Lilli.

"Yeah, yeah," Lilli said in a warm and comforting voice as she smiled and hugged Ava once more.

Lilli offered each of them a cold drink and they accepted as the three of them walked toward a few chairs in the yard. Ava and Alex sat down while Lilli went to get the beverages. Lilli returned a few minutes later and took a seat with them. All three of them lit cigarettes and opened the sodas Lilli had brought with her. Though Lilli had gotten married and started a family, memories of Sonya continued to create many feelings of hatred and contempt for her mother in her heart.

"You can stay here for as long as ya need to," Lilli said to Ava in a caring voice.

Ava, still reeling from the recent confrontation with Sonya, was only able to offer a weak smile and a slight nod.

"When's driver's ed start?" Lilli asked in an effort to help Ava move away from her feelings of confusion and sadness.

"Starts Monday," Ava answered. "S'posed to be there at eight."

"Okay, I can take you," Lilli said kindly as she offered a smile.

Ava looked up and noticed the smile on Lilli's face. The sight of her sister's warm smile eased her upset a great deal and she was able to return the expression.

"Ya know," Lilli began, "Ma tried the same kinda shit with

me when I was still home. I'm really glad I got outta there. Wish I coulda gotten you guys outta there too." she continued.

"I don't even know where it came from," Ava said. "We were just watchin' TV and she just started screamin' at me. I didn't know what to do."

Ava's eyes again cast toward the ground as she tried to find some sort of sense in the situation.

"Well, I don't know, but it's bullshit," Lilli said. "Doesn't make any sense."

The three of them sat in the shade of a large tree and talked for several hours, the conversation eventually drifting away from Sonya and toward Lilli's children, the farm, and sleeping arrangements for Ava. Lilli's husband, Shane, eventually arrived home from work and went into the house. Lilli, Ava, and Alex decided they would go into the house as well to explain to Shane what had happened and inform him about Ava staying with them. The three walked into the house and each took a seat at the kitchen table, where Shane was already sitting, smoking a cigarette and drinking a soda.

"Ava needs to stay with us for a while," Lilli said to Shane in a somber tone.

"Why?" Shane responded with no concern in his voice.

"Ma kicked her outa the house," Lilli replied.

In response, Shane only made a "humph" sound and took a drink of his soda.

"Well you're guna have to help around here," Shane said in a rough voice.

"Okay," Ava responded, obviously intimidated by Shane.

Ava did not know Shane very well, but the impression she had always gotten from him was, he was not an individual who was concerned about much more than himself and she had never witnessed a time when he had extended any sort of caring reaction to anything or anyone. He stood about 5'10" and weighed about 180 pounds. He wasn't an unattractive man but Ava was unsure about what Lilli saw in him. Lilli had met him when she lived with her foster family in Korin and the two had been together for several years. In the infancy of their relationship Shane was married to another woman and had gotten Lilli pregnant with twins. He had forced her to abort the babies to protect his secret, apparently not concerned about the unborn children or Lilli's psyche concerning the event. Secretly, Lilli carried a scar on her heart reflecting the remorse she felt as a result of the terrible act. Eventually, Shane divorced his wife and became exclusive with Lilli.

It seemed clear to Ava Shane was not happy about having another person in the house and she felt the need to avoid him as much as possible. The four of them sat at the table for quite some time talking, though Shane said little. Shane finally decided to shower and go to bed while Lilli, Ava, and Alex remained seated at the table talking about various things. Finally, Lilli turned the conversation back toward Sonya and what had happened earlier that evening.

"Did she let ya take anything with you?" Lilli asked Ava.

"I didn't even try," Ava answered. "I just had to get outta there."

"Okay," Lilli said. "I'll stop there tomorrow and pick up some clothes for ya. Do ya wana go along?"

"Might as well," Ava said. "I'll have to face her eventually anyway.

"Okay," Lilli said. "There's an empty bedroom upstairs you can use while you're here," Lilli said as she continued to try to move the conversation forward.

"Thank you," Ava said, nodding her head as shame colored her face.

Lilli had two children with Shane, both of whom were visiting their cousins in Nathia for the weekend. They continued to talk about their plans to stop at Sonya's, what was needed for Ava to attend her driver's education class, and what would be expected of Ava while she lived in the house.

It had gotten late and Lilli was ready to go to bed as well. Ava walked Alex out to his truck and the two said farewell, at least until the next day.

"I'll come out to see ya tomorrow," Alex said.

"Okay," Ava responded. "I can call ya when Lilli and I get back from town."

"Sounds good," Alex said, offering a sweet smile. "It'll be okay," he continued as he hugged her.

"I know," Ava said, unsure of whether she was trying to convince Alex she believed him, or if she was trying to convince herself it was true.

Alex climbed into his truck and turned the key. The engine roared to life and he shifted the truck into reverse.

"See ya tomorrow," Alex said as he winked at Ava.

"Okay," she replied with an exhausted smile.

Alex drove out of the driveway and Ava returned to the house. Lilli had gathered some blankets for the bed in the spare room and led Ava up the stairs. Lilli helped her make the bed and Ava climbed under the blankets. Neither of them spoke but before Lilli switched the light off she looked at Ava and offered a smile which warmed Ava's heart. To Ava's surprise she was able to fall asleep quickly and slept through the night with no trouble, the sense of a constant impending threat completely gone from her mind for the first time she could remember.

The following day Lilli and Ava ventured to Sonya's house to pick up some of Ava's clothes and other things she needed. When they arrived Sonya was sitting on the couch watching a soap opera. Lilli was well aware of Sonya's tactics and she was completely prepared for the possibilities of what may transpire. Lilli felt she must protect Ava and was completely prepared to do so. She was unaware of Ava's willingness and ability to physically protect herself against Sonya and had mentally prepared herself for anything.

Sonya said nothing when Lilli and Ava entered the house. She glanced toward the door then immediately turned her attention back to the television screen. Ava walked purposefully through the living room toward her bedroom while Lilli waited by the door. After Ava had been in her room for a few minutes, Sonya finally decided to speak.

"What are ya doin'?" Sonya asked Lilli with irritation in her voice.

"Came to get some of Ava's stuff," Lilli answered, matter-of-factly.

"Ya guna let her live with ya?" Sonya questioned, still not averting her eyes from the television screen.

"Yup, as long as she needs to," Lilli answered flatly.

Sonya remained silent for several minutes before speaking again, sipping her coffee as if she was completely comfortable with her decision to kick her daughter out of the house. She still held a grudge against Lilli for getting herself sent away when she was young and still struggled to interact with her in a pleasant way.

"Well, she don't have to," Sonya said, clearly irritated at the situation and Ava's decision to go to Lilli's house.

"She said ya kicked her out," Lilli replied. "Where else is she supposed to go?"

"I didn't kick her out," Sonya defensively scoffed as she stood from her seat on the couch.

Lilli was not interested in arguing with Sonya and already knew she would say anything she could think of to make herself look good in the situation.

"She just took off, I didn't kick her out!" Sonya continued in an effort to convince Lilli.

Lilli watched as Ava stepped out of her bedroom and walked toward the bathroom to get her toothbrush. Sonya did not notice Ava in the room and continued her attempt to assure Lilli Ava had simply left on her own.

"She said ya weren't guna let her go to driver's ed if she didn't break up with Alex. Then she said ya told her to get out," Lilli recalled with no emotion in her voice.

"She's a lyin' li'l bitch! I didn't say anything like that!" Sonya retorted as she plopped back on the couch.

Lilli noticed Sonya's face had taken on a look of disgust, a look she had seen on her mother's face many times before. She knew Sonya was lying and resolved to refrain from any further conversation on the matter. Ava appeared from the bathroom and walked toward Lilli.

"I'll be at Lilli's," Ava said in a flat tone as she walked behind her mother toward the door.

Sonya said nothing, unable to think of another way to deny what had happened the night before in front of Ava. She knew Ava would contradict her in front of Lilli if she tried to say anything. Lilli and Ava walked out of the house without saying another word and got into Lilli's car. As they drove away from the house Ava felt a twinge of sympathy for her mother.

She could not understand where the caring feeling was coming from. After the way Sonya had treated her throughout her life she rationalized she had every reason to hate her mother but something inside her forced her to feel remorse as she left the house.

Over the next few months Ava attended her driver's education class, helped on Lilli and Shane's farm, and spent time with Alex. She was able to get to know Lilli's children and enjoyed spending time with them. She felt so relaxed with Lilli and loved the time she was able to spend with her. Alex was welcomed by Lilli each time he came to visit Ava and everything seemed to be going very well. Still, Ava felt a certain emptiness in her heart, caused by the feelings of sadness and guilt, about leaving her mother's house. On a daily basis, she struggled with whether or not she was to blame for the way her mother had treated her, but would always return to the realization she had done nothing to provoke the years of terrible abuse and neglect.

Even though Ava was comfortable living with Lilli, she was still incredibly uncomfortable around Shane. He was away from home for the majority of each day while he worked, and Ava was thankful. His mannerisms and booming voice, paired with the lack of any caring nature, frightened Ava and she hated the thought of being alone with him. She did all she could to avoid contact with him and seemed to be successful much of the time.

One afternoon Lilli approached Ava as she sat in her room reading a book.

"Hey, I gota take the kids to the doctor," Lilli said as she sat on the edge of Ava's bed. "Ya wana go?"

"Nah, I think I'll stay here," Ava answered apologetically. "Alex is coming out in about an hour so I wana be here when he gets here."

"Oh, okay," Lilli said with an understanding smile as she stood and walked toward the door of Ava's room. "See ya later," she continued happily as she walked out of the room.

"See ya," Ava answered as she opened her book again and continued to read.

As Ava sat quietly in her room she could clearly hear the sounds of Lilli getting the children ready and leaving the house. Only a few minutes after she heard the front door close, the telephone rang. She made her way down the stairs and into the kitchen to answer it.

"Hello?" she said politely into the receiver.

"Ya know, ya can come home," the voice on the other end of the line said scornfully.

Ava immediately recognized her mother's voice and was at a loss for words. After a few seconds she found her voice once again and spoke.

"Okay," Ava said with no emotion. "Thanks."

"Well are ya guna?" Sonya asked, her voice unmistakably impatient.

"I don't know," Ava answered.

"Well, whatever," Sonya said. "I guess you'll just get sent away like Lilli."

"What do ya mean?" Ava asked.

"Ya don't wana be at home so I'm callin' the cops and they'll send ya away," Sonya said in a malevolent tone.

In reality, Sonya knew she would never call anyone to get Ava sent away. She was only trying to scare the girl into coming home before anyone became aware of the new living arrangements. Sonya knew, if Ava was with Lilli long enough, she would likely decide never to return home and she would ultimately lose her welfare. The tactic did not work immediately, as Sonya had hoped, but the seed was planted in Ava's mind and the fear of being separated from Alex and Lilli began to grow. Ava was unable to find the words to contradict her mother and wanted the conversation to end.

"I gota go," Ava said quietly.

She hung up the phone and stood motionless, staring at the receiver for a few seconds. She hated the idea of being sent away the way Lilli had been, ultimately because she was afraid of losing Alex. She turned slowly and made her way back up the stairs to her room. Returning to her seat on the bed, she picked up her book and tried to distract herself from her fears with the words on the page.

Lilli had only been gone for a short time when Ava heard the unmistakable sound of the front door closing as someone entered the house. She did not concern herself with who had come in but paid close attention to the noises coming from the first floor of the house. It sounded to Ava as if Shane might have come home but it was much too early in the day. After listening closely for a few seconds, she concluded the person who had come into the house must be Shane and gave the situation no more thought as she returned her attention to her book once again.

After a few minutes, she heard the distinctive creak of the bottom step. She waited, as the faint sound of footsteps continued up the staircase, toward her room. She wondered why Shane would be climbing the stairs. He stepped into her room and closed the door. Ava immediately felt uncomfortable as she looked at him and forced a timid greeting. Shane's face looked different than it normally did and even though his look typically made Ava uneasy, the change in his expression sparked even more trepidation in her mind.

"Hi, Ava," Shane said as he smiled at her.

She said nothing and tried hard to force a half-hearted smile to mask the alarm she felt. Shane crossed the room toward the bed and sat on the edge. The bed was large and Ava was sitting in the middle, leaning on the headboard with pillows behind her back.

"What are ya doin'?" Shane asked with a sickly sweet tone in his voice Ava had never heard before.

"Reading," she answered timidly, completely confused about what was happening and why Shane was sitting on the edge of her bed.

Shane leaned toward Ava, as if to see which book she was reading, repositioning himself closer to her with his feet now completely off the floor.

"What book ya readin'?" he asked, trying to flood his voice with innocence.

Ava was unable to answer, only able to look past the book and stare at the blankets on the bed. Her inability to answer seemed to make Shane uncomfortable so he spoke again.

"Where's Lilli?" he asked.

"She took the kids to the doctor," Ava answered dutifully, still not able to look at Shane.

"She'll be gone for a while then," he said, as if continuing a normal conversation.

Ava sat very still, hoping Shane would simply stand up and walk out of the room. He looked around, as if he had never been in the room before, as he consciously decided what to do next. In an effort to convey her disinterest in talking with Shane, Ava returned her eyes to the pages of her book and pretended to read. Shane sat quietly for a few seconds then, to Ava's relief, raised himself from his seat on the edge of the bed. Though Ava thought Shane was standing to leave she was terribly mistaken. Instead of walking toward the door he lifted his right leg onto the bed and abruptly leaned toward her, putting his weight on his right knee and left hand as his right hand reached for Ava. His movements were fluid, as if he had practiced the maneuver many times before, the entire approach taking less than two seconds. Ava had no time to pull away and was obviously surprised by his approach. His right hand reached the left side of Ava's face and lithely guided her head to turn toward him as he continued to lean closer to her. Her mind was filled with astonishment and she opened her mouth in an attempt to verbally object to Shane's advance. Before she was able to utter a sound Shane's lips were upon hers and his tongue in her mouth. The bewilderment of the situation, and her constant fear of Shane, forced her body to stiffen and freeze. She was unable to think clearly as the confusion flooded through her. Shane continued the kiss for a few seconds, and Ava could hear soft sounds of approval coming from his throat. When the disgusting intrusion was finished, he pulled away from Ava, as quickly as he had approached her. He once again stood next to the bed looking at Ava and wearing a smile unlike any she had ever seen on his face before. Her whole body was trembling with fear as she anticipated what might happen next. Her muscles began to respond in preparation for escape in the event he approached close to her again.

"I'm just so lonely," Shane said to Ava as if she had asked why he had kissed her. "Lilli won't fuck me anymore."

Ava could not respond. She wanted to scream at him to get away but her voice had hidden from her, just as it had when she was six-years-old and John had stolen her innocence from her. Shane stood motionless and gazed out the window, for what seemed like forever to Ava, before he spoke again.

"Don't say a fuckin' word about this to anybody," he said

without looking at Ava. His words had regained their typical tone and the sound of his voice made Ava's fear grow even more.

"Not a fuckin' word," he repeated, this time looking directly at Ava as he pointed his finger at her.

She continued to look down at the blankets on the bed, wishing for Shane to leave the room. She wished she had gone with Lilli and wanted her to come home. The lack of response from Ava seemed to satisfy Shane and he turned and walked from the room. After only a few seconds Ava leapt from the bed and closed the door to her room. She was finally able to relax her muscles but she was completely unable to comprehend the situation which had just taken place. She wanted to tell Lilli about everything but the fear of hurting her sister, and what her reaction might be, seemed to scare her more than Shane's advances. She thought about telling Alex what had happened but the fear of losing his affection, in her mind, outweighed her own comfort and safety. Silent tears began to roll down her cheeks as she once again realized she was completely alone in the situation and had no one to turn to for help. She feared Shane would return to her room and continue his advancements so she decided to go outside and wait for Alex to arrive.

As she sat quietly outside she lit a cigarette and thought about the conversation she had with her mother on the phone earlier in the day. She tried to decide if it would be better to return to her mother's home or remain at Lilli's house. By the time Alex's truck pulled into the driveway she had decided she would go back to her mother's house. Even though living there was horrible for her, she felt her presence in Lilli's home had somehow fostered Shane's advances and rationalized, if she had not been there, he would not have tried anything with her.

Ava and Alex sat together outside talking until well after

Lilli had returned home and darkness had settled upon them. Alex seemed to know something was wrong but did not press the matter, assuming Ava must have talked to her mother vvv day.

The next day Ava was helping Lilli fold laundry at the kitchen table. The television was on and the two of them intermittently watched as they worked their way through the laundry.

"Think I'm guna go back to Ma's," Ava said.

"Oh, okay," Lilli answered with subtle shock in her voice. "Why?"

"I don't know, just feel like I should," Ava answered with a sad tone.

"Okay," Lilli said. "You can come back anytime you need to," she continued.

Ava glanced at Lilli and smiled. "Thanks," she said as she reached for another shirt to fold.

"When ya guna go back?" Lilli asked.

"Prob'ly today," Ava answered solemnly, without looking up.

Lilli nodded her head to indicate she understood as she began to put stacks of folded laundry back in the basket for easy transport. She had a feeling there was another reason Ava wanted to go back to Sonya's house but was not sure what it was. She silently wondered if Ava had overheard any of the arguments she and Shane had had regarding Ava's presence in their home. She rationalized, if Ava had overheard any of the arguments, it would likely be enough to provoke her to leave. She worried for Ava's safety but knew she had very little influence over what would transpire.

Ava gathered her things the next afternoon and prepared to return to Sonya's house. Alex arrived at Lilli's and was informed of the decision. After a brief conversation about the issue Ava and Alex left Lilli's house and headed back to Sonya's. When they finally reached the house Alex wheeled the pickup into the driveway and turned off the engine.

"Are ya sure ya wana do this?" Alex asked, clearly skeptical.

"Yeah," Ava answered. "I have to."

Alex did not completely understand the meaning of Ava's response but she had opened the door and climbed out of the truck before he could question her any further. Ava felt as if living with Sonya was the only thing she could do considering what had happened the day before with Shane. Ever since he had kissed her, she felt incredibly uncomfortable in the house, regardless of whether or not he was there. Ava had not told anyone about Shane's advance and did what she could to avoid explaining her decision to move back home in detail.

Alex got out of the truck and followed Ava into the house. When they walked through the door they saw Sonya sitting at the table with a beer can in front of her. She looked up when she heard the door open and sat quietly, waiting to see who would appear in the doorway. When she saw Ava she immediately began to speak.

"Decided to come back, huh?" Sonya said with a tone of triumph in her voice.

"Yep," Ava answered with no emotion.

"Good choice," Sonya said with disdain.

Ava chose not to respond and made her way to her bedroom. She tossed her belongings in the corner of the room and sat heavily on her bed. Alex walked into the bedroom as well and sat next to her. He put his arm around her and she leaned into his chest as she started to cry quietly. He said nothing, sensing she simply needed time to cry.

Sonya watched as Ava walked to her bedroom and felt a wave of relief the girl had chosen to come home.

"At least now I won't lose my money," Sonya thought to herself as she took a drink from her beer can. Alex walked by her, on his way to Ava's bedroom, without looking at Sonya. She chose not to say anything more to either of them for the rest of the night for fear Ava would change her mind and return to Lilli's house.

With Ava's driver's education class completed she was free to enjoy the rest of her summer. She and Alex spent every day together, most often alone but occasionally with Rachel and Eliza. Julia was not allowed out much after her father picked her up at the park the day she had introduced Ava and Alex. At least twice per week Ava and Alex went to the local bar and played pool, a game Ava seemed to have a natural talent for, and really enjoyed. Intermittently, Rachel and Eliza would join them but didn't seem to be as interested in the game as Ava always was.

Sonya continued to keep Ava's self confidence at a minimum and diligently worked to keep her from finding any promise of anything that might give her any type of a positive outlook on life. Sonya's tactics were subtle and Ava would not be able to realize the source of her low self-esteem for many years.

School would be starting again soon and Ava prepared herself for yet another year of social unrest. Though she would have liked to have been involved in extra curricular activities at school, she chose to avoid them, due to the constant fear of being made fun of and the possibility of failure. It seemed Sonya's endeavor to destroy her had been mostly successful on both the emotional and mental levels.

Chapter Nine

Over the next few years Ava and Alex continued their relationship and by the time Ava turned sixteen Alex had proposed to her. Sonya was beside herself with anger and jealousy and attempted to destroy the bond between the young couple on a daily basis. Even though she tried, her attempts seem to grow weaker by the day, as if she had finally begun to lose interest in separating them. Ava began to drift further away from her friends at school, as she was completely consumed with Alex, and seemed to have tunnel vision regarding escaping her mother's care. Over the years, Ava had learned how to manipulate others from her mother's example, and after Alex proposed she began to unconsciously use manipulation on Sonya in an attempt to gain permission to marry Alex before the age of eighteen. Sonya was well aware, since Ava was her last child, she would lose her welfare when Ava finally left home. Sonya was left with no other choice than to find a job and once she did it seemed as if she was more easily convinced to let Ava marry Alex and move out.

During Ava's junior year in high school, she learned she had an opportunity to graduate early and endeavored to do so. In spite of the abusive environment from which she had come, she excelled, lettering in academics. The endeavor to escape the social unrest of school drove her forward. To

Ava, the idea of graduating early was an alluring one, as she strived to leave home and separate herself from the ridicule she endured from her peers. She rationalized, once she could become independent from her mother and finish school, a new life would somehow materialize for her and she might finally find peace and happiness. During the entire time she and Alex had been together he was an attentive, loving, and caring individual, continuously making her feel loved, appreciated, and significant. To Ava, the decision to marry him and escape her terrible past was made in her mind, without a doubt, before he had even asked the question. Sonya still put forth some effort to change Ava's mind about moving out, but regarding her conviction to leave home, Ava had become so much stronger than Sonya. No amount of persuasion would ever change her mind and she counted the days until she would finally be free from her mother's torments.

At the start of her senior year in high school, Ava followed the channels that would allow her to graduate early, such as taking double classes to complete the required credits. The commitment she displayed to fulfilling the requirements of graduation was only paralleled by the fact she had somehow, miraculously avoided suicide. After a great deal of planning, Ava and Alex were married in mid-December 1994 which was, without contest, the happiest day of Ava's life. It was a very small ceremony, with only a few people in attendance. Sonya was there, and seemed to portray the behaviors of a happy mother, though Ava was suspicious it was only an act. In spite of the traditional happiness a bride might feel on her wedding day, Ava's happiness was ultimately rooted in her final escape from her mother. Of course, she was happy to be marrying Alex but that happiness was dwarfed in her mind by the fact she was finally able to live her life without constant manipulation and abuse from Sonya. Ava's last day of school came in January of 1995 and she finished with her name on the A honor roll. She and Alex had already been married for about a month and she felt like she was on top of the world.

In spite of everything that had happened between Sonya and Ava throughout Ava's life, after getting married and finishing school, Ava felt as if she must try to create a new relationship with her mother. A new relationship, possibly based on adult ideas, rather than the hatred Sonya had always felt. Even though Ava had actually finished school in January, the graduation ceremony would not be held until May of that year and Ava desperately wanted Sonya to attend and finally show some sort of positive interest in her. During the months before the graduation ceremony, Ava attempted to find out if her mother was planning to attend. It seemed as if Sonya was planning to go, and that fact made Ava feel a twinge of happiness, but ultimately she knew it was not a guarantee. A few days before the commencement ceremony Ava stopped to visit with her mother in order to give her a ticket for the event. Ava walked into Sonya's house to find her sitting on the couch, drinking coffee, and watching television. It seemed as if Sonya's drinking had decreased considerably, to allow her to go to work on the days she was scheduled, something Ava was ultimately happy to finally witness.

"Hi," Ava said as she walked through the door.

Sonya said nothing and chose to continue watching the program flickering on the screen in front of her. Ava took a seat at the opposite end of the couch and waited for her mother to acknowledge her. After a few minutes, Ava decided to speak again, in spite of Sonya's silence.

"I brought your ticket for my graduation," Ava said as she extended her arm to hand the ticket to Sonya.

Sonya glanced in Ava's direction while reaching out to snatch the ticket from her hand.

"Thanks," Sonya said, clearly upset about something.

Ava had hoped the visit would be a pleasant one, even though she knew it would likely be filled with tension.

"I don't know if I'm goin'," Sonya scoffed without taking her eyes away from the television.

"Why?" Ava asked, her voice faltering slightly as the sadness leaked into her words.

"Why should I?" Sonya suddenly snapped. "Ya don't wana be with me anyway! All ya wana do is be with Alex!" she continued, still not looking away from the television.

Ava was unable to speak as she tried hard to wrap her mind around the words her mother had just spoken.

"He's my husband," Ava said, sadness now flooding her words. "All I've ever wanted was for you to love me," Ava continued as she looked down at the floor.

"Oh, bullshit," Sonya growled. "Fuck you, I'm not goin'! Ya wanted to be with him and now ya are so go fuckin' be with him!" She hissed.

Ava felt the sadness inside of her rush into her mind and heart as her eyes welled up with tears. She wanted to scream at her mother but her emotions overwhelmed her, leaving her speechless. She sat motionless and completely silent as a hurricane of thoughts and emotions filled her mind. She began to recall all of the things her mother had done to her and the significant moments her mother had missed or tried to take away as she grew up. The anger inside of her, ultimately rooted in sadness, began to consume her and she stood up like a shot.

"What the fuck have I ever done to make you hate me?" Ava screamed.

Ava's outburst shocked Sonya and her head snapped toward the girl, their eyes locking. She stood staring at Sonya, waiting for a response, as the tears rolled down her face. Sonya was unable to hold her gaze and turned her eyes away from her daughter. With sadness and pain in her heart Ava realized her mother would likely not respond.

"All I've ever wanted was for you to love me! What about me makes it impossible for you to do that?" Ava yelled at Sonya.

Sonya closed her eyes and continued to sit in silence, an expression of inconvenience on her face.

"And now, after eighteen years, I am finally asking you outright, what the fuck I did, and ya can't even answer me? What the fuck?" Ava continued, still shouting.

Sonya remained silent and Ava noticed tears welling in her mother's eyes. Ava stood, still waiting for some kind of response from her mother, but none came. After several minutes she finally gave up, the last trace of hope for her mother's love finally draining permanently from her heart.

"I give up," Ava finally said, matter-of-factly. "I don't get it. I never have and obviously I never will. I'm done," she continued, no longer shouting. She had finally lost the will to strive for any kind of relationship with Sonya. Turning to leave, she paused and looked at Sonya. "See ya around, I guess," she said quietly, then walked out of the house.

Ava went to her graduation and Sonya held true to her claim she would not be there. Alex and his mother attended the ceremony and even though they were there to support her, Ava still felt an empty space in her heart, created by her mother's absence. It was ultimately a bitter-sweet day for Ava. After the graduation ceremony she decided to wait for a while before trying to talk with Sonya again. Even though her heart was riddled with emotional scars from Sonya, missing the graduation had created a gaping wound which would not heal for quite some time.

Even though Alex had always been perfect in Ava's eyes, it seemed she had let the upset with Sonya cloud her vision. Ava turned eighteen at the end of March 1995, and it seemed she was finally free, her new life now underway. By May of that year, the month of her graduation ceremony, Ava had begun to notice a difference in Alex's behavior toward her but rationalized the changes must be due to stress at work. Just before their wedding the previous year, the couple had moved into a large house, only a few blocks away from Sonya. The front yard was enormous with the house sitting at the rear of the property. Even though they were only renting the house Ava finally felt as if she belonged somewhere. Ava and Emma had started to reconnect since Ava's graduation from high school, and Ava decided to invite Emma and her family to visit for the day. It was a Saturday in early June when Emma, Lee, and their two boys arrived. The boys played in the front yard while Emma and Ava sat at the kitchen table talking and Lee and Alex talked in the living room over a beer. After about an hour Ava decided to start cooking a meal for all of them while she and Emma continued to converse. Ava had prepared to make spaghetti for the meal that day, and while she was filling the pot with water, Alex left the living room and went to the basement. Lee walked into the kitchen and sat at the table with Emma.

"What's Alex doin'?" Ava asked Lee.

"I don't fuckin' know, he just went downstairs. He seems pissed off about somethin'," Lee said as he cracked another beer open.

"Oh, really?" Ava asked, more to herself than to anyone else.

The pot of water Ava had put on the stove had not yet begun to boil and when she heard about Alex going to the basement her thoughts of cooking quickly left her mind. Without thinking, she dumped the spaghetti noodles into the pot, and turned to go to the basement to check on Alex.

"Ya wana watch that?" Ava asked Emma as she walked by her on the way to the basement.

"Sure," Emma answered, sounding a little concerned as her eyes followed her sister's movements.

Ava walked across the enclosed porch and down the basement stairs. When she stepped into the basement she noticed Alex busy with something but was not sure what he was working on.

"Whatcha doin'?" she asked playfully.

"Nothin'!" Alex barked back at her as he spun around.

The surprise of Alex's response stopped Ava in her tracks. He stepped away from the bench at which he had been standing, and stood in front of whatever he was working on, clearly trying to block Ava's view from the items behind him.

"Get your fuckin' ass back upstairs before I fuckin' knock ya out!" Alex screamed at Ava.

Ava was unable to move, fear suddenly gripping her. She had no idea what to say or do. As soon as the words flew from Alex's mouth she could feel her whole new world start to crumble around her. He had been acting strange over the previous months but had never yelled at or threatened her. Alex had been distant and seemed preoccupied spending little time at home. Suddenly, Alex barked at her again.

"Ava!" he yelled. "Get your fuckin' ass back upstairs!"

She was only standing about ten feet from him and in a flash he rushed her, grabbing her by the wrist. The surprise and force of his movements made her falter and she almost fell backward. She winced in pain as his hand squeezed her wrist. She quickly looked down and tried to pry his hand away with her free hand. Before she could even begin to escape, his other hand was around her throat. He held her firmly in place, his hands still restraining her. She felt a twinge of panic as she realized she must struggle to take a breath. He leaned close to her face, the tip of his nose almost touching the tip of hers.

"This is my part of the house and you'll stay the fuck outta here, got it?" he hissed at her.

Ava was unable to utter a sound with the pressure of Alex's hand on her throat. She did all she could to nod her head and indicate she understood.

"Now, I'm guna let go of ya and you're guna get your fuckin' ass back upstairs and finish cookin', got it?" Alex growled, purposefully enunciating the words.

Once again, Ava nodded her head slightly in spite of his grip. At the same time, Alex released his grip on Ava's wrist and neck, but did not back away. Ava, still reeling from the incident, turned slowly and made her way up the basement stairs. She stood silently at the top and tears began to fall down her cheeks as she realized she was trembling from fear. Her new, happy world was quickly fading and she wondered what she had done to provoke this kind of behavior from Alex. She tried to regain her composure and wiped the tears from her face. With all the inner strength she had she tried to keep what had just happened to herself as she walked back into the kitchen and to the stove.

"Ya put the noodles in too soon," Emma said with a giggle in her voice.

Ava said nothing and tried to salvage the meal with no success.

Lee was still sitting at the table, three empty beer cans in front of him.

"You're about fuckin' worthless," he said, letting a mocking chuckle weave through his words. "Ya can't even cook spaghetti," he continued, now laughing at her.

Emma said nothing and walked to Ava's side.

"Guna have to throw this out," Ava said quietly, doing all she could to ignore Lee's ridicule. "Suddenly I'm not feeling very good, Emma," she continued. "Can we do this some other time?"

Emma was unaware of what had transpired in the basement and was clearly surprised at Ava's request.

"Yeah, sure," Emma answered with an irritated tone in her voice. "We'll just go visit Ma," she continued.

Ava remained silent, staring at the noodles in the pot with her head down so no one would notice the tears welling back up in her eyes.

"Bye," Emma said as she and Lee walked out the door, clearly put off by the sudden change in plans.

Ava could not believe what had just happened with Alex. She drained the water from the pot and dumped the half-cooked noodles into the garbage can. Without cleaning up the rest of the cooking supplies she walked from the kitchen to the bedroom to lie down. As she lay on the bed she and Alex shared, her mind drifted back to suicide and how wonderful it would be to not have to worry about any more abuse. As she thought about ending her life she cried quietly and slowly drifted off to sleep.

It seemed as if Ava had either been too preoccupied with all of the turmoil with Sonya, or was simply too blind to see the things in Alex that may have hinted toward his abusive side. Regardless of the reason Ava was unable to see it, she was now married to him, and could not just walk away. She hoped she would be able to find the reason for Alex's behavior and help him to overcome it.

Toward evening, hours after the incident occurred in the basement, Alex returned to the first level of the house in search of Ava. He found her asleep in the bedroom and stood watching her for a few moments. Finally, he decided to wake her. He sat on the bed next to her and gently touched her arm. She awoke immediately and pulled away from his touch, innately trying to protect herself and escape any further physical attacks. Alex looked down at his hands, clearly ashamed of his actions. He extended his right hand in an attempt to touch Ava's leg but she pulled away again, her eyes locked on him and fear coloring her face. He slowly lowered his hand to the bed and guilt clouded his eyes.

"I'm so sorry," Alex said in a quiet, gentle voice. "I shouldn't have hurt you or yelled at you."

Ava stared at him in silence, unable to find the courage to speak. Once again, she found herself in the company of an individual whom she feared. Alex raised his eyes to hers and looked at her apologetically. She felt a pang of sympathy for him but was still afraid. She wanted to forget about what had happened and never look back again. Alex looked down once again and began to sob, his face wet with tears after only a few seconds. She watched him as he cried and her heart began to soften once again.

"Why did you do that?" she asked quietly, still unsure if she should speak.

He looked at her with hope in his eyes, tears streaming down his face.

"I don't know what came over me," he answered soberly. "I'm so sorry."

"I can't handle that shit," Ava said, as kindly as she could. "Ya know what my mom did to me. I can't handle that again." she continued in an attempt to explain why she had pulled away from him.

"I know. I know, and I'm so sorry. I've just been so busy at work and they're really ridin' my ass about shit," Alex said with sorrow in his voice, still sobbing.

Ava watched him as he cried and finally began to feel sorry for him as she felt herself forgiving him. She moved toward him and put her arms around him. He hugged her back and continued to sob.

"I'm so sorry. I'm so sorry," he repeated through his tears.

"I know," Ava whispered. "It's okay," she said as they held each other.

Their embrace continued for quite some time while Alex cried. Ava thought about what had happened and tried to rationalize the situation.

"He's been under a lot of stress lately and work is really stressful for him," she thought to herself. "I'm sure he won't do it again," her thoughts continued.

Finally, the two of them repositioned themselves under the blankets and once again held each other. Ava just wanted the fear to subside and the incident to be buried in the past. They fell asleep holding one another, Alex's pillow wet with tears.

Within the next few days, the incident in the basement had been tucked away, chalked up to a mistake and stress. Alex had promised to never hurt Ava again and she had accepted the statement as truth. More often than not, Ava and Alex went to Bonwhall to visit Emma and Lee on the weekends, though occasionally they spent time with Lilli and Shane as well.

Ava was still very uncomfortable around Shane because of what he had done when she lived at Lilli's house two years before. Since then, he consciously avoided talking to her, likely because he was afraid she would reveal what he had done. She was just as uncomfortable around Lee but for different reasons. Lee was a heavy drinker, exactly the way Sonya had always been. In addition, he was terribly sarcastic and rude virtually all of the time. He had always made sexually explicit comments to Ava and she hated it. There had even been an instance, when Ava was only about eleven, when Lee had chosen to watch a pornographic film while Ava was visiting. While Emma was out of the house, he had forced Ava to watch the movie with him, and Ava recalled being scared to death of what he might try to do to her. Thankfully, Lee had gotten drunk and passed out before he was able to do anything to her, if that had ultimately been his plan.

Ava and Alex went to visit Emma and Lee during the second week of June and Emma shared her and her family were in the process of buying a house across town. Emma suggested Ava and Alex move to Bonwhall and buy the trailer house she and her family currently lived in. Alex seemed to be very excited about the idea and Ava ultimately just wanted to see him happy. It seemed to Ava, Alex was simply looking forward to starting over in a new town, with a fresh outlook. In reality, however, she was completely wrong. Alex had run into some problems at his current job, having purchased tools and a tool box with a combined worth of several thousand dollars. He had failed to repay the supplier and his tools and tool box were close to being repossessed. In addition to his failure to pay for his tools, Alex also knew he was about to be terminated for missing too many days of work. Even though Ava believed he was going to work everyday, in reality, at least once a week he would skip work and spend the day getting high with a few of his friends. Ava had never known Alex to be a drug user because he had hidden his actions from her very well. Alex had also purchased a vehicle from a dealership and had stopped making payments to the bank. He rationalized, if they moved to a new town in a different county, it would likely take longer for the bank to locate him and repossess the vehicle. Ava was completely in the dark concerning all of Alex's dishonest behavior, never having been alerted to anything as he was very good at concealing his many reckless and dishonest choices.

When they arrived that afternoon Alex, Ava, Emma, and Lee sat around the table in Emma and Lee's kitchen and discussed the idea of Ava and Alex moving into the trailer house.

"So, you guys could move in with us until our house is ready and then you would be able to buy this from us," Emma suggested.

"Sounds great to me," Alex said with a smile.

Lee had very little to contribute to the conversation but seemed to agree to whatever Emma was suggesting. In reality, Lee was simply too intoxicated to care about what was being discussed and since his construction job took him away from home for a week at a time he did not concern himself with the details. Alex had also been drinking but was not intoxicated, having not even finished one can of beer. Emma and Ava had chosen to drink soda instead of alcohol so both of them were completely sober. After more discussion about the purchase of the trailer house Emma asked Ava if she would help her hang laundry on the clothesline in the back yard. Ava agreed and joined Emma in her task while Alex and Lee remained at the table drinking.

Ava and Emma ventured to the back yard and began hanging the laundry on the line. A large dome tent had been set up by Lee, somewhat close to the end of the clothesline, in an effort to let it air out before his job took him on the road again. Ava and Emma talked about various things while they worked, seemingly happy with what they were doing. When they were about half finished hanging the laundry Alex appeared in the back yard and reported Lee had decided to go to bed. Even though it was only about six in the evening, Lee had been drinking since about eight o'clock that morning, a regular practice for him.

After Emma and Ava had gone to the back yard to hang the laundry, Lee had finished his beer and gone straight to bed, leaving Alex alone in the kitchen. When Alex was sure Lee would not return to the kitchen he fished around in his overnight bag until he found the plastic baggy of pills he had brought with him. The pills were a concentrated form of barbiturate that provided a euphoric high for him. What he didn't realize was, when he mixed the barbiturate with alcohol, he became very angry and violent. While Ava was busy getting ready for the short trip he had gotten the pills from a friend of his before he left Nathia for the weekend. He popped one of the pills and guzzled the rest of his beer to wash it down. After letting out a loud belch, he opened another beer and went outside to join Ava and Emma in the back yard.

A large garden spread across the back yard, behind

the clothesline, and Alex walked around it talking about everything he would like to plant once he and Ava got settled. Even though it was too far into the summer months to start a garden, he told Ava he would like to plant various vegetables the next spring. Ava liked it when Alex made plans and felt as if she would be included, even if he didn't say it out loud. She felt so happy, looking forward to a new start with Alex in a new town. Little did she know, the evening was about to take a severe turn for the worse and her life would begin to change, once again, in a terrible way.

After Emma and Ava finished hanging the laundry on the line the two of them, along with Alex, stood in the back yard and each lit a cigarette. The three of them stood in a small group, talking and laughing, until Emma finished her cigarette and decided to go back inside the trailer house to check on Lee and the kids. Ava and Alex stood together, by the end of the clothesline, and silently looked around the property. Ava glanced toward the end of the trailer house and watched as Emma rounded the corner of the structure, disappearing as she made her way to the front door. Ava then directed her attention back to Alex who was already staring at her. She was surprised at the look he wore on his face, one of anger and contempt. The pill he had taken had finally started to affect him. Ava felt a tinge of fear in her heart but attempted to conceal it with a loving smile. She had no idea Alex had taken the pill and was struggling to understand why he was looking at her as if he wanted to hurt her. The instant the smile spread across her face, Alex reacted in a way she could never have prepared for.

Alex's right hand held his beer while his left hand shot out in front of him, his fingers clamping as tightly as an eagle's talon around her throat. His movements were quick and strong, as if he were part machine. Immediately, she tried to loosen his grip with both of her hands as she struggled to fill her lungs with air. In an instant, he lifted her completely off the ground and with blinding force, slammed the back of her head against the "T" shaped pole securing the end of the clothesline. Ava's vision was instantly blurred as Alex released his grip on her and she fell to the ground coughing and trying to breathe. He said nothing, simply turning to slowly walk away from her. As she tried to regain her breath and vision, she felt a wave of uncontrollable anger flow through her. She began to shake from the adrenaline rushing through her and from her hands and knees she stumbled to her feet, still unable to breathe regularly or see clearly. Without thinking, she sprinted to catch up to Alex, his back to her as he continued to walk away. She leapt onto his back, wrapping her legs around his waist, as if she were astride a bareback horse. Holding her position on his back with her legs, she assaulted him with a barrage of punches directed at the back of this head, neck, and shoulders, connecting solidly each time. After she landed several punches, he began to lose his balance and, taking several steps backward, he finally fell into the tent Lee had set up in the yard, collapsing the entire structure. Though Alex's weight had landed directly on top of her she could not stop hitting him.

"Don't you ever fuckin' hit me again!" She screamed as she continued to throw punches, connecting wherever she could.

Alex was finally able to get away from Ava, crawling a few feet on his hands and knees, before he struggled to stand. She had exhausted herself with the burst of violence she had fired at him and could not pursue him after he escaped her initial attack. Back on her hands and knees in the grass, she was barely able to watch as Alex stumbled away from her. Her head was pounding from the blow to the steel pole and her vision was still blurry. She glared at him as she panted, trying to catch her breath from the extreme amount of energy she had just expended. As soon as he was out of sight she began to calm down and the tears began to flow from her eyes. She could not imagine what could have provoked him to do such a thing to her. She struggled to stand, feeling as if her legs were completely unable to support her weight. Making her way to the front door of the trailer house, she was forced to use the walls to help her walk.

"What happened?" Emma exclaimed when she saw the look on Ava's face and her clumsy struggle to stay upright.

"He grabbed me by the throat and slammed my head against the clothesline pole!" Ava said, her voice filled with disbelief.

Ava's eyes searched for Alex and found he had already passed out on the fold-out sofa Emma had prepared for them. She glared at him and found herself unable to find any more words.

"Why?" Emma said, clearly concerned about her sister.

"I don't know," Ava answered, now starting to regain normal breathing.

Anger washed over her again and she wanted to launch another attack on Alex.

"What the fuck?" Emma exclaimed, clearly confused about how things could have gone so badly so quickly.

"All I know is the mother fucker better make sure I'm knocked out or dead before he turns his back on me the next time he tries that shit," Ava growled loudly, hoping Alex was only pretending to be asleep.

Emma sat in silence, unable to find any words that might

help Ava through the traumatic event. She had no idea Alex was capable of attacking Ava physically, still completely unaware of what had happened in the basement during their visit a few months earlier.

"You guna be okay?" Emma asked as Ava made her way to the table and sat down.

"Yeah," Ava answered, not looking up to meet Emma's gaze.

Ava really had no idea whether or not she was really alright but she was trying to protect Emma from having to worry. After a short time Emma decided to go to bed after making sure Ava was able to make it to the fold-out sofa bed. After Emma turned off the lights, Ava lay motionless next to Alex, wondering what had provoked him to attack her. She began to feel as if she was in an even worse situation than she had been with her mother rationalizing, at least she was stronger than Sonya, and could protect herself. Regardless, she felt as if she must do something to help Alex with whatever was making him behave in such an aggressive way. Though it seemed ridiculous to remain in the relationship, Ava felt as if she had to try to make the marriage work. She loved Alex deeply and felt if she showed him how much she loved him he would remember how great their relationship had once been. Her thoughts and rationalizations were textbook examples of an abused wife's typical response to acts of violence, but her eighteen-year-old mind was completely unaware of the dangers and she felt as if she had to try.

The next morning Lee was up at five o'clock and making coffee. Immediately, he began to complain about Ava and Alex still asleep in the living room. Emma was up shortly after Lee and tried to keep him from complaining too loudly and waking them up. Shortly after Ava awoke, her head still pounding from the night before, she joined Emma and Lee at the table. Only a few minutes later Alex began to stir, moaning as if he was in pain. He rolled over to face the others and opened his eyes.

"How ya feelin'?" Emma asked, snickering because she knew he must be sore.

"My fuckin' head, neck, and shoulders are killin' me!" Alex exclaimed with a thick, low voice.

"I wonder why," Emma answered, still with a hint of humor in her voice.

Ava sat in silence glaring at Alex. She wanted to scream at him but the adrenaline she had felt before was not coursing through her now. She was angry, hurt, and sad and could not clear her mind enough to say anything to him. It was obvious he had no idea what had happened and Ava began to wonder how he could simply not remember. He had only had two beers the night before, not even finishing the second after he dropped the can in the grass when she had pounced on him. Suddenly, she seemed to be fully aware of the cause, and concluded he must be on drugs of some kind. She felt so stupid. She was fooled into thinking he was a great man, one who had so much potential.

"What the fuck did I do last night?" Alex said as he attempted to sit up, only to lie back down immediately due to the pain.

No one answered. Emma had told Lee about what had happened the night before, and Lee assumed Ava had done something to provoke the attack, so he chose not to say anything. Ava walked back to the fold-out sofa and sat on the edge, next to Alex as he lay on his back in confusion. She leaned close to his ear and began to speak.

"You really don't remember what happened?" she asked in a whisper.

"No!" Alex answered in a quiet voice, completely innocent.

"Well, I'll tell ya," Ava said with a quiet hiss in her voice. "Ya grabbed me by the throat and slammed me into the clothesline pole so I jumped on your back and wailed on ya," she continued in a calm whisper, anger saturating her words.

Alex did not respond, well aware Ava's words were likely true. He honestly did not remember what he had done and knew the pill he had taken was likely the reason for his absent memory.

"I did?" Alex said, his voice cracking as he tried to whisper.

"Yeah, ya did," Ava answered in gruff whisper. "I can't do this anymore, Alex. I'm done," she continued.

He knew she loved him deeply and he was sure he would be able to talk her into staying if he put forth the effort.

"I'm sorry," he said as his eyes closed slowly. "Maybe the beer affected me more than I thought."

"I don't believe you," Ava said, her voice wavering as she prepared to tell him their marriage was over.

Alex tried to roll onto his left side in order to face away from Lee and Emma in the kitchen. It was clear he was in pain and his movements were excruciating.

"I'm truly sorry, Ava," Alex said as he softly touched the small of her back.

Ava looked down at the carpeted floor beneath her feet, remaining silent for what seemed like an eternity.

"Yeah, well, I'm telling ya now," Ava began. "If ya ever touch me like that again I don't know what I'll do to you, but I do know I will leave."

Alex nodded his head slightly to indicate he understood, though he knew he could keep her with him as long as he wanted.

Ava stood from her seat on the edge of the bed and busied herself with a few chores she had agreed to help Emma with. As she worked, she began to realize he was no better than the others she had dealt with in her life. No better than John, Jeff, Lee, Shane, or Sonya. She felt so deflated and taken advantage of, not to mention trapped in this new hell she had once thought to be a positive change in her life. Once again, another layer of bricks was added to the wall around her heart, and she chose not to speak of the incident any further with anyone.

The following week Ava and Alex prepared to move to Bonwhall, fulfilling the agreement they had made with Emma and Lee to purchase the trailer house, on contract. After moving in and getting settled, Ava began working at a sewing factory in Pinewood, a small town only about ten miles from Bonwhall. Alex had found a job in Pinewood as well, working for a farmer's cooperative. Their places of work were directly across the street from one another but Ava and Alex never seemed to see one another during the day.

Ava had not made any real friends in the sewing factory but hung out with a few of the women who worked there while they smoked cigarettes during breaks. Alex had made a friend at the co-op, one who was into drugs even more than he was. Once he had made the connection, it was only a matter of time before he would get high again, his reactions to the drugs usually not consistent. Alex had not attacked Ava since the day in the back yard, giving her hope he may have stopped using which was a huge relief to her, though she was sadly mistaken. Alex did not always get violent, sometimes he would be happy, and sometimes he would just get tired and go to sleep. Only a few short weeks after Ava had started her job at the sewing factory, Alex began to behave violently once again, his words and actions suggesting he would likely attack her at any time. One night, when Alex thought Ava was across town visiting Emma, she arrived home early and found him at their neighbor's house, a woman about Alex's age. When Ava asked if Alex was there the woman had attempted to lie but Ava would not be fooled. She pushed past the woman and walked into the house to find Alex hiding in the bedroom. Now, not only was Alex violent, but she knew he was having an affair as well. She had not actually caught him in the act of sex with the other woman but she knew what was really happening.

It was a Saturday, and Ava was home doing what she could to keep the trailer house clean and organized. All of the unpacking had been done and she worked to keep the home warm and inviting to Alex in an effort to subdue his violent and deceitful tendencies. She had planned to confront Alex about his drug use after he got home and had some time to unwind the workday. Since the couple had started their life together not long before, their belongings were still sparse, having only one television. Both Ava and Alex enjoyed watching TV at night before going to sleep so much of the time the fold-out sofa Emma and Lee had left for them served as their bed. Ava had folded the sofa in during her cleaning routine that day but had not yet moved the coffee table back into place in front of it. She had decided to take a break from her busy day and sit on the couch to watch a few minutes of television before returning to her chores. Rain started to fall lightly outside but she thought it would not be enough for Alex to get sent home early from work. Apparently, however, rain had already been falling much harder and for a great deal longer in Pinewood as Ava soon heard Alex's truck pull into the driveway. He burst through the front door and his eyes immediately locked on Ava, and angry fire burning within them.

"What the fuck are ya doin'?" Alex screamed at Ava as he slammed the front door.

Immediately, fear inundated Ava and she attempted to answer.

"I've been cleanin'," she said in a shaky voice. "I just sat down for a minute to take a break."

With no verbal response, Alex threw his lunch cooler on the floor in the kitchen, the contents spilling out across the linoleum. He rushed at her so quickly she had no time to make a move. With one hand on each of her arms he picked her up off of the couch and threw her toward the wall. Her entire body slammed into the wall with such force it seemed the entire trailer house shook. She fell in a crumpled pile on the floor as Alex turned back toward the couch and pulled the cushions from it. Yanking on the front of the fold-out portion of the couch he clumsily unfolded the bed and flopped on it.

"Get your fuckin' ass up and clean that kitchen!" he screamed at Ava from his place on the makeshift bed.

Without responding, Ava immediately stood and made her way around the sofa-bed, toward the kitchen. Before she could get all of the way around the bed Alex was up again and coming at her. Both of his hands griped her upper arms once again and he violently repositioned her so her back was toward the kitchen. She tried to back away but she was no match for his drug-fueled strength. In a flash, he let go of her arms and pulled his left hand back to hit her. With a closed fist he struck her right jaw so brutally the force knocked her backwards. She fell between the wall and the coffee table which had not been replaced in front of the couch that day. Her limp body crashed to the floor, her left jaw bouncing off of the edge of the wooden coffee table on the way down. Unconscious, she lay on the floor, her face already swollen and bruising deeply. Alex stood above her, contemplating what he had just done, but was unable to think clearly. He had taken some pills his friend had given him and chased them with a few beers at the bar after he was dismissed from work because of the rain. After a few minutes, he made his way to the bedroom, leaving Ava unconscious on the living room floor with no concern for her.

Ava awoke in a daze a few hours later, her head pounding and her face incredibly sore. She used the coffee table to support herself as she tried to stand. She felt as if she must escape at that moment, but to her dismay, she noticed Alex sitting on the edge of the sofa bed staring at her.

"Get over here!" he barked at her.

She clumsily stood, her balance clearly affected by the blows to her head. She took a step toward Alex then changed her mind.

"No," she said with conviction.

"What?" Alex asked, clearly confused about her response as the look on his face changed to one of angry disbelief.

She began to back away from him slowly, only able to cover a few feet before he was upon her once again. Using his entire body, he herded her backward toward the kitchen sink, as she stumbled to stay upright. She was unable to escape him as his weight forced her lower back to ram into the edge of the countertop.

"You'll do what I fuckin' tell ya to do!" he screamed at her, his face so close to hers she could smell the beer and cigarettes on his breath.

He took a step back, and before she was able to protect herself, his fist connected solidly with her mouth, just under her nose. The force of the blow caused her head to fly backwards, then bounce forward, as if she had been rear-ended in a car. Immediately blood poured from her nose and mouth like bright red water from a faucet. She attempted to slow the bleeding by covering her nose and mouth with her hand. Alex turned around and walked to the living room, once again flopping haphazardly on the sofa bed, as if he could no longer stay conscious. She took her hand away from her mouth and turned to clutch a dish towel hanging next to the sink. She could not breathe through her nose, as the blood continued to drain from it, so she opened her mouth to take a breath. She immediately heard the sound of something small and hard hitting the floor. She looked down and saw two of her teeth lying in the puddle of blood which spread across the white linoleum. She squatted down and picked up the teeth. He had knocked both of them out by the roots with the force of the punch to her face. Absentmindedly, she shoved the teeth back into the gaping holes in her gums, from which they had just been dislodged, holding them in place. Alex was still lying on the sofa-bed on his stomach, seemingly with no plans of moving. Ava tossed the dish towel over the pool of blood on the floor and retreated to the bathroom. Leaning forward over the sink she attempted to clean the blood from her face with a cold wash cloth while she held the teeth in their places with her tongue. After only a few moments Alex was at the bathroom door and burst into the room. The door opened inward, and once he was inside the room, he slammed the door shut behind him. With no words, he once again grabbed Ava by the throat and picked her up, completely off of her feet. He swung her toward the door behind him and slammed her into it. The instant her body made contact with the door, the jam on the outside of the doorway seemed to explode, allowing the door to be forced open the wrong way as the hinges twisted and broke. Directly across the hall from the now broken bathroom door was the metal back door of the trailer house which always remained locked. Her consciousness began to fade, but she was still aware of what was happening, as he slammed her small, limp body into the back door as well. The lock broke free and the entire door knob flew from the door, as the door sprung off of its hinges, from the force of her body's contact upon it. The door fell to the ground in front of the trailer house, Alex deciding to let go of Ava the instant the door broke free. Simultaneously, Ava and the door crashed to the ground. The door landed flat, the interior facing up. Only a fraction of a second after it hit the ground Ava's lifeless body landed hard on top of it. She desperately tried to remain conscious as she looked up at the gaping hole in the wall of the trailer, where the door had been. She saw Alex standing there, his fists still clenched, and saliva dripping from his chin. She faded into unconsciousness, wishing for death, the will to live draining from her as her eyes slowly closed and her muscles relaxed.

Light rain had continued to fall on the grass around Ava as she lay unconscious from the beating Alex had given her many hours before. As she regained consciousness, she did not know what time it was, and her entire body ached horribly. Even though it was only the end of June, the temperature was unseasonably cool, and the continuous rain had soaked her. She shivered from the cold and tried to move but the pain throughout her body was excruciating. After several minutes, she was able to pull herself across the wet grass to the rusted metal stairs, which served as meager access to the back door. She wanted to escape but her desire to live had not returned since she awoke. She tried to think clearly but the pain and cold throughout her body drove her to seek warmth within the trailer house. Unable to stand, she crawled up the stairs and through the open hole in the trailer house wall where the back door once hung. As quietly as she could, she crawled the short distance to the bedroom, only a few feet away from the back door. In the dark she was able to find the bed and pull a blanket from it. Unable to support herself any longer she slowly lay on the hard, carpeted floor of the bedroom, and covered herself, in an attempt to find some warmth. She lay on the floor shivering, each tiny movement creating repeated waves of pain throughout her entire body. Eventually, exhaustion overtook her and she once again lost consciousness.

The next day Ava awoke to bright sunlight shining through the windows into the bedroom. She could hear the birds chirping outside and wished everything that had happened had only been a nightmare. She tried to lift her head but the pain was too great. She could feel the dried blood on her face and remembered putting her teeth back into their sockets. She moved her tongue forward in an attempt to find out if the teeth had remained where she had put them. To her surprise, both of her front teeth were still in place, and seemed to be solid though touching them even with her tongue sent pain shooting through her mouth and into her nose. She winced and once again attempted to move. Everything hurt but she forced herself to slowly lift her broken body from the floor. Tears rolled down her cheeks as a result of the pain she was experiencing, but she pressed on, using the edge of the bed for support to help her stand. She turned toward the bedroom door and made her way down the hall, all the while leaning against the paneled walls to remain upright. As she entered the kitchen, she noticed Alex was nowhere to be found, and felt a hint of relief. She made her way to the sofa-bed which was still folded out, the physical trauma she had endured forcing her to sit down. Her head was spinning and the pain she felt finally overtook her and she lost consciousness once again.

After Alex had slammed Ava through both of the doors, and she had landed outside, he stood watching until he was sure she was dead. When her eyes closed, he finally felt satisfied he had killed her, and stumbled back to the living room to pass out on the sofa-bed. He fell asleep immediately with no feelings of remorse in his mind or in his heart. When he woke the next day he checked to see if Ava was still lying in the yard. He rationalized, if she was still out there he would have to get her inside before someone called the police. He didn't remember everything that had happened the night before, but fleeting memories helped him to realize he had done something terrible, though he did not feel saddened about anything. After he noticed Ava lying on the bedroom floor, he turned and left the trailer house, making his way to the neighbor's house with whom he was having an affair. He did not mention what had happened the night before and proceeded to have sex with her.

After several hours, Alex thought he should return to the trailer house, and take care of the mess waiting for him. When he entered the trailer house, he found Ava lying on the sofa-bed, unconscious. He decided he would leave her alone for a while and take the time to fix the back door. Rummaging around in some boxes of various items from the garage in Nathia he found some hinges and a door knob which would suffice for some sloppy repairs. He fixed the back door, the task taking him only a few hours in spite of the damage to the door. He chose to simply remove the bathroom door, rationalizing he would be living there alone soon anyway. Ava remained unconscious on the sofa-bed for the remainder of the day and

Alex checked on her periodically only to determine whether or not she was still alive.

By Monday the rain had returned and Alex did not have to go to work. As a co-op employee rain was almost a guarantee he would have the day off. Ava was supposed to be at work by six o'clock Monday morning but did not regain consciousness until about eight. After waking up she tried to raise herself from the sofa-bed to call in sick to work. Alex sat next to her on the sofa-bed, watching television, as if nothing had happened.

"What are ya doin?" Alex asked calmly without taking his eyes away from the screen.

"Gota call in to work," Ava answered, no longer afraid of him since she welcomed another beating which might kill her.

"Just quit," Alex ordered. "I know there's a guy there you're fuckin' and I don't like it. He comes to see ya once a week and you thought I didn't know," he continued.

Ava thought hard to determine what Alex was talking about. She remembered the man who came to the factory once a week, sent by the parent company several miles away, to work on the sewing machines. She had not even spoken to the man before, let alone had an affair with him. She thought about challenging Alex's accusation, but something inside her kept her from it. She still felt as if she wanted to die, but that same feeling inside her heart from when she was younger, seemed to convince her to continue life regardless of what was happening to her. She slowly made her way to the phone and called her workplace to quit her job.

Ava wanted to escape Alex but it seemed as if the pain in her body would never go away. She was unable to move quickly, the bruises she wore going very deep into her muscles. Alex remained home for three days straight as the rain continued. Ava slept much of the time and while she slept Alex visited his mistress. By the fourth day the rain had finally stopped and

Alex was called back to work. Even though Ava's pain was still great she noticed she was able to move more easily than before. After Alex left for work she showered and gathered a few of her things as she prepared to leave and escape her abusive hell. She had to force herself to ignore the pain in her body while she loaded a few things into the small hatchback car Alex had given her to drive. It only took about an hour to load the car and she was finally ready to go. She pulled the small car onto the highway, and pointed it back toward Nathia, unsure of where she would go.

After only driving a few miles, she noticed a vehicle approaching from behind, more quickly than it should be. She recognized Alex's truck and felt a rush of fear and panic. The car she drove was a model well known for exploding when rear ended and she was sure Alex would ram into the back of the car. At the last second, however, he slammed on his brakes and pulled onto the wrong side of the road to drive next to her. His windows were down and she could hear him clearly as he screamed at her.

"Go home or I'm runnin' ya off the fuckin' road!" he shouted from the driver's side of the truck through the passenger window.

Ava tried to ignore him, but when she didn't answer, she saw the side of his truck rushing toward her car. She swerved slightly, in an attempt to avoid impact, but had little room between her passenger wheels and the edge of the road. The ditch was very deep and the drop-off at the edge of the road was enormous. Ava lifted her foot from the gas pedal and slowed the car. Alex noticed her choice to slow down and matched her speed. He knew all of the field driveways by memory and knew there was one coming up he could force her into. He inched the passenger side of the truck closer to the driver's side of her car until her car came up on the field driveway. She spotted the driveway and swerved the car toward it as soon as she could, narrowly avoiding contact with Alex's truck. The car slid to a stop and the truck matched the maneuver. Alex slammed the truck into park and slid across the bench seat in order to scream at Ava through the passenger window.

"Where the fuck do ya think you're goin'?" he barked at her.

"You don't want me so why do you care?" Ava barked back at him as tears ran down her cheeks.

"You ain't goin' anywhere 'til I fuckin' tell ya to!" Alex retorted, his voice even louder than before. "Get you're fuckin' ass home and stay there!"

Alex knew his behavior struck fear deep in Ava's heart and he was confident she would do exactly what he told her to do. With her car still running, she shifted the transmission into reverse. That act indicated her obedience and he inched his truck away from her car. She hoped he would simply drive away, but today she would not be that fortunate. He allowed enough room for her to pull out of the field drive and followed her all of the way back to Bonwhall. Ava pulled into their driveway with Alex close behind her. She heard the tires of the truck slide to a stop on the gravel of the driveway and the engine shut off. She got out of her car and closed the door as Alex ran toward her. He reached the back of the car and slammed his left forearm down hard on the window of the hatchback, shattering it. Blood drained from the numerous cuts on his arm but he seemed not to notice. With his right hand he gripped Ava's upper arm and forced her into the trailer house.

"Clean this shit up!" Alex screeched, referring to the cuts on his arm.

Ava did not argue and simply wet a dish towel and cleaned the blood from his arm. After she finished Alex looked at her, his eyes not clouded as they seemed to be during the other violent attacks. She was sure he was completely sober and completely aware of what he was doing.

"Don't fuckin' leave again," Alex ordered as he poked Ava very hard in the chest with his finger.

She cast her eyes toward the floor and slightly nodded her head to indicate she understood the order and would obey.

Alex turned away from her and made his way to the door, slamming it on his way out. Ava walked to the window and watched as he went to the neighbor's house. She felt so worthless and empty. She felt as if she did not deserve to be happy. She made her way to the sofa-bed and sat down, but only for a moment. Her thoughts wandered quickly to the gun Alex had inherited after his father had died. The gun was a beautiful over and under shotgun, which Alex always kept loaded in the spare bedroom just off of the living room. She felt the need to find the gun. She searched the closet in the spare bedroom and found it. She admired the beauty of the firearm and deliberately clicked it open. She removed the shells from the gun, as something inside her compelled her to do so. For some reason, she felt she must make sure it was not loaded. The rest of the shells were in a small box on the shelf at the top of the closet and Ava found them right away. She knew Alex had only one box of ammunition, and with the shells she had removed from the gun, the box was once again full. In an effort to hide the ammunition, she removed the cover from one of the heat runs in the spare bedroom, and placed the box in the open hole. She replaced the cover to the vent and returned to her place on the sofa bed. Once again, the pain of the beating she had taken a few days earlier was becoming unbearable, and exhaustion overtook her. She had not eaten since before Alex had attacked her, and hunger was contributing to her fatigue, just as much as her pain.

After Alex forced Ava to return to the trailer house he had made her clean the wounds on his arm before he visited his mistress once again and had sex with her. After they finished having sex both of them smoked a joint to relax as they lay naked on the bed together. Alex returned to the trailer house several hours later to find Ava asleep on the sofa-bed in the living room. Even though he felt calmed from his visit with his mistress, he could not help but think Ava would turn him in for beating her so severely. He stood over her as she slept, and thought about what he could do to keep her quiet, rationalizing if he killed her it was likely no one would notice. He remembered the shotgun he had gotten when his dad died and the thought of losing his dad seemed to provoke feelings of anger within him which compounded with the irritation of his wife. He went to the closet where the gun was kept and retrieved it. He knew he had loaded the gun before he had set it in its place in the corner of the closet, so without checking to see if it was still loaded, he cocked the gun and walked back into the living room. He held the barrels of the gun only millimeters from Ava's forehead and after only a few seconds he pulled the trigger. The gun clicked loudly as the hammer snapped forward but it did not fire. He pulled the trigger again but the gun only made another loud click. Ava's eyes snapped opened and Alex realized, she must have unloaded the gun in anticipation of the event, and anger flared up inside of him.

Ava slept soundly, not waking when Alex returned to the trailer house. She did not feel his presence in front of her as he stared at her while she slept. He was quiet when he retrieved the gun from the closet and since he cocked it in the spare bedroom the walls of the room helped to muffle the sound. It was not until he pulled the trigger the first time that Ava was pulled from sleep. She heard the loud click the hammer made as it slammed forward against the firing pin. Then another loud click rang through the silent room as he pulled the trigger the second time. She opened her eyes to see the two black holes at the end of the shotgun's two barrels. She was unable to move as she refocused her eyes and saw Alex holding the gun to her head. Fear exploded inside of her as she expected him to successfully fire the gun and end her life. Even though she wanted to die, the familiar feeling inside of her would not let her give up. She recognized the anger on Alex's face as he realized she had unloaded the gun. She sat up like a shot, the adrenaline created by fear helping her ignore the pain surging through her body. Alex said nothing as he snapped the gun open and looked for the shells he knew he had put in it. When he realized the gun was, indeed, not loaded his gaze immediately shot back to Ava and he glared at her.

"You're fuckin' lucky," he hissed.

Ava said nothing and tried to keep her face from showing her fear.

Alex turned to replace the gun in its original place in the closet then stepped back into the living room. He climbed onto the sofa-bed next to Ava and lay down next to where she sat.

"Lay down," Alex ordered, as if speaking to a dog.

Ava did not move and within seconds Alex grabbed her arm and slammed her to the mattress next to him. She lay as stiff as a board next to him and he put his arm over her stomach. He was tired from the day's events and wanted to sleep. With his arm over her he felt confident he would wake up if she tried to move. Once he fell asleep, she slid out from under his arm and made her way to the door. She knew she had to leave and something inside her urged her to leave at that very moment. Her car was still packed and, even though the back window was broken, she seized the opportunity to escape. Alex did not wake up as she opened the door, so she slipped out, unnoticed by anyone. She started her car and backed out of the driveway, once again pointing the car toward Nathia. This time she was able to escape since this time, Alex's mistress had not noticed her leaving, and failed to warn him the way she had earlier.

When she finally reached Nathia, she made her way to her mother's new apartment and pulled into the parking lot. Sonya had been forced to move from the house in which Ava had grown up since she could no longer depend upon welfare and rental assistance to support her. Ava hated the idea of living with Sonya again, but knew she could not stay in Bonwhall, and could not bear to go back to Lilli's house. She prepared herself for the barrage of ridicule she would likely hear from Sonya, collected herself, and knocked on the apartment door. Obvious surprise blanketed Sonya's face when she opened the door to find Ava standing in the hallway.

"Can I stay here?" Ava asked soberly.

Sonya could not help but notice all of the bruises Ava wore on her face, neck, and arms. Suddenly, Sonya felt as if she must help her daughter, something completely out of character for her.

"Can ya help pay bills?" Sonya questioned ignorantly, concern nowhere in her voice.

"As soon as I find a job," Ava answered matter-of-factly.

Sonya hesitantly opened the door and stepped to the side to allow Ava to enter the apartment. Ava walked to the couch and sat down cradling her head in her hands. With no words Sonya walked to the couch and sat next to her. She put her arm around Ava and hugged her, in the first real display of true affection she had ever extended to her. Ava was not sure how to take the sudden change in Sonya's behavior, but simply did not possess the energy to question it. Ava sobbed uncontrollably, and as if Sonya had always been a caring mother, she continued to hold her daughter as she cried.

Chapter Ten

$\mathscr{T}$he tender moment between mother and daughter lasted only minutes before Sonya separated herself from Ava and returned to her seat at the table. Ava continued to cry but she felt as if her tears would soon run out.

"You can stay here but you'll have to help pay for stuff," Sonya said with no emotion as she returned her gaze to the television screen.

Ava chose not to respond. She knew she would be able to get a job with little effort and had planned to do so before Sonya had even spoken. She simply nodded her head to indicate her understanding as she closed her eyes and positioned herself to fall asleep on the couch. Her exhaustion had once again overtaken her and she was unable to stay awake any longer as she drifted into a very disturbed sleep.

Sonya pretended to watch television, ignoring Ava's obvious suffering with spiteful ease. Even though sympathy was not a natural feeling for her, she felt a pang of emotion in her heart as she looked at her daughter's bruised face. She closed her eyes as the memories of many beatings at the hands of Simon and Lars wafted through her mind. She struggled to remain rigid and ultimately was able to keep her composure and force the memories from her mind. Ava had already fallen asleep and Sonya sat alone thinking of the different ways she could gain some sort of financial benefit from her daughter's return. She retreated to her small bedroom and allowed Ava to sleep through the night without disturbing her.

When Ava awoke the next morning, her eyes were still wet with tears, as she had cried periodically throughout the night as she dreamt about the violence she had endured with Alex. She lay quietly on the couch thinking of the tornado of upset that had befallen her marriage. She thought about the time they had spent together before they were married and tried to remember whether or not Alex had shown any signs of possible violence. She was unable to recall anything that may have served as a warning but ultimately concluded she would have married him, regardless of any palpable cautions, if only to escape Sonya. Ava knew she would have to wait until the bruises on her face healed before looking for a job and decided she would take the time to attempt to find herself. She sadly reflected on the fact her marriage had lasted little more than seven months and, once again, found her self-esteem plummeting. She knew she was a failure and began to rationalize her mother may have been right about her all along.

Sonya eventually appeared in the kitchen and brewed a pot of coffee. After pouring herself some, she took her usual seat at the table, and silently sipped from her cup.

"Do ya have any soda?" Ava asked, her voice raspy from crying.

"Some," Sonya answered.

"Can I have one?" Ava dared to ask.

"I guess," Sonya said, a touch of irritation in her voice and clearly showing on her face.

Ava slowly rose from the couch, her body still aching from the violent beatings she had endured. She walked to the refrigerator and opened the door, immediately spotting the soda, and took one from the shelf. Before closing the door she noticed the refrigerator held no alcohol. She quietly closed the door and returned to the couch.

"I didn't see any beer in the fridge," Ava said with curiosity.

"I quit drinkin'," Sonya volunteered quietly, a touch of shame in her voice, as if avoiding alcohol was somehow a failure in her life.

"Why?" Ava asked soberly.

"'Cause I wanted to," Sonya answered with an annoyed tone.

Ava chose not to comment any further as she took a seat on the couch once again. Neither of them spoke for several minutes, both seemingly content with sitting in silence. Finally, Sonya spoke.

"So what the fuck happened to ya?" She asked with no emotion.

"Alex beat the shit outa me," Ava answered matter-of-factly.

"Humph," Sonya responded. "Wondered how long that would take," she said with a hint of undeserving pride in her voice.

Ava chose to remain silent, as she did not possess the energy to argue with her mother.

"So ya guna be here for a long time or are ya goin' back?" Sonya asked.

"I don't know," Ava responded. "I can't think right now."

Sonya looked at her coffee cup thoughtfully and took a sip. She wanted to remind Ava she had not wanted her to marry Alex, but chose not to, remembering Ava's willingness and ability to defend herself.

"There's a spare bedroom," Sonya said. "Ya can sleep in there instead of on the couch," she continued. "How much stuff did ya bring with ya?"

"Not much," Ava answered without looking at Sonya. "Just what I could get in the car."

Sonya again did not respond, attempting to show Ava she cared little about what had transpired.

Ava rose from her seat on the couch, once again, and set her soda on the table.

"I gota go out and get stuff outta the car," she said. "Alex busted the back window and I don't want everything to get wet if it rains."

Sonya again chose to remain silent and intentionally ignored Ava as she walked toward the door of the apartment. Though she spoke no words, the expression of irritation and imposition was still clearly etched in every detail of her face.

It took Ava three trips to get everything out of her car, and with each trip, the pile of her things in the corner of the spare bedroom grew. Sonya made no attempt to help Ava carry her belongings, even though she assumed the work was excruciating to Ava's beaten body, as she rationalizing the pain was a justifying punishment for defying her wishes and marrying Alex in the first place. Once Ava had finished transferring her things into the apartment she sat on the edge of the single bed in the spare bedroom. She hated everything about where she had ended up and once again the tears of defeat began to flow from her eyes. While she cried, Ava heard the telephone ring. She had forgotten her mother had gotten a phone. Even though she hated being around Sonya, she stood and walked back into the living room, hating the feeling of being alone even more. Sonya hung up the phone and turned toward Ava.

"That was Alex," Sonya said with a tone of playfulness which did not at all belong. "He wants to come and see ya."

Ava looked at the floor as she tried to understand why he would want to see her after everything he had done to her. She said nothing as she picked up the can of soda she had been drinking and returned to the couch.

"What did he say?" Ava asked, ultimately afraid of the answer.

"Said he wants to see ya and he'll be here in a few hours," Sonya answered.

Ava continued to sit quietly with downcast eyes and thought about what might happen when he arrived. She found herself unable to make sense of Alex's desire to see her and chose to concentrate on the program flickering on the television screen across the room. Sonya and Ava chose to remain silent for the next few hours as they waited for Alex to arrive. Sonya wondered silently about what Ava must have done to provoke Alex. Ava knew her mother cared little about what had happened to her and chose not to divulge any details, unless asked directly, but possibly not even then.

Finally, there was a knock on the door and Sonya rose from her seat to open it. Alex stood in the doorway, holding a single rose, a look of shame and innocence on his face. Sonya said nothing and opened the door wide so he would have room to walk through. Ava looked up when he stepped into the living room, immediately noticing the look of shame he clearly wore.

"Can we go somewhere and talk?" Alex asked Ava sheepishly.

Ava stood from her seat but said nothing. She turned and made her way to the spare bedroom with Alex following close behind her. She sat on the edge of bed and waited for him to enter the room.

"You okay?" Alex asked quietly as he appeared in the doorway.

Ava nodded her head, indicating she was okay, but did not want to speak.

He walked to the bed and sat down next to her. Extending the rose in front of her, he waited for her to accept it.

"I'm sorry," he said gravely.

Ava reached for the rose and took it. She knew he was sorry, but was not sure if he was sorry about hurting her, or sorry about letting her escape. Alex said nothing as he sat beside her and stared at the floor in front of his feet. After several minutes Ava finally spoke.

"I'm filing for divorce," she said softly with no emotion in her voice.

Out of the corner of her eye she could see Alex nodding his head to indicate he understood. Within seconds she heard the unmistakable sounds of weeping coming from deep in his throat. She had no more understanding to offer him and chose to sit motionless.

"I should go," Alex said through his tears, his voice squeaking as he tried to regain his composure.

"Yeah, probably," Ava answered as silent tears began to fall from her eyes.

"Please don't make me go," he finally said after several minutes.

Ava closed her eyes, unable to offer a reply.

"I love you," he said weakly as he attempted to hold her hand.

She pulled away and stood up, afraid she would give in to him. He began to cry louder but remained seated on the bed.

"You almost killed me, Alex," Ava said in an even tone. "Why would I go back to you?"

"I don't know what happened," Alex whispered from behind her. "I'm not guna do drugs anymore," he continued, still weeping. "I promise."

"I don't believe you," she said, anger leaking into her voice. "Ya been fuckin' the neighbor for God knows how long, and ya 'bout fuckin' killed me!" she continued, speaking louder and with more conviction as she whirled around to face him.

He looked at her, his tears suddenly no longer flowing. She could see the look of anger beginning to wash over his face but stood her ground.

"Fine," Alex said, his voice no longer weak with tears, as if someone had flipped a switch.

He stood and walked out of the bedroom, making his way toward the front door. Ava turned to look out the window, and after only a few seconds, saw him walking toward his truck in the parking lot. She knew she would not likely see him again, and a feeling of relief washed over her, combined with a renewed feeling of failure. She returned to her bed and lay down on her back, holding the rose above her. She studied the flower, looking closely at its deep red pedals and sharp thorns. It was such a beautiful blossom, one that usually represented love and caring. In this instance, however, Ava realized it was only a lure, a weak attempt to fool her into returning to a life of abuse. At that moment, she seemed to fully understand things are not always as they seem, and no matter how wonderful things seem to be in one's mind, reality will inevitably prove to overtake everything. She closed her eyes and let her left arm relax, the rose still in her hand. Slowly, she released her grip on the stem of the beautiful flower, and as the rose dropped to the floor, yet another layer of bricks was added to the wall around her heart.

After Ava's bruises healed she was able to obtain a full time job at the only factory in Nathia. She filed for divorce and Alex did not contest the proceedings. The dissolution took little more than a month and finally she was able to put the whole thing behind her, though she would ultimately come to find, the effects of the abuse would change her forever. There were a few people living in the apartment complex, with whom Ava got along very well, so she spent a great deal of time with them during her time off from the factory. Everyone in her new group of friends seemed to drink a great deal and Ava followed suit. She found, when she drank, her feelings of failure and emptiness seemed to diminish and she was thankful for that.

Soon after she started her job several men asked her out but she had not yet accepted any offers. After becoming comfortable with her coworkers, Ava began to feel as if she belonged, and began to hang out with them outside of work as well. Ultimately, all of the coworkers with whom she spent time drank alcohol as well and they all seemed to get along wonderfully. Over the next few months she developed a habit of drinking every night and was fully aware she was falling into the trap of alcoholism. She cared little about her own life, with frequent thoughts of suicide still dominating her thoughts, and rationalized she would not likely live to the age of twenty-five. Her reality allowed her to throw caution to the wind and continue to try to erase the horrible memories of her life.

Ava finally found a house to rent and, when she informed Sonya of her impending move, Sonya was livid. She had grown used to Ava paying half of all of her bills and tried to convince Ava she would not be able to make it if she moved out. Ava knew her mother was only trying to use guilt to keep the financial assistance of her paychecks, so she ultimately thanked her mother for helping her when she left Alex, and proceeded to move out on her own.

A few weeks after moving out, Ava began to feel the empowerment of independence, and a wild spirit within her seemed to be unleashed. She drank even more, having parties and joining her coworkers at the bar on a regular basis.

Finally, she decided to give in to one of the men with whom she worked and had a few sexual excursions with him. Though the relationship did not blossom, the attention she received from him seemed to feed a hunger deep inside of her which had been ignored for much too long. On one occasion, Ava joined some of her friends at a party and met another man, who she ultimately allowed to accompany her home. It was the first time in her life she had ever experienced a one night stand, and though the time spent with the man seemed to fulfill a need for her, she still felt very incomplete. The connection between them was merely sexual and made her longing for a real connection even more vivid in her heart and mind. The next morning she felt even emptier inside, fully understanding she had, once again been used as a sexual object. This understanding ultimately supported her unconscious acceptance of the world in which she lived, one devoid of real love, the very thing her heart and mind desperately needed.

Throughout the next few months Ava had grown superficially close to a few of her coworkers and, for the first time in her life, felt as if she had genuinely been accepted into a social circle. One of the supervisors at the factory, Mark, had shown a deep interest in her and began to strive to spend time with her. He began to frequent the bar with her and her friends and was blatant about his interest in her. Finally, Ava began to show an interest in him as well, and a relationship slowly began to form. To Ava, the relationship seemed genuine, but she failed to realize it was fostered by frequent alcohol use. Ava and Mark dated for only a few months, before moving in together and drinking alcohol seemed to be their favorite pastime. Ava rationalized, the short time together before taking a serious step did not have anything to do with whether or not the relationship would be a success. She remembered she and Alex had been together for almost four years before getting married and the amount of time together did not seem to matter. Ava and Mark seemed to be very happy together and Mark was very attentive. He made her feel loved and constantly strived to let her know he loved her. After only living together for a few months the couple decided to get married and plans were made. On a rainy day, late in May of 1996, Ava and Mark became man and wife. Emma was there with her family and even Sonya attended the ceremony. Lilli, however, was not allowed to attend. Shane had decided Ava was a bad influence on Lilli, and did not allow the sisters to speak to one another at all, his guilt governing his decision.

Within a week after the wedding Ava began to notice remarkable changes in Mark's behavior. Before they had gotten married it seemed Mark was a man who would allow Ava to be herself and do what she liked. Ultimately, however, that was not the case and once the vows had been taken a whole new persona seemed to cloak him, changing him completely. He began to demand Ava not see the friends she had become close to at work and was even more demanding about severing her friendships with the individuals from the apartment complex. Ava tried to rationalize the situation but was unable to understand how and why he had changed his behavior so abruptly and drastically.

Drinking continued to be the couple's most frequent leisure and they spent a great deal of time at the local bar. Ava was only allowed to spend time with Mark and his friends, as he had been adamant about his distrust for her, fearing she would cheat on him if allowed to spend time alone or with people he did not know or approve of. Ava felt trapped once again but hated the idea of being alone. She wanted to make the marriage work and rationalized, since Mark was not physically abusive, she could deal with his obsessive control. She had no idea the control Mark exercised over her was ultimately a type of abuse as well, one which would inevitably create a feeling of inadequacy, unintelligence, and a need to constantly prove herself, even to strangers. One positive attribute, for Ava, seemed to be the abundant opportunities to play pool. She inevitably used the game as an outlet for her frustrations and seemed to find comfort in getting lost in the game. Mark played as well and decided to recruit some of his friends, along with Ava, forming a team in order to join their local pool league. Ava found joy in the nights she took part in league competition and found she was able to partially escape the emotional prison Mark had constructed around her. Ava finally found herself endeavoring to play pool as much as possible and was able to convince Mark to shoot on another league, on a different night as well, with a different team.

After playing the majority of the league season, Ava and Mark learned they were eligible to take part in a large tournament at the state level, which involved multiple events and hundreds of people. Mark decided, as long as he was able to control what Ava did during the events, their team could participate. Involvement in the events at the state tournament opened up opportunities to escape their daily lives by taking a miniature vacation, staying in a hotel room, and leaving their responsibilities behind for the span of about four days. As the events approached, Ava's excitement continued to build, and Mark made plans with his teammates to drink excessively and visit the strip club located very close to the venue where the tournament events were scheduled to take place.

Each of the team members participated in their respective single player events and Ava took part in the women's events. She ultimately finished with second place in her bracket and learned she would be considered a master player for at least the next three years. The team she and Mark belonged to competed in the team event, and seemed to shoot well, but did not finish very well in the tournament. Ultimately, however, Mark seemed to be relaxed around his friends and Ava found he was much easier to get along with. With this observation, she rationalized his change in behavior must be due to his supervisory position at work, though it was a feeble attempt to continue the relationship with hope in her heart.

It was Saturday afternoon and Mark and Ava's team had just been beaten out of the team event at the state pool tournament. As the small group gathered and tried to decide what to do next they each opened a beer, and those who smoked, lit up.

"So what now?" Mark asked, directing his question at everyone in the group except Ava.

Ava knew better than to suggest anything and simply remained silent waiting for plans to be made for her. She knew Mark would not consider any ideas she might have.

"Let's go to the titty bar!" Josh, Mark's best friend, suggested excitedly.

Ava's heart sank as Mark and the rest of the team happily agreed. She was the only female on the team and immediately felt out of place with the pending plans.

"Soon as we get done with our beers, let's go!" Mark barked playfully at his teammates.

Ava felt anger building within her. She could not understand why Mark would want to go look at other women, especially when she was right there with him. Without thinking she leaned toward Mark to offer her opinion.

"I don't wana go to the strip bar," Ava whispered with anger and conviction in her voice.

Mark giggled, in an effort to create the illusion Ava had said something funny to him. He leaned close to Ava and put his right arm around her back and his left hand on the right side of her face.

"You'll go to the fuckin' strip joint, bitch," Mark growled softly in her ear. "If ya don't, I'll knock you're fuckin' head off," he continued in a tone which immediately sparked fear in Ava's heart.

She knew he was serious about his threat and felt as if she were powerless against him. She felt she had no other choice but to join the team in their plans. Mark moved away from her and tipped his beer can up to indicate he was finished. After draining all of the beer from the can he set it down hard on the tabletop with a loud crack, the sudden, loud noise making Ava jump slightly.

"Let's go!" Mark barked happily.

The other members of the team quickly finished their beers as well and everyone in the group rose from their chairs to follow Mark to the door.

The strip bar was only a few blocks from the tournament venue and the team walked together, as a group, for about a half of a block before Mark decided to speak.

"Hey guys, I gota talk to Ava for a sec," he said in a jovial tone. "We'll catch up with ya in a minute," he continued with an innocent smile on his face.

The rest of the team walked ahead, laughing and joking amongst one another, as Mark guided Ava to the side of a building, out of sight of the others and seemingly, everyone else.

"Don't you ever put me in a position like that again ya little bitch!" Mark hissed at Ava, his nose almost touching hers.

She could feel his hot breath and smell the stench of the beer he had just finished. She was immediately enveloped in fear and felt as if her muscles had instantly turned to stone. She was unable to move or even speak. Before she realized what was happening, Mark's large, open hand made contact with the right side of her face. The slap produced a loud crack and she instantly felt excruciating pain throughout her cheek and around her eye. Without waiting for Ava to respond Mark's left hand reached for the back of her head. He intertwined his fingers throughout her hair and jerked her head forward as he turned to continue to the strip bar. Ava had no choice but to follow, Mark's grip on her hair already burning her scalp.

"Move your fuckin' ass and don't start fuckin' bawlin'!" Mark barked as he dragged her behind him toward the strip bar. "Maybe it's amateur night," he continued in an eerie tone. "If it is, your ass is gettin' up on the stage and you're gettin' naked!" he ordered, a deviant vein saturating his voice.

When they reached the door of the bar, Mark's face and behavior changed instantly as he crossed the threshold, in order to convey he and his wife had simply had a tender moment before walking into the establishment. As Ava stepped into the strip bar, a terrible smell flooded her nostrils, making her gag instantly. She unconsciously covered her mouth and nose with her hand in an effort to avoid the horrible stench. The air inside the establishment smelled as if the women who were stripping had been sexually active repeatedly and had not showered in days. Music was blaring and the lighting was dim. The carpet was a deep, royal purple and the walls were a very dark red. The place was buzzing with men, and to Ava's surprise, several women as well. Within seconds of entering the bar, Mark spotted the rest of their group, and approached them joking and laughing loudly. Ava followed Mark obediently, as if she were a beaten dog, avoiding eye contact with everyone. Mark and the other members of the team positioned themselves so they were able to see the stage and watched as the women danced. Ava felt like running away but she knew her punishment would be much worse than being forced to sit in the establishment. She tried to lose herself in her thoughts but they were littered with pain, self-loathing, and sadness. Mark requested a lap dance for the youngest member of the team, and the other three stood close by watching intently, tucking dollar bills into the woman's g-string, whistling, and loudly yelling obscenities. When the stripper finished the lap dance Ava noticed Mark talking to her.

"Is it amateur night?" Mark asked the stripper, yelling so she could hear him over the deafening music.

"No," the stripper answered as she shook her head, a promiscuous smile on her face.

"Any way I could pay someone to let my wife dance?" Mark inquired, glancing at Ava and pointing toward her.

"I don't think so," the stripper responded. "That's Wednesday nights."

Mark smiled and tucked another dollar bill into the stripper's g-string, this time his hand sinking into the front. The stripper stood still for a moment and closed her eyes. She smiled and slowly turned to walk away from Mark, looking back to offer a wink. Mark made his way toward Ava, wearing an innocent smile on his face, as if no one was able to see what he had just done.

"You're fuckin' lucky!" Mark yelled in Ava's ear, attempting to conceal his message. "Amateur night is only on Wednesdays!"

Ava let out a relieved sigh which went completely unnoticed by everyone else in the entire bar. She knew Mark would have forced her to get on the stage, and if she had refused, she was certain he would have beaten her. The group remained at the strip bar for another few hours before going back to their hotel rooms. Ava remained silent for the rest of the night and continued to portray the behavior of an abused dog. Mark continued to behave as if he had done nothing wrong and he and the rest of the team had a great deal of fun drinking, laughing, and joking until very late into night. The next morning Ava and Mark awoke, gathered their things, and made their way back to their daily lives, the tournament events marking the end of the league season until the following fall.

Over the next six months Ava did her best to continue with life as usual. Mark's threats became more frequent and the physical confrontations between the two of them became more aggressive. Mark repeatedly accused Ava of having various affairs with different men with whom she worked, and though the grounds of the accusations were never founded, she was completely unable to prove her innocence to him as he refused to listen to anything she had to say. Each time he accused her of an affair, he conveniently remembered she had been away from home or had come home late from work, though each time she had been home with him and the two of them rode to and from work together every day. Ava was unable to understand where the accusations were coming from but continued to try to figure it out. Ultimately, though Ava would not become aware of the fact for some time, Mark was repeatedly imagining the alleged adultery in his own mind. Eventually, Ava quit her job in the factory where Mark was employed, in order to pursue a more promising and better paying position with another company. She had become a welder during her time at the Nathia factory and had a skill she could offer in order to better herself. She was hired with the new company, which was located in Ropschon, as a steel welder though she had extensive experience with aluminum welding as well. With the new job, Ava felt as if she would be able to escape Mark's control, at least during the work day.

As the days passed Ava was able to spend the majority of each day at work as overtime was mandatory. The small group of people with whom she worked accepted her immediately and she seemed to fit in perfectly. Though she enjoyed her job Ava dreaded going home each night. In order to avoid any confrontations with Mark she adopted a routine and did her best to keep from upsetting him. Since she no longer worked for the same company, the accusations of adultery seemed to stop immediately, and she felt a hint of relief with the change though Mark continued to treat her as if she had cheated on him. During the work week Ava followed the same routine every day. Every morning she would wake at four o'clock, shower, and go to work. Each day upon arriving home she would lie on the couch in the living room and fall asleep. Each night about eleven o'clock she would wake and go to bed, after Mark had already been in bed and asleep for a while. Each Friday, her coworkers enjoyed going to the bar for drinks after work, and even though she knew Mark would be furious she joined them for some social time. It seemed the social time at the bar with her coworkers was the closest thing she could find to feeling accepted, feeling as though she was not welcome in her own home, because of the abusive way Mark treated her. She continued to drink and welcomed the relaxing state that swept over her. She found once again, while she was drinking, she did not worry about what would happen when she arrived home, nor did she worry about whether or not Mark actually loved her. She once again felt trapped and did what she could to find comfort in the situation.

After some time, Lilli ultimately refused to let Shane continue to control her and she divorced him. Lilli's divorce was not only prompted by the control Shane had forced upon her but also due to his sexual indiscretions with the wife of one of his best friends. In addition, Shane had begun to speak of sexually atrocious things concerning Lilli. During one of the last arguments between Lilli and Shane, before the divorce was final, he attempted to prove to her how much he loved her by telling her one of his secrets. He told Lilli, if she were to die in her sleep, he would have sex with her dead body before calling the authorities, because he would want to be with her just one more time before they would take her body away. Though Shane had shared his secret in an effort to express his deep love for Lilli, ultimately he only created feelings of fear and suspicions of harm in Lilli's mind. During the divorce, Lilli and Ava became close once again, and the sisters spent a great deal of time together. Emma and Lee continued to be a part or Ava's life, though the geographical distance proved to be a challenge. More often than not, Emma would visit Lilli's house, and Ava would join them. Even though Emma and Ava had continued contact throughout the years it seemed the frequent visits between the three sisters drew them all closer together than ever before.

Niles, now known as Able, had returned from his time in the Navy and tried to be a part of the sibling connection as well. Ultimately, the sisters loved him and wanted to accept him, but his behavior and attitude about life, religion, and women in general posed a great obstacle. Able continually judged the choices each of the girls made, seemingly on every level, and had no reservations about telling each of them how they should live their lives. His mental state was very unstable and the three sisters chose to hold their tongues in order to keep him from getting upset. Eventually, Able befriended Mark and the two men became very close friends. With the new friendship, Ava felt even more alienated from her home, and sought to spend as much time as she could at work and with Lilli.

While in the Navy, after he changed his name, Able had endured a terrible breakdown and had connected with his unit's chaplain for counseling. The chaplain was able to help him accept Jesus and renounce his Atheist ideals. Able studied the Christian faith in depth, but ultimately, seemed to embrace ideals that suited him instead of seeking the ultimate, divine truth. He continuously kept a wall between himself and his sisters, openly sharing his belief that all of the world's problems were the fault of the female gender. This belief was rooted in his interpretation of the story of Adam and Eve, perceiving the story in a way which deleted any responsibility by Adam. He believed, since Eve was the first to eat the apple, she corrupted Adam with her sexual temptations to do the same, therefore taking the blame off of Adam and justifying his belief of the evil which resides inside every woman, and their potential to bring down civilization if not continually subdued by men. This perception dismayed Lilli, Emma, and Ava but Able stood by his ideals and would prove to do so for the rest of his life, continuously attempting to push his delusional perception of Christianity on everyone he encountered, including his sisters.

Mark did not necessarily believe in all of Abel's Christian ideals but he embraced Abel's position on keeping women subdued. Though he did not share his abusive behavior toward Ava with Abel, or anyone else, he spoke with him on many occasions, convincing him Ava was a terrible person who treated him badly and cheated on him repeatedly. Abel's idealism of women facilitated his belief of Mark's claims about Ava and eventually Abel reached the decision, Mark was a great guy, and Ava did not deserve to be with someone so wonderful. This stance was something Ava could not ever hope to overcome, so she felt she had no other choice than to emotionally pull away from her brother, to protect herself from yet another attack on her emotional and mental wellbeing, this time from a religious standpoint.

Ava and Mark continued to live their lives, Ava continued to work and drink a great deal, and Mark continued to accuse her of multiple affairs though she was not unfaithful. One Saturday, while Ava and Mark were sitting in the living room watching television, Mark seemingly attempted to reconnect with Ava on a sexual level. Typically, Ava would sit on the couch and Mark would sit in his chair, and they would not converse at all. Out of the blue Mark rose from his chair and took a seat on the couch next to Ava. She felt tense and innately readied herself for some sort of physical blow.

"Hey," Mark said in a soft tone Ava had not heard since they had started dating.

She said nothing but forced a half-hearted smile in response.

"I've been thinkin', we haven't been the same for a while," Mark continued.

Ava still remained silent, unable to process the abrupt and

unrealistic change in Mark's behavior. He put his arm around her gently and pulled her close to him, hugging her. Ava's heart leapt and she suddenly felt he may actually love her.

"I think we should try something new," he said affectionately.

"What?" Ava inquired softly with skepticism.

"Let me take some pictures of ya," he said with a flirtatious smile on his face.

"What kind of pictures?" Ava asked, unsure of his motives.

"Ya know, pictures," Mark answered, winking at her playfully like he had when they had first gotten together. "It's kinda always been one of my fantasies."

As Ava watched his face, she immediately remembered the good things about him, and loved that he was being so nice to her. She felt so warm and loved at that moment, and wanted to do whatever she could to make him happy, in the hopes the affection would continue and they could finally be happy with one another. Though she had no idea at the time, she had become a textbook example of an abused wife, and a perfect illustration of the confusion and damage that is the result of an abusive relationship. She wanted to escape but was immediately fully reinvested once Mark offered even the slightest hint of affection. Though from the outside, it would be easy for anyone to see the unhealthy and abusive setting, once trapped inside it was virtually impossible for Ava to see a way out.

Mark ultimately convinced Ava, doing new sexual things together would renew their relationship, and bring them closer together than ever. She wanted so much to do whatever she could to make her husband happy so she apprehensively agreed to let him photograph her in sexually explicit positions.

"I think we should tell each other our fantasies," Mark

encouraged with an innocent look on his face as his voice took on a seductive tone. "I think it'll help us."

Ava let herself be captivated by the sudden changes in Mark's behavior, simply because she wanted so much to be happy with him. She was much too shy to share her fantasies with Mark but he was much freer with his thoughts. As Mark described the positions in which he wanted Ava to pose, and snapped several pictures, he described another sexual fantasy involving videotaping himself with Ava during sex so they could watch the tape together later. Intoxicated on the attention Mark was lavishing over her Ava agreed to do whatever he wanted her to do.

After Mark had taken the pictures he wanted to take they went into their bedroom and Mark set up the video camera. He encouraged Ava to bring herself to orgasm on camera before they had sex and she agreed, though she was full of reservation, incredibly self-conscious and ashamed. All the while she lay on the bed in front of the camera, she felt as if Mark was really interested in her again, for the first time in what seemed like forever. She did all she could to be as free and uninhibited as she could possibly be, fully enveloped in the belief the night marked a new beginning for their marriage, and feeling her hope for true happiness may finally be coming to fruition. Mark talked to her as he videotaped her and she was completely swept away. Once she brought herself to orgasm Mark undressed and came into camera view with her. The couple had sex for quite some time, and to Ava, it was the best sex she had ever had with Mark. She was so excited about the new possibilities of a happy and intimate marriage her heart soared.

After they were finished and the camera was shut off they lay in bed together holding each other. Mark spoke of random things and Ava felt free to converse with him. It was like they had just met and it was the first time they had been intimate with one another. To Ava, the entire night was a dream come true and she was so happy Mark had decided to return to the relationship. After lying together and talking for about an hour Mark drifted off to sleep. Soon after, Ava's eyes slowly closed and she drifted off to sleep as well, her thoughts inundated with wonderful feelings of acceptance and love.

The next morning Ava awoke still feeling all of the warmth and love from the night before. For the first time in a long time she was not afraid and she wore a smile even before she opened her eyes. Rolling over in bed Ava found Mark's side of the bed empty, the blankets still pulled back from when he had gotten up. She got out of bed and wrapped a blanket around herself in order to go find Mark. She wanted to tell him how much the night before had meant to her and how much she loved him.

As Ava crossed the bedroom toward the door she could hear the television in the living room. She stepped out of the bedroom and found Mark sitting in his chair as he always did. Still smiling, she walked to the couch and sat down.

"Good morning," she said with a loving tone in her voice.

Mark said nothing and continued to stare at the screen as it flickered in front of him.

"Ya wana come sit on the couch with me?" Ava asked sweetly.

Mark continued to ignore her without looking away from the television.

Ava was so swept up in the wonderful feelings from the night before she gave no thought to the possibility Mark had reverted back to his abusive behavior. Without thinking, Ava rationalized Mark had not heard her.

"Honey?" Ava said, still in a loving tone.

"What?" Mark barked loudly at her.

Ava was surprised at his tone and froze. After a few seconds she spoke again.

"Do ya wana come sit with me?" she repeated.

"I fuckin' heard ya the first time! No, I don't wana come sit with ya!" he screamed at her, his eyes full of hate.

Ava's eyes welled with tears as the sting of his scream immediately drained all of the warm, tender feelings from her heart.

"Why are you acting like this?" Ava asked timidly.

"Actin' like what? Leave me the fuck alone!" Mark barked back at her.

"Last night-" she began.

Mark cut her off in a fit of rage and stood from his chair.

"Shut the fuck up!" he screamed as he stomped toward her. "I just wanted some fuckin' last night and I didn't wana leave the house!"

Ava did not know what to think. As Mark stomped toward her she seemingly tried to sink into the cushions of the couch as she lowered her head to protect her face. She was unable to process the feelings his words produced and the tears stung her eyes as they continued to flow.

When Mark reached Ava he leaned close to her head and continued to shout.

"What the fuck did ya expect ya little whore?" he screamed. "Did ya actually think I really love ya? Think again! Ya fuck around on me so much I just thought I should get a turn too!"

Ava felt so much fear and sadness as Mark screamed at her. She wished for death at that moment so she would no longer feel as if she were worth nothing. She had not cheated on Mark but knew there was no way to prove her innocence on any level. Without thinking she attempted to dispute his accusations.

"I haven't cheated on you!" she cried with dismay.

"Bullshit!" Mark growled back at her. "Everybody tells me what you do!"

"No!" Ava said with sadness and defeat saturating her voice.

Mark had heard enough. He reached toward the back of Ava's head and grabbed a handful of hair so he could force her to look up at him. As he held her head up he brought his face toward hers and slammed his forehead into hers with great force. Immediately, Ava felt intense pain creep through her skull and felt as if she would be sick as she squeezed her eyes tightly closed.

"Here's what you're guna do, bitch," he growled at her. "You're guna go find a guy to fuck, bring him back here, and fuck him while I hide in the closet and watch. Ya won't tell him what's goin' on and ya won't see him again afterward. After you're done I'm guna fuck ya so ya know the difference between sex with other men and sex with your husband 'cause obviously you're too fuckin' stupid to know the difference!"

Tears continued to stream down Ava's face and she tried to plead with Mark to change his mind.

"I didn't cheat on you!" she cried with sadness flooding her voice. "I don't want anyone but you!"

"Bull fuckin' shit," Mark hissed.

"I don't wana do that," Ava said with pleading sorrow in her voice.

"Too fuckin' bad, bitch! You're guna fuckin' do it or I'm guna beat the fuck outta ya!" Mark screamed.

The sudden high volume in Mark's voice made Ava jump. The grip he still had on her hair made her muscles pull against his grasp and her neck twisted slightly creating even more pain through her head and back. Mark assumed Ava was trying to escape his hold and became even more furious. He pulled his right hand back and brought it hard across her face as he held her head still with his left hand. The impact of his large hand instantly made the entire left side of her face turn bright red and her left eye begin to swell. A trickle of blood ran from the left side of her nose as Mark used the grip he had on her hair to violently throw her head into the back of the couch. He clumsily stepped backward and turned back toward his chair. He sat down heavily as he continued to shout at her.

"You're nothin'!" he shrieked. "Ya ain't good for anything except fuckin'! That's all ya know how to do ya fuckin' piece a shit! I shouldn't have married ya I should've just kept fuckin' ya!"

Ava held her face in her hands and sobbed. She could not make sense of what was happening. She rose slowly from her seat on the couch, pulling the blanket tightly around her naked body. She slowly made her way back to the bedroom to get dressed. After dressing, Ava walked slowly to the bathroom to wash her face. Her nose had stopped bleeding but blood still colored the left side of her upper lip and chin. She washed her face with cold water, gently dabbing the bloody water off of her skin as tears continued to pour from her eyes. Cautiously, she stepped from the bathroom and quietly returned to her seat on the couch. Mark paid no attention to her and looked as if nothing had happened. Suddenly, there was a knock on the door. Mark jumped from his chair and rushed to the door with the excitement of a child. He opened the door and a smile immediately spread across his face.

"Hey!" Mark said happily as he saw who was standing on the other side of the door.

"Hey!" Josh answered in the same happy tone as he stepped into the living room and closed the door behind him.

Josh looked at Ava and his face changed immediately.

"What's wrong with you?" Josh asked Ava in somewhat of a joking tone.

"Who the fuck knows," Mark quickly answered for her. "Prob'ly raggin'," he continued as he let out a convincing laugh. "She cries all the fuckin' time for nothin'."

"Oh," Josh said with doubt coloring his response as he noticed the left side of Ava's face.

Ava sat soundlessly on the couch, unable to understand how Mark could be so vicious with her and only minutes later behave as if he had no idea what caused her tears. It was as if another personality had taken over and he really did not know what had happened.

Josh sat on the opposite end of the couch from Ava and began talking with Mark as if nothing was amiss. They discussed work, people they both knew, and the upcoming pay per view event they would be watching in only a few hours. The two men laughed and joked, both ignoring Ava's presence completely. Ava sat quietly thinking to herself, her thoughts a whirlwind of confusion as she tried to understand what was happening.

"I wish my life would end," Ava thought silently to herself. "I wish I could just close my eyes and not wake up."

She began to think of different ways she could end her own life and remembered Mark's .357 Magnum in the drawer under the bed. Slowly, she rose from the couch and turned to walk toward the bedroom.

"Where ya goin'?" Mark asked with a hint of irritation in his voice.

"To lay down," Ava answered with no emotion.

Mark said nothing in response to Ava and simply returned to his conversation with Josh.

Ava walked into the bedroom and closed the door softly

behind her. She made her way to Mark's side of the bed and reached inside the drawer. Grasping the handle of the heavy handgun, she lifted it from its place in the drawer. Gently, she placed the gun on the bed and reached inside the drawer once more, this time to find the bullets for the gun. She sat down on Mark's side of the bed and opened the box. She held the partial box of bullets and looked at them intently, studying the circles in the bases of each one. The perfect empty circles, where bullets had been removed from the opaque, yellow plastic box reminded her of a beehive but she barely noticed the thought consciously. She realized, as she stared at the remaining bullets in the box, her mind was completely quiet. She wasn't worrying. She wasn't sad. She wasn't happy. Her mind was finally quiet. She then began to wonder if death would be similar, if she would finally be able to quiet her mind.

Ava was not very well practiced with guns but she had watched Mark handle the .357 enough to understand how to load and fire it. She gingerly placed the box of bullets on the bed next to the gun and shifted her attention to the weapon. She carefully picked it up and admired it. She had always thought it was beautiful. She studied the gun closely, taking in every detail. It was very heavy and cold in her small hands. The long, silver barrel shined as if it were constructed of chrome glass. The handle was made of pearl and the white swirls seemed to create an infinite nothingness in which she could lose herself forever. Though to most the gun would be considered plain, Ava thought it was the most beautiful gun she had ever seen. As she held it, turning it over and feeling its curves, she felt as if it would save her from her terrible existence by helping her to quiet her mind and escape Mark's abuse. Unconsciously, Ava clicked the loading gate open, pulled the hammer back part way then reached for the bullets. Slowly and intently, she slid a bullet into each of the six chambers and purposefully snapped the loading gate shut. She then pulled the hammer back the rest of the way so the revolver was ready to fire. As she continued to contemplate ending her life she felt a desire to feel the cold steel of the barrel against her face. She gripped the handle of the gun and gently nestled her finger next to the trigger. As she closed her eyes she brought the barrel of the gun to her face and lay it against her skin. The cold steel felt good, somehow relaxing and calming. Without thinking, she gently dragged the gun down the right side of her face until the end of the barrel was pressed gently against the under side of her chin. She sat quietly, asking God to forgive her for what she was about to do. Though Ava had not been raised in a religious home, she was well aware God considered suicide a sin. Her finger tightened on the trigger and she felt the steel give way as the trigger moved. Suddenly, the bedroom door flew open and Mark stomped into the room. The surprise of Mark bursting into the room made Ava jump and her hand tighten on the gun. Her finger squeezed the trigger and the gun fired, producing a deafening boom as the hammer slammed against the first bullet in its chamber. The slight movement of Ava's startled jump at Mark bursting into the room caused her right hand to move as well, pulling the barrel of the gun away from the under side of her chin. As the gun fired the bullet narrowly missed Ava's face and lodged into the ceiling of the bedroom. Ava looked at Mark with a calmness about her that made the hairs on the back of his neck stand on end.

"What the fuck are ya doin', ya dumb bitch?" Mark screamed at her.

The adrenaline which had begun pumping through Ava's body when the gun had fired immediately began to slow and she suddenly felt as if the gun in her hand weighed a hundred pounds. She dropped her hand, still clutching the revolver, to the surface of the bed. Mark stomped toward her and forcefully took the gun from her. He noticed her grip on the gun was remarkably strong and it took a great deal of effort for him to pry it from her hand. The gun shot had deafened Ava and she was completely unable to hear the words coming from Mark's throat, though she could read his lips and understood him perfectly.

"Ya wana fuckin' die?" Mark screeched at her. "Huh?"

Ava didn't answer. She simply lowered her head and closed her eyes. She didn't feel ashamed at all. She was saddened by Mark's interference in her attempt to end her own life. She felt the silence and peace of death slipping away from her and wanted so much to grasp it. Mark grabbed the box of bullets from the bed and whirled around to leave the room. Josh had gone to the store to get some beer and had not heard anything. Ultimately, the only reason Mark had entered the room when he did was to scold Ava for letting Josh see her cry. He had waited until he was sure Josh had pulled away from the house before he had gone into the bedroom. He was furious about Ava's tear-stained face because the sight of it had produced questions from Josh and Mark was forced to contrive answers. He found it easy to lie to his best friend but he was still very irritated the questions had come up at all.

Ava did not regain the ability to hear in her right ear for more than a week after the suicide attempt. For quite some time after she felt numb, unable to produce any emotional responses to anything. She ultimately felt that the numbness was the closest she would get to peace until she could finally die. Mark ordered Ava to see a counselor and badgered her until she made an appointment. He repeatedly told her she was crazy and should be institutionalized. Ava knew her mental state was unstable due to the years of abuse that had preceded her marriage to Mark, as well as the abuse she had endured while she was with him. Even though she had come so close to ending her own life at only twenty-one, something inside her began to shine through once again and she was able to push on, attending the first appointment with her counselor. Neither Mark nor Ava shared anything about the suicide attempt with anyone, but for very different reasons. Mark held his tongue for fear of someone blaming him for Ava's actions and Ava said nothing because she did not care to have the attention it would likely produce. She wanted to pull away from everyone, and simply exist in a world, completely alone.

Chapter Eleven

The day arrived for Ava to see her counselor for the first time, and before leaving the house, she conversed with Mark briefly.

"I'm guna go," Ava said flatly, unable to muster any emotion.

Mark only looked at her with an expression of contempt on his face. She walked to the door and turned the knob, but stopped and turned back to face Mark.

"I don't think we should be together anymore," Ava said, her voice thick with conviction.

"Humph," Mark scoffed, fully aware in his own mind Ava was not strong enough to leave him.

Ava remained in front of the door for a few seconds, looking at Mark's jagged expression, then turned to leave.

"If ya don't come back I'll find ya," Mark warned with a growl as she pulled the door closed.

After about an hour drive, she arrived at the counselor's office and parked the car. She felt somewhat nervous about the initial appointment and her mind continued to return to the warning Mark presented to her as she left the house. She knew he would find her if she tried to escape him. She refused to let her mind wander and think of what he would do to her if she tried to run.

She had arrived several minutes early for the appointment, so she decided to have a cigarette before going into the office. She pulled a cigarette from the pack and absent-mindedly put it in her mouth. Flicking the disposable lighter, she brought the flame up to the cigarette and drew air through it so it would ignite. She dropped the lighter back into her purse and sat back in the driver's seat of the car. The sun was very warm as it seeped through the glass of the windshield. The warmth felt good to Ava, as if something was trying to tell her everything would be alright. She wondered why Mark had not come with her to the appointment, reasoning that if he really cared for her, he would want to make sure she had made it safely. The thought quickly wafted from her mind, as she took the last few drags from the cigarette, then dropped it out the window to the ground. Looking at her watch she decided it was time to go in so she grabbed her purse, rolled the window up, pulled the keys from the ignition, and made her way to the front door of the building.

After informing the receptionist of her arrival, Ava took a seat in the small waiting room, and tried to look as if she did not need to be there. She felt as if everyone in the room could tell she had tried to shoot herself and could clearly see she and Mark were having problems. Once again, she felt as if she was less of a person, as if she did not deserve life, let alone a happy life. The years of abuse she had endured had whittled away at her self-esteem until only a shadow of confidence remained. Though she knew in her heart she was worthy of happiness, the sadness, pain, and continuous abuse throughout her life ultimately shrouded her self-worth and she was unable to find any good within herself. She still felt numb inside, as if her soul had been removed, and what remained was a vessel simply waiting to expire.

She was brought back to the present abruptly when she

heard a man's voice speaking her name. She looked up to see a man of about forty-five, with thinning hair, looking at her. He wore a warm smile on his face and his eyes seemed kind. She rose from her chair and offered a half-hearted smile in return. The man turned and walked down a short hallway to one of the doors on the left side. Opening the door, the man stood aside and gestured for Ava to enter the room. She obeyed the gestures and stepped past him.

"Please, have a seat," the man encouraged in a kind and gentle voice.

Ava took a seat in the large, purple armchair nestled in the corner of the small office. The man sat in an office chair adjacent to her and promptly picked up a note pad and pen. Turning to face her, the man spoke.

"Hi, Ava," he said, "I'm Dr. Fox."

Ava made a weak attempt to smile and said nothing. She felt as though she wanted to cry but fought it.

"What brings you here today?" Dr. Fox asked kindly.

"My husband made me come," she replied.

"Oh?" he said with curiosity in his voice.

"I tried to shoot myself, and he told me I was crazy, so here I am," she said matter-of-factly.

Dr. Fox looked at Ava intently, as a concerned expression washed over his face. He did all he could to mask his emotional disquiet, but she could see it clearly enough.

"Why did you try to shoot yourself?" he asked gently.

"Just can't take it anymore," she answered soberly.

"You can't take what anymore, Ava?" he asked.

"Everything," she answered as she brought her hand to her forehead. She could feel the tears burning her eyes and knew she would not be able to hold them in much longer.

"Tell me about your marriage," Dr. Fox said.

"Well," Ava began, "we've been married for a few years and things have gone to shit already."

"How so?" Dr. Fox inquired.

Ava proceeded to explain her relationship with Mark, in detail, including the many accusations of infidelity as well as the physical abuse and the way Mark spoke to her on a regular basis. Dr. Fox listened attentively to everything Ava told him, and observed her body language and facial expressions as well. He was able to conclude that everything Ava shared was truthful and she was, indeed, being severely abused.

"He even told me he wants me to go find a guy to bring home and have sex with so he can hide in the closet and watch," Ava continued, shame filling her voice. "Said if I don't he'll beat me. I told him I don't think we should be together anymore but I'm afraid if I leave he'll find me. He even told me that today when I left to come here."

After listening to her story Dr. Fox looked at Ava as if she had just shared devastating news about someone in his own family. Though still maintaining his professional composure, he was unable to mask the expression of the fear he felt for her.

"You need to get out of there," Dr. Fox said with concern flooding his voice. Though it was unprofessional to blatantly offer advice to a client, he was unable to keep the words from flooding out of his mouth.

Ava looked at him with inquisitive eyes and felt a spark of confidence deep inside her heart.

"No one should have to endure the things you are going through," he continued, clearly afraid for her.

Ava eyes dropped to the floor in front of her feet and she studied the light beige carpet. A smirk spread across her lips as her eyes lifted to meet Dr. Fox's concerned gaze. She could see the question forming in his mind from the expression on his face and decided to answer before he had a chance to ask it.

"Ya know, it's funny…" Ava said.

What's that?" Dr. Fox asked.

"Mark sent me here 'cause he said I'm crazy and said you would tell me to stay with him 'cause there's no way I can make it on my own," she answered thoughtfully.

"On the contrary," he began, somewhat offended, "I don't think you'll make it if you do stay with him."

Ava looked at Dr. Fox with an expression of curiosity as tears quietly ran down her face.

"You said you sleep much of the time you are at home, correct?" he asked, remembering the description of her daily routine.

Ava nodded her head slightly.

"I believe you are sleeping so much because you are trying to escape your situation," he continued. "And, I truly believe if you continue your life with Mark, eventually, you won't wake up."

Ava nodded her head again in agreement.

"Every day I hope I don't wake up," she said as her eyes dropped to the floor once more.

"Do you really want that?" he asked softly.

She shrugged her shoulders and fresh, hot tears replaced the ones that had slowed.

"I just don't know what else to do," she said, as she tried to keep her voice from reflecting her desperation.

"Escape," Dr. Fox said, offering a comforting smile. "You are strong enough and you are smart enough."

Ava smiled faintly and nodded her head. She knew she could make it on her own, but had ultimately lost the will to try. Throughout her life it seemed as if she was always forced to simply survive and the effort it took to do so clouded her vision of what a future without abuse might hold for her.

"Looks like our time is up for today," Dr. Fox said

apologetically, clearly unsure of whether or not Ava would be able to salvage her life.

Ava stood from her seat and made her way to the door as she thanked Dr. Fox for his time. She left the office without setting up another appointment and drove home. When she pulled up in front of the house she turned the ignition off and walked to the front door. As she opened the door she heard the same familiar sound of the television and immediately saw Mark sitting in his chair. He wore a smug smile and watched her closely as she made her way to the couch and sat down.

"So?" Mark asked with a tone of arrogance.

"So, what?" Ava answered without looking at him.

"What did he say?" he asked, staring at her. Without giving her a chance to respond, he continued condescendingly, "He told you you're a nut job, right? He told ya you're fuckin' crazy if ya think you're guna leave me, right? Yeah, that's what I fuckin' thought, ya dumb bitch."

"He said I should get the fuck outta here," she answered, in a matter-of-fact tone, still not meeting his gaze,

"Bullshit," Mark replied, shaking his head. "No counselor would ever say somethin' like that."

She knew he would not believe her, no matter what she said, so she chose not to continue the conversation. Mark remained silent, staring at the television for quite some time before he decided to speak again.

"So, ya guna go find a guy to fuck tonight?" he said, once again looking directly at Ava.

She hated what Mark was suggesting and tried to ignore him.

"It's Friday, and ya don't have to work tomorrow, why not?" he continued, trying to get her to agree as he wore a sadistic smile on his face.

She looked at him and shook her head in disgust.

"I haven't cheated on you and I'm not guna," she said with conviction as she looked back at the television.

"But ya have my permission so it ain't cheatin'," he argued, as the creepy smile on his face spread even further.

Ava continued to stare at the television but she could still see him in her peripheral vision. She just wanted him to drop it. Mark continued to stare at her and she knew he wasn't finished. An evil chuckle came from deep in his throat as he rose from his chair and walked toward her. He sat on the couch next to her and leaned forward so she could no longer see the television screen. His eyes seemed to hold a strange and terrible soft tenderness within them and the smile on his face transformed, suggesting he may have changed his mind. He gently placed his right hand on her leg as he began to speak.

"If ya don't go out and find a guy to fuck I'll beat your fuckin' head in," he said in a gentle and tender voice, creating an avalanche of confusion and fear within Ava's mind.

The confusion created by the conflict between his body language, facial expression, tone of voice, and the words he had just uttered prompted an innate survival response to protect herself. It was as if she hadn't heard the actual words he had said. Everything about the way he was presenting himself, including his voice, suggested love and understanding but the words he spoke were dark and dreadful. The entire interaction was enough to make her want to run away from him and never look back. Her mind was conflicted between the opposing reactions the differing subtleties produced. She sat quietly, fully aware Mark was completely serious in his threat. She hated the idea of being beaten and wondered if he would stop before he killed her.

"Bring him back here, but call me when you're on your way so I can watch for ya. Ya know where I'll be when ya fuck him in our bed," he said, as the expression on his face changed to one of wicked amusement.

Ava tried to keep from thinking about the horrible thing Mark wanted her to do. She suddenly felt as if she must get out of the house and put distance between herself and her husband. The fear she felt inside her heart prompted her to respond.

"Fine," Ava answered. "I'll be back later."

Excitement seemed to wash over Mark's face but a look of jealous anger colored the excitement and created an expression she had never seen before. She left the house and got into her car. She had no intention of sleeping with anyone that night. She simply wanted to escape Mark, if only for a few hours. She would tell him she couldn't find anyone she liked and maybe he would eventually forget about the entire absurd thing. In the back of her mind, however, she knew he would not forget and she would be forced to either do what he ordered or face a horrific beating. She pulled away from the house and headed for Ropschon. She had no idea where she was going but kept driving, none the less.

Ava thought about calling a few of her friends, but decided not to impose on them, rationalizing she did not want to make her problems anyone else's. She wondered if she should call Lilli, but chose not to, since Lilli had just started a new relationship and seemed to be happy. She knew if Lilli was aware of her situation she would worry and her happiness would be disrupted. Emma was too far away, and she couldn't go to Able, simply because Able and Mark had become such close friends. She found herself simply driving around Ropschon, with no particular destination, wasting time. As she drove through the city she let her mind wander and thought about her marriage to Mark. She knew she could kill herself but something inside her continued to warn her of the divine consequences. She would go to hell if she took her own life. Though she knew little of religion, she believed in her heart there was a God and He would save her, though she was still uncertain how long her life would last. Her thoughts continued as she drove and she felt a spark of hope when she consciously thought about leaving Mark. Recalling Dr. Fox's words helped her begin to put things into perspective. The strength she found within the doctor's encouragement, helped her salvage what little self-respect she had left. She purposefully turned the car toward Nathia and drove home with a renewed sense of self and a feeling of confidence she had not felt in so very long.

Often, Ava felt as if the way Mark treated her may somehow be her fault but she could never determine what she had done, exactly, to make him behave the way he did. Each time, she would abandon the effort of trying to pinpoint the reason and simply envelop herself in the illusory realization that she must be to blame, since Alex had beaten her too. Her mind would then wander back to the beatings she had received from Sonya and she felt even more to blame for the horrible situations in which she repeatedly seemed to find herself. Though her mind continued to vindicate the idea she was ultimately to blame, her heart seemed to dispute the assertion. She couldn't help but find flaw in the idea she had been the cause of the pain that had befallen her throughout her life.

She pulled up in front of the house she and Mark shared and turned the ignition off. She sat quietly in the driver's seat and looked at the house. Soft light spilled from the living room windows, creating the appearance of a welcoming home. She knew, however, what awaited her was anything but welcoming and she wished she could simply close her eyes and fast forward through time, to a moment in the future when she would no longer have to fear going home. It was no use. She knew she had to face Mark. She made her way to the house and walked inside, ready for whatever he would do to her. As she stepped through the door Mark peered at her with a startled expression, as if wondering why she had not called as he had instructed her. With no words, Ava took her seat on the couch and attempted to behave as if she were not upset.

"So?" Mark said, clearly questioning her.

"Didn't find anybody," Ava answered flatly.

"Did ya look?" he asked skeptically.

"Not really," she answered without thinking.

She was tired of being afraid and felt if she lied to him about looking for another man to sleep with the lie would only create more fear. She simply wanted to be done with the entire thing and if he was going to beat her for it she hoped he would just beat her to death.

"I told ya to find a guy to fuck," he snapped.

"Sorry, she said, "I'm not doin' that."

"Then I'm guna beat you're fuckin' head in. I thought I was pretty fuckin' clear about that before ya left," he said in the same eerily calm tone he had used before.

"Then beat my fuckin' head in," Ava snapped back at him with anger in her eyes as she looked directly at him. "I don't fuckin' care anymore! I'm sick of this shit and I'm not guna be here long anyway so ya better do it while ya have the chance!"

A look of betrayal, combined with confusion, washed over Mark's face as the realization of her words sunk into his conscious mind.

"What the fuck do ya mean you're not guna be here long?" he barked, his voice getting louder with each word. "What are ya guna do, fuckin' kill yourself? Ya tried that, remember, ya couldn't do it!" he scoffed. "Ya fuckin' chickened out and couldn't go through with it, ya fuckin' coward!"

Ava was well aware of what she had tried to do and she

knew exactly why she wasn't able to shoot herself. It had nothing to do with an inability to go through with it. Mark had simply walked into the bedroom and surprised her and her natural reflexes had jerked the gun away from its original target. Mark assumed her failed attempt suggested she was unable to take her own life, due to an inner weakness, but his assumption was ultimately mistaken. In reality, had he waited another ten seconds to burst through the bedroom door, he would have found Ava dead on his side of the bed. She had felt no fear when the barrel of the revolver was pressed into the soft tissue between her chin and throat and miraculously, even though she was facing a violent assault, she felt no fear as she refused to follow Mark's sexually deviant orders.

Mark had risen from his chair and, in response, Ava stood as well. She was tired of being his punching bag and felt as if she needed to take a stand and defend herself, even if the attempt was futile. He outweighed her by at least one hundred forty-five pounds and was at least nine inches taller. It was as if a train was screaming toward her and she stood directly in the middle of the tracks. She stood her ground and never flinched as his large right hand wrapped around her throat and picked her up. Her feet were no longer touching the floor and she could feel the incredible pressure his hand created, suddenly finding it impossible to take a breath. Even though Mark was not an incredibly strong man, the anger he felt seemed to be driving his strength to new levels. He looked up at her as a disturbingly wicked smile spread across his face. She began to feel the urgent need to breathe and she instinctively began to try to pry his hand from around her throat. Silent tears began to fall from the corners of her eyes, streaming down both sides of her face. She did not necessarily want to die, she just wanted to be free from Mark's abusive treatment as well as escape the memories of her past which continued to haunt her. She felt

Mark's hand tightening around her neck and realized she had no chance of forcing him to release her. She surrendered to the idea that her life would be over in the blink of an eye and stopped struggling. Relaxing her body, she closed her eyes and waited for death to come. Finally, she would be free from everything.

"Please God, please, save me," she prayed, waiting for her soul to be lifted up and her consciousness to end.

All at once Mark let out a loud bellow that seamed to echo through the house. He wanted so much to end Ava's life. She had not turned out to be the woman he thought she would be and it infuriated him. He wanted a wife who would be obedient, not one who wanted to be an individual. He wanted to be able to control every facet of the relationship but Ava seemed to want to have a voice. He felt his hand tighten around her neck and knew she would be dead soon. He hated her for thinking she deserved to have an opinion about anything.

"I'm the man and I deserve to control her. Fuck you, bitch! Fuck you!" Mark thought to himself as he watched his wife struggle to breathe.

Soon, he felt her body relax and he wondered if he had, indeed, killed her. Her face held no expression and she looked as if she were asleep as he held her in the air. Suddenly, an overwhelming urge to let go of her washed over him. In a fraction of a second he reacted and had no time to willfully validate it. He began to release the grip on his wife's throat, as if to lower her gently to the floor, but his anger took over once again just as suddenly as it had been interrupted. With all the strength he could muster he hurled Ava's limp body toward the wall only about four feet away. The back of her head was the first to make contact with the sheetrock covering the wall, her lower back immediately following, the impact of each producing a distinct noise, before she fell to the floor in a rumpled pile.

Ava heard the garish bellow coming from Mark's throat and felt herself sailing through the air. As her head struck the wall she saw thousands of bright, white points of light behind her closed eyelids and felt sharp, shooting pain throughout her head. As her lower back made contact with the wall a surge of excruciating pain ran through her legs and up her back. Even though it took less than two seconds for Mark to throw her against the wall, it felt to Ava as if it had all happened in slow motion. She found herself in a heap on the floor, barely conscious, and gasping for air. She could not move and the terrible pain she felt from the impact with the wall proved to be more powerful than her will to move her body. She remained in the disheveled heap in which she had landed and finally lost consciousness.

Mark stood over Ava and watched her closely to see if she was still breathing. He could make out only faint movements that suggested she was still alive and he found himself wanting to kick her. Instead, he turned and walked to his chair, picking up the television remote as he flopped down hard on the seat. He felt exhausted. He found the channel he wanted, flipped the foot rest of the chair out, lit a cigarette, and took a drink of the soda sitting on the end table next to him. Calmly, he smoked his cigarette as he gazed at the screen. When he was finished smoking he crushed out the cigarette in the ashtray and closed his eyes. Within minutes, he was sound asleep, a feeling of calming relaxation throughout his body. His last thought, before drifting into a remorseless slumber, was a cognizant hope that Ava would never regain consciousness.

Ava's eyes fluttered open and she was immediately aware of the excruciating pain in her back and legs, as well as the throbbing ache that seemed to resonate in the back of her head. Slowly, she attempted to move, every muscle in her body screaming with agony. The memories of the event which left her on the floor flooded back into her mind and fear gripped her heart as she cautiously tried to figure out where Mark had gone. The living room was dark, the only light coming from the television program flickering on the screen. She was unable to concentrate on the dialog of the actors on the program as she struggled to bring herself into a sitting position. The room seemed to spin slightly as she squinted her eyes in an attempt to determine whether or not Mark was in the room. As the program went to a commercial, the light from the screen increased for a moment, and she was able to make out Mark's contour as he slept in his chair. She wanted so much to leave at that very moment and the fear, shame, and anger she felt seemed to drive her to escape. She repositioned herself so she was on her hands and knees as she prepared to pull herself to a standing position. She struggled to stand but her back felt as if it had been broken. The muscles in her legs would not obey the commands of her mind and she was unable to move either of them enough to support her own frame. She refused to give up and drug herself toward the end of the couch in order to use it to pull herself up. Again, her legs refused to cooperate. After wrestling to stand for several minutes, exhaustion overtook her and she could no longer struggle. As gently as she could, she lowered herself to the floor and laid on her back. She squeezed her eyes tightly closed as tears began to sting her eyes once again. Silently, she laid on the floor and sobbed as she felt the tragic defeat of the horrific situation encase her. Her head continued to pound, and with no warning, she lost consciousness once again as her head rolled limply to the side.

Though Ava remained unconscious for several hours her tears continued to fall as she unconsciously cried in her sleep. Images of the brutal encounter she had endured continued to waft through her subconscious and she felt as though it was happening all over again. Mark awoke as the sun peeked through the open blinds hanging in the picture window of the living room. He stretched and yawned as his mind recaptured the events of the night before. He lazily turned his head in the direction he had left Ava to die and noticed she had moved at some point in the night. He realized she must still be alive, and his eyes immediately found her on the floor, next to the end of the couch. He had to use the bathroom so he forcefully folded the foot rest back into the chair and stood up. He reached for his cigarettes and pulled one from the pack before heading to the bathroom. After lighting it, he walked toward Ava, and stopped next to her head. Taking a long drag from the cigarette, he inhaled the smoke deep into his lungs. He stared at Ava's face as he released the smoke through his nostrils. He knew he had to wake her up, in case someone stopped to visit. He didn't want to explain why she was lying on the floor. He had not taken his cowboy boots off before he had fallen asleep, his anger creating an adrenaline rush which had robbed him of his energy, before he could even think about removing the boots from his feet. He drew his right foot back and brought it forward with determined force. Ava's head was facing away from him as she lay on her back. The pointed toe of his boot connected with the back of her head, near the base of her skull. The impact abruptly brought Ava back to consciousness and her eyes snapped open as she felt the force of the boot against the back of her head.

"Get up!" Mark screamed at her.

She tried to roll away from him and her muscles finally cooperated with her. Though she was riddled with pain she slowly lifted herself to a standing position, with the support of the couch.

"Go to bed," Mark snarled, "ya lazy bitch!"

Without dispute, she turned slowly and made her way to the bedroom. Every muscle in her body ached, as if she had been trampled by elephants. As she reached the bed she was no longer able to stand. Before she was able to purposefully lie down, she once again lost consciousness and limply fell to the mattress on her stomach, her right leg still hanging off the side of the bed. She lay there, virtually lifeless, for the rest of the day.

Over the next few days Mark made no effort to check on Ava, nor did he care about how she was doing. She remained in the bedroom, exiting only to visit the bathroom. She was due to return to work on Monday, however, she was still too sore to move well so she called in sick. Mark went to work and Ava was able to exist in the house without fear, at least for part of the day. She hadn't eaten since the day before Mark had attacked her and she felt the weakness her hunger was causing. As she lay in bed, she again began to wish for death to overtake her, but the peacefulness she imagined would accompany death never came.

Later that night, Ava finally felt as if she would be able to function, at least with partial normality. She chose to remain in the bedroom, however, in an attempt to avoid any further attacks. By the next morning she was determined to return to work, if for no other reason than to escape the looming threat of what Mark may do next. During her lunch break from her physically demanding job, she exited the factory to have a cigarette. She usually liked to join her coworkers who also smoked, but this time she just wanted to be alone. Instead of exiting the building through the door she normally did, she decided to go to a side of the building not usually inhabited by others who took break outside. There, sitting alone, she found another coworker, Leo, who apparently took his breaks alone as well.

"Hey, Ava," Leo said in a surprised and jovial tone.

"Hey, Leo," she responded with no emotion.

"Are you okay?" he asked softly.

Ava shrugged her shoulders slightly and looked down at the ground as she took a long drag from her cigarette.

"You look upset," he continued, trying to get her to share her troubles.

"Ah, it's no big deal," she said, still not willing to look at him.

They had worked together long enough, and spoken to each other often enough, that Leo felt as if he knew her pretty well. He had always had a secret interest in Ava and had paid very close attention to her mannerisms, personality, and habits as he attempted to learn more about her. He knew she was married and had heard scuttle from other people at work about suspected problems in the marriage. He felt a deep sympathy for her as he began to realize she was doing all she could to hide her emotions.

"I don't believe you," Leo said in a gentle tone.

Ava's eyes lifted to meet his and he could see the tears welling as she tried to fight them.

"Mark tried to kill me Saturday night," Ava blurted without thinking.

"Oh my God!" Leo exclaimed, clearly shocked by her words. "That is a big deal, Ava!"

She closed her eyes as her tears overtook her effort to hold them back. Leo immediately stood and stepped toward her, putting his arms around her and pulling her close in an effort to console her. She fought the tears back and after only a few seconds pulled herself away from him.

"I can't..." she said as she wiped the tears from her face.

"You can't what?" he said with concern in his voice.

"I can't keep doing this," she answered. "He's guna kill me."

"If you need a place to go you're welcome to stay at my place," Leo offered with complete innocence. "No strings attached."

Ava slightly nodded her head and offered a weak smile to convey her gratitude. She had no intention of going to Leo's house but the offer helped her feel a little better. Lunch time ended and they returned to their obligations. Ava's mind reeled throughout the rest of her shift as she tried to decide how and when she would make her escape from Mark.

Over the next few months Ava and Leo continued to take lunch together and he did all he could to help her talk through her difficulties. Ava began to feel a closeness to Leo that seemed to help her escape the constant upset that plagued her heart and mind. She desperately wanted to end her marriage to Mark and it seemed Leo's support facilitated her courage and confidence to do so. Mark continued to accuse Ava of cheating, but she had given up on trying to dispute his allegations. Instead of wasting her energy on finding ways to defend her innocence, she concentrated on developing a plan so she would be ready, when the time was right, to make her escape. She knew Mark would do everything he could to keep her under his control and she was well aware she would need to orchestrate her escape with careful diligence. Mark paid very close attention to the bank account they shared, and even though the factory in which he worked had closed down and he had not put forth an effort to find another job, he felt as if all of Ava's income was his to do with what he wished. Mark had even begun to check the odometer in Ava's car each day when she would arrive home from work. In addition, he documented the hours in which she claimed to be working and compared his calculations with each paycheck she brought home. Numerous times, he accused her of lying to him about where she had been, and declared she was also lying about the number of hours she claimed to work. Each time Mark felt Ava had lied to him she received a brutal beating, typically leaving her unconscious and unable to defend herself. Mark also repeatedly attempted to force Ava to fulfill his fantasy of allowing him to watch from the closet as she had sex with another man. She persistently refused and each time she was severely beaten. Ultimately, Mark was able to keep Ava subdued by continually keeping her in pain and unable to escape.

Lilli had suspicions that Ava was being abused and tried repeatedly to urge her to reveal the details of the situation. In an effort to recruit help in coaxing Ava to disclose what was happening, Lilli spoke to Emma about the situation in depth. As Lilli and Emma conversed about the circumstances, they both realized they had witnessed interactions between Ava and Mark that suggested the abuse was severe. Though Mark would never raise his hand to Ava in the presence of any of her family members, the nuances of the interactions seemed to shriek of abusive behavior when no one else was around. Lilli had even tried to speak with Sonya about the situation but quickly realized she was completely engulfed in her own plans to move to another state to be closer to one of her sisters. Ava continued to be vague about the abuse to Lilli and Emma because she did not want either of them to have to worry. The close friendship between Mark and Able seemed to interfere with any indication of the abuse she endured, and Ava knew Able would not believe her even if she wanted to tell him, so she chose not to mention anything. Lilli tried to talk with Able about Ava's situation, but he only made excuses for Mark, citing the many times Mark had claimed Ava had been unfaithful. Lilli knew Able could not be reasoned with and dropped the subject almost as quickly as she had brought it up.

On a Friday evening, early in July of 2002, the night came when Ava was finally able to break free from Mark's fierce control. With Leo's connections, Ava had been able to secure an apartment in Ropschon, without a deposit, since her circumstances made a financial transaction impossible to conceal. The company for which she worked stopped production every year during the week of Independence Day, so Ava had plenty of time to execute her plan without the threat of missing work. She felt confident she would be able to break free, though she knew Mark would not take the news well. After she arrived home from work she took a shower and gathered her clothes, packing them into her car along with some other essentials, before Mark returned home from a visit at his parents' house in a neighboring town. After completing the task, she sat on the couch and calmly awaited Mark's return. She thought about how the circumstances seemed to be working in her favor. She had a week off of work, an apartment already waiting for her, and Mark's physical attacks had not been bad enough to render her unable to function in the recent days. Though he had beaten her within the last few days, she had promised him she would finally go find a man to bring home as soon as the weekend arrived, in an attempt to avoid being debilitated. Ultimately, she knew the smartest thing to do would be to leave without telling Mark, but she felt as if leaving that way would only confirm his negative idea of her. She did not know why she cared so much about his perception of her but she refused to walk away without telling him she would not return.

Ava heard Mark's truck come to a stop in front of the house. She listened as the engine quieted and the driver's door slammed shut. She could feel a confusing combination of emotions begin to boil in heart, though no doubt entered her mind. The realization she may not be able to leave, if Mark beat her severely enough, suddenly settled in the front of her mind and she began to regret wanting to tell him she was leaving. Even though fear had begun to grip her heart, she felt as if she must take a stand and be outspoken about her decision, though in reality the fledgling attempt at honor held the potential to be fatal. Mark entered the house and immediately flopped into his chair without acknowledging Ava's presence. He lit a cigarette and flipped the television on, continuing to ignore her. She gathered her courage and took a breath to speak.

"I'm leaving," she began.

Mark continued to stare at the television screen and said nothing as he took a long drag from his cigarette. She stood and began to walk toward the door. Mark's eyes quickly darted toward her and he noticed she had showered and changed clothes.

"Goin' to find a guy?" Mark asked calmly. "Don't forget to call me when you're on your way back."

Ava stopped about three feet from the front door and turned back to face Mark.

"No, I'm not goin' to find a guy," she said coolly. "What you want me to do is disgusting and I'm not guna."

Mark's face took on an expression of disdain as he stared at Ava.

"Then where the fuck do ya think you're goin'?" he asked in a demanding but matter-or-fact tone.

"I told ya, I'm leavin'," she answered, holding his gaze.

"Huh," Mark responded thoughtfully, as if he were trying to understand her simple statement.

Ava turned toward the door once again. As she took a step forward she heard the unmistakable sound of the footrest of Mark's chair slam back underneath.

"Oh, you're leavin' me?" Mark said, clearly angry and surprised at the turn of events. "Do ya think ya can fuckin' survive without me?" he continued, his voice erupting with anger.

Ava froze and closed her eyes. She feared what would happen next, but her drive to survive seemed to keep her from getting lost in the immeasurable fright which always accompanied his cruel words, and her anticipation of the usual physical attack. She took another step toward the door as the booming sound of Mark stomping toward her filled her ears. She grasped for the door, but before she could reach it, Mark was upon her. He grabbed her arms and spun her around, forcing her lower back to crash into the doorknob. She winced in pain, almost losing her balance, but was able to support herself against the wall and keep from falling to the floor. He leaned toward her and touched his nose to hers. She could feel his breath on her face and dread began to grip her. His hand slipped around her throat, and she could feel the pressure beginning to cut off her air supply, once again. She knew she had to do something quickly or she would not have a chance. Still pinned against the wall, Ava wriggled to her left until her right shoulder was off of the surface of the steel door, but Mark did not move at all. As she continued to gasp for air her right hand found the doorknob and twisted it. With a burst of strength she pulled the door open. As the heavy, steel door swung inward it connected with Mark's forehead, producing a deep, solid thud. With stunned surprise he immediately released his grip on her throat and brought both of his hands to the front of his own head. The force of the blow from the door caused him to lose his balance, and fall backward, landing on the floor. In the instant Mark's hands left her throat, she desperately sucked air into her lungs. She was able to breathe once again, and as she panted, she watched as Mark toppled backward. Just as quickly as he had hit the floor, he scrambled to get back up, now even more furious than he had ever been before. Without waiting to see what would happen next, she slipped through the opening and pushed on the small handle of the storm door to open it. She was already out the door and sprinting toward her car by the time Mark was able to stand. She got in, her hands shaking furiously as she tried to put the key in the ignition. Finally, the key slipped into the slot, and the engine roared to life. Mark pursued her but immediately realized the blow he had taken from the door had given her the few seconds she needed to get away. She glanced back toward the house in time to see Mark burst through the storm door and onto the sidewalk. He knew he would never be able to stop her but in his state of manic rage he continued toward the car. Shoving the car in drive, she stomped on the gas pedal and tore away from the house. Glancing back toward Mark, she noticed he had finally stopped chasing her. He stood as still as a statue pointing at her, and she knew it was far from over.

As Ava's car rounded the corner and disappeared from sight, Mark's hand slowly dropped back to his side as he stood on the sidewalk panting in anger and pain. He turned around and went back into the house, making his way to his chair. Sitting down heavily, he lit a cigarette and looked out the window. He could not believe Ava had left him. Tears began to well in his eyes as he sat silently in the living room with only the sound of the television to keep him company.

Ava continued to tremble as she drove to Ropschon, her eyes repeatedly searching the rearview mirror, as she anticipated the reflection of Mark's truck on the road behind her. She sped toward Leo's house so she could pick up her apartment keys but realized Mark knew where Leo's house was. She immediately decided to call Leo on her cell phone. She dialed the number and waited for him to answer.

"Hello?" Leo said, completely aware Ava should be on her way to Ropschon by then.

"Leo," Ava said with an urgent tone, "I don't think I should come to your house. Mark doesn't know where my apartment is so I think it'll be safer if ya meet me there with the keys."

"Okay," Leo answered. "When will you be there?"

"I'm on my way now," she said. "Should be there in about ten minutes."

"Okay, I'll head over there now," Leo said quickly, the urgency in Ava's voice producing alarm in his own.

"Thanks," Ava said, then ended the call.

She wanted to stay alert, and keep a watchful eye on the traffic behind her, in case Mark had decided to try to follow her. She drove directly to her apartment building and parked. Exiting the car, she locked the doors and waited for Leo to arrive. Leo's car pulled into the parking lot only a minute later and took the space next to her car. He got out of his car and locked the doors, then made his way toward Ava, as she stood in front of the building waiting for him. Without saying anything, Leo handed Ava her keys, and followed her to her apartment on the third floor. Once they were inside the apartment, Ava lowered herself to the floor in the middle of the small living room, and began to sob. Her back was throbbing from the contact with the doorknob. She continued to tremble, but more severely now, as she realized she had finally broken away from Mark. Leo sat next to her and attempted to console her. He had no idea what exactly had transpired, and chose to wait for a little time to pass before asking any questions. About thirty minutes passed before Leo noticed Ava's sobs diminishing. He continued to sit quietly next to her with his hand on her back while she cried. Finally, he decided to speak.

"Are you okay?" He asked quietly.

Ava nodded, to indicate she was okay, but he did not believe her.

"What happened?" he asked softly.

She wiped the tears from her face, took a careful breath, and recounted the events which had taken place after she had arrived home from work that day. Leo listened intently as Ava told her story, and when she had finally finished he simply hugged her, unable to think of any other way to help her. Leo remained at Ava's apartment for several hours, until he was sure she was really alright, before leaving to go to his own home. He was happy she had finally escaped Mark's abuse but knew Mark would likely continue to torment her.

After Leo left, Ava transferred her belongings from her car to the apartment, in an effort to keep her mind from wandering. She rationalized she should get everything moved before nightfall so she would not have to worry about Mark lurking in the shadows. When she had completed her task, she locked the door and tried to relax. Between getting the apartment and leaving Mark, Ava had been able to sparsely furnish her dwelling, at least enough to be comfortable. Since she did not yet own a bed, she decided to try to get some sleep on a couch she had gotten from a friend at work. After only a few minutes she drifted off to sleep, for the first time in a long time, not haunted by fearful thoughts.

At around two o'clock the next morning, Ava's cell phone rang. She had been asleep for a while, and in her groggy state, did not think about checking the screen to see the caller's number before answering the phone.

"Hello?" Ava said, her voice flooded with sleep.

"Where the fuck are ya?" Mark's voice demanded.

Ava suddenly snapped from her sleepy state and sat straight up. She felt as if he was able to look into her window, and see her in the apartment, though she was on the third floor and there was no way he possibly could. Just his voice coming through the phone made her feel as if he were intruding on her. As if his hand would reach out of the phone at any second and grab her by the throat. Just as quickly as her mind wandered, it came back to reality and she began to feel safe again, as she felt courage building inside her.

"I'm not tellin' ya," she answered calmly.

"Ya better fuckin' tell me, ya little bitch!" Mark exclaimed, clearly frustrated and angry about not being able to find her. "If I find ya on my own I'm guna fuckin' kill ya!"

Ava said nothing for a few seconds, as she attempted to keep her cool, and not let Mark gain the upper hand in the conversation.

"Don't call me anymore," she said with conviction. "We're done."

"I'm guna find ya, bitch, and I'm guna fuckin' kill ya!" he growled into the phone.

Ava took the cell phone away from her ear and ended the call. She felt freer than she had in a long time and knew she did not have to keep talking to Mark. Setting the phone down on the floor next to the couch, she tried to return to sleep, but struggled. Finally, she once again drifted off to sleep, only to be disturbed again by the ringing of her cell phone, within the next thirty minutes.

Over the course of the next fourteen hours, Mark placed seventy-two calls to Ava's cell phone, each time leaving messages that involved threats on her life, as well as Leo's life. Leo had once been a deputy, based in Ropschon, but had been forced to quit due to a personal vendetta the sheriff held against him. Since Ava and Leo had become close friends, and Leo was aware of the laws, he encouraged her to file a no-contact order against Mark in an effort to protect her. A few days after the calls had finally stopped, Leo accompanied her to the courthouse to file for the no-contact order. It took very little time for the judge to determine, Mark had not done enough to have a no-contact order filed against him, in spite of the multiple threatening messages left on Ava's cell phone.

Mark continued to harass Ava by phone, continually calling her and leaving messages. On a few occasions he even called from different numbers in an attempt to trick her into answering. Ava and Leo spent more and more time together, quickly developing a romantic relationship. She felt safe with Leo, as if he would do anything to protect her. The safety she felt when she was with him was unlike anything she had ever felt before. At no time in her life had any man made her feel safe and she was swept away by the new and warm feeling. Leo put forth an exceptional effort to win Ava's affections, taking her out on dinner dates, bringing her flowers, and joining her whenever she went to play pool. It seemed she had finally found a man, who would love her for who she was, instead of trying to change her. She finally began to feel as if she may find happiness after all.

Chapter Twelve

Leo's protective behavior in the relationship was something Ava had never experienced. Whenever she was with him, for the first time in her life, she felt truly safe. They spent every moment they could together and enjoyed one another's company completely. Leo fully supported Ava's strive to play pool and accompanied her to league every night she played. Though Leo was not a smoker, he did not outwardly judge Ava for smoking, and she never smoked in his house when the couple spent time there. It seemed as if Ava was finally destined to have a life full of love, safety, and happiness. Mark continued to verbally harass her, but she felt as if he could no longer hurt her. His threats still filled her heart with dread, but Leo's company seemed to generate a fog around the fear, giving Ava the ability to push it to the back of her mind.

The shut down week Ava and Leo had enjoyed came to an end and it was finally time to return to work. Leo had taken a job, within the company, as a security guard and Ava continued in her position as a welder. Since Leo had taken the security position, he was scheduled to arrive at work at five o'clock in the morning, whereas Ava was not scheduled to start her shift until seven o'clock. Ava had gotten up at six o'clock and began getting ready for work. After she showered and dressed she went outside to smoke a cigarette. She stood on the tiny balcony at the back of her apartment while she enjoyed the sounds of the early morning. From inside the kitchen, she heard her cell phone ring, and thought it strange someone would call her so early. She walked into the apartment and looked at the screen of her phone to see the number of the caller. She expected to see Mark's number, or a number she did not recognize, however, this time it was Leo's number that appeared on the screen. Ava answered the call and greeted Leo in a joyful tone.

"Hello?" Ava said happily.

"Ava, you need to get to work," Leo began, his voice shaky. "Come in through the office. Don't come in through the employee entrance."

"What's goin' on?" She said, her voice clearly displaying her immediate worry and apprehension.

"I'll tell ya when ya get here. Just go straight into the conference room." Leo said gently but sternly.

"Uh, okay," Ava answered with concerned confusion. "I'll be there in a few."

"Okay, bye," Leo said.

"Bye," Ava answered, then ended the call.

Her mind began to race. Once again, fear seemed to envelop her and she began to tremble. She frantically wondered, what could possibly be going on, that would cause Leo to instruct her to go directly to the conference room. She knew the situation had to have something to do with Mark, but she had no idea what it could be. She gathered her things and left the apartment and, as she drove to the factory, her mind continued to race with no hope of figuring out what was going on. At one point, Mark had threatened to kill himself if she divorced him, but she thought it to be only an idle threat. She pulled into the employee lot and parked the car. Walking quickly to the office entrance of the building, she pushed the door open. Once inside, she made her way straight to the conference room, where she found Leo sitting at the conference table, along with her supervisor, Tim, and the general manager of the plant, Tom. Leo quickly rose from his seat and closed the door behind her as she stepped into the room.

"What's goin' on?" Ava said, concern saturating her voice as she looked at each of the men in the room.

"You better sit down, Ava," Leo said as he carefully guided her to a chair across the table from the others.

Ava sat down, and Leo took a seat in the chair next to her, as he looked at Tim and Tom. Both men gestured for Leo to speak and remained silent.

"Um," Leo began unsteadily, "Mark was here early this morning and threw pictures of you all over the parking lot."

"Okay," Ava said with uncertainty in her voice. "What pictures?"

"Nude pictures," Tim said with sympathy in his voice. "We found ninety-six copies throughout the parking lot. The wind carried some of them to the surrounding ditches, but we think we got them all," he continued, unable to meet Ava's gaze.

Ava closed her eyes and took a deep breath. She had forgotten about the pictures Mark had taken of her a few years before. He had used the fear he had instilled in her mind, combined with a superficial promise of love and happiness, to convince her to pose for the shots. Tears pushed past her closed eyelids and silently rolled down her face.

"As far as we can tell, there were only four people that actually saw them. Leo, myself, Tim, and Charlie, one of the maintenance guys," Tom said in an effort to calm Ava.

Ava remained silent, and simply sat motionless, a feeling of helpless guilt and drowning embarrassment flooding her mind.

"Are you okay, Ava?" Tim asked softly.

Ava nodded slightly then dropped her head as shame washed over her. She cried silently for a few minutes while Leo, Tim, and Tom conversed about the situation. Finally, Ava raised her head and spoke.

"Where are they?" Ava asked in a sober and emotionless tone as she tried to regain her composure.

"Here," Tom said, gesturing toward a thick file folder lying on the table.

"I would like to take them," Ava said as she stared at the folder.

"Sure, they're all yours," Tom answered, as he slid the folder across the table toward her.

She reached for the folder and gently picked it up. The rumpled pages inside made the folder appear much thicker than it really was. Ava hugged the folder close to her chest, unwilling to let anyone else have a glimpse. She wondered how Mark could do such a thing. Her heart pounded as she continued to weep silently, and found herself thinking about the beatings she had received from him over the years. She knew the pain from the horrendous beatings could never compare to the pain she felt at that moment as she desperately tried to maintain her composure. Leo touched her shoulder gently, trying to offer compassion, but at the same time trying to remain professional.

"You can take a few days off if you want to," Tom said. "Under the circumstances it would be understandable."

Ava sat quietly for a few seconds, closely studying the random woodgrain pattern of the table top, then looked at Tom as unwavering determination began to intrude upon her tears.

"No, thanks," Ava said, trying to keep her voice from

faltering. "If I go home it'll only prove I'm weak. I'm not weak. I'll stay and work."

Tom, Tim, and Leo silently looked at one another, with admiration veiling their expressions of skepticism. Ava slowly rose from her chair and walked toward the door of the conference room.

"If you need anything, let one of us know," Tom said in an effort to help Ava feel confident with her decision to work.

"Thanks," Ava said, trying to convey her gratitude without diluting her determination.

The three men rose from their chairs as well, unable to help following Ava's courageous example. After depositing the photographs under the driver's seat in her locked car, she walked back through the office to the door leading to the factory, and looked through the window. She watched, as people scurried about doing their jobs, and collected herself in preparation to walk out onto the production floor. Her mind seemed to go blank as she turned the knob and pulled the door open. The familiar sounds of the factory filled her ears as she walked toward her work area. Some of her coworkers stopped and stared as she walked by, but she paid little attention to them. She wasn't sure if they were staring because they were impressed by her presence, or because they were secretly laughing at her. Tom had explained that the security system had not yet been installed so no images of the act were captured, however, he was able to speak with one of the employees who arrived very early each morning, and found Mark must have driven through the parking lot before five o'clock that morning. Ava continued to her work area and proceeded to do her job. The three men who worked directly with her seemed to be sympathetic, and did not say anything belittling. To Ava's surprise, the majority of the workers in the factory chose to ignore the situation involving the photographs and treated Ava as they always had, at least to her face. A few days after the incident, some of the men who worked on the line tried to get under her skin by making fun of her and shouting derogatory comments, but she was able to hold her head high and ignore them. The week finally came to an end and Ava was able to put the entire incident behind her. Though time seemed to be helping to fade the incident, it sat just at the back of her mind along with all of the other horrible, embarrassing, and painful events of her past, ready to rush into her consciousness at a moment's notice.

Ava and Leo had sought legal assistance regarding the photographs scattered over the parking lot. Combined with their previous complaint regarding the numerous phone calls, the police were finally able to arrest Mark. He was charged with stalking, harassment, and extortion. With that, Ava was finally able to successfully request a no-contact order that was issued for a three year duration. The legal restraint on Mark helped Ava feel a little safer but she knew, in reality, it was merely a piece of paper.

Within the next few months, plans were made for Ava to move into Leo's house, and the day finally came for the move to ensue. It took the couple less than a day to move all of Ava's belongings and the rest of the day was spent unpacking. Leo helped Ava settle into her new home and she felt as if she belonged with him. His house seemed to feel like home to her right away.

Ava continued to play pool on both of the leagues she and Mark had played together and she joined a team on a women's pool league as well. Leo, though not well practiced in the sport, strived to be a part of Ava's world and joined one of the teams. After a while, Ava became very close to two of the women with whom she played pool, and it was easy to see their friendships would likely last a lifetime. Sophie, a woman about eighteen years older than Ava, was the captain of the women's team for which Ava played. She was a very kind person, and the friendship she extended to Ava, was warm and honest. The other, Peyton, was a few years younger than Ava, but seemed to have a fun, yet maturing mindset. Though Peyton was younger than Ava, she and Ava seemed to bond very quickly. The three of them together seemed to produce the perfect balance of humor, seriousness, maturity, and fun Ava had desperately been looking for in her search for friends. It was the first time in Ava's adult life she had felt comfortable with other women and she loved it. She knew she could trust both of them with her life and they knew they could trust her with theirs.

It seemed Ava's life had finally come together, and she felt as though she could finally leave the past behind her, though such a feat was not as easy as it would seem. Ava and Leo did all they could to become involved in each other's interests, and spent as much time as possible together. Leo had become involved with pool, enjoyed spending time with Ava's friends, and even accompanied Ava and her team to state tournaments. Ava joined the local search and rescue team, to which Leo belonged, and loved the feeling of helping others. Leo was also involved in SCUBA diving, so Ava joined him in that hobby as well, taking classes to become an advanced diver. Motorcycle riding was another hobby the couple shared, and all day rides seemed to be their favorite. Ava eventually earned her motorcycle license and was able to ride alone as well. Life seemed splendid.

After many months, Leo finally proposed to Ava and she happily accepted. It seemed like a fairy tale to Ava, and her family was overjoyed about the upcoming nuptials. Finally, in the summer of 2004 Leo and Ava were married. Before the wedding, Ava had become a member of Leo's church, and the couple faithfully attended services every Sunday. At the age of twenty-six, Ava was finally baptized and her ever-increasing knowledge of Christianity seemed to open her mind to positive views, chipping away at the thick wall of hate and trepidation she had built around her heart. Though she finally felt as if she had triumphed over her past, it seemed as if it still somehow continuously haunted her. Though many of the thoughts she had did not present themselves consciously, she could feel herself seemingly transform into another person from time to time, as if only a shadow of herself existed inside her mind.

Ava opted to share her concerns with Leo and he was supportive of whatever she felt she needed to do. She knew the scars from her past were causing the upset in her mind, so she chose to see a psychologist, in order to help work through her struggles. Ultimately, the psychologist's diagnosis was one Ava had suspected for quite some time - that of Depressive Personality Disorder (DPD) as well as Post-traumatic Stress Disorder (PTSD). Visiting with the psychologist regularly helped Ava immensely, and it seemed as if the more she worked through her past issues, the stronger and more confident she became. However, at the same time, her new-found confidence seemed to transform her into a fearless woman who wanted to experience life to the fullest. Though she was successfully wading through her past and felt confident, the issues that still remained seemed to get in the way, consistently creating incredible frustration in her mind. Ultimately, her conscious mind was lucid and aware of all of the positive facets of her new life with Leo, but somehow her subconscious seemed to ruthlessly involve the past at every opportunity, sabotaging her endeavor to exist in the happy and nurturing atmosphere.

As she became more and more self-assured, it seemed as if her mind was relentlessly immersed in an emotional battle with the shadow of herself. Trying to recover from everything in her past seemed to consistently exhaust her. As she worked to free herself from the chains of depression and PTSD, it seemed as if she were becoming more tightly entwined in the shackles, much of the time fearing she may never break free. It was as if one moment she felt free to fly, but the next bound to a stake in the ground, unable to move even an inch. Her confidence eventually gave way to independence and she began to feel as if she could conquer the world on a whim. The confidence and independence intoxicated her and she embraced it whenever possible. The more independent she became, the more Leo noticed the changes in her, and protested. Though he wanted her to be happy and strong, deep down, he was afraid she would no longer need him to protect her and she would eventually leave.

As Ava changed, so did Leo. He stopped playing league with her and eventually stopped going with her all together. He protested the amount of time she dedicated to pool and began to pressure her about it. Her new-found strength, combined with her incessant psychological battles, proved to be a recipe for an acid capable of dissolving any emotional connection between the two of them. On one hand, she understood Leo's concern about her wellbeing during league and tournaments, but on the other hand the exhilaration created by her confidence was something she was much too afraid to release, for fear of never grasping it again. Her conscious mind rationalized that Leo loved her and wanted to spend time with her, but her psyche was not yet willing to let go of the abuse and demeaning control she endured at the hands of those from her past. She was simply unable to see through the dark cloak that had been wrapped around her as she struggled to free herself from all of the pain and sadness of her past. Ava's subconscious screamed warnings of her relationship with Leo, turning sour and restrained about Leo trying to control her. The warnings her mind presented were not tangible, but she struggled to differentiate between real and perceived threats, ultimately deciding to protect herself at all costs. Over time, she pulled away from Leo, and began to live as if she were alone in the world, while Leo fought desperately to save their marriage. It seemed, however, the harder he tried to get close to her, the more she pulled away.

During the summer of 2005 Ava tried to stop smoking at Leo's request. She tried diligently to break free from her addiction to nicotine and was seemingly successful. By using a transdermal patch, she was able to gradually decrease her dependence on nicotine, with much less discomfort than if she had tried to stop without any cessation support. She faithfully used the patches for the recommended duration, trying hard to remain faithful to the decision to stop smoking. After about a week with no nicotine in her system, she felt rejuvenated and full of energy. She knew the chemicals within each cigarette caused her to be lethargic and less energetic and the change was a welcomed one. Leo was very pleased she had stopped smoking and was sure to congratulate her whenever possible. Even though turmoil still existed in the relationship, the couple tried to return to the once happy relationship they had shared.

The second week without nicotine proved to be a difficult

one for Ava. She began experiencing severe dizzy spells, each lasting well over two hours. It seemed as if nothing, in particular, prompted the dizzy spells and they occurred almost daily. In addition to the dizziness, Ava began to experience debilitating migraine headaches, which would render her unable to tolerate light of virtually any kind, without vomiting and severe abdominal pain. At times, the migraines would last for days, varying in intensity, and the abdominal pain seemed to be persistently present. Ava and Leo discussed the situation, and rationalized the headaches and dizziness must be a result of the nicotine leaving her system, as her body endeavored to produce dopamine on its own once again. They also reached the conclusion the abdominal pain was likely a result of the rest of her body trying to cope with the lack of nicotine as well. Over the next few weeks, however, the dizziness and headaches worsened and the abdominal pain stayed consistent. The couple began to fear the cause was something more than recovery from nicotine addiction.

With all of the pain, and Ava's reluctance to drive for fear of having a dizzy spell, she abruptly stopped seeing her psychologist. An appointment with her regular physician was made and the following week the appointment was kept. Leo was unable to accompany her to the appointment, so she knew she had to be very careful while driving the forty-five minutes to the doctor's office. Once inside, she checked in and sat nervously in the waiting room, until her name was called. After she was led into one of the examination rooms the nurse explained that her regular doctor was not in, due to having back surgery, so Ava would be examined by another physician, Dr. Andrews, who was filling in. Ava felt a twinge of uncertainty but felt she had no other choice but to be examined by Dr. Andrews. After completing her duties, the nurse exited the room and Ava waited silently while her mind raced.

The door opened and a man of about sixty-five entered the room. He was tall and thin and wore a concerned look on his wrinkled face.

"Hi, Ava," he said as he extended his hand to her. "I'm Dr. Andrews."

"Hi," Ava said, shaking the man's hand.

"What brings you here today?" he asked, matter-of-factly.

Ava explained, in detail, the symptoms she had been experiencing over the past weeks, making sure to include information about her headaches, dizziness, and abdominal pain. Dr. Andrews listened intently as Ava described her symptoms, only interjecting when he needed clarification. He physically examined her, concentrating on her eyes, neck, reflexes, and balance. He then proceeded to examine her abdomen, pushing in different places in an effort to feel something, if it was there.

"Okay," Dr. Andrews said, a new level of concern flooding his voice. "I would like to do a blood test now, then send you for some other discovery tests, is that okay?" He continued, trying to cover his concerned expression with one of reassurance.

"Okay," Ava agreed quietly.

Dr. Andrews led Ava to another room in the small clinic and instructed one of the nurses to draw the blood. Ava sat quietly, watching as the needle pierced the skin in the fold of her elbow. She followed the crimson blood, as it seemed to magically climb the needle, and collect in the tube above it. After only a few seconds, the nurse finished her task, and covered the small hole in Ava's skin with a cotton ball and piece of surgical tape.

"Okay," the nurse said warmly as she offered a smile, "you're all set."

Ava smiled slightly to convey her gratitude and returned to the examination room as Dr. Andrews had instructed.

"I'd like to send you for an MRI and an ultrasound to see if we can find what is troubling you, okay?" Dr. Andrews said in a warm and sympathetic tone.

"Okay," Ava agreed once again as she slightly nodded her head.

"Once you have the MRI and ultrasound, and I get the results back, we can set up another appointment so you can come back in," he said. "Then, if the pictures show me anything, we can decide where to go from there, okay?"

Ava nodded her head to show she understood but remained quiet. She wanted so much to immediately know the cause of her symptoms but knew there was no way to find out until after the tests. Dr. Andrews wrote some notes in Ava's file then stood to exit the room.

"I'll be right back," he said, smiling kindly at her.

She offered a half-hearted smile in return then lowered her eyes to the floor. After about five minutes, Dr. Andrews entered the examination room again to give Ava her next instructions.

"Okay, all set," he began. "I've got orders here for an MRI and an ultrasound, both of which you can have done at any time at any hospital. It's up to you when you go, but I encourage you to do it as soon as possible," he continued as he handed the papers to her.

"I'll go there as soon as I leave here," she said meekly, as she reached out to take the papers from him.

"Good," he said with a reassuring smile. "As soon as I get the results I'll give you a call to come back in, okay?"

"Okay," she said quietly.

Though Dr. Andrews was not her regular physician, and she had initially felt skepticism, the interaction with him made her feel confident he would be able to help her.

Ava called Leo to let him know what had been said and

to inform him she was going directly to the hospital for the other tests. Leo could not camouflage his concern, but tried to blindly reassure her everything would be alright. She ended the call and drove to the hospital in Waterburn to have the tests done. Ultimately, her visit at the hospital took a little more than three hours, as she had to wait for others who had arrived before her. She was informed the results would be sent to the clinic and she need not worry about waiting for anything other than a call from Dr. Andrews. She left the hospital and carefully drove home with a heavy heart and a mind full of questions.

A few days after Ava had seen Dr. Andrews she received a call from the doctor's office informing her that her test results were in and Dr. Andrews wanted to set up another appointment as soon as possible. The appointment was set for the next day and, once again, Leo was unable to accompany her. Ava arrived at the clinic, and did not have to wait long, before she was called to one of the examination rooms. Dr. Andrews entered the room only a few minutes later, with a look of grave seriousness on his face, immediately sparking fear in Ava's mind.

"Hi, Ava," Dr. Andrews said.

She offered a smile and waited for him to continue.

"Well, I found a few things I'm concerned about," he began. "The blood test we did was a CA 125 test that shows possible suggestions of cancerous cells. If the CA 125 in the blood is elevated, it could mean there is cancer present. Your CA 125 was elevated a little, and the ultrasound showed a thickening of your uterine wall, as well as some cysts on your ovaries, that may or may not be problematic."

"Okay, so what does all that mean?" Ava asked with unmistakable concern in her voice.

"Well," Dr. Andrews began, "it means there is a possibility you may have uterine *and* ovarian cancer, but I would like to send you to a specialist for further testing and diagnosis to determine if it is, indeed, cancer. I will refer you to an OB/GYN as soon as possible."

"Okay," she said, her voice now saturated with defeat.

"The MRI, on the other hand, showed something else," Dr. Andrews said. "I can't be sure but I believe you may have a very rare condition known as Chiari Malformation of the Brain."

"What?" Ava said in a confused tone. "What's that?"

"Well, again, it's a very rare condition. The brain herniates into the spinal column, and creates pressure on the brainstem, due to the underdevelopment of the skull in the back of the head," he explained. "I think I have a book, I'll be right back," he continued as he left the room.

Ava sat perfectly still, trying to process all of the information Dr. Andrews was presenting to her. She suddenly felt numb, as if all of her nerves had been removed from her body. She felt like she wanted to cry but was simply unable.

Dr. Andrews quickly returned to the examination room with a large, thick book. He opened it, and found a diagram of the condition he suspected was plaguing her. He explained the diagram as Ava looked at it, trying to help her understand as much as she could. After explaining everything, he set the book aside and looked at Ava.

"Will it kill me?" Ava asked soberly as she looked into the doctor's eyes.

"I don't know," he answered in an apologetic tone. "You'll

need to see a neurosurgeon in order to get a definitive diagnosis. I will refer you to one your insurance will approve and let you know about both of the referrals as soon as I know."

Ava still felt numb. She did not know what to think. It was as if escaping all of the torment in her life was something she was being reprimanded for, and she began to wonder why God was punishing her. She was still unable to cry or show any emotion at all. She finished her conversation with Dr. Andrews, thanked him, and left the clinic. As she drove home, she began to feel incredible anger building in her heart, and her body began to tremble.

"Looks like I would have been better off if Mark had waited another ten seconds to walk into the bedroom," she thought to herself, referring to her suicide attempt with the .357 Magnum.

Tears began to silently fall from her eyes as the miles disappeared under the tires of her car. She drove home in a daze, barely able to believe the words the doctor had said to her. Before she left the clinic, she had asked Dr. Andrews to make copies of the diagram in the book, so she could show them to Leo and he had readily agreed. Once she arrived home, armed with only the copies of the diagram, a vague sense of self, and the inability to fully process what she had learned, she walked into the house and attempted to explain the situation to her husband.

That weekend, Ava and Leo invited both of their immediate families to a cookout at their house. Emma and Lee came with their family and Lilli and her boyfriend came with Lilli's children. Sonya had moved to another state, so it was no surprise she did not attend. Able refused to attend, as he was still very close with Mark, and still blamed Ava for being unfaithful, rationalizing the divorce was entirely her fault. Leo's sister and her family lived too far away to attend, but Leo's parents, along with his step-sister were glad to be there.

Upon inviting everyone, Ava and Leo had only explained there were some important things that needed to be shared, and they wanted to share them with everyone at the same time, instead of trying to explain things to everyone separately. As the meat sizzled on the grill Emma and Lilli helped Ava prepare the rest of the meal in the kitchen. The three sisters happily conversed about trivial things, laughing and giggling, until the suspense of the gathering finally got the best of Lilli.

"Ava, are you pregnant?" Lilli asked with a smile on her face.

Surprised at the question, Ava looked at Lilli and smiled back. Ava simply shook her head, to indicate she was not pregnant, and picked up a bowl of salad to take outside. Lilli and Emma followed Ava's lead, and carried the rest of the serving dishes to the garage, and set them on the table.

The sound of murmuring voices filled the air, accompanied by the laughter of the children as they played in the driveway, just outside the open garage doors. It had not occurred to Ava or Leo that one or more of their family members would assume a baby was on the way.

"Okay, everybody," Leo said in a booming voice. "Once everybody gets their food we'll go ahead with the news."

Everyone obediently filed into a line, chose what they wanted from the buffet-style set up, then filtered to their seats to get ready to hear the news. Once everyone was seated, Leo gestured for Ava to join him in front of everyone. Listening carefully, no one made a sound as Leo began to speak.

"Thanks for comin' everybody," he began. "We have some news we knew you would all want to hear and we thought it would just be easier to tell everybody at once."

Leo looked at Ava, as if to ask if he should make the announcement, or if she want to. Ava understood the silent cue and knew it was finally time to tell everyone about her medical dilemma.

"I know some of you think we are having a baby," she began, in an attempt to lighten the mood, "but that's not it. There is a possibility that I have uterine and ovarian cancer, along with a condition known as Chiari Malformation of the Brain."

No one uttered a word. Even though everyone had been silent before Leo and Ava began to speak, it seemed as if even the birds had stopped chirping in utter disbelief. After a few seconds, Lilli was the first to break the silence.

"What has to be done? What do you need help with?" she asked, clearly upset and worried about her little sister.

Ava proceeded to explain she would be seeing specialists to either prove, or disprove the suspicions of each possibility, and the room seemed to fill with questions and concerned statements directed toward both Ava and Leo. Throughout the rest of the evening, Ava and Leo spent time with their families talking, explaining things, and answering questions. The news seemed to blanket them all in the realization that no one can ever be certain of continued good health, nor can anyone guarantee they will even be alive from day to day. The families seemed to bond together, on a higher level that evening, sadly the news of possible medical turmoil being the hands that spread the blanket over all of them.

Ava finally received a call from Dr. Andrews, informing her of the details of her appointments with the two specialists. The OB/GYN was located in a city about fifty miles south of

Ropschon, and her appointment was not scheduled for another six weeks. The neurosurgeon she was to see was located in a city about forty miles north of Ropschon, and that appointment was not scheduled to take place for another four weeks. After thanking Dr. Andrews, Ava ended the call and sat down, again in a daze. She couldn't believe she would have to wait so long to find out more information. The unknown was beginning to wear on her, and she felt as if she were stuck in some sort of limbo, unable to control her own life. Over the next few hours she and Leo called their family members and informed them of the appointment dates. Each seemed to have a complaint in defense of Ava and wondered why it would take so long. Ultimately, the root cause of the delay was the insurance Ava was forced to carry, through her place of employment. The insurance was not very good and only allowed its policy holders to see certain physicians and specialists. A hospital only a few hours away, perceivably one of the best hospitals in the Midwest, was completely out of reach for Ava, as her insurance would not allow her to seek treatment there.

With all of the stress thrust upon Ava involving her possible medical issues, the upset in her marriage, her psychological issues, and the common stress of working full time, she eventually began smoking again in an effort to reclaim some sort of normalcy in her life. Within a few weeks after Dr. Andrews had called her, Ava's headaches seemed to subside, the dizzy spells were reduced to barely noticeable lightheadedness, and the abdominal pain completely went away. Though her symptoms seemed to lie dormant, the knowledge of what may be determined still floated at the front of her mind, constantly weaving through her conscious thoughts with each waking moment. Smoking, for some unknown reason, seemed to be some sort of significant factor within the entire situation.

Finally, the day came for Ava to see the neurosurgeon

and she was eager for the appointment time to arrive. Leo accompanied her to the neurosurgeon's office, and when her name was called, she followed the nurse into the examination room with Leo close behind. The nurse instructed Ava to remove her upper garments and replace them with a paper shirt that came to her waist and tied in the back. Ava did as she was instructed, then sat patiently on the examination table awaiting the doctor's arrival. When the doctor finally entered the room he seemed cold, aloof, and uninterested in Ava's well-being.

"I hear you have Chiari," the doctor stated, as if it were as common as a cold.

"That's what my doctor believes, yes" Ava answered, clearly unsettled by the neurosurgeon's indifferent attitude.

"Well, you do," the doctor said matter-of-factly.

"So, what does that mean for me?" Ava asked.

"It means your brain is protruding into your spinal column," the doctor replied in a mocking tone, as if he were a taunting child on a playground.

Ava looked at the doctor with an expression of offense and disbelief. She could not believe his uncaring and sarcastic behavior concerning her condition.

"I know it means my brain is protruding into my spinal column," Ava said, her voice not yet reflecting the irritation she felt. "I meant, do I need to have surgery? Is it fatal? Should I avoid certain activities?"

"Well, you could have surgery, but it wouldn't do any good," the doctor replied, as he turned his back to Ava and began shuffling through some papers.

Ava looked at Leo with an expression of contempt on her face, a direct reflection of the frustration she felt, as a result of the detached and uncaring disposition the doctor held regarding her condition. She had been completely unprepared for the doctor's unkind and callous attitude. Ava had a feeling the doctor was not as familiar with Chiari, as he would like others to believe, and she simply wanted to get dressed and leave the office. Her insurance, however, completely restricted her ability to seek care from another physician. She felt anger begin to boil deep inside her and knew she would not be able to hold her tongue any longer. The neurosurgeon's lack of answers to her questions, as well as his apathetic attitude, made it virtually impossible for her to keep her composure, as fear of the unknown seemed to overtake her mind.

"What do you know about Chiari?" Ava asked in a callous tone as her eyes narrowed.

Without bothering to turn and face her, the neurosurgeon said nothing, and continued to shuffle through the stack of papers in front of him.

"I've found out some information on the condition, but I was hoping you could tell me more. It is possibly fatal, it can interrupt many things in my body, and it may or may not be hereditary," Ava continued, attempting to coax information from the doctor, no longer able to mask the animosity his behavior had prompted.

"I suppose you read that on the internet," the neurosurgeon responded, in a pretentious and derisive tone, as he turned to leave the examination room.

"Uh, no, that is what my doctor told me," Ava spat in response.

The neurosurgeon continued toward the door and swung it open. Ava could no longer hold her anger.

"So, are we done here?" she asked shortly.

"Yep, you can leave," the doctor responded without turning to look at her.

As the doctor forcefully pulled the door closed behind

him Ava felt an overwhelming determination to reveal what she thought of him.

"Ya know, you're fuckin' worthless!" Ava said loudly, her voice flooding with frustration. "I don't think ya know a damned thing about Chiari! Thanks for fuckin' nothin'!" Leo stood and tried to calm her, in an effort to avoid confrontation, as she began to cry.

The movement of the examination room door slowed briefly as she spoke, then accelerated, the door finally slamming shut. Ava dressed quickly and exited the neurosurgeon's office without a word. Leo followed, trying to keep up with her all of the way to the parking lot. Tears still streamed down Ava's face, as she put her seatbelt on, and lit a cigarette. Leo got into the car as well, choosing not to speak, as he knew there would be nothing he could possibly say to calm his wife. After driving for about ten minutes, Ava finally broke the silence.

"Guess I'll have to figure this shit out on my own, as always," she said, her voice full of hatred, frustration, and fear.

"Well, we can see what we can find on the internet," Leo responded, still clearly uncertain if he should even speak.

Nothing more was said as the couple continued home. Ava's mind, still not healed from her past, began to fill with a new fear. She had always been used to other people attacking her and had learned how to fight back. Now, however, she was excruciatingly aware her own body was now the source of her pain and torment. The new fear she felt resonated from the realization she was defenseless against her condition, and the only medical help she was able to pursue, was seated in a man who did not seem to care about the situation or the impact it had on her life. Once again, she felt as if her back was against the wall. Leo tried to offer support but the disarray of Ava's mind seemed to close him out. She had a distinct problem controlling her anger, and seemed to find solace in being alone, or around people who only knew her superficially. She unconsciously felt, if others did not know about her medical condition or the demons she was fighting in her mind, they would treat her like a normal person and she would not have to deal with any of it. Little did she know, the demons in her mind had a firm hold on her personality and would push her to her limits, repeatedly.

A few weeks later, Ava kept her appointment with the OB/GYN and tried to face the possibility of cancer with a brave heart. The typical examination took place and biopsies were taken. She was then sent down the hall for an ultrasound. After the ultrasound was completed, and she had returned to the original examination room to dress, she was lead to an office where she found the doctor waiting for her. He explained that the biopsies would be sent to the lab and the ultrasound would be read. He assured her, as soon as the results were determined, she would be contacted. She thanked the doctor and left the office. As she drove back to Ropschon her mind wandered. She was unable to consciously control her thoughts, or even remember all of the thoughts crawling through her mind, from moment to moment. Silent tears once again began to fall from her eyes as she began to wonder if her life was worth all of the trouble. She felt that her existence, the relationships she had been a part of, the worry about her physical health, and the desperation she felt had ultimately created terrible upset for the people who cared for her. She truly believed, in her heart, the world would have been better off if she had ended up in the ditch to die on the way to the hospital some twenty-eight years earlier. Her tears continued to fall as she contemplated her own demise, but not from fear of death. She cried because she seemed to understand a silent message, from an unknown source, assuring her of how much her family and friends would miss her. Her psychological issues, physical conditions, love for her family and friends, and her own self-loathing seemed to create a pressure chamber from which something would eventually have to explode.

Within a few days of her original OB/GYN appointment, she was called back to the office to be informed of the results. She was informed she did not have cancer of any kind, and she need not worry. The doctor took the time to explain the possible indicators of the cancers were also commonly occurring issues involved in a normal menstrual cycle. He expanded on the information, to be sure she understood everything completely, and she was grateful. She thanked the doctor for the optimistic news and left the office. Leo was relieved to hear the news as well, and the couple wasted no time in calling their family members to pass it on. Ava seemed to be so enveloped by all of the other issues she faced she seemed literally unable to find even the smallest amount of hope.

Ava did not resume counseling after being diagnosed with Chiari, though it would have likely been the best thing for her. A new sense of unrest had befallen her psyche, and she seemed determined to trudge through things alone. Though Leo strived to help her, it was as if she was ultimately unable to allow herself to recognize the care he extended to her. Leo tried desperately to protect her from herself, but she was only able to recognize his efforts as acts of control. It seemed to Ava that, the more independent she wanted to be, the more Leo endeavored to control her.

Ava researched Chiari on the internet, but was not able to find a great deal of information. Even though she no longer felt the physical pain of Chiari, aside from the headaches she had become accustomed to, the fear of the condition occupied her thoughts continuously. Her marriage to Leo continued to dissolve, and she finally succumbed to the low self-esteem and self-loathing that had been planted deep within her mind, throughout the years of abuse she had endured. She began to pull away from Leo drastically, and recklessly sought attention from another man, in an effort to drown her feelings of repeated failure and inferiority. She spent even more time at tournaments and increased the amount of alcohol she consumed. Ultimately, she was once again on the path to her own destruction and was well aware of it. She had once again stopped caring about her own well-being, and unconsciously decided to face her own demolition head on, with full force. She was determined to be in control of her own fate instead of allowing Chiari to overtake her. At that point, it was as if she had lost the ability to control herself, but in reality, she had simply stopped caring and felt the undeniable compulsion to destroy herself.

By the spring of 2006 Ava and Leo's marriage had succumbed to the pressures of all of the changes Ava had gone through. She was no longer the woman Leo had proposed to, and he feared the marriage would end very soon, though he did not want to stand idly by and let it happen. Ava had begun a romantic relationship with another man in Ropschon but it was kept secret. Leo seemed to sense her unfaithful actions and tried desperately to keep her from pursuing the relationship. Finally, the marriage ended and Ava was free to pursue the relationship she had begun with the other man, Corey. The divorce was very peaceful, and was finalized only a few short days, after it was filed. Leo and Ava remained friends, in spite of the horrendous pain they both felt as a result of the failed union.

In addition to Chiari, Ava had also struggled for several years with terrible pain in both of her feet, which continuously radiated up both legs and into her hips. Finally, she discovered the pain was ultimately due to the bones in her feet being gradually displaced. She opted to have surgery on both feet, one at a time, to correct the bones. Leo offered to let her recover under his care, likely in an attempt to salvage the sense of closeness the two had once shared. Ava politely declined Leo's offer and the first surgery was scheduled. Her left foot would be the first one to be operated on.

Corey had moved to a small town about three hours south of Ropschon a few weeks before Ava's surgery, after being hired as a salesman for a large implement company. He informed Ava he would not be able to be there for her surgery and suggested Leo accompany her to have the procedure. Corey's mother, Sylvia, who lived just outside of Ropschon, had become very fond of Ava and did not understand Corey's indifference to Ava's pending procedure, any more than Ava did, but was unable to convince Corey to change his mind. Ava seemed to be blind to Corey's rationale and simply concluded it was due to the newness of their relationship. The procedure took place and Leo was there to help. After the procedure, Leo drove Ava to Sylvia's house so she could recover from the anesthesia. Sylvia thanked Leo and proceeded to do all she could to help Ava feel comfortable. Ava was not fully alert when Leo helped her into Sylvia's house, but she was aware enough to extend a heart-felt thank you, before he left. The next day, Ava drove the three hours to Corey's new apartment, and once again felt as if she would be able to start anew. In reality, Ava did not want to take her own life, but she would soon find out she would be unable to continue the fight that was incessantly sustained within her own mind.

Chapter Thirteen

When Ava arrived at Corey's apartment he warmly welcomed her. Since she had taken a medical leave of absence from work, she was able to spend as much time as she liked with Corey, at the new apartment. He continued to go to work every day, and Ava was waiting for him when he returned. The couple began to discuss moving Ava into the apartment as well and excitement of the transition mounted. It seemed the two of them got along wonderfully, but just under the surface, Ava was curious about Corey's personality and characteristics. She had not known anyone like him before and thus, was captivated by him. With that captivation, it seemed as if she excused things he said and did that may have otherwise caused her to abandon the relationship. Ultimately, the newness of the relationship was an opaque blindfold covering her eyes.

Ava's surgery had left her unable to walk without crutches and she was forced to rely on Corey for some things. The couple sat in the living room, Ava reading a book and Corey working on his computer. Ava had prepared a meal for the two of them to share, however, since she was unable to maneuver her crutches and carry things, Corey happily transported their plates into the living room so they could watch television as they ate. Corey was sure to situate Ava's meal first, then his own. As he sat down to begin eating, Ava sweetly asked if he would fetch her glass of milk that still sat on the counter. Corey glanced at Ava, with a look in his eyes she had never seen before, and it startled her. Slamming his fork on his plate, he scoffed and walked swiftly to the kitchen.

"Why didn't ya fuckin' ask me when I was up?" Corey spat at her.

"I'm sorry," she began in a meek voice, "I was tryin' to get situated so I could reach my plate."

Corey handed the glass to her, and she meekly took it.

"Do ya need anything else?" He asked in a frustrated and irritated tone.

"No," she said, unsure of why he was so upset with her. In reality, she wanted the salt shaker from the kitchen, but because of his tone, she was immediately afraid to ask for anything else.

Corey, returning to his meal, sat down heavily in the chair. Nothing else was said between the two of them for the rest of the meal as Corey stared at the television and Ava wondered what was happening. When the meal was finished, Ava tried to take her own dishes to the kitchen in order to avoid another unpleasant interaction with Corey. As she stood and fumbled with her crutches, Corey tried hard to ignore her struggling. Finally, unable to ignore her any longer, he rose and took his dishes to the sink. Returning to the living room he approached Ava as she tried to figure out how to carry her dishes with the crutches.

"Here," he said with irritation in his voice, grabbing the dishes. "I'll take 'em. Just sit down."

She reluctantly accepted his help, though she was completely aware of the irritation he felt toward her. She once again took her seat on the couch and tried to figure out why he was so annoyed.

After Corey returned to the living room and sat down he

resumed his computer work. Ava waited only a few minutes before speaking to him again.

"What's wrong?" Ava asked in a timid voice.

"Nothin'," Corey barked sharply.

She knew his answer was a lie, and felt that if only they could talk about things, the tension would leave the room.

"I know there's somethin' botherin' ya," she continued, trying to help him understand he could talk to her.

Corey rolled his eyes then turned toward Ava in his chair.

"Why'd ya wait 'til I sat down before needing your milk?" he said with irritation dripping from his words.

"I didn't do it on purpose," she said, her voice starting to waver. "It was on the counter next to yours so I figured you'd bring it in with my plate. I didn't realize you hadn't brought it in until you had already sat down. I'm sorry."

"Whatever," Corey hissed, no longer willing to discuss the matter, as he turned back to his computer.

Ava dropped the subject as well, hoping her explanation was satisfactory, but felt as though the tiny incident would never be forgotten. She returned to her book but had difficulty reasserting herself into the story. After a few hours, Ava was ready for bed and Corey followed soon after. Nothing was said after retiring to bed, and soon both of them had fallen asleep.

The next morning, Ava prepared to return to Sylvia's house, as she was scheduled for a check up on her foot the following day. Corey was scheduled to travel for his job for the week, so Ava planned to stay with Sylvia until he returned. When it was finally time for her to depart, Corey walked her to her car to say goodbye. The couple hugged and Ava drove away. As the miles disappeared under her tires, her mind wandered, thinking about what had happened the night before and Corey's disposition toward her. She recalled all of the plans the two of them had made, to get married, have a family, and live happily ever after. She wondered how she could possibly be happy with him or anyone else, considering her track record with marriage. She also recalled some of the comments Corey had made regarding marriage over the last week, and could not help but worry that he had changed his mind. When she finally reached Sylvia's house, she was tired and needed to put her foot up. She and Sylvia talked as Ava rested and Sylvia was beside herself with the information Ava shared. Sylvia knew Ava loved Corey very much, but also knew her son could be selfish and ineffectual, when things proved to be inconvenient for him. This was a side of Corey Ava had just begun to recognize, and upsetting thoughts continued to rush into her mind. Would he be there for her during her next surgery? Could she trust him to be faithful to her? Would he be resolute in the promises of happiness and family he had made? Would she be able to depend on him if Chiari rose up to attack her again? So many questions flooded her mind and she sought comfort in the conversations she had with Sylvia.

Ava and Sylvia became very close and each referred to the other as if they were family. Sylvia recalled a failed pregnancy she had, and declared Ava must be the baby she had lost, somehow reincarnated so they could meet under different circumstances. Ava felt a strong connection with Sylvia and felt as though she was the mother she should have had. Sylvia had spoken with Sonya on the phone and through letters, finding the nuances of selfishness to be present in every sentence. Sylvia felt as though she needed to be there for Ava, understanding Sonya had not been a good mother. As time went on, Ava and Sylvia became closer and closer, as if they were actually mother and daughter. This relationship between Ava and Sylvia seemed to upset Corey and he would voice his disapproval openly, as he felt like Ava was trying to take his place in his mother's heart, though the only thing Ava wanted to do was feel as if she belonged – somewhere.

Once Ava was able to walk without her crutches, though having to be very careful, she loaded her things in Corey's pickup and made the move to be with him. She and Corey had spent the night with Sylvia and planned to drive the three hours to the apartment the next day. That night, as Ava thought about how things had ended with Leo, she cried. Corey took the tears to mean she was upset about the move, however, the tears ultimately were Ava's way of saying goodbye to her life with Leo as she looked forward to yet another promising start. The morning arrived and Ava and Corey prepared to depart. Ava drove Corey's truck, filled with her belongings, and Corey drove his company car. As they drove to the apartment, they conversed on the phone in what seemed to be a lighthearted and loving way. After about two hours of driving and talking, Corey said the words that would forever mark a turn in their relationship.

"Ava, I'm not sure about you moving in with me," he said with nervousness in his voice.

Ava immediately assumed Corey was joking.

"Um, it's a little late now," she said, giggling.

"I'm serious, Ava," he said, his tone assuring her he was not joking.

Ava was speechless. She had no idea what to say or how to feel.

"Are ya fuckin' kiddin' me?" Ava said, a combination of

anger and desperation filling her voice. "We're only an hour from the apartment and ya wait 'til now to tell me this?"

He said nothing, and she could hear him as he began to cry quietly. Immediately, upon hearing his muffled sobs, her heart softened and the anger left her mind. She chose to comfort him instead of criticizing him any further.

"Do ya wana turn around and head back to Ropschon?" She asked kindly. "I can find an apartment and we can figure things out. If you're not sure then we shouldn't do this."

"No," he said, his voice cracking with his tears. "Let's just get there and figure it out. I'm sorry I said anything."

Ava tried to assure Corey that everything would be alright, and once they were able to discuss things face to face, they could reach a conclusion. Corey decided he wanted to end the phone conversation to give himself time to think for the last hour of the drive. Ava agreed and the call was ended.

As Ava set her phone on the seat next to her, she began to realize that Corey was not going to be the wonderful husband he had promised he would be. The realization that marriage would not even happen struck her, and once again, she felt her anger begin to mount.

"What the fuck is goin' on with him?" she thought to herself as she drove. "What the fuck am I guna do?" She knew she couldn't go back to Leo, nor did she want to, for fear of hurting him again. She knew that if her relationship with Corey did not work she would strive to make it on her own instead of rushing into another relationship. Before she knew it, she had reached the driveway of the apartment building and slowed to pull in. Only minutes after she arrived, Corey pulled into the driveway as well. Both of them exited the vehicles and walked toward one another. Ava was unsure of what would happen next and was completely surprised at Corey's actions as he hugged her tightly with tears running down his face.

"It's okay," Ava said as she hugged him back. "What's goin' on?"

"I don't know," Corey began, "maybe I'm just scared because of what happened in my first marriage."

"I'm not your ex-wife, Corey," she assured him. "I want to be with you. She obviously didn't."

"I know," he said, still crying. "I'm sorry."

Hugging again, the two of them seemed to understand things would be alright, and the move was still happening. As they began to unload Ava's belongings, Corey's mood seemed to lighten and they were both able to giggle and make the chore fun. Finally, everything was in the apartment and they were able to sit down and rest. As Corey looked around the apartment at all of the boxes filled with Ava's things, his face seemed to take on a glow of happiness. He put his arm around her and kissed her forehead.

"I'm glad you're here," he said lovingly.

"Me too," she said as a smile spread across her face.

"It's late," he said. "We should go to bed."

"Yeah," she agreed. "I'm tired.

They walked to the bedroom together and were happy to lie down and sleep. Though earlier, the connotation of Corey's words had stricken upset in Ava's heart, it seemed as if the issue had been resolved and he no longer had reservations about the move. Ava once again felt the warm feeling of possible belonging and fell asleep feeling loved and happy.

Monday arrived and Ava was scheduled to be in surgery that afternoon. She and Corey headed toward Ropschon to keep the appointment. He had concluded Ava had been right to wonder about his indifference during her first surgery, and pledged to be by her side for the second one. They arrived at the hospital and walked in together. As the intravenous sedative dripped into the tube, and Ava became drowsy, Corey dutifully sat with her and talked. Once she was drowsy enough to be taken into the operating room, she was moved and Corey waited patiently until she returned to recovery to wake up. Once she was able to leave the hospital, Corey carefully and lovingly helped her to the car, and drove to Sylvia's house to spend time with his mother and let Ava rest. Corey seemed to be so caring and tentative both Ava and Sylvia were surprised. The time finally arrived for the couple to drive the three hours back to the apartment and Ava had gotten plenty of rest. Though she was in pain from the surgery, she was happy to be with Corey, and that happiness seemed to dilute the physical pain she felt.

Because the second surgery had involved Ava's right foot, she was not only forced to use crutches to walk, but was also unable to drive. She worked around the apartment when Corey was at work or traveling, finally seeming to be on the path to their promised life of happiness. Though they had not yet begun to discuss marriage, Ava felt the discussion was imminent. Though housework was difficult while using crutches, she kept herself busy with situating the apartment and getting everything put in its place. She began searching online for a job in the area, to be prepared when her foot was finally healed. She was excited about leaving the factory she had worked in for so long and starting a new adventure. As the next few weeks passed, however, the happy and nurturing Corey seemed to transform into a doubt-filled and upset man who was ultimately unsure of everything in his life.

After only about four months in the apartment, Corey

began to feel homesick and wanted to move back to Ropschon. He found a job in one of Ropschon's neighboring communities and planned to move in with his brother, refusing to live with Ava again. Ava was then forced to find a place of her own to live, deciding to move back to Ropschon as well. She was glad she had not yet gotten a new job and still had the factory to return to. Corey's decision to move back confused Ava, and his refusal to live with her in the apartment she had found hurt her terribly, and fueled her fear of losing him. In reality it would seem that, at that point, she had already lost him. It seemed as if there were so many small things that did not seem right between them. She rationalized that the turmoil in the relationship must have a great deal to do with her, unconsciously defending Corey from attack and making excuses for his behavior. She once again began to feel the urge to take her own life in an effort to escape the difficulty she seemed to constantly face. Though she did not share her urge to die with anyone, nevertheless, the urge was very real. She decided to return to her psychologist and resume sessions, in an effort to help herself trudge the rest of the way through the thorns of her past, in an effort to find her way.

Ava's right foot had finally healed and she was able to return to work in the factory. Now living on her own, she decided to take a second job to keep herself busy, and earn more money to stay afloat. Rent, utilities, car payment, and gas seemed to devour her paycheck every week, and she had little money left for anything else. She was able to secure a second job as a bartender at a bar owned by a friend of hers. She enjoyed the work, but the late nights proved to be trying, as she worked in the factory early in the morning. With both jobs taking up much of her time and energy, Sylvia was happy to help her with laundry and other small tasks. Sylvia visited often and she and Ava remained close, even though it seemed as if Ava's relationship with Corey was gradually dissolving. With the frustration and unhappiness Ava felt regarding her relationship with Corey, she was happy to return to her psychologist, Ben, for her first appointment. Ava was beginning to feel as if she were drowning in midair, unable to find a way to save herself. The day of the appointment finally arrived and she eagerly waited to be called back to the psychologist's office. Once inside the office, she felt free to speak and hopeful she would be able to find her way.

"How are things, Ava?" Ben asked caringly.

"Not great," she answered.

"What's goin' on?" He asked with concern.

"Well, I'm struggling with my boyfriend, struggling to make ends meet, working two jobs, and I'm thinking of suicide again," she said matter-of-factly.

"Oh, okay," he answered, surprised at Ava's candor. "Let's talk about your relationship with…"

"Corey," Ava offered.

"Corey. Okay, what's happening with him?" Ben continued.

"I don't know. It's weird, ya know?" She began. "It's like one minute he wants to marry me and have kids then the next minute he changes his mind."

"Hmm," Ben said with confusion on his face. "Why do you think that is?"

"No idea," she said, unwilling to even try to conclude why Corey behaved the way he did.

"How'd you two meet?" Ben asked.

"Well, through friends, I guess," Ava recalled. "We had an affair while I was married to my ex-husband, Leo. It didn't start well."

"Oh, okay," Ben said thoughtfully.

"Corey's different from anyone I've ever met," she said.

"How so?" Ben asked.

"Well, he seems so confident and sure of himself but at the same time it's like he can't make up his mind about anything," Ava said, recalling the many times Corey had shifted in his convictions. "With jobs, with me, with where to live, it doesn't seem to matter. It's confusing."

"Maybe he isn't the one for you," Ben said caringly.

"Maybe," she answered thoughtfully.

"You said you have been thinking about suicide again," Ben said, trying to keep the session moving along.

"Yeah," Ava said as her eyes dropped to the floor.

"Why?" Ben questioned softly.

"It seems like as soon as I start to feel happy I fall back in a hole. It's so frustrating. I feel like I can't trust anyone and like everyone else would just be better off if I wasn't here," Ava answered, shame coating her words. "I mean, I just don't know how much longer I can take trying to dig out of this muddy hole I feel like I'm in."

Ben nodded his head thoughtfully and waited for Ava to continue.

"Have you told anyone you want to kill yourself?" He inquired.

"No, I don't wana upset anyone. I just wana one day be gone so nobody has to deal with my shit anymore," she said as tears began to fill her eyes. "I just feel like no matter what I do it's wrong, ya know? I've tried to have relationships and be happy but I've fucked that up three times already."

"It sounds like you don't like yourself very much," Ben said.

"I hate myself," she answered, without thinking. "I let Alex and Mark beat the fuck outta me and I thought Leo was trying to control me. What the fuck is wrong with me?" she asked, somewhat rhetorically as she met Ben's gaze.

"I don't think there is necessarily anything *wrong* with you, Ava," Ben began. "I think you are a victim of your past and throughout the years things keep building up. You've been forced to fight for your life and, isn't it possible, that you are feeling insignificant because you are so critical of yourself?"

Ava shrugged her shoulders and tilted her head to indicate Ben's thoughts could be right.

"Even though we haven't had a session in a while, I know your history, and I know what you've been through. Why are you so hard on yourself?" He questioned with warmth.

"I don't want to let anyone be right about me," she said, new tears now staining her face. "People said when I was a kid that I was garbage and would never amount to anything. After I got outa school, they said I was a whore and was on drugs. I've only ever tried pot once and it was disgusting. I drink and smoke cigarettes but I don't do anything else. Now, I work hard and try to be happy but when I play pool a lot of the women on the leagues think I'm tryin' to fuck their husbands and I'm not. I just wana shoot and have fun."

"You've accomplished a lot in your life, haven't you?" Ben said, trying to lead Ava into positive thoughts about herself.

"Not really," she answered, unable to follow his lead.

"Did you graduate high school?" Ben asked.

"Yeah, then got married too soon and fucked off college," she said bitterly, still not taking the positive bait Ben dangled in front of her.

"How'd you finish in high school?" He questioned.

"Oh, I don't know, I think with a 3.9 grade point average," she said, clearly unimpressed with her own accomplishment.

"On a 4.0 scale? That's impressive!" Ben said with excitement in his voice. "With everything you were dealing with involving your mother, I'd say that is quite a big accomplishment!"

"I guess," she said, shrugging her shoulders. "Since school though it seems like I've just made one bad decision after another. Look where I've ended up."

"Well, just because you have made some bad decisions doesn't mean you are less of a person," Ben assured her.

"I feel worthless. Like I'm a bother to everyone," she said softly.

"You obviously didn't feel like a bother to Corey when you first got together. Why do you feel like a bother now?" Ben asked.

"I don't know, it's like he only wants me around if I don't need him, but if I didn't need him I wouldn't want to be with him. I don't think he gets me, ya know?" Ava answered. "And since he is so much different from anyone else I feel like I don't know how the hell to do anything right. It's like I've learned to ride a motorcycle and now I have to learn to ride a different one where the brake and clutch are switched. Like my instincts are constantly wrong, ya know?"

"It seems like your relationship with Corey may not be heading in a positive direction," Ben surmised.

"It doesn't feel like it is," Ava said. "It feels like the harder I try to make things go well, the worse they end up."

"You can't be the only one putting effort into the relationship, Ava," Ben said. "He has to be willing to put the work into it too, and if he's not willing, you can't force him."

"I know," she said sadly. "I just love him so much. I feel like we could really be happy together, if he could just step outside of himself long enough to understand other people are just as significant as he is."

"It sounds to me like he has portrayed himself differently than he actually is," he said carefully, trying to convey the message without upsetting Ava too much.

"That's exactly what he did," she said, understanding what Ben was suggesting. "He told me he wanted to marry me and have kids. He promised we would be so happy and do everything together and my dumb ass fell for it." She shook her head slightly as her gaze dropped to the floor, indicating the shame and embarrassment she felt for once again being taken advantage of.

"You wanting to be happy and giving a relationship a chance doesn't make you a dumb ass," he said. "It simply means you wanted to be happy, chose him, and he lied. It's as simple as that."

"I thought that, since he said he loved me he would be there for me, no matter what. If he needed me the way I need him I would be there for him. With all of his indecision, I've always been supportive and tried to help him figure things out. When I struggle with past stuff though, he just wants to run away. I don't get it!" She said, tears still running down her face.

"Maybe it's time to make yourself happy instead of waiting for him to do it. No one else can *make* you happy, Ava. You have to be able to make *yourself* happy. That way, if things do go sour, you won't feel so much hatred toward yourself believing you could have done something to make him, or someone else appreciate you. Be happy with who *you* are and understand that life is not about being perfect. It's about being able to enjoy your own growth and development and not putting all your stock in what someone else thinks of you," he explained.

"I know, I just don't know how to do that. I've been judged my whole life and all I know how to do is judge myself. And

I judge myself harshly," she answered, clearly searching for a way to help herself. "I feel like I'm stuck in my own head and can't escape myself. It's like my brain is a huge maze and I can't find my way through it because there are no lights. When something good happens, a little light seeps into the passages but if I get too far away from that light I can't see anything anymore. Maybe that's why I try so hard to keep what I think makes me happy. Maybe I try to rekindle the light after it goes out. So I'm not in the dark anymore, or at least for a little while. I don't know how to light the lights in the passages and I can't seem to carry one with me. It's like I'm always in that maze and it's always dark. It's a pitch black maze and I feel like the only way I'll find my way out is by accident. But, I'm thinkin' that's not guna happen either, so I'm trapped in that black maze all of the time. It terrifies me. I can't escape."

Ben looked at Ava as if she had just given him all of the information he would need to help her. He was astonished at her perception and he knew she would eventually work her way through things.

"Do you think the light you can carry with you can be lit by finding happiness in yourself? That way, you wouldn't have to cling to anyone else to find the light. Then you could find your way through the maze on your own and wouldn't have to depend on anyone else to provide light for you," he offered.

"Maybe," she said thoughtfully.

"We're out of time for today," Ben said. "How about we make another appointment for next week and we can continue the discussion.

"I'll have to check my work schedule," she answered. "I'll just call and make another appointment when I can.

"Sounds good," Ben said with a smile. "See you next time."

Ava left the office and drove back to Ropschon. She thought about what she and Ben had talked about, and seemed to feel a new energy inside of her, though it was small. She knew the session with Ben had helped greatly and she was determined to go back again.

Fall had arrived and Ava was invited to play pool on the same two leagues as the year before. She was happy to reunite with Sophie and Peyton and the comradery between the three of them helped her see things a little more positively. Ava confided in both of them about her struggles with Corey. They both wanted to help but knew there was very little, if anything, they could do aside from being there for her when she needed to talk.

During league one night, Sophie and Ava discussed some of the issues Ava had been dealing with. She told Sophie about her feeling of being trapped in a maze. Sophie tried to help Ava talk through some of the issues and even had a suggestion.

"I don't know how the fuck I'm guna get through all this, Sophie," Ava said with desperation in her voice.

"What about doing a role-play session?" Sophie suggested.

"What's that?" Ava questioned inquisitively.

"Well, you write letters to the people who have hurt you, then give the letters to people who can act like those people. Then, you can yell, talk, whatever, and you will feel better because you will get to express your feelings," Sophie explained.

"So I can get my thoughts out and not hurt anyone," Ava reflected in an effort to discover whether or not she had understood Sophie correctly.

"Yeah," Sophie said with a smile.

"Will you help me?" Ava asked politely.

"Sure," Sophie agreed.

"Sweet, thank you!" Ava exclaimed. "I'll write the letters this week."

Ava and Sophie resumed their participation in the night of pool and Ava had a good feeling about using Sophie's suggestion. Just to be safe, however, Ava wanted to ask Ben about toying with psychological issues without a professional present.

The next day, Ava made another appointment with Ben for a few days later. The week seemed to fly by, and before she knew it, the time came to return to Ben's office to keep her appointment. The appointment went well and Ava was able to keep her tears to a minimum. She inquired about Sophie's suggestion and Ben elaborated on the subject.

"When role-playing to remedy psychological situations such as yours, I believe you would be safe to do it at home or in my office," he said. "I would be happy to observe if you like, but if you would rather do it in private that is acceptable as well. I think Sophie's suggestion is a good one and I believe you will benefit from it."

"So, is there a chance of someone getting hurt?" Ava questioned, knowing she would likely lose control of her anger during the reenactment.

"Absolutely," Ben confirmed. "You should have someone there to help control the situation if needed."

"Okay," Ava said, happy Ben had told her Sophie's idea was a good one. "So, why will role-play help me? I mean, why can't I just talk through the stuff with you or my friends or somethin'?"

"Well," he began, "when traumatic things happen in our lives, the way things have happened in yours, each of these situations creates a virtual niche within the psyche. If the situation is not rectified, or if you do not have the opportunity to achieve closure, the virtual niche remains and the subconscious returns to it when something is reminiscent of the situation such as a sound, a smell, someone's attitude, etc."

"I must have a buncha niches then," Ava remarked thoughtfully.

"Why do you say that?" Ben inquired.

"Well, 'cause when things get outta hand I feel like I'm driving a bus and a deer runs out in front of me. Instead of reacting the way I should, I seem to freeze up because I have all these thoughts in my head at once. Like there are fifty people on the bus I'm drivin' yellin' at me to do different things. Then I can't seem to do what I know is right, ya know?" She explained.

"That would make sense," Ben said. "If you have several niches in your psyche, and one aspect of the situation at hand is reminiscent of all or many of the niches, it would stand to reason that your subconscious is unable to draw from only one or two sources of reference to handle the situation. It would be as if all or several of the people on the bus are yelling at you to do different things, rendering you unable to decide what to do for yourself. The people on the bus yelling at you would be the various niches in your psyche, creating reactions."

Ava looked thoughtfully, everything Ben had explained making perfect sense to her.

"To describe it in even more detail," Ben began, "each time a niche is formed in your psyche that niche remains at the age in which it originally occurred. For example, you were unable to confront John about what he did to you when you were six so the niche that was created at that point will remain six years old. Therefore, the rationale and experience from that point in your life, regarding aspects of your life now that are reminiscent of those situations, will remain as if that part of your psyche is only six years old. Does that make sense?" Ben asked.

"Yes, it does," she answered, seemingly in awe of the explanation Ben had given her. Everything seemed to be making so much sense to her. Her new understanding seemed to give her a glimpse of hope and she felt relieved.

She left Ben's office and decided to see if Sophie was busy. She had to let her know she wanted to go through with the role-play. Calling Sophie, she told her what Ben had said and Sophie was excited about the role-play as well. She wanted Ava to find peace, hating the idea of her friend having to deal with so much pain. During their conversation, Sophie and Ava decided the best person to help with the role-play would be Corey. Ava told Sophie she would set everything up with him, finish the letters, and find a time when the role-play would work for all three of them. Ava called Corey, explained the situation, and asked him to help. He skeptically agreed and plans were made to meet at Sophie's house the next weekend. Everything seemed to be going smoothly and Ava felt calmed.

Over the course of the next week, Ava had begun to struggle once again, feeling as if she could no longer go on. Returning to her apartment after a long day at the factory, she attempted to find solace by calling Corey to talk. It was a Thursday and Ava knew Sophie and Peyton would be at her apartment by five-thirty to pick her up for pool.

"I really just need to talk," Ava said to Corey.

"About what?" he asked, his voice faintly colored with irritation.

"I don't know, just stuff. I feel really sad right now, and Sophie and Peyton will be here soon to get me," she explained.

"I don't think I can help ya, Ava," he said. "I feel like all ya ever do is feel sad and I feel like I caused it."

"What do ya mean ya feel like you caused it?" she asked, surprised.

"Well, whenever we talk it's like you're unhappy," he said. "Why do ya always wana talk to me when you're sad? Ya need to learn to stand on your own two feet and deal with stuff. I can't do it anymore."

Once again, it seemed as if Corey was trying to make the situation about himself and how he felt. It was becoming very clear to Ava that he was not able to step outside of himself long enough to help her. The selfishness she had always suspected seemed to be showing itself more and more every day.

"Ya know, this isn't about you," Ava said, her voice beginning to shake. "I need help and you're my boyfriend. Why wouldn't I turn to you?"

"I'll help ya this weekend, like I said I would, but I don't wana talk anymore unless it's positive stuff," Corey declared. "Ya know, like when we first got together."

"A lot's happened since we got together, Corey," Ava said. "You promised we would be together and you tell me you love me yet here I am in my own apartment with you nowhere around. You want me to deal with shit on my own and when I ask you for help you act like it's not your problem. Seems to me you haven't wanted to be with me for a while unless it benefits you."

"Whatever," he said with indifference. "Get ready and go to pool."

He hung up the phone without giving Ava time to reply and she chose not to call him back. It would only make things worse. She sat down on the couch and lit a cigarette. As the cigarette burned in her hand, she once again began to cry. It felt as if her life was caving in around her and there was nothing she could do about it. The man she loved did not seem to care about her and he had told her he was no longer willing to help her deal with anything. Soon after she sat down on the couch she heard a knock at the door. Ava knew it was Peyton and Sophie, there to pick her up for league. She walked to the door and opened it to find Peyton standing in the doorway. With one look at Ava's face, Peyton was immediately concerned and stepped into the apartment.

"Are you okay?" Peyton asked.

"No," Ava said, "I can't do it anymore."

"You can't do what anymore?" Peyton questioned, now very concerned.

Ava shook her head and returned to her seat on the couch. "I can't shoot tonight, Peyton," she sobbed. "I can't let anyone see me like this. Will you tell the other girls I'm sick? Please? Please don't tell them what is really wrong?" Ava begged.

"What *is* really wrong?" Peyton asked as she crossed the room to sit on the couch next to Ava. "You aren't guna hurt yourself are ya?"

Ava sat silently staring at her cigarette and rolling it between her fingers.

"Promise me you won't hurt yourself, Ava," Peyton pleaded.

Ava looked at Peyton and immediately felt the concern in Peyton's heart. She couldn't hurt her that way.

"I promise," Ava said softly, trying to offer a comforting smile through the terrible anguish she wore on her face.

"Okay, I'll stop back if ya want me to after pool," Peyton offered.

"No, don't worry about me. I'm okay. I'm just feeling a lot of anxiety and I just want the weekend to get here so Sophie and I can do the role-play. Hopefully that'll help," Ava said, still very distant.

"Ya promise you're not guna to hurt yourself, right?" Peyton asked again.

"I promise," Ava repeated. "Thank you."

Still very concerned, Peyton rose to leave. "We'll take care of finding a sub tonight," she assured Ava.

"Thank you," Ava said.

Peyton hugged Ava then left the apartment. Even though she was still very worried about Ava, Peyton believed her when she promised she wouldn't hurt herself that night. Peyton walked to the car and got inside.

"Ava's not comin' tonight," she informed Sophie.

"How come?" Sophie asked, immediately concerned.

"She's really strugglin'," Peyton answered. "Cryin' and everything. I'm not sure what all happened but I'm sure it's got something to do with Corey. Fuckin' dick. She wants us to just say she's sick but she's not. I'm worried about her."

"Me too," Sophie said. "I'm lookin' forward to this weekend. I hope it helps her."

Sophie backed her car out of the parking place and drove onto the road. Peyton called Lila, the captain of the Thursday night team, to inform her Ava would not be playing, and that they needed to find a sub.

"Hello," Lila happily answered.

"Hey Lila," Peyton said, "Ava isn't guna be able to make it tonight."

"What the hell's wrong with her?" Lila said, immediately irritated by the news.

"She's sick," Peyton said.

"Oh, great. Would've been nice if she could've given me some fuckin' notice," Lila spat, clearly angry about Ava's absence.

"Well, she just got sick and was feeling shitty after work," Peyton said in an effort to covertly defend Ava.

"Whatever," Lila said. "Guess I'll have to call Jill."

"Okay," Peyton said. "See ya when we get there."

Lila hung up without saying goodbye and proceeded to find a sub for Ava. Ava hated leaving the burden of finding someone to shoot for her on the others, so she had sent a text to Jill as soon as Peyton left, to see if she could shoot. Jill had agreed and was already on her way to the bar before Lila even contacted her. Lila called Jill and she happily answered the phone, already knowing what she would ask.

"Hello?" Jill said.

"Jill, can you shoot tonight?" Lila asked, her voice clearly compelling her upset with the situation.

"Yeah, Ava sent me a text and I'm already on my way," she answered.

"Nice," Lila spat. "She didn't give me any fuckin' notice and says she's sick."

"Yeah, I know," Jill said. "Why are you pissed?"

"Because she waited 'til the last fuckin' minute to say anything and then didn't even call me. She had to have Peyton call me," Lila said, her voice sounding angrier with each word.

"So she's sick," Jill spat back at Lila. "We all get sick and who cares if Peyton called ya. Ava asked me to sub and I'm happy to do it. No reason to be all pissy about it!"

"See ya when ya get here," Lila said and then hung up the phone.

Jill felt anger toward Lila on Ava's behalf and decided at that moment she would tell Ava what Lila had said, if for no other reason than to let Ava know what kind of person Lila was, if she did not already know.

Sophie and Peyton arrived at the bar and walked in. Jill was already there and welcomed them with a smile. Cheryl, the fifth member of the team, was the first to speak to Peyton and Sophie.

"Is Ava really sick or are her and Corey fightin' again?" Cheryl scoffed.

Peyton was offended for Ava at Cheryl's comment and immediately stepped up to defend her. "She's fuckin' sick! Big deal! We all get fuckin' sick! Drop it!"

Cheryl said nothing else and Lila chose to remain silent as well. In response to Payton's defense of Ava, Cheryl and Lila exchanged a spiteful and irritated glance. The night went on and the games were played. As Peyton and Sophie drove back to Ropschon Peyton called Ava to check on her.

"Hello?" Ava said in a groggy voice.

"How ya doin'?" Peyton asked.

"Okay, I guess. Been sleepin'," Ava answered, her voice thick with sleep.

"Okay, I'll let ya go back to sleep. Just wanted to check on ya," Peyton said.

"Okay, thanks," Ava said. "Bye."

"See ya," Peyton said, then hung up the phone.

"How's she doin'?" Sophie asked.

"Okay, said she's been sleepin'," Peyton replied. "I'll call her tomorrow."

"Think I will too," Sophie said.

Peyton and Sophie both called Ava the next day and each talked for quite some time. Ava was able to calmly explain the situation the night before to both of them and both listened without judgment. Both Peyton and Sophie told Ava about the things Lila and Cheryl had said and Ava was furious.

"What the fuck?" Ava said to Peyton on the phone. "They automatically think I'm just guna fuck the team, huh?"

"Yeah," Peyton answered. "It was horse shit. Lila was a total bitch about it and asked what the fuck was wrong with ya. Didn't even ask if you'd be okay. Just started bitchin'."

"Nice," Ava said, at that moment concluding she would not consider Lila a friend any longer.

"And Cheryl was just as bad," Peyton continued. "She wanted to know if you were really sick or if you and Corey were fightin' again. She didn't ask if you were okay either."

"Well, they're both gettin' a piece of my fuckin' mind when I see 'em again," Ava said. "Fuck 'em. I don't need this shit from people who claim to be my friends. I have only missed pool one other time in all the years I've played! Guess I have to be perfect for them to care about me too, right?"

"No shit, right?" Peyton agreed angrily.

After the phone conversation with Peyton ended, Ava's phone rang again, this time with Jill's number showing on the screen. Jill told Ava the things Lila had said on the phone and what she had heard at the bar. She assured Ava she was not telling her to cause problems, but so Ava would be aware of what her so-called friends were saying about her. Ava told Jill what Peyton and Sophie had told her as well and then thanked Jill for the information. Ava was ultimately set in confronting Cheryl and Lila but knew she had bigger things to worry about that weekend. It was time for the role-play and Corey would be arriving in only a few minutes to pick her up to go to Sophie's house.

Corey arrived and Ava got into his car. They drove the ten miles to Sophie's house with minimal conversation.

"How ya doin'?" Corey asked.

"Okay, I guess," Ava replied, unwilling to tell him the truth. Changing the subject, she continued, "I need ya to promise me you'll do everything ya can to keep me from hurting Sophie," Ava said.

"Yeah, I will," he assured her with no concern in his voice.

"I really don't want to hurt her," she said, clearly concerned about the situation.

"Yeah," he said, "it'll be fine."

They arrived at Sophie's house and went inside. Ava and Sophie talked about what would be happening and Ava gave Sophie the letters.

"Do you want to do all these people today? Like at the same time?" Sophie asked, referring to whether or not Ava wanted the reenactment to involve all of the characters.

"If ya think we can, yeah," Ava said. "I just wana get it done."

"Corey can do the male voices and I can do the female voices," Sophie suggested.

"Sure, whatever," Corey agreed, clearly indifferent to the situation.

"You'll need to read these two letters then, so you know what's comin'," Sophie said to Corey as she handed the letters to him.

Sophie and Corey sat down and read through the letters. Once she was finished reading, Sophie suggested Ava choose a character to start with and the others could then be brought in. Ava agreed, then to mentally prepare for the role-play interaction, Sophie and Ava sat down to have a cigarette together.

"I really don't want to hurt you, Sophie," Ava said in a nervous and apologetic tone.

"Well, Corey's here to help make sure that doesn't happen," she said, reassuring Ava everything would be okay.

"If you'd rather not do this I would completely understand," Ava said, giving Sophie another chance to change her mind.

"I wana do it," Sophie said. "I wana help you."

Ava offered a crooked smile to relay her gratitude.

"I'm nervous," Ava said in a somewhat lighter tone.

"I am a little bit too," Sophie said, offering a smile. "Are ya ready?"

"Yeah, ready as I'll ever be," Ava breathed, clearly unsure of what was going to happen next.

"Corey, are ya ready?" Sophie asked.

"Yep," he answered, confused about why Ava was nervous and why Ava was afraid she might hurt Sophie.

What Corey did not realize, regardless of the several times Ava had informed him, she tended to lose control of herself when she was very angry. He wrote it off as a false or exaggerated claim and did not worry about the admonitions. He knew he outweighed Ava by at least fifty pounds and that he was stronger than her. He assumed he would have no problem keeping her contained if needed. He was definitely in for a surprise.

Chapter Fourteen

With all three participants seemingly ready to initiate the role-play exercise, Ava, Sophie, and Corey gathered in Sophie's living room, to settle the last minute details, before beginning. Sophie was set to portray Sonya, Ava's mother, a role that would prove to capitalize the session. Corey was to represent Able, Ava's brother, and John, the man who had raped Ava repeatedly when she was six years old. Ava and Sophie had decided to start with the three major individuals in Ava's life who had begun the upset that later created a gravity that continually threatened to pull Ava into the ground.

"Okay, so basically we're guna help Ava recreate some of the times in her life that were upsetting," Sophie began, speaking directly to Corey.

"Okay," he said, clearly not yet possessing the understanding he needed to be an effective participant. "We're guna act out the bad stuff she went through?" he questioned with concern.

"No," Sophie said, "we're just guna try to act like these people toward her so she can say what she needs to say to them without actually having to see them."

"Oh, okay," Corey answered, confusion still coloring his face even though he nodded as if he understood completely.

"All that needs to happen is for you guys to talk to me

the way they did so I can get upset, say what I need to say, and get closure," Ava volunteered in an effort to help Corey understand.

Corey nodded his head again but the expression on his face conveyed a suggestion of many more questions.

"So, in your letter to John ya said a lot of stuff about him rapin' ya. Ya don't wana act it out, ya just wana yell at him, right?" Corey said to Ava in an attempt to clarify his own understanding.

"Yeah," Ava answered, relieved Corey had begun to grasp the idea of the exercise. "Ben, my psychologist, says I just need to say what I feel to each person, or someone representing each person, in order to get closure and hopefully start to heal."

"Oh, okay," Corey said, nodding his head yet again. "I get it."

"So, do ya get how to talk to her as John?" Sophie asked Corey, still unsure whether or not he completely understood his role.

"Yeah, I think so," Corey replied.

"'Cause when she yells at ya you're guna wana stop," Sophie explained, "but ya can't. Ya gota keep goin' with it 'til I tell ya to stop."

"Okay," Corey said, his voice gaining a hint of reluctance as he spoke the single word.

"Tell us how to speak to ya as each person," Sophie said to Ava. "We have to know what will set ya off in order to really get ya goin' in this."

"Well," Ava began, letting out a sigh. "John always had a soft voice and would say sexual stuff to me, even though I was only six. Of course, the stuff he said wasn't sexual innuendo type stuff... it was really direct. Like after my mom left the house, he'd tell me to take my pants off 'cause I looked better that way, then he'd rape me. He'd always remind me not to tell Ma, 'cause I'd get in trouble. Of course, I believed him. I was only six and my mom was a fuckin' bitch."

"Okay, so you'll have to talk to her like she's six and you want her to get naked so you can have sex with her," Sophie instructed Corey.

While Sophie spoke the words to him, Corey began to realize the extent of the role-play exercise and his part in it. His face took on a collective look of disgust and fear as the information sunk into his mind.

"That's sick," Corey said to Sophie as his face distorted to reflect his revulsion.

"I know," Sophie said, "but we have to do this if we wana help her."

Corey nodded his head slightly, to indicate he understood, then looked at Ava.

"Do ya think it's a good idea for me to be the one to do this?" he asked with skepticism.

"I don't know," Ava said, "but who else would be able to do it?" she asked, her face taking on a look of defeat as she realized Corey may be trying to avoid participating.

He shrugged his shoulders slightly, and looked down at the floor in front of his feet, revealing his guilt about trying to escape the situation.

"Are ya guna do this?" Sophie asked bluntly.

"Yeah," he replied weakly without looking up.

"Okay, so what was Niles like?" Sophie asked Ava.

Of course, Sophie was referring to Ava's brother, Able, who had changed his name. Many of the people who had known him before he had changed his name still referred to him as Niles, Ava being one of them. Since Sophie did not know him personally, she referred to him as Niles because that was the name Ava always used.

"He was always loud and seemed pissed all the time," Ava

said as her mind briefly wandered back to a time when she and Niles still lived at home with Sonya. "It's like, most of the time he talked to me he was blamin' me for somethin' or chewin' my ass about somethin', ya know?"

Corey was abruptly jerked from his thoughts about how to portray John and listened intently.

"So, I gota be loud and bitch at ya?" Corey asked Ava.

"Yeah, he always got pissed when I'd go in his room, try to be around him, or ask him questions about stuff he thought I should know, even though I was only a little kid," Ava said. "I really just wanted to be around him 'cause I loved him. I never met my father so he was the only guy I trusted. I think maybe that's another reason I was such an easy target for John. I needed a male figure in my life and Niles didn't seem interested," Ava said, her eyes showing the shadow of the saddening memories as she spoke.

Corey looked at Sophie and she returned his glance. He nodded at her to indicate he understood what was expected of him.

"So, how'd you're mom talk to ya?" Sophie asked.

"Well, she was always drunk and yelled at me for everything," Ava said, her eyes clearing as she was pulled from her memories of Niles. "Called me a little fuckin' bitch and little fuckin' whore all the time. Always threatenin' to beat my ass and went through with it. When I'd come home from one of my friends' houses she'd ask where the hell I'd been then call me a name. Happened all the time."

"Okay," Sophie said, preparing to begin the role-play. "Corey, are ya ready?"

"Yep," Corey said, still clearly uneasy with the entire situation.

"You ready?" Sophie asked Ava with concern in her voice.

"Before we start," Ava said in a shaky voice, "I gota make

sure we're all on the same page about making sure nobody gets hurt."

Corey and Sophie quietly waited as Ava lit a cigarette. Sophie decided to take the opportunity to join Ava as she smoked and lit one of her own. Ava took a long drink of her soda then took a deep breath as she prepared herself to speak.

"Um, I know ya don't think it's a big deal, and think ya can control me when I'm mad, but I'm worried 'cause I know me and I know how I get," Ava said, directly to Corey as she intently looked him in the eye.

"Nobody's guna get hurt," Corey said, with no doubt in his voice, unable to hold Ava's gaze.

"I know ya think that but you've never seen me mad enough to hurt someone," Ava argued.

"I've seen ya pissed, Ava," Corey said matter-of-factly. "You've been pissed at me plenty of times!"

"That's different," Ava said with grave seriousness in her voice as her eyes searched his face for understanding. "I've never wanted to literally kill *you* so no, ya haven't seen me that pissed."

The look on Corey's face slowly changed as he realized the gravity of the situation, and for the first time, began to realize the amount of hatred Ava held in her heart toward Sonya, John, and Niles.

"You actually wanted to kill them?" he asked, his voice thick with curious alarm.

"Well, not so much Niles, but I definitely wanted to kill my mom and John," Ava said. Though Niles was mean to her most of the time, he had not done the things Sonya and John had, therefore, she did not hate him completely. She rationalized that even though Niles seemed to treat her like a piece of garbage, he at least stood up for her when he found out what John had done. That alone seemed to gain Niles a pardon in Ava's heart that would remain forever, even if she eventually disconnected herself from him.

"What are you afraid is guna happen?" Sophie asked Ava in a caring voice.

"I don't know for sure," Ava said, as her gaze shifted to her friend. "I just don't wana hurt either one of ya."

"Hurt us how?" Sophie asked.

"Physically," Ava said. "I know I get fuckin' nuts when I get mad, and it seems like the older I get, the harder it is to control. I know you guys are both bigger than me but I don't trust myself not to hurt ya. Ben said I could go into a type of hypnotic state and if that happens I won't even know what I'm doin'. It scares me."

"Well," Sophie began, "Corey will be able to protect me and I'll be able to protect him," she said in an effort to help Ava feel comforted and reassured.

Ava looked up to once again meet Sophie's gaze, then looked at Corey. Both of them were looking at her with confident expressions and she believed things would be alright.

"Okay," Ava said reluctantly. "Let's do it, I guess."

"Ya wana take a little break before we start?" Sophie asked.

"Yeah," Ava said, "I need to regroup a little and go pee."

While Ava was in the bathroom, Sophie and Corey spoke briefly about what was about to happen.

"Do ya really think she could hurt either one of us?" Corey asked Sophie.

"Oh yeah," Sophie replied as a nervous, but serious chuckle rose in her throat. "This kinda shit can bring things up that are hard to control. We aren't guna be talkin' to the Ava we know. We'll be talking to the Ava that went through all this shit. The reason she might be dangerous is 'cause she's got years of hate and anger built up that's guna explode. We gota be careful – for ourselves, and for her."

Corey did not respond to Sophie verbally, but she could clearly understand his unspoken thoughts by the expression on his face, and saw that he was unable to argue with anything she had told him. He knew Ava had been through a great deal but had not completely realized the severity of the situation until that very moment.

After Ava finished in the bathroom she crossed the room to Sophie.

"Thank you for doin' this," Ava said as she hugged her friend.

"You're welcome," Sophie said, hugging her back and offering a comforting smile.

Ava hugged Corey as well, also thanking him for helping with the role-play.

"I know it's guna be uncomfortable for ya and I'm glad you decided to help," Ava said to him She knew Corey usually avoided situations involving upset, and ultimately had been surprised he had agreed to help at all, especially once he found out he would be participating instead of only protecting Sophie.

"I just have one question," Sophie said to Ava. "Who ya wana start with?"

"Um, well, it'd probably be better to start with the one who pissed me off the most, right?" Ava reasoned.

"Yep," Sophie answered.

"Looks like we'll start with Ma then," Ava decided, without hesitation.

Corey was relieved he would not have to start things off

and felt more comfortable that Sophie would be setting the pace.

"Okay," Sophie said. "Ya ready?"

Ava nodded her head slightly and stood in front of Sophie, only a few feet from her.

"Where the fuck ya been ya little fuckin' bitch?" Sophie screeched at Ava.

The unnatural way the words fell on Ava's ears made her wince and her eyes slammed shut. She continued to stand in front of Sophie and immediately felt the anger begin to build inside her. Ava opened her eyes slowly, and simply looked away from Sophie's face, as Sophie understood her words had sparked something deep.

"What, ya think you can just do whatever ya want ya little fuckin' whore?" Sophie screamed at Ava, stepping closer to her.

Ava leaned slightly backward away from Sophie but stood her ground. She was not able to look at Sophie and she could feel herself beginning to tremble as her anger continued to grow. Corey stood to the side and was poised to interfere if something went awry, though he had no idea what he would do. Sophie took another step toward Ava and continued to shriek judgmental obscenities at her. Sophie's words flew at Ava, seemingly from every direction. Ava was still lucid and knew it was not her mother yelling at her, but was unable to stifle the eruptive anger that was welling inside of her. Ava took a step back. She felt her calf touch the front of the couch that was behind her, and knew she could not back up any further.

"Stop," Ava said in a voice that was almost inaudible.

Sophie continued to screech at Ava, the way her mother had, drawing from the letter as well as the many conversations she and Ava had throughout the years as Ava described the horrible experiences from her childhood.

"Stop," Ava said again, her voice only slightly louder than before.

Sophie heard Ava's meek command, though the words were little louder than the squeak of a slightly rusted hinge. She knew Ava was starting to become overwhelmed with her own anger and used the momentum to push Ava closer to her goal.

Corey stood close by, watching as Ava's face changed. He suddenly realized he was not at all prepared for the fierceness of the confrontation, but knew it was too late to try to avoid participating. The volume of Sophie's voice and the horrible things she was saying to Ava had taken him by surprise and his mind whirled. He knew that if he was the one who had started the interaction, as soon as Ava said to stop, he would have. He struggled to understand how Sophie could say the things she was saying, the larger picture of how the exercise would help Ava still eluding him.

"Stop," Ava said again, this time with more conviction, in a voice that was easily heard.

Sophie relentlessly continued, never moving her face away from Ava's. As Ava turned her head from side to side in a feeble attempt to avoid Sophie's verbal attack, Sophie moved with her to increase the provocation of Ava's temper even more. As Sophie shrieked at Ava, using many of the same phrases Sonya once had, it became more and more difficult for Ava to control herself. Finally, Ava had reached her breaking point.

"Stop it, Ma! Please!" Ava shrieked as she covered her face and fell back on the couch right behind her.

Ava drew her feet up in front of her and hid her face behind her knees. As she sat on the end of the couch, curled in a ball as if she were a child, Sophie knew she had finally pushed her back into the past that was trapped in her mind. Sophie continued to scream at Ava, barraging her with what seemed like a lifetime of insults. Ava felt as if she were a child again, and her eyes were tightly closed, as Sophie continued to verbally attack her. She had succumbed to the hypnotic state, of which Ben had spoken, and was no longer completely aware of the present moment. She was utterly submerged in the reenactment that was taking place and was once again the little girl Sonya had abused so viciously.

After several minutes of cowering on the couch, Ava felt as if she had to do something to fight back. It was as if several years had gone by in only a few seconds, and she was able to find the courage to stand once again. Sophie had stepped back slightly, allowing only a few feet between herself and the front of the couch upon which Ava sat. Ava took the opportunity to shoot to her feet and began screaming back at Sophie, though she was only able to see Sonya as her memories engulfed reality.

Sophie knew Ava had gone into a hypnotic state and continued to fire insults at her. Ava was now completely active in the role-play and followed Sophie's prompts immediately. From the letter Ava had written to Sonya, Sophie was able to mock some of the worst confrontations that had taken place throughout the years and her performance was flawless. Each time Sophie referenced a confrontation, Ava was able to respond as if she were in the moment, reliving every second. The battle between Ava and Sonya seethed for quite some time, before Ava was finally able to reach a point in her entranced state, where she began to reveal the things she had always wanted to say and do to her mother. She began to boldly step toward Sophie and Sophie responded by reluctantly retreating. In order to keep Sophie from escaping her, Ava reached out with both hands and grasped her wrists. Sophie, still portraying Sonya, began to bark objections to the physical contact, but Ava refused to let go. The grip she had on Sophie's wrists was so tight her fingernails began to break the skin as she squeezed and twisted. She wanted to inflict pain on Sonya, the way Sonya had inflicted pain on her so many times before.

Corey was still standing by and had begun to interfere when Ava reached for Sophie. Sophie immediately rejected his intervention with a commanding look and Corey stepped back. As the minutes passed Ava forcefully guided Sophie toward the couch that sat next to the one she had initially fallen back on. The other couch was at a right angle to the first one, creating an "L" shape of furniture. Sophie felt the backs of her legs touch the second couch, and knew she had to step to the left if Ava attempted a more threatening attack. Ava's hands swiftly slid up and forcefully seized Sophie's upper arms. Sophie felt an instant urgency to step away from Ava, but before she could act, Ava began to lift her vertically off of the floor. Sophie was surprised at Ava's ability to lift her but knew the adrenaline pumping through her veins was likely the source of her incredible strength.

Sophie's eyes quickly shot toward Corey as her feet left the floor, and he immediately understood it was time to intervene. He swiftly reached for Ava's shoulders, and as his hands touched her, he could feel the rigidity of every muscle and knew that coaxing her to let go of Sophie would be harder than he had first assumed. Trying to force Ava's hands off of Sophie's arms seemed to only tighten her grip. He tugged at Ava's forearms, then tried to force himself between Ava and Sophie, so Ava would have to step away and release her. Before he was able to even begin to overpower Ava, a burst of adrenaline, ultimately caused by his interference, allowed Ava to throw Sophie backward onto the couch. Sophie hit the couch heavily and Ava stood her ground, ready to continue her attack with a new tactic. Corey's interference had interrupted Ava's memories and she took a brief second to look directly at him after throwing Sophie onto the couch. Ava was unable to make out the features of Corey's face, as he was not an original part of the memory. She could only see a densely shadowed outline of a face, with features that seemed to blur together, rendering them impossible to define. Quickly and unconsciously deciding the interfering person was no match for her, Ava resumed her attack on Sophie.

"I'm guna fuckin' kill you!" Ava screeched repeatedly at Sophie, still only able to see Sonya as she stepped toward her friend, and began to come down on her.

Reaching toward Sophie, Ava's hands closed around her throat and tightened. Sophie tried to stop Ava's advance but her attempt to protect herself was futile. Corey's continued attempts to pull Ava off of Sophie were no more effective than an ant trying to move a car. Sophie's eyes began to reflect her increasing fear as Ava sustained her grip. Sophie could feel her air supply being cut off and tried desperately to break free from the relentless pressure Ava's hands created on her throat.

"I'm guna fuckin' kill you!" Ava continued to scream at Sophie. "I'm guna fuckin' kill you!" Repeating the phrase over and over.

"Ava!" Corey screamed. "Ava, it's me, Corey! Let her go! That's not your mom! It's Sophie! Let her go!"

Ava's grip remained tight as Corey tried to wake Ava from her dreamlike state. She could only see Sonya in front of her and she wanted nothing more than to kill her.

"Ava!" Corey barked again, still physically trying to force her to release her fatal hold on Sophie's throat. He continued to scream at her and repeatedly ordered her to let go of Sophie.

Several seconds after Corey began yelling at Ava, she slowing began to loosen her grip on Sophie's throat, and within only a few more seconds had released her completely, her hands resting limply on Sophie's neck. Ava clumsily stepped backward, away from Sophie, but was clearly still in the hypnotic trance. In reality, Ava had let go of Sophie because she was still trying to figure out who Corey was. At the point in time brought about by hypnosis in Ava's mind, she had not yet met Corey, and was completely confused by the name.

"Are you okay?" Corey asked Sophie, lightly touching her arm, and panting from the escalation of the situation.

"Yeah, I'm fine," Sophie panted, out of breath and shaking. "It's your turn. Ya gota keep it goin'. Do Niles. Now!"

Swept up in the excitement of the situation, Corey immediately turned to Ava and began yelling at her. Ava stood in the middle of Sophie's living room, her eyes fluttering, as her hypnotized mind tried to make sense of the interruption and the unknown person. She was still completely absorbed in the role-play, having remained in the depths of her own mind. Ava's reaction to Corey's portrayal of Niles was not nearly as severe as the interaction between Ava and Sophie. Ava seemed to be completely ready to attack her brother, and as soon as she began to hear the familiar phrases, she was immediately ready to fire back at him. Ava unleashed an assault of words that seemed to fly from her mouth like bullets from the barrel of a machine gun. Ava had never wanted to physically hurt Niles, she simply wanted to be able to tell him what she thought. She had never been able to disclose any of her thoughts to her brother, because he was always ready to yell at her if she opposed him in any way. She desperately wanted his approval, but was unable to earn it, no matter how hard she tried. Ultimately, during her early twenties, just after her divorce from Mark, Ava had completely abandoned any hope of ever gaining Niles' approval for anything.

Several minutes passed and Sophie had time to largely recover from the attack Ava had unleashed upon her. It was clear that Ava only needed to be able to unload her thoughts on her brother, and Corey seemed to be unable to argue with her.

Sophie could see Corey was still nervous about the role-play, so she encouraged him to verbally engage with Ava by nudging him in the back. Finally, Corey was able to remember some of the things in Ava's letter to Niles, and resumed verbal combat with her. Ultimately, Corey knew he needed to slowly retreat his words to allow Ava to speak her mind and he ineptly did so. After Ava had said her peace to Niles, she simply turned away from him, crossing her arms across her chest with tenacity. That was Sophie's cue to tell Corey to switch characters and start interacting with Ava as John.

"Ava?" Sophie said, trying to determine whether or not she was still in the unsophisticated hypnotic state.

"What?" Ava barked back angrily.

Her response was enough proof she was still confined in her past, and Sophie gestured for Corey to begin his part as John.

"Ava, Niles is gone. It's me, John," Corey said in a calm voice.

Ava did not move. Sophie and Corey watched nervously as Ava's mind seemed to visibly shift and prepared to face the man who had repeatedly raped her when she was a little girl. Ava's slowly lowered her arms to her sides and her hands began to form fists. She turned her head to the side, as if to hear John's voice better, to ensure it was him. Sophie and Corey watched as Ava's muscles tightened once again. Sophie could see Ava's body trembling, and knew the interaction was going to be successful, as well as violent. Again, Sophie nudged Corey, indicating it was time to say something sexual.

"Take off your pants," Corey said, his voice shaky and weak. "Ya look better without 'em. But don't say anything or you're guna be in trouble."

The words seemed to fuel Ava once again and she slowly

turned to face Corey. This time she only saw John standing in front of her, and her eyes were filled with sweltering hatred.

"You sick fuck!" Ava growled, as small droplets of saliva flew from her mouth. "You deserve to die for what you've been doing to me!"

Sophie and Corey simultaneously felt a chill of fear as they looked at Ava. Neither of them had ever seen her with such a look of complete detestation on her face.

"You sick mother fucker!" Ava screeched as she rushed toward Corey, her voice exploding like a crack of thunder powerful enough to shake the Earth.

She was upon him before he could react and her hands gripped his arms. She continued to scream obscene insults at him, her face only a fraction of an inch from his. As the words formed and flew from her mouth, more saliva flew with them, as if she was a rabid animal viciously attacking a domestic pet. Immediately, Corey tried to break free of Ava's hold, but before he could move she was shoving him backward, her strength surprising him. He tried to object, but her ears were deaf to his words. Shoving him violently, he was unable to keep his footing. As he began to lose his balance, Ava had yet another burst of strength that allowed her to physically throw him backward and to the left. He landed hard on the couch Ava had been on when the role-play session had first started. The force of the impact, as his body connected with the cushions, knocked the breath from his lungs, and he immediately gulped for air. Ava continued to advance upon him with a look of absolute disgust in her eyes, her hands extending toward his throat. Sophie wrapped her arms around Ava, pinning her arms to her sides.

"Ava!" Sophie said in a calm but very stern voice. "Wake up! John's gone! Wake up!"

Sophie shook Ava slightly, and continued to encourage her

to come out of the murky depths of her own mind, believing Ava had endured quite enough for one day. After only a few seconds, Ava's body began to relax, and her breathing began to slow. Sophie loosened her grip around Ava and Ava's body continued to relax. Sophie did not want to completely release her hold on Ava, until she was sure she was out of the trance-like state. Ava's knees began to wobble and suddenly gave out. Sophie did not expect Ava to fall, and was unable to support her weight, as her legs failed underneath her. Corey had regained his breathing, and quickly stood to help Sophie keep Ava from falling, adrenaline now fueling his motions. They slowly lowered Ava to the floor and allowed her to be free from any confinement.

"Ava?" Sophie said, in an attempt to keep Ava from losing consciousness.

Ava's head swiveled, as if she were severely intoxicated, but no words came from her throat.

"Ava!" Sophie exclaimed, unwilling to leave her alone until she answered.

"Yeah," Ava replied, almost inaudibly, in a very tired and scratchy voice.

"You okay?" Sophie asked, very concerned.

"Yeah," Ava repeated, slowly nodding her head slightly.

Suddenly, a gagging noise resonated from Ava's throat. She had completely returned to reality and felt incredibly weary. She knew she was going to be sick and tried to scramble to her feet. Every muscle in her body felt as if it had been severely bruised, and she was unable to stand. She clumsily rolled over and was able to get on her hands and knees. She gagged again and began crawling toward Sophie's bathroom. Since the house was small, she was able to cover the distance quite quickly, driven by her refusal to vomit on Sophie's carpet. She barely made it to the toilet before she retched, but only a small amount of fluid came up. She had not eaten much in several days, due to the anxiety she had been experiencing, so after the small amount of fluid had been expelled she could only dry heave. After several minutes, Ava's abdominal muscles stopped contracting, and she was able to relax. Putting her arms across the seat of the toilet, she rested her head on them in an attempt to regain her composure. She felt as if she had been through a violent car crash, every muscle and joint in her body filled with pain and exhaustion.

Sophie entered the bathroom to check on Ava while Corey took Ava's belongings to the car in preparation to leave.

"You okay?" Sophie asked in a warm and caring tone.

"Yeah," Ava said, her voice echoing into the bowl of the toilet as she spoke.

Ava raised her head slightly in an attempt to look at Sophie. Her eyes looked as though she had not slept for days. She tried to stand, but was completely unsuccessful. Corey reentered the house and crossed the dining room to the open door of the bathroom.

"How's she doin'?" he asked Sophie.

"Okay, I think," Sophie said, "but I don't think she's guna be able to walk to the car.

Corey entered the bathroom and knelt next to Ava.

"Can ya walk?" he asked.

"I'll try," Ava said in a weak voice, as she tried to position herself to stand.

Corey helped her to her feet, but her legs were simply too weak to support her frame. She began to falter, but Corey helped her stay upright.

"I'll just carry her," he said to no one in particular, as he lowered the lid of the toilet and guided Ava to sit on it.

Repositioning himself with his right arm behind her back, and left arm under her knees, he lifted Ava and began to walk toward the door. Sophie hurried in front of him and opened the door, prepared to help any way she could. She then rushed to the passenger side of the car and opened the door. Corey set Ava in the passenger seat and pushed the car door shut with a slam.

"Thanks," Corey said, turning to Sophie.

"Yep," Sophie replied. "I'll call her later to see how she's doin'."

"Okay, see ya," he said with a half-hearted smile as he made his way to the driver's side of the car.

Corey drove Ava back to her apartment and helped her to her door. She had been able to regain her ability to walk, though not well, by the time they had driven the ten miles back to Ropschon. He helped her make her way to the couch in her living room, and covered her up with a blanket.

"Okay, I'm guna go," he said.

"Okay," Ava said, saddened by his declaration. "See ya. Thanks."

Corey left the apartment and drove back to his brother's house. Ava reached for the remote control and turned the television on. She wondered why Corey had not stayed with her. Tears silently soaked the throw pillow under her head, and she drifted off to sleep with the sound of the television program lending only slight comfort, as if someone were there to make sure she was alright.

The next day Ava awoke to sunshine spilling through the blinds that hung on her living room window. Her mind felt refreshed from the several hours of sleep, but her body was still incredibly sore. It seemed as if the role-play session had a positive impact, at least regarding sleep. She had slept so deeply after the session she was not even able to remember her dreams. It was refreshing to awake without being haunted by the hazy recollections of the memories that habitually plagued her. It was only eight o'clock, and had it not been for her need to use the bathroom, she would have happily rolled over and fell back to sleep.

She stiffly stood from the comfortable couch and stretched her tired, sore muscles. After relieving herself, she walked to the refrigerator and took a soda from the shelf. Returning to the couch, she sat down, lit a cigarette, and cracked the top on the soda can. She felt so very thirsty and the cold liquid seemed to sooth her sore, scratchy throat. For a brief moment, she wondered if she might be coming down with something, but immediately remembered her throat must be sore because of overuse the day before during the role-play session with Sophie and Corey. Picking up the remote control, she flipped through the channels until she found a program she wanted to watch. It only took a few seconds for Ava to decide she would be doing little that day, in order to give her body and voice time to recuperate.

At around noon, Ava's phone rang and Sophie's number appeared on the screen.

"Hello?" Ava said lazily, her voice reflecting the soreness of her traumatized throat.

"How ya doin'?" Sophie asked, a combination of concern and excitement flooding her voice.

"Good," Ava said, "my whole body hurts and my throat is killin' me, but otherwise I'm okay."

"Do ya think it helped?" Sophie inquired.

"It must have," Ava said. "I don't remember any of my

dreams from last night and I didn't wake up 'til eight. I haven't slept that good in a long time."

"That's good," Sophie agreed. "Do ya feel any different?"

"I don't really know yet," Ava said with slight disappointment leaking into her words. "I was hoping I would feel like a different person when I woke up, but I guess that's askin' a little much, huh?" Ava laughed hoarsely.

"Yeah," Sophie agreed with a giggle. "Maybe it'll take a few days to really notice anything."

"Prob'ly," Ava said. "I have to believe I'll have to be in some different situations before I'll know if it really helped."

"Yeah, that makes sense," Sophie agreed. "Okay, well, I just wanted to call and check on ya. Is Corey still there?"

"Oh, no," Ava said in a voice that immediately took on a cynical tone. "He helped me to the couch when we got here yesterday, gave me a blanket, then left. Haven't heard shit out of him since."

"Really?" Sophie remarked, disbelief clearly coloring her words. "What the hell?"

"I don't know," Ava said, her voice gradually sinking with each word. "I was upset about it yesterday when he left but when I woke up today I don't seem to give a shit."

"Well, maybe that's one way you can tell yesterday helped!" Sophie remarked in a positive tone, a smile clearly riding upon her words.

"Maybe!" Ava said with a raspy giggle.

"Okay, well, I gota go," Sophie said. "Let me know if ya need anything, okay?"

"Okay," Ava agreed. "Thank you so much for yesterday and for calling today. I don't know what I'd do without ya."

"You'd have done the same for me!" Sophie said happily.

"Yep," Ava said with a smile.

"Love ya," Sophie said.

"Love you too," Ava answered.

The call was ended and Ava set her phone on the coffee table in front of the couch. She hadn't realized it until she spoke the words to Sophie, but she really did not care if Corey called to check on her that day. She somehow felt as if she would be alright, regardless of how things turned out with him. She smiled to herself and for the first time she could remember, and felt a warm feeling in her heart, one that seemed to come from the happiness she felt inside. The happiness she had facilitated herself and carried out with Sophie's help. Of course, Corey had helped as well, but he had not caused her to feel the happiness. Taking the step to heal herself had ultimately produced the outcome, and that outcome was the warm, happy feeling she was enjoying at that moment.

Ava returned to work the following Monday, and seemed to have a different outlook on virtually everything. She knew her relationship with Corey would likely crumble, but that understanding no longer created panic in her heart. When league night finally rolled around again, Ava was able to confront Cheryl and Lila with conviction, exercising her anger, but still keeping her cool. Though she could feel the explosive anger deep inside, she seemed to inexplicably have a better understanding of how to control it. Lila and Cheryl apologized for the things they had said, and she decided to give them both another chance, though she knew it would be a very long time before she would trust either of them. She bluntly assured both of them that if either of them ever betrayed her again, she would erase them from her life as friends, and would not even acknowledge them as distant acquaintances. Ultimately, Ava would eventually find that Cheryl had truly understood her mistake, and over time, proved to be a true and loyal friend. Lila, on the other hand, chose to betray her once again, and Ava held true to her promise. Only months after the initial warning, Ava informed Lila she was no longer a person she wanted to know. She demanded that Lila behave as if she did not know her, and she would do the same.

Though in the back of Ava's mind, she knew her relationship with Corey would likely not survive, she accepted his invitation to once again share a home. Without her input, he had purchased a house in Wheaton, a town only about twenty minutes south of Ropschon. Ava did all she could to help him put the finishing touches on several of the rooms in the new house, in order to make it their own. After all of their belongings were put in their places, Ava strived to keep the house clean and welcoming for Corey when he would arrive home from work each day. She had finally obtained a different job, one entirely different from the one she had known for so many years. She had accepted a position at a local motorcycle dealership, retaining her job at the bar as well. Her days off each week were Sunday and Monday, and on Mondays she enjoyed sleeping in due to all the hours she worked between both jobs during the week. After only a few weeks, Corey became upset with her if she slept past nine in the morning on her days off, giving no regard to how tired she must be after working two jobs, and keeping the housework done. He initiated arguments with her on several occasions about the issue, until she finally grew tired of his judgment, and simply gave in to his demands.

Over time, Ava and Corey argued more and more about trivial things, and Ava was able to clearly recognize the continued breakdown of the relationship. With each passing day, Corey's actions, comments, and behavior seemed to convey his undivided attention to the material things in his life. At every opportunity, he was adamant about his ownership of the house in which they lived, as well as vehicles, furniture, and even the small dog he had. Ava had tried to explain to him, many times before, that she wanted nothing material from him, only his love. Ultimately, she wanted him to consider the material things as shared property, at least while they were a couple, though she had no actual interest in any of it. The desire Ava had for Corey to consider everything he had as shared property had nothing to do with Ava's desire to actually own any of it. Ultimately, she knew his material possessions were more important to him than anything, aside from his money, and felt that if he would refer to his possessions as *theirs* it may indicate she was even more important to him than the material things. He refused, claiming he did not understand why it was important for him to refer to *his* belongings as *theirs* when it was all, in fact, *his.* After trying every possible way to explain the reason for her desire, she ultimately gave up and concluded his possessions would always be more important to him than she would ever be. It was a very difficult realization for her, but the revelation helped her to look back on the relationship, and clearly recognize the many times he had chosen materialism over their relationship.

Though Ava tried hard not to recognize Corey's obvious indifference to her, it would prove to be more and more difficult for her to deny with each passing day. When she had her first foot surgery, Corey had chosen to abandon her so he could work and make more money, even after promising he would be there to take her to the hospital, take her home, and take care of her. After she had hit a deer with her vehicle, repairs needed to be completed before she could drive it once again. When she asked to borrow one of Corey's vehicles until hers was repaired, he had refused, and she was forced to ask Sylvia if she could use one of hers. Instances such as these seemed to occur regularly, and each time, Ava was able to see Corey a little more clearly for what he really was. The only exception was when she had loaded her belongings in his pick up in order to complete the move to the apartment Corey had obtained when he had taken the sales position with the implement company. He had expressed his excitement at Ava's move to join him in the apartment, and seemed to be one hundred percent invested in the relationship, though that illusion was quickly dissolved.

Corey's unparalleled attentiveness to his material possessions and concentration on money was something that unsettled Ava more and more each day. She sadly wondered if she would ever be able to equal these things and, time after time, Corey seemed to demonstrate she would likely never be able to compete. It seemed to Ava that Corey used each insignificant issue that arose as yet another foothold to escape her. The unrest in the relationship continued to grow and Ava felt as if she was losing Corey even more with each passing day. As he slipped away from her, she tried everything she could think of to bring him back, but the harder she tried the faster he seemed to fall away.

Finally, the time had arrived to venture to the state pool tournament once again. It was mid-March, 2009 and Ava was looking forward to the fun she would have with her friends, as well as Corey. She held the hope this small get away might rekindle some of the love Corey had proclaimed so readily when they had first started dating only a few years before. Though she held the hope, reality continued to interfere, and suggest it would not ever be possible to return to that happiness. Even though their relationship was anything but stable, plans had been made for the two of them to share a room with the rest of Ava's team. They were about to embark on what would prove to be a life-changing trip for Ava. Though she had attended each state tournament since the year 2000, this would be the most significant and metamorphic one of all for her. Little did she know, she was about to face her own mortality yet again, as she allowed her past to ambush her and force her to fall harder than she ever had before as she desperately grasped for help from someone who refused to catch her.

Chapter Fifteen

The day was bright and sunny and Ava impatiently waited for Peyton to arrive to pick her up for the state pool tournament. Though the temperature was warmer than it recently had been, the air was still crisp and cold. Hearing a vehicle round the corner a block away, Ava looked up excitedly and saw Peyton's truck driving slowly down the street. As the vehicle wheeled into the driveway, Ava was already holding her suitcase. As she opened the door, a smile spread across her face, and it was answered by the smile Peyton wore on hers.

"Hi!" Ava said excitedly.

"Hi!" Peyton answered with equal excitement.

Ava flipped the passenger seat forward and placed her suitcase on the floor of the truck's extended cab. Peyton had thoughtfully left plenty of room for Ava's things, and she walked back to the front door of the house to retrieve the rest of her luggage. After making sure all of her things were securely positioned, she placed her cue case atop the rest of the luggage, next to Peyton's. She pushed the passenger seat back into its original position, and climbed into the truck. When her door was closed, Peyton shifted the vehicle into reverse and backed out of the driveway.

"So, when is Corey guna come down?" Peyton questioned politely.

"He's headin' down when he gets off work, later tonight," Ava answered, somewhat absent-mindedly.

Peyton acknowledged Ava's answer with a slight nod. She had always had a disconnection with Corey that kept her from really liking him, possibly due to the way he treated Ava, and capitalized her time. Ultimately, however, Peyton had finally accepted Ava's relationship with Corey and did her best to be his friend though she still did not really like him.

Both of the girls rolled their windows down about an inch and each lit a cigarette. While they drove, they talked about the fun they would have and reminisced about past tournaments, when they had so much fun. Every trip to the state tournament involved drinking, laughing, and having a great deal of fun as they partied with various people from different teams on their league. Pool was the highlight of Ava's life and it had quickly become the same for Peyton.

"When's Sophie guna be down there?" Ava asked.

"She's riding with Lila and Cheryl," Peyton answered. "She couldn't get off work in time to head down with us. Besides, if she had ridden with us, we would've had to take your truck."

"We could've taken mine," Ava said, wishing Sophie was with them.

"She said she didn't mind," Peyton offered. "Said the fun doesn't start 'til we get to the hotel anyway," she laughed.

Ava responded with a laugh as well, and the two continued to converse about different things for the remainder of the drive. When they arrived at the hotel, Ava checked in and returned to the vehicle with a cart to transport their luggage to the sixth floor room they had been assigned. After loading all of their things on the cart, Ava rode the elevator to the second floor and Peyton went to park the truck. Peyton took the skywalk from the parking garage to the hotel and met Ava on the second floor. They got back in the elevator, laughing and talking, and proceeded to take their things up to their room. Sophie, Cheryl, and Lila would be sharing a room with them, along with Corey. It was a two-room suite, and by sharing a room between all of the members of the team, the cost was surprisingly low for the very nice accommodations.

Once in the hotel room, Ava and Peyton unloaded the cart and parked it by the wall. They were saving it for Sophie and the others to use when they arrived. Since they did not have to worry about playing pool until the next day, Ava and Peyton decided to get the party started before the other three women arrived. They dragged the cooler full of beer over to the end of the small counter in the kitchenette, found an ashtray, and sat down to talk.

"How's things goin' with Corey?" Peyton asked.

"Not great," Ava began. "It's fucked up. It's like one day he loves me more than life itself and the next day he doesn't give a shit about me at all. Pretty confusing." Ava took a long drink from her beer can and set it softly on the counter in front of her.

Peyton offered a slight nod in response but said nothing right away. She took a drink of her beer and belched loudly, prompting childish giggles from both of them.

"I wish he'd treat ya better," Peyton said with concern in her voice.

Ava nodded in response as her eyes fell to her beer can.

"Don't think it'll ever happen," Ava said softly, speaking partially to Peyton and partially to herself. "I'll know when I've had enough." The phrase had been offered to both Peyton and Sophie a number of times, and they both knew, when she had had enough she would undoubtedly act. Saying the words, however, seemed to help Peyton and Sophie continue to be at ease regarding her relationship with Corey, even though they still constantly worried for her.

Peyton offered another slight nod, clearly at a loss for what to say next. It seemed as if Ava had always been the one that knew what she wanted and would stand up for herself. Seeing her now, seemingly trapped in a relationship with a man who treated her like dirt, confused Peyton. Deep in her heart, however, she knew Ava would find her way out of the relationship and be on to better things.

"Fuck it," Ava said, unexpectedly loud and happy. "Fuck all this sappy shit. Let's have fun this weekend!"

Peyton readily agreed and the two women clanked their beer cans together as if a toast had been proposed. They decided to play cribbage until the rest of the team arrived, and Peyton could tell without a doubt Ava no longer wanted to discuss her relationship with Corey.

Ava and Peyton had already had three beers each by the time Ava's phone rang. Sophie had called to let them know that she, Cheryl, and Lila had finally arrived. Immediately, Ava and Peyton took the luggage cart down to the lobby and met the other three women. After handing each of them a key, their luggage was loaded on the cart and Ava, Peyton, and Sophie took the cart to the room while Cheryl and Lila parked Cheryl's car in the parking ramp. After all five women were in the room, Cheryl, Lila, and Sophie unloaded their luggage and pushed the cart to the second room of the suite. They always hoarded the luggage cart for the entire weekend, as it was so difficult to find one when it was time to load up and go home again. Seemingly, the housekeepers at the hotel never noticed, or at least never said anything, because the cart always remained in the room until it was time to leave.

Though Ava and Lila did not get along well, the two tolerated each other for the sake of the team. The upset between them had occurred rather late in the league season, and Ava knew there was not enough time to get a new player sanctioned. Lila continually tried to fuel animosity in Cheryl against Ava, but Cheryl did not allow her to upset their friendship the way she had before. After the incident when Ava was unable to make it to pool, and Cheryl had apologized for the things she had said, the two women had begun to strengthen their friendship and Cheryl was quickly becoming one of Ava's closest friends. Cheryl seemed to simply let Lila say what she would, and not relay the information to any of the other women on the team, in order to keep the peace. Cheryl knew the things Lila said were rooted in jealousy, so she simply let them go in one ear and out the other, knowing her words were meaningless. The five women interacted with happiness, and seemed to let any type of discontent drain away, at least during the state tournament.

Ava had still been dealing with the headaches she had become so used to over the years, but it seemed they were worsening with each passing week. She tried to explain the pain in her head to Corey, informing him that when she slept she could escape the pain. She knew the headaches were a result of the Chiari and pangs of fear would wash over her as she imagined the worst. Day by day, she dealt with the headaches, and pushed through life. Pool was no exception. She was adamant about having fun, and not letting her team down, as she dealt with the constant pain. Corey held no sympathy for Ava regarding her headaches, and accused her of using the Chiari as an excuse to complain, so she could sleep in and get out of cleaning the house. Ultimately, had he taken the time to care about Ava's condition, and listen to her explanation of the symptoms, he would have likely understood and may have found a little sympathy for her. He would proclaim he had headaches also, but he did not let it stop him from standing on his own two feet, and taking care of what needed to be done. He had no idea how much pain and suffering Ava dealt with on a daily basis, nor did he attempt to understand the severity of her condition, on any level whatsoever.

Though her headaches proved to be unbearable at times, most of the time Ava was able to contend with the pain without letting on that she was uncomfortable. With everything she had been through, the physical pain of abuse seemed to equip her with an ability to endure a great deal of physical pain. The Chiari headaches became yet another agony she must endure, and she did it very well. Her pain tolerance had risen far above that of most people, and for the most part, she was able to continue her daily life without letting the headaches interfere significantly. Just as always, Ava's head was pounding, but she was able to mask her pain while she interacted with her friends. Sophie, Cheryl, and Lila joined Ava and Peyton in drinking and having fun, as they changed the game from cribbage to something suited for five players. Laughter filled the two-room suite as all five of the women had fun talking and joking with one another. Eventually, Corey called Ava to let her know he had arrived.

"I'm in the parking ramp," he snapped. "Where are you?"

"We're in room 609," Ava responded. "Do you need any help with your stuff?"

"No," no, he answered with an irritated tone.

"'Kay," she responded, with an unconcerned tone in an effort to disguise Corey's obvious sour mood to her friends. "See ya when ya get up here."

Without responding, Corey ended the call. Ava was sure he was upset with her about something, though she had no idea what it could be. After placing her phone on the counter next to her beer and cigarettes, she looked up at the others. She noticed that Sophie and Peyton were looking at her with concern, as Cheryl and Lila continued to joke and talk. Sophie raised her eyebrows, as if to ask if everything was alright, and Ava raised her eyebrows back in a way that conveyed the existence of some sort of upset on Corey's part. Ava looked at Peyton and the same interaction took place. Peyton, Sophie, and Ava were so close to one another, they were able to have entire conversations without words at times - something that proved to be helpful when they wanted to keep things between only the three of them.

After about fifteen minutes, there was a soft knock at the door. Cheryl sprang from her chair and opened the door to find Corey standing in the hallway. His face wore a happy and innocent expression, one that was contradictory of his tone of voice when he spoke to Ava on the phone a short time earlier.

"Hi honey!" Cheryl chirped, obviously happy to see Corey. "What took ya so long?" she teased playfully.

Corey laughed but did not respond as he stepped past Cheryl into the hotel room with his suitcase in his hand.

"Hey, Corey!" Lila chimed with a giggle.

"Hi, Lila!" Corey said happily as he raised his free hand in a wave.

Ava watched Corey as he greeted Cheryl and Lila. His eyes finally found hers and she offered a meek smile. Corey said nothing and looked away as he placed his suitcase by the chair on the other side of the room. He then made his way to the counter and found a beer in the cooler. After popping the top on the beer, and taking a long drink, he proceeded to address the others.

"Peyton," Corey said with a smile.

"Corey," Peyton replied, forcing a smile in return.

"Hi, Sophie," Corey said, still wearing the smile he had offered Peyton.

"Hi, Corey," Sophie responded with a half-hearted smile.

Ava sat quietly waiting for Corey to acknowledge her. When he finally looked at her, she again offered a smile. Once again, Corey chose to look away with an indifferent expression on his face.

"What are we playin'?" Corey said, acting interested in the game the women were playing.

Cheryl and Lila happily explained the game to him as Peyton, Sophie, and Ava remained quiet. Corey turned down the opportunity to join the game, but remained at the counter drinking beer, watching, laughing, and joking with Cheryl and Lila. It was as if Ava and Corey were not a couple. As long as she did not try to interact with him, everything seemed to go well. Peyton and Sophie seemed to transform their moods when Corey arrived, ultimately because they were concerned for Ava, and disgusted by the way he treated her. Both of them wanted to take him aside and talk to him, but neither of them could find the words, nor did they want to create any problems for Ava by letting him know she shared things about their relationship with them. They could only remain silent and worry about Ava while trying to seem as if they were not concerned.

As the evening progressed, Ava decided not to concern herself with whatever Corey was upset about. Instead, she chose to have fun with the team and keep her mood happy and light. Lila was the first to go to bed and Cheryl followed shortly after. Sleeping arrangements had been made before the trip and Peyton had informed Ava she did not want to share a bed with Corey. Since Sophie was a more agreeable personality than Peyton, at least regarding Corey, she agreed to share the king size bed with he and Ava. Finally, everyone who was still awake decided to conclude the night and turn in. Peyton fell asleep next to Lila and Cheryl had fallen asleep in the recliner. Corey was the first to climb into the bed, Ava joining him on one side, and Sophie on the other. Ava chose to continue to ignore whatever was upsetting Corey earlier in the evening, and not ask about it, nor did he offer an explanation. All three of them quickly fell asleep.

The next morning, Ava awoke to a small sliver of bright sunlight creeping through the heavy curtains. Sophie and Corey had already gotten up, and Ava was in the large bed alone. Her head pounded but it was bearable. She slowly rose, her lower back aching terribly. It seemed that no matter how soft the bed was, her back would always hurt. She made her way to the bathroom and found it unoccupied. After emptying her bladder, she made her way to the main room of the suite. Cheryl still sat in the recliner in which she had slept, Lila was drinking coffee, Peyton was rummaging in the cooler to find a soda, Sophie sat quietly on the end of the fold-out sofa bed where Peyton and Lila had spent the night, and Corey sat next to her. Everyone except Cheryl and Corey were smokers and it seemed to be the first thing they would all do after opening a soda or pouring a cup of coffee.

Ava submerged her hand in the ice cold water of the cooler, several cubes of ice bumping into her hand as if they were tiny lifeboats seeking rescue from a watery demise. She finally found the kind of soda she wanted, and pulled her hand from the frigid water. The can dripped and created a ring of water as she set it atop the counter to pop the tab. After taking a long drink, she pulled a cigarette from her pack and lit it. Sitting gently on one of the bar stools at the counter, she said nothing. Corey offered no conversation with her either, and the others simply milled around the room, getting ready for their day of pool. Very little conversation in the morning was the norm for the women when they went to state tournaments. Typically, they had all had too much to drink the night before, and it was ultimately all they could do just to get ready for their day. As time passed, and they were awake longer, conversations began to slowly develop and they would be on their way.

Ava was the first to finish her cigarette and make her way back to the bathroom to shower, brush her teeth, and get ready to go.

"I'm guna go get ready," she offered to everyone in the room. "Anybody need the bathroom before I get in the shower?"

Everyone answered that they did not need to use the bathroom before she went in, so she proceeded with her morning routine. Once out of the shower and dressed, she informed the others she was finished with her shower, and that the next person could get in. Peyton responded by taking her turn. After Peyton was in the shower, Ava returned to the bathroom to finish her routine and put her hair in a ponytail. Next was Sophie, showering as Peyton completed her morning routine, then Lila, then Cheryl. Corey waited for all of the women to finish before showering himself, as it would not be appropriate for him to be in the bathroom while any of them were, except for Ava. Corey was not shooting in the men's division singles tournament that year, but all of the women were shooting in the ladies divisions, Sophie, Peyton, Lila, and Cheryl in the Open and Ava in the Masters. As a group, they made their way from the hotel to the event venue, and milled around in an attempt to find a few tables to practice on. Ultimately, the practice simply meant they were trying to get back into their shooting routines and get a feel for the tables. Sophie spotted a table toward the middle of the lower room and the group headed toward it. Since Ava and Peyton were scheduled to play their matches sooner than the others, the two of them were the first to shoot. After a short time, they both had to find their tournament tables and begin play. Once they left, Sophie, Cheryl, and Lila took turns shooting on the open table, until it was time for their matches to start as well. Corey remained with Sophie, Cheryl, and Lila after Ava and Peyton had left for their matches.

"Aren't ya guna go watch Ava?" Sophie asked Corey, irritation clouding her voice.

"Yeah, eventually," he responded, clearly not interested.

Sophie chose not to say anything else, but his continued indifference to Ava deeply annoyed her. After about thirty minutes, Corey stood and stretched.

"I'm goin' to see how Ava's doin'," he said to no one in particular.

"I thought you might come watch me," Lila said with a tone of deviant, flirtatious humor in her voice.

Corey smiled, letting out a giggle before he walked away, as if to indicate that he would rather watch Lila play. Ultimately, however, he made his way to Ava's table and proceeded to sit down to watch. Her match was a tough one, and she was unable to capitalize over her opponent and advance. After finishing her match, she discovered she had two hours before she was scheduled to play again. She was upset about the loss and ultimately distracted by the fact that she and Corey had not even conversed since he had arrived at the hotel room the day before. Corey followed Ava without saying anything, though she informed him of what she planned to do.

"I'm guna find Sophie 'n Peyton's tables and watch them for a bit," she said flatly.

Though he did not acknowledge she had said anything, he followed her to watch the other two matches. Peyton and Sophie were playing only a few tables apart, so Ava was able to watch both matches at the same time. Corey sat down next to her, and neither of them spoke, for what seemed like an eternity. The longer the silence continued, the more Ava wanted to ask what was bothering Corey. Finally, she could not remain quiet any longer.

"What's wrong?" Ava asked him, as she remained seemingly interested in the pool games taking place on the tables in front of her, in an attempt to mask the unrest that resided in the simple words.

"Nothin'," he answered with irritation.

"Well, ya haven't talked to me since ya got here. What'd I do?" She pressed.

"I just don't know why I *had* to come down here," he said, irritation now flooding his voice as he turned to look at her.

"Ya didn't *have* to come down here," she responded, now looking at him as well.

He said nothing and turned away from her. His face was flush with frustration, and Ava could not understand why he thought he had to join her at the tournament.

"Why do ya think ya *had* to be here?" She questioned shortly.

"'Cause if I wasn't you'd find a way to make me feel like shit," he answered. "Plus, then those guys would think I was a dick," he said, referring to the rest of Ava's team.

"What are you talking about?" She said, clearly upset by his statement.

"Forget it," he hissed. "I'm here and ya got your way."

"What?" Ava said, her face turning red as her temper began to boil.

"I'm not talkin' here," Corey said sternly.

"Fine, let's go," Ava said as she quickly stood.

Corey shook his head but stood anyway. He followed her through the venue and up the escalator to the second floor. She led him to a stairwell that offered at least a little bit of privacy. After descending to the first landing, Ava stopped and turned to face Corey.

"Now, what the fuck are ya talkin' about?" She asked harshly, attempting to keep her voice low.

"I didn't wana come down her but ya begged me so here I am!" he exclaimed, also trying to keep his voice low. "If I hadn't come ya would've found a way to pester me until I did. I don't wana be here!"

"Then leave!" She said with conviction. "I didn't beg ya to come down here, so just go home."

Corey began to feel a pang of guilt. He knew Ava had not begged him to join her at the tournament. In reality, he was in a bad mood because of work, and really did want to be there. He was also irritated he had not signed up for the men's division, and felt as if he were missing out on the fun of shooting. He had lashed out at Ava in an attempt to blame someone other than himself for his own issues, as if Ava needed any more issues to deal with beyond her own. Corey seemed to have a knack for pushing Ava's buttons, and seemed to strive to do so with every opportunity.

"I didn't mean it," Corey confessed immediately, shame veiling his face.

Ava simply stood and looked at him, unable to make sense of why he would say such a thing. Ultimately, she had asked him if he wanted to go to the state tournament with her, and when he had not answered right away, she assured him it was fine with her whether or not he decided to go. Without words, she slowly stepped past Corey and walked up the stairs. He followed her and remained silent. Ava walked to the bracket and checked her match time. She had about thirty minutes before having to play again, so she decided to use the restroom, get a beer, have a cigarette, and go to her table.

"I'm goin' to the bathroom," she declared, as if speaking to the air around her.

Corey followed her and waited dutifully outside the restroom until she returned. She went to the bar and ordered a beer then carried it, along with her cue, outside to smoke. Corey stood outside with her for only a moment before speaking.

"I'm guna go see how they're doin'," he said, referring to Sophie, Peyton, Lila, and Cheryl.

"Whatever," she answered without looking at him. She was baffled by his behavior since he arrived at the hotel, and she fumed even more when she recalled his apology. "Like him sayin' he's sorry will fix it," she thought to herself. "Fuckin' dick." Her angry thoughts began to drift and she tried to figure out why he would be the way he was with her. She went through so many scenarios in her mind regarding possible reasons for him to treat her poorly. She thought of a seemingly unending number of reasons, all rooted in her actions, behaviors, and personality. Ultimately, she was once again able to blame herself for his indifference toward her. This time, however, finding the so-called reason for his behavior created no tranquility in her heart. She felt as if she were empty inside, and discovering the unfounded reasons for Corey's behavior had not helped to make her feel whole again, even though it usually did, at least for a little while. She checked the time and headed for her next match. The match began and she did her best to play well, however, her mind was captivated elsewhere. The match came to an end and even though she had played well, she was not at the top of her game. The second loss marked her defeat in the tournament, and now she would be free to watch her teammates, have fun, and drink without worrying about paying attention to her own stroke.

As Ava returned her cues to their case, Corey approached with Peyton and Cheryl behind him.

"Did ya win?" Corey asked.

"Nope," Ava answered without looking at him.

"Me either," Peyton offered in an attempt to help Ava feel better about her loss.

"I'm a loser too," volunteered Cheryl with an annoyed giggle.

"How'd Lila and Sophie do?" Ava asked no one in particular, without looking up.

"Last I saw, Sophie was down two to one and I don't know how Lila did," Peyton said, matter-of-factly.

"I'm guna go see where Sophie's at," Ava said quietly as she swung the cue case over her shoulder.

No one else said anything, but all of them followed Ava to the bracket. As they approached the giant piece of paper that hung on the wall, Ava spotted Sophie walking toward them. As Sophie and the group came closer together, Peyton was the first to speak.

"How'd ya do?" she asked Sophie.

"Not good," Sophie said with a defeated chuckle.

"Are you out?" Ava asked.

"Yep," Sophie said, as an expression of irritation crossed her face.

"Nice," Ava said to everyone. "So far we're all done and out except for Lila."

"She's done too," Sophie said. "I just saw her in the bathroom. She went in as I was coming out. I saw you guys and she asked me to wait for her here."

The group stood and looked around the venue. They had the rest of the afternoon and night to have fun and socialize.

"What do you guys wana do?" Ava asked the group in general.

"I wana go eat," Sophie said.

"Me too," Cheryl agreed.

"Sounds good," Peyton offered. "What are you guys guna do?" speaking to Ava and Corey.

"I don't know what I wana do yet," Ava answered. "Except take my cue back to the room. I don't wana carry it around if I don't have to and I don't think they'll be runnin' any mini tournaments until ten or eleven tonight at the earliest, if they do at all."

Lila had approached the group, and they all agreed to go back to the hotel room together, and decide where and when to meet up later that evening. After arriving at the hotel room, they each went about their business and participated in making plans to meet back at the hotel room. Lila had decided to join Sophie, Peyton, and Cheryl, leaving Ava and Corey to decide what they wanted to do on their own.

"Wana go eat?" Ava asked soberly.

"'Kay," Corey answered. "Where ya wana go?"

"I don't know," Ava said. "Let's go and figure it out on the way.

Corey scoffed slightly but did not challenge her. The couple left the hotel room and walked silently across the skywalk that led from the hotel to the multi-level parking ramp. The afternoon air was cold and moist, and the sky had become overcast with grey clouds that looked heavy with snow. As they entered the parking ramp on the second level, Corey decided to speak.

"If we leave I'll lose my parkin' spot," he said, clearly irritated.

Without speaking, Ava simply turned around to walk back to the skywalk.

"If you're guna be like that we'll just go," he said, still clearly irritated.

Ava stopped and turned to face him, but said nothing as she looked at him, awaiting his decision.

"Well, let's go," he said as he began walking toward his car again.

She followed and knew the entire weekend would be full of this kind of behavior from him. Since she had ridden with Peyton, she resolved to tell him during their meal he need not stay if he wanted to go home. After they both got in the car, Corey started the engine and began the descent toward the parking ramp exit. He had originally been parked on the second level, just outside the skywalk entrance, so it took very little time to reach the street. They drove only a short time, before deciding which restaurant they wanted to go to, and arrived at their destination shortly after.

Ava had heard many couples, who had been married for many years, describe their marriage as uneventful and separated. To her, as they entered the restaurant, it felt as if their relationship closely compared to all of them. They did not speak, nor did they laugh or converse. It was saddening. They chose their table and ordered before either of them spoke. Ava was the first.

"You can go home if ya want," she began. "I rode down here with Peyton and I can ride home with her. No need for you to stay if you are not happy about being here."

Corey thought silently for a moment before responding.

"Whatever," he said softly as he shook his head.

"I'm just makin' sure ya know ya don't have to stay down here," she continued. "Ya made it perfectly clear earlier that ya didn't wana be down here so go home if ya want. I don't really care."

"Yeah, right," Corey scoffed. "If I leave we'll just fight about it when ya get home."

"We won't unless you bring it up," Ava fired back. "I'm sick of fighting with you. I'm sick of fighting everything."

Tears began to burn Ava's eyes and she quickly looked away from Corey.

"Oh, good," he said mockingly. "Here we go with the fuckin' tears."

Ava said nothing. She wanted to talk to Corey. She wanted so much for him to listen to her, in a loving and caring way, as he had once done. She knew she should not say anything about how she felt, but with each passing minute, it proved to be more and more difficult to hold back the words.

"What the fuck is wrong with ya now?" Corey snapped, trying to keep his voice as low as he could. "Shut up! Don't fuckin' cry, we're in public!"

Silent tears rolled down Ava's cheeks even though she was trying hard not to cry. She remained silent and withdrew her mind from the conversation. She was done. She knew there was nothing more she could say to him, and it seemed once again, she was failing at life. It seemed as if every negative thing in her life was mounting on top of her, each instance adding tremendous weight. She felt as if she had once again lost her grip on the slippery, wet sides of the muddy hole she had fallen into so many years ago. Once again, her mind felt like a black maze where no source of light was available. At a dead end in her maze, she felt the terrible burden of striving to succeed weigh on her heart and mind. She felt as though she was completely alone, no warmth, no light, and no hope. Standing motionless at a dead end in one of the maze passages, unable to discern which way she had come and which way she needed to go, she looked at Corey with a blank stare and said the words that would prove to be too much for him handle.

"I don't wana be here anymore," she whispered, as her gaze fell to her lap and tears fell from her eyes.

"Then let's fuckin' go," he said as he stood up like a shot, and violently grabbed his coat from the booth.

Ava continued to look down at her lap, knowing he had not understood the meaning of her statement. Instead of trying to clarify herself inside the restaurant, she chose to wait until they had gotten in the car. As Corey stomped to the counter to pay for their meal, Ava silently walked out the door and onto the sidewalk. Pulling a cigarette from her pack, she lit it as she crossed the parking lot to his car, her hands shaking uncontrollably. She hadn't even touched the food she had ordered, and felt bad for leaving it sitting on the table. She slowly made her way toward Corey's car while she smoked. He did not allow her to smoke in the car, so she wanted to finish it before he came out. When she had smoked only about half of the cigarette, she noticed Corey walking swiftly toward the car. His body language and facial expression screamed volumes of his irritation and anger. He said nothing as he unlocked the car and got in. Ava threw her cigarette on the asphalt and got in the car as well.

Corey was silent as they made their way back to the hotel parking ramp. Finally, Ava broke the silence.

"Ya didn't understand what I meant before," she began.

"What, then?" Corey barked, hitting the steering wheel with an open hand.

"I don't wana be here anymore," she repeated deliberately.

"Where?" He screeched, as he slapped the steering wheel in frustration once again. "Where don't ya wana be? Ya don't wana be at state, ya don't wana be with me, where don't ya wana be?

"Alive," she answered soberly.

"I'm takin' ya to the fuckin' nut house!" Corey yelled at her.

"If ya don't take me back to the hotel I'll jump outta this fuckin' car," she proclaimed with conviction and calmness in her voice.

Corey continued to yell as he drove back to the hotel. He knew Ava was serious about her claim to jump from the moving car. She was unable to hear him as her past began to flood into her mind and mix with her present day life. She was no longer able to find the positives in life, and was being overtaken by a sadness she knew she would likely not recover from. She knew Corey was still yelling, but she had no idea what he was saying. It seemed as if her mind wanted to keep her from hearing anything else from him. All at once, her body felt as if she hadn't slept in days. She began to feel nauseous and her head pounded harder than it had in many weeks. She was only able to clearly see the road signs, which indicated the way back to the parking ramp, while everything else around her was ultimately a blur. Finally, as the car slowed to turn into the parking ramp, her vision cleared and she could see everything as sharply as ever. Corey had stopped yelling, but Ava could still feel the unrest in the atmosphere of the car. As they slowly ascended through each level of the ramp, looking for a parking space, Corey grumbled about having left in the first place. His disgust with having to park on the top level of the ramp further fueled his anger.

Without speaking, Ava exited the car and slowly walked away from Corey. He sat in the driver's seat, unable to bring himself to say or do anything. He simply watched her walk toward the side of the ramp, his blood still boiling. It was still daylight and Ava breathed in the sharp, cold air. It seemed to chill her from within, as if she were locked in a giant freezer.

As she walked away from Corey's car, she kept her eyes on the concrete guard walls of the ramp. Though she seemed to be floating across the floor, she could feel the structure shudder as other cars found their way to the top level. She could hear the rush of the nearby river and felt the cold wind on her face. She realized nothing would matter after she was gone. She heard the faint sound of a car door slamming shut but paid no attention. All at once she heard Corey yelling for her. She stopped and turned toward him, as if to acknowledge his call, but her stare was blank and her face expressionless.

"Where the fuck do ya think you're goin'?" he screeched.

She said nothing and simply stared at him. She felt neither cold nor warmth. She felt nothing.

"Well?" Corey yelled at her.

"I told you," Ava said in a calm and even voice. "I don't wana live anymore. It hurts too much and I can't do it anymore. I just can't." No tears fell from her eyes and her body no longer trembled. She was neither smiling nor offering a frown. Though she looked at Corey, and could see him, it seemed to him as if she were ultimately looking through him. She was utterly and completely numb.

"Fuck you!" Corey screamed. "Ya wana fuckin' kill yourself then fuckin' kill yourself, ya crazy fuckin' bitch!" As he finished the insult, he spun around and briskly walked back to his car. Slamming the driver's door, he started the car and rammed the transmission it into reverse. His tires squawked as the car lunged backward. Shoving the car into drive, he slammed the gas pedal to the floor and sped past Ava toward the ramp's exit lane.

Ava knew it had just been a matter of time before Corey would show his true self. It was clear to her he did not care for her. She found herself in a whirlwind of thoughts that seemed to lift her off of her feet and carry her to the edge of the parking ramp. She stood, gazing down at the concrete below, for what seemed like hours. She knew her sisters and true friends cared for her, but she felt as though her existence was somehow connected to the negative things that happened in their lives as well. She felt as if the end of her existence would allow those she cared about to deal with things much more important and worthy of their attention than her bad decisions and constant mistakes. "I seem to hurt everyone I come into contact with, one way or another," she thought silently. "When I get into relationships I seem to do something to screw them up. I've managed to hurt my sisters, alienate my brother, and create upset wherever I go," she continued, thinking to herself.

In reality, Ava's illusionary state had been created in her mind, by the years of abuse she had not been able to face or overcome before venturing into adulthood. The thousands, if not millions of times she had been told she was worthless, had created a strong foothold in her psyche and her attempts to remove it had been virtually unsuccessful. Her mind began to focus on the cold, hard concrete at the base of the parking ramp. Though she stood only four stories above the sidewalk, she was certain a head-first impact would kill her. The bitter wind of the March air stung her face, but she consciously felt nothing. Her cheeks were bright red, and her hands had begun to turn white as she gripped the cold, steel guardrail that ran along the top of the partial concrete wall. She leaned over the wall and continued to stare down at the sidewalk. Traffic passed below her on the street, but she took no notice. Once again, she felt as if death was her only way out of the pitch black maze that seemed to imprison her mind. Slowly, she lifted her left leg and placed it on the other side of the guardrail. Deliberately and precisely, she balanced herself on the thick tubing, as if astride a frigid steel horse. With her hands still gripping the guardrail in front of her, she leaned forward and touched her forehead to her hands.

"God, please don't send me to hell," she prayed as tears began to fall from her eyes. "I've spent my whole life there."

As she finished her short, but meaningful prayer, she felt herself begin to give in to her desire to die. Slowly, she shifted her body weight to the outside of the guard wall, and began to slip slowly off of the steel rail as gravity took hold of her body. Closing her eyes, she felt all of the sadness, trepidation, pain, sorrow, and fear slip swiftly from her heart and mind. Finally, she would be free of the mental and emotional prison so many people had contributed to the construction of over the years. Finally, she would no longer feel pain. She would no longer feel sadness or worry. Finally.

Suddenly, Ava felt a hand grip her upper right arm with a great deal of force. Before she knew what was happening, she had been pulled from atop the guardrail, and landed heavily on her back. Someone had kept her from falling to her death. Being torn from her dazed state, it took only seconds for her to find the individual responsible for interrupting her suicide attempt. She could see a figure standing above her, but the force of landing on her back had blurred her vision. As her vision cleared, she began to make out the features of the person who had saved her. It was Corey. He stood above her, panting as if he had just ran a mile. Fear, anger, and disbelief veiled his face as he struggled to catch his breath. "He came back for me!" Ava thought excitedly, giving no thought to how close she had come to death, yet again. Her excitement was destroyed, however, when Corey finally found his voice.

"I am not guna have this on my fuckin' conscience," he hissed as he bent at the waist and pointed at her, his finger only inches from her forehead.

Her heart sank as she began to feel the pain of his rejection once again. This time, however, her feelings of sorrow were overtaken by a cocktail of other feelings. She felt anger at all of the people who had hurt her in her life, sadness and mourning for all of the parts of herself she had lost, and anxiousness and exhilaration about the many possibilities in her future. She was overwhelmed by the indication that it was not yet her turn to die. She felt guilty about trying to end her own life, regretful of all of the lives she had upset, humiliated for allowing others to take advantage of her, and weary of her unending efforts to try to keep her relationship with Corey alive. Ultimately, the barrage of diverse feelings that culminated inside her created a whirlwind of new determination, strive, and ambition, to construct a successful life from what she wholeheartedly believed was less than nothing only a few short minutes before.

As Ava's mind came back to the reality of the situation, she rose from the place she had landed and dusted herself off. Corey's words finally began to resonate in her mind. She replayed his words in her mind silently as she stood staring at him. "I am not guna have this on my fuckin' conscience," he had said. The gravity of the statement weighing on her mind, and she grasped it with all she had, to keep it from pushing her back down the slippery slope into the muddy hole she tried so desperately to escape. He had not returned to check on her because he cared, nor had he saved her because he loved her. He had pulled her from the wall because he did not want to feel guilty about her death. It was a sobering realization for Ava, but that realization was the first step in her journey to improve and succeed in her life.

Ava chose not to say anything to Corey as she walked by him and toward the stairs that led to the skywalk.

"Where the fuck are ya goin' now?" He squawked.

She said nothing, and continued to walk at a relaxed, but determined pace. With no response from her, Corey decided to follow as confusion washed over him. Would she try to kill herself again? Would people think it was his fault? Several thoughts ran through his mind as he trotted to catch up with her. She continued walking in silence as she descended the stairs.

"We need to talk about this," Corey demanded in an uneasy tone.

Again, Ava said nothing. Her mind was rushing through all of the things she wanted to do to improve her life, and she barely heard his words. Finally, Corey reached out and grabbed her right arm to force her to stop. She jerked her arm out of his hand and looked at him.

"Leave me alone," she growled, her eyes full of hate.

Corey was clearly shocked by her response and was not able to find any words to protest. Ava turned back around and continued to walk down the next flight of stairs. He followed her all the way back to the sixth floor hotel room, continually barking orders for her to talk to him, and demanding she tell him what she planned to do. She continued walking without acknowledging his words. When she slipped her key card into the lock on the hotel room door, it disengaged, and she turned the handle to open the door. Peyton and Sophie were sitting at the counter talking, and Lila and Cheryl were watching television. It occurred to Ava, by the looks on Peyton and

Sophie's faces, they had been worried about her. Though Ava wanted to portray she was fine, her eyes deceived her. They knew something was going on but did not dare ask any questions in front of Corey.

She walked to the cooler and fished a beer from the ice cold water. Peyton and Sophie watched attentively as Ava moved around the room. Situating herself at the end of the counter, Ava opened the beer and lit a cigarette. After taking a long drag from the cigarette, and a large drink from the beer can, she offered a look of determination to Sophie and Peyton. They both felt a sense of calming from the look, as if they knew she had made a life-changing decision, though they had no idea what the decision was or what had led to it. With the reassuring look Ava had offered them, they both felt as if they could resume their conversation and did so. Corey walked to the bathroom and closed the door. Ava did not say a word to any of the women in the room, and Cheryl and Lila continued to watch television, oblivious to what was happening. Ava continued to sit at the counter and simply listened to Sophie and Peyton converse. A few minutes later, Corey approached Ava.

"Let's go talk," he demanded quietly.

"Leave me alone," Ava answered, as she looked him in the eye.

"Ava," he continued, "c'mon, let's go talk!"

"Leave me alone!" she said, louder this time and with conviction, as she turned her head slightly away from him.

"We can talk out here in front of everybody, then," he continued, now almost yelling at her.

Ava closed her eyes and tilted her head back slightly, as if to indicate frustration. When she opened her eyes she looked at Peyton and Sophie who both suddenly seemed very uncomfortable. In order to keep her relationship issues from ruining the rest of the team's weekend as much as possible, Ava crushed her cigarette out and rose from her chair. Turning slowly, she walked toward the second room of the suite. She did not want to talk about anything with Corey, but she did not want to upset anyone else either. As she walked past Lila and Cheryl, she noticed a concerned look on Cheryl's face and one of irritated indifference on Lila's. Once inside the second room, Ava walked to the bathroom. She just wanted to escape his incessant howling for a few minutes. That, however, would prove to be impossible. He was right on her heels as she entered the bathroom. She was becoming more and more irritated with each passing second, and when Corey followed her into the bathroom and would not leave, she finally lost control.

"I have to pee," she said evenly.

"So, pee," he retorted.

"Please leave so I can pee," she said, still in the same even tone.

"No," he argued, as he crossed his arms in front of him.

Ava felt as if she were talking to a malevolent child. She proceeded with the task of emptying her bladder, then stood to wash her hands. Corey continued to bark at her, most of his words wafting past her ears without the ability to penetrate her mind. Finally, however, she had had enough. In a flash of movement, Ava slammed the bathroom door shut behind Corey. A look of sheer terror washed over his face as he had never seen her so upset with him. His memory immediately flashed back to the role-play he and Sophie had helped her with, and he recalled her intense strength, and the anger that fueled it. Ava stepped toward Corey, and guided him backward, toward the door. When his back was against it, she held her face only inches from his.

"Ya wana talk?" she growled, "Then let's talk."

Corey had never seen the anger and hatred in her eyes that he was now witnessing. He was scared of her, and for good reason. He was unable to speak as she stood her ground, unwavering.

"Well?" Ava sneered. "Talk!"

He began to speak in a weak and squeaky voice, one she was barely able to understand. He accused her of cheating on him and told her he did not feel the way that he once did about her. Then the words came that would make Ava take yet another step toward her freedom.

"I almost didn't come back for ya," he said quietly. "But I didn't wana feel guilty if ya killed yourself or have people think it was my fault."

Ava's eyes dropped away from Corey's as she realized she had been right about him on the top of the parking ramp. She was happy he had finally been honest with her, but his words made her furious. Before he knew what was going on, she had drawn her right hand back and punched the door right beside his head. She watched as his eyes followed her arm toward her hand, as if to confirm she had really hit the door so close to him. A new wave of fear, mixed with relief, seemed to color his face as he realized she hit the exact point she meant to. Once again, she leaned toward him and stopped with her nose only a fraction of an inch from his.

"We've talked," she growled. "I'm done. Leave me alone."

Corey's eyes seemed to relay his acknowledgment of her demand, and she slowly backed away from him. Without taking his eyes off of her, he reached behind his back and found the door handle. Slowly, he opened the door and backed out of the bathroom as she stood stone still, watching him. Corey quickly gathered his things from the hotel room and left without saying anything to anyone. A few minutes later, she walked back to the main room of the suite.

"Corey isn't guna stay so I'll cover his share of the hotel cost along with mine," she said in an even, matter-of-fact tone.

Without paying attention to her words, Lila slipped by Ava and headed for the bathroom, grumbling. Ava only caught a few of the words Lila had said, but thought she better wait to say anything to her until after she used the bathroom, in the event Ava got mad enough to make Lila pee her pants. Cheryl stood from her chair in front of the television and took a step toward Ava.

"You okay?" she asked, concern filling her voice.

"Am now," Ava said soberly, offering a superficial smile.

Cheryl chose not to say anything else, and returned to her seat in front of the television. Peyton and Sophie stared at Ava, seemingly a new respect developing for her, as they watched. Raising her eyebrows, Payton spoke.

"All good?" she said, with concern on her face.

"Yep," Ava said, as she let out a deep breath.

Sophie and Peyton stood from their seats and approached Ava to hug her.

"If ya need to talk, I'm here," Peyton offered with caring, as she hugged Ava.

"Thanks," Ava responded, as she returned the hug.

"Finally had enough, huh?" Sophie said, with empathy and a little smile in her voice as she hugged Ava.

"Yeah," Ava said, and a slight smirk curled her lips as she returned Sophie's hug.

"So," Peyton barked with a grin, "Are we ready to have some fuckin' fun?"

Cheryl had joined Ava, Peyton, and Sophie at the counter and they all shared a smile and a giggle.

"Almost," Ava said slyly, as yet another crooked, devious smile formed on her lips. "I just have one more thing to do." She turned around and faced the doorway to the second room of the suite as Lila appeared from the bathroom. Cheryl, Peyton, and Sophie shared a glance and a smirk, knowing Ava was about to correct the older woman.

Ava stepped toward Lila quickly, and was upon her before she realized what was happening. The shock of Ava's movement almost made her lose her balance and fall backward.

"What the fuck did you say to me when ya walked by?" Ava demanded, her nose only inches from Lila's.

"I said that there are other people in this room that might need to use the bathroom," Lila said, stupidly challenging Ava's confrontation.

"Is that so," Ava growled. "So you only worry about yourself and can't support your friends, huh? Oh, that's right, we aren't friends. You've clearly proven that to me. After this tournament, you're done on this team. Find someone else to put up with your selfish shit!"

"Well, maybe I'll just leave now," Lila said, her voice cracking as she tried to keep her composure.

"Go ahead," Ava hissed. "You rode with Cheryl. Let's see if she wants to leave. Cheryl, are you leaving?" Ava posed the question to Cheryl without taking her eyes off of Lila.

"I'm not goin' anywhere," Cheryl answered immediately.

"Alright then," Ava said. "I guess if ya start walkin' now, she can pick you up on her way home Sunday. It's Thursday night now, so shit, you might be able to make it home before she can even pick you up!" Ava continued with twisted humor lacing her voice.

Lila could no longer hold Ava's gaze and knew she had been defeated. She was not about to leave without a ride and no one was going home until the end of the tournament.

"Listen," Ava continued, now speaking in a more even and superficially friendly tone. "I'm sick of all the drama bullshit from Corey, and from you. Let's just get through this weekend and we won't ever have to talk again. Agreed?"

Lila nodded her head slowly in fearful agreement. If she found another ride home and left before the team event on Saturday, she would forfeit her entry fee and break the trust the rest of the team had in her. She had already lost Ava's trust, but did not want to lose Cheryl's, as Cheryl was her camouflage when she wanted to spend time with one of her many boyfriends, behind her husband's back.

The rest of the night proved to be quite relaxing and everyone except Lila had fun drinking, talking, laughing, and playing cards. Cheryl joined the fun also, tired of having to miss out on fun because of Lila. The women went to sleep in the early hours of Friday morning and slept late. After they woke the next day and got ready, they ate and continued their party as they watched their league mates play matches, drank beer, and laughed. Though it had proven to be a tough beginning for Ava, the weekend was evolving into one of the most fun and significant she had ever had.

Ava, Sophie, Peyton, Cheryl, and Lila went on to participate in the team event on Saturday. Though they only played two matches and were beat out of the tournament, they still made the most of the weekend. They drank more beer, played in some mini tournaments, and laughed until they got home. Everyone except Lila, anyway.

Once the tournament concluded, Ava returned to her life with Corey, and it was clearly different than it had ever been before. Ultimately, he behaved the same way, but Ava did not. She had become confident and deliberate in her actions, and her disposition seemed to have changed a great deal. As the days passed, she found herself more and more excited about making her life into something she could be proud of, without worrying about what anyone else thought.

Chapter Sixteen

By July of 2009, Ava had finally had enough of the constant bickering and unreciprocated affection she continually tried to offer Corey. The day was warm and the air was fresh and clean. She had contemplated the right time in which to approach Corey about the shambled condition of their relationship, and finally decided, the time had come. Corey sat in kitchen, as she walked in from the bedroom with determination, preparing to confront him.

"Corey, we need to talk," she said in a matter-of-fact tone, clearly wearing an expression of fortitude.

He looked at her questioningly and said nothing.

"Are you happy?" she asked soberly.

Still, he said nothing, a look of irritation now beginning to color his face as he immediately assumed she wanted to bother him with his perception of her unending drama.

"I was just wonderin' 'cause I'm not," she said, ignoring the fact he had chosen to remain silent. "I can't do this anymore."

"Do what?" He hesitantly asked, now clearly confused.

"This. You and me. The fighting. I can't do it anymore," she clarified. "I'm not happy. Are you?"

"No," he admitted as he broke eye contact with her.

"So, I'm thinkin' we're done," she declared.

Corey looked at her with disbelief. She had always seemed

to cling to the promises he had made to her when they had first started dating. Her calm, confident conviction seemed to startle him, and send his mind into a spiral. When he first met her, she had been so strong and confident, and seemed to be the exact type of woman he had always wanted. Over time, however, he watched as her confidence and independence seemed to diminish, and the reality of her need to lean on him caused him to pull away from her quickly. Even though she had told him she would likely need him to be her emotional crutch from time to time, he had always imagined it would be only brief instances, and had never realized how much she would *actually* need him. It seemed as if, at that very moment, he began to rediscover his feelings of love for her as he was able to once again see the woman he had first fallen in love with. Whether or not he realized it at that moment, had he been the man he had made himself out to be in the beginning, he would have been able to enjoy a wonderfully loving, life-long relationship with a woman who would have done virtually anything for him.

Though he believed she had lost her confidence and will to be independent, in reality, it was only shrouded by the struggles he had forced her to face alone. The confidence inside her had continued to build during her emotional and psychological struggles, but he was simply unwilling to see it, as he emotionally disconnected himself from her. Had he truly been the man he had claimed to be from the start, he would have been able to help her through the difficult and trying times. He would have been able to once again enjoy the woman he had known her to be, and with his help and support, her confidence would have grown much more quickly. Instead, he had chosen to hide from the commitment and devotion he had proclaimed in the beginning, as the reality of being a true companion revealed itself. He simply had chosen to give up, and avoid the hard work which would have eventually produced a loving, devoted, and fulfilling relationship with her.

"Yeah, I guess," he replied, clearly taken aback by her sober and unemotional disposition.

"Okay, so I'll be out as soon as I can," she assured him with a brisk nod.

"You can stay as long as ya need to," he offered, his voice continuing to reveal the curiosity her new-found, confident behavior seemed to foster. "I'll sleep on the couch and you can have the bed."

"I'll be out by the end of next week," she said flatly, paying no attention to his feeble attempt at being caring.

"Ya don't have to hurry," he debated, as a tinge of desperation leaked into his voice.

"Well thanks, but I'll be out by the end of next week," she repeated with no emotion.

Corey simply looked at her with a blank expression as she turned and walked back to the bedroom to begin packing her things. The friend of hers for whom she worked at the bar owned a house in Carlisle, a small town about thirty-five miles north of Ropschon. She would be about the same distance from her job at the dealership, but would be much closer to her job at the bar. She had spoken to her friend the day before, knowing she would be approaching Corey about ending their relationship the next day. Her friend had informed her the house would be ready for her to move into by the end of the following week, if not sooner, and Ava simply could not wait for the day to come. Recruiting a few of her friends, the small group of four was able to pack, load, and move all of her belongings in one day. Corey chose to avoid any interaction while she prepared to leave the house, by choosing to spend the day away from home. As she walked toward the door to leave the house for the last time, she paused in the kitchen and looked around. The house had never really been her home, a fact she had been painfully aware of the entire time she had lived there. She gingerly placed her house key on the counter, then made her way to the door. Without looking back, she closed the door behind her, and stepped into her new life. It was finally time for her to live her own life, this time depending on no one but herself. She felt completely comfortable, walking into the world on her own, with no one beside her. Excitement, curiosity, hope, and confidence were the feelings that enveloped her and she loved it.

The caravan headed toward Carlisle with Ava in the lead. She rode her motorcycle, Sophie drove Ava's truck, Peyton drove her own truck, and Ava's close friend, Dave, brought up the rear with his truck and trailer. Every vehicle was full of Ava's belongings, and it was relieving to know the move would be done in one day.

Prior to moving day, Ava, Peyton, Sophie, and a few other friends had worked hard to get the house ready to occupy. The disarray in which the previous tenants left the small house proved to be quite a challenge, even for a team of people to clean. The carpet in the living room and downstairs bedroom had been replaced, the floors cleaned, and the rest of the house diligently scoured. As Ava slowed to pull into the driveway of her new home, a feeling of triumph washed over her. Of course, she would always need her friends, but she finally began to understand the many opportunities available when not worrying about a relationship. As the recruited movers made trip after trip into and out of the house, her belongings were stacked in this room and that room, in an attempt to simply complete the job. Once everything was unloaded and everyone departed, she was left to enjoy her new home in peace. It was late, and she decided not to tackle the huge job of putting things away, until the next day. As it was Sunday night and she had every Monday off, she would be able to work at the daunting task after she got some rest.

She had purchased a couch and love seat from a thrift store, and the two pieces of furniture were already in their places. She had already purchased a new television, and in the two weeks prior to moving in, had gotten her cable and internet connected. She watched television as she smoked a cigarette and sipped on a soda.

"This is amazing," she thought to herself. "I don't have to feel upset. I can do what I want to do. I'm finally free."

She smiled to herself as she became lost in the flickering of the television screen. It had been so long since she had truly relaxed. Even though her headaches still persisted, she felt as though she could live with them for the rest of her life, if she could only feel this free every day.

Several days passed, and in between her scheduled work hours at both jobs, she was able to put her home in order quite quickly. Using the downstairs bedroom as her office, she used her laptop to search for different schools she could attend to obtain her bachelors degree in psychology. There were many to choose from, however, the first school to contact her assured her she would be unable to obtain a psychology degree entirely online. This seemed to take a little of the wind out of her sails, but she resolved to press on, and find an alternative. Finally, a school contacted her and she was able to speak, at length, with the admissions counselor. She extended her concern about being unable to earn a degree in psychology completely online. The admissions counselor assured her she could earn her degree entirely online and the school specialized in psychology and business. Ava was ecstatic. She made plans to start in late fall of 2009 and could not wait to begin. She had already resolved to do the best she possibly could, and graduate at the top of her class.

Ava's life continued to improve, and Corey eventually showed a new interest in her, reminiscent of when they first began a relationship. Corey called her to aske if she would like to watch a movie with him. He explained he wanted to tell her a few things, and she reluctantly accepted his offer. She was not sure why she had accepted, but she felt as if she would be strong and stable enough to make the right decisions, no matter what the situation presented. Corey arrived at her house and rang the doorbell. She answered the door, and found him standing there, looking very similar to the man she had once fallen in love with.

"C'mon in," she said with a smile.

He stepped into the house and closed the door. She showed him around her new home and described the amount of work that had gone into making it livable. He readily displayed reactions of awe, and was clearly impressed, at least that is what he portrayed.

"I hope he pays ya back for all the money you're puttin' into the house," he said, referring to Ava's landlord.

"My rent is the repairs I complete on the house," she responded. "We figure out how much I spend and he prorates it so my rent is covered. He buys the bigger stuff, like siding, but I take care of things like ceiling fans and give him a copy of the receipts. It's all worked out."

"So what movie ya wana watch?" Corey asked as he showed her the movies he had brought with him.

"Whatever you want to watch is fine with me," she responded.

Corey chose a movie and Ava took her normal seat at the left end of the couch. After starting the movie, he chose the seat on the couch right next to her. He reached out for her hand and held it in his. Old feelings of love began to well inside Ava's heart as she remembered how loving he once was. She was confused about the feelings that seemed to rise inside her heart, having never felt the conflict of denying a perceived acceptance. She had always felt she needed to cling to anyone who would love her, but now she felt something completely different. She knew she no longer needed to subject herself to anything that may prove to be destructive, and she chose to protect herself from letting the familiar feelings control her heart and mind. When the movie ended, Corey stopped it and put the disc back in its case.

"Good movie," he said with enthusiasm.

"Yeah," she agreed, barely remembering any of it. Her mind had been running a million miles a minute, and she had not been able to pay very close attention to the television screen.

Corey looked as if he had something meaningful to say, and Ava decided to ask him about it.

"Ya look like ya got somethin' to say," she said evenly.

"Well," he began, "I do. I miss you. I miss ya being in my house. I miss how ya used to fold my laundry. I just miss ya."

Ava nodded her head slightly to acknowledge his declaration. She was unable to respond, however, as her mind continued to race.

"I want ya back," he continued, his confidence building with each word he spoke.

Ava remained silent as he continued.

"I'm not sayin' we'll be married in a year, but we'll definitely be engaged within a year," he professed. "I'm not real sure when we'll have kids either, but that's on the list too."

She could not believe her ears. He was finally saying aloud, the words she had longed to hear, for what seemed like forever. The dream she once held so highly in her heart was finally coming true. It was surreal. He missed her and loved her. She was utterly stunned.

After a few minutes, her mind came back to reality and she realized Corey was looking at her, awaiting an answer. Blinking her eyes to clear her mind, she raised her eyes to meet his enthusiastic gaze, as she thought about his promises. She had heard promises similar to these from him before. She rose from her seat on the couch and reached for the pack of cigarettes on the coffee table in front of her. Lighting one, she picked up the heavy, glass ashtray and stepped toward the love seat. After sitting down on the floor in front of the love seat, and placing the ashtray on the floor next to her, she thoughtfully looked at Corey as he eagerly awaited her response.

"Why would I put myself back in that situation?" she said soberly, posing the question not only to him, but out loud to herself as well.

He was clearly shocked at her words and began to look very uncomfortable.

"I know I fucked up, Ava," he said pleadingly. "Now I know what I had when I had you."

She looked down at her cigarette, watching the greyish-white smoke curl from the lit end, as she rolled it between her fingers. She had always liked the way the smoke would rise from the end of a lit cigarette, seemingly free from any type of bonds or barriers. Returning her gaze to Corey, she spoke again.

"Ya promised all of that stuff before, Corey," she began. "What's to say ya won't go back on it again?"

He looked down at his hands as they nervously fumbled with the movie case he still held.

"I won't back out this time," he promised, with a determined look on his face.

She sat silently as she contemplated his promises. He had no idea what she would decide, and the suspense was killing him. After what seemed like an eternity, she decided to speak once again.

"I don't believe you," she said matter-of-factly as she raised her gaze once again to meet his. "I refuse to put myself back into that situation again."

Corey's eyes immediately welled up with tears, as he realized she would not be as easily swayed as she had been before.

"Please, Ava," he said, his voice thick with sadness. "I miss you."

"I'm sorry, Corey," she said. "I'm just not willing to risk my heart again with you."

She could see in his face, he wanted to keep trying to talk her into what he wanted her to do, but he chose not to. She knew, no matter what he said, she no longer loved him and she would be able to withstand his charms. Ultimately, Corey realized it too, and knew he had lost her forever. Tears streamed down his face as he collected his movies and made his way to the door. Ava remained seated on the floor, knowing if she offered any kind of sympathy, he would likely take it as an invitation to keep trying. She did not want to make him feel the way he had made her feel, though she knew he deserved the experience. He turned to look at her as he walked through the kitchen doorway. His eyes were apologetic and his face was soft and fragile. He said nothing and turned to leave. She let him walk out the door without a word, and once he had driven away from the house, she reflected on the situation. She felt as if she had overcome another very large obstacle in her life at that point, having the strength to turn away from something she had once wanted so desperately, completely aware it would likely have proven to be destructive to her.

Though Corey tried a few more times to reconnect with Ava by calling her, she had moved away from the empty promises she once held on to so tightly, and made that clear to him. It had become even clearer to her that, even when people say they love you, they are still interested only in what will benefit them. She finally felt free to pursue her own aspirations, without the intrusive impediments of men, she had grown so accustomed to. At one time in her life, she feared being alone, but that fear had disappeared, somewhere along the way. She enjoyed living alone in the small house she now called her home. Ironically, she had spent her life trying to find a place where she felt she belonged, attached to another person, but finally realized she needed to feel as if she belonged somewhere on her own before she could even hope to find the unconditional love which had so far evaded her.

She quickly grew accustomed to the routine of her new life, working full time at the dealership, as well as part time at the bar. She stayed true to her decision to live on her own for a while, though several men asked her out, each of whom she graciously rejected. She knew she needed to give herself time to regroup, and understand what she needed in life, before she should pursue any type of romantic relationship with anyone.

So much of the work of settling in had already been completed on the small house, making it livable, and even comfortable for her. It was cozy and reflected her personality, throughout each and every room. She had settled in well, but needed to pick up some items to maintain her now clean and organized home. As the sun began to creep across the western sky, Ava pulled out of the driveway of the dealership, her vehicle headed toward Ropschon. The early evening was warm, and she enjoyed the relaxing awareness she did not have to work again until the following Tuesday. Having the weekend away from bartending, she had made plans to get the final details of her home in place. As she drove toward the only department store in Ropschon, she reviewed the items she needed, and imagined how she might spend her free time once she had finished everything. Her thoughts helped the short drive seem even shorter, and before she knew it, she had arrived at the store. As she drove slowly into the large parking lot, looking for a space somewhat close to the entrance, she noticed a black motorcycle parked next to the main entrance. Of course, she had always loved motorcycles, and even more so since she had learned to ride on her own.

She wheeled her vehicle into a parking space and shifted into park. After collecting her purse and keys, she locked the vehicle, and began to make her way to the entrance of the store. She noticed a man beside the motorcycle, but paid little attention as she continued the short walk across the parking lot.

"Hi!" She heard the man say happily.

Ava instantly recognized the man's voice, and slowed her pace as she directed her attention to him.

"Well hey!" She replied, in a jovial tone.

It was Charlie, the maintenance man from the factory, who had helped to collect the photos Mark had so cruelly scattered to shame her. She had only seen him a few times since she had decided to leave the factory, and had no idea where his life had taken him.

"What are you up to?" He asked, still noticeably happy to see her.

"Not much," she replied. "Just workin' a lot. Have to get some stuff for my house in Carlisle, so thought I'd stop before I left town."

Charlie nodded his head, still smiling at her. "Carlisle?" He said, unaware she had moved.

"Yeah," she said, "I moved into a house there about a month ago."

"Last I knew you were living in Wheaton," he said with an inquisitive tone.

"Yeah, I was," she replied. "That all came to an end and I moved out. Now I'm livin' alone and lovin' it."

Again, Charlie nodded his head with interest. He had seen Ava at the dealership a few times, but had only said hi, though he had wanted to talk to her more. He knew she had been living with Corey, but had no idea the relationship had dissolved, and she had moved out.

"Well, I better keep movin'," she said. "Wana get home and get a few things done."

"Yep," he responded. "See ya later."

She turned and walked into the store, and Charlie turned his attention back to the task he had abandoned while he spoke with her. He finished closing up the saddlebag on his motorcycle, swung his leg over the seat, and nudged the kickstand so it would spring up and out of the way. The motorcycle roared to life, as he continued looking at the entrance of the store, a small part of him wishing Ava would come back out and talk to him more. He twisted the throttle, and the bike began to creep forward as he settled into the seat, and steered it toward the parking lot exit.

As the heavy motorcycle drifted effortlessly onto the four-lane highway, Charlie let his mind return to the plans he had made with some friends for that night. He was on his way to Leahwill, a mid-sized city, only about thirty miles west of Ropschon. His friends had made arrangements for him to meet a friend of theirs, in hopes he would be able to find companionship with her, since he had been single for so long. His first marriage had ended badly, and the day he had arrived home from work to an empty house, was almost more than he could bear. As the tires of the motorcycle seemed to devour the asphalt beneath them, his mind drifted back to Ava, and the sort conversation the two of them had just had. He was already about half of the way to Leahwill, when he let off of the throttle and steered the bike toward the inside lane, in order to turn onto a gravel U-turn access way. He felt an overwhelming impulse to return to Ropschon, to see if she was still at the store. As he navigated the motorcycle back onto the highway, this time in the opposite direction, he began to feel an undeniable excitement in his heart.

He had always felt a flutter of excitement any time he spoke with Ava, ever since he had met her in the factory, the first time he was called to repair her welder. His mind automatically drifted to a memory of one instance, when Ava's welder had needed maintenance, and he had been called for the task. She had already gone for the day, but when he arrived to repair the machine, he had found a small note attached to the side of the housing unit. It simply read:

"Charlie, Thank you for fixing my welder! If you have any questions, give me a call. Ava. J"

She had included a smiley face beside her name, and her phone number followed. When he found the note, he had felt the same tingly flutter in his heart he always felt when he was around her. He had entered her phone number in his cell phone and tucked the note carefully into his toolbox. Of course, he had no questions about the machine and was able to fix it rather quickly, with no need to contact her. He had wished, however, he would have needed to call her just so he could talk to her.

Though he had not spent a great deal of time talking with Ava directly, he had heard a great deal about her from the other workers in the factory, and knew she struggled with many things. He knew her life had been full of pain and sadness, though he knew only sparse details, and just wanted to get close to her to save her from it all. As his mind drifted back to the present moment, he slowed the motorcycle, and merged onto the exit that would lead him back to the parking lot where he had just talked to her a short time before. It occurred to him, as he slowed to a stop before turning onto the next street, he did not know exactly what had made him turned around. He suddenly felt nervous, as if he were a school boy, about to ask a girl out for the first time. He truly felt as if God were guiding him back to the store to talk to Ava, even though he had no idea what the outcome would be. From somewhere in his heart, he felt irrefutably compelled to talk to her again, as if it were his one and only chance. His heart began to beat rapidly with joyful anticipation, as he once again slowed the motorcycle to make the turn back into the parking lot. Immediately, he spotted her vehicle, and his excitement continuing to mount. Parking next to her truck, he turned the motorcycle's engine off, and decided to simply wait for her to come out of the store.

Ava made her way around the store, selecting the items she needed, and eventually made her way to the checkouts. She had already spent about thirty minutes in the store, and wanted to get home, so she could get some things done around the house. As she collected the few bags full of the items she had just purchased, she was glad to be finished shopping, and on her way out the door. She stepped into the vestibule of the store, and peered through the outermost set of doors, toward her vehicle. Immediately, she saw Charlie parked next to her truck, sitting on his motorcycle.

"If he askes me out, I'm just guna tell him no," she thought to herself with determination.

With everything that had happened with Corey, as well as the other disheveled relationships she had been in, she just wanted to be on her own for a while. Charlie had asked her out several years ago, but she had turned him down, since at the time she was involved with Leo. As she exited the outer door of the store, she briefly recalled the memory of when Charlie had asked her out. He had invited her to one of the local bars, stating he had needed to tell her something, and she had hesitantly agreed to meet him. During the short conversation between them, the only thoughts in her mind involved Charlie's size, and her relationship with Leo. He had asked if he could take her out for dinner, but she had declined the invitation, citing her relationship with Leo. Charlie was gracious about the rejection, completely respecting her ambition to be faithful to her boyfriend. He did attempt to discredit Leo, to a slight degree, but immediately recognized his efforts were futile. She had been relieved she was able to cite her relationship as a reason for declining the dinner date, given she would have otherwise likely accepted the invitation, even though she was secretly afraid of him. Of course, she had no rational reason to be afraid of him, but her past had conditioned her to be afraid of all men. Not only was Charlie a man, he was also over six feet tall, and build quite solidly. Even though she had always found him to be very handsome, his physique sparked fear in her heart, as she was completely aware of how badly he could physically hurt her if he chose to do so. What Ava did not realize was, Charlie was a man unlike any other she had ever known.

As she approached her vehicle, she acknowledged Charlie.

"Hello again," she said with a slight chuckle.

"Hey," he responded, clearly nervous about something.

She looked at him with an inquisitive expression, clearly confused about why he was next to her vehicle.

"What are you still doin' here?" She asked.

"I made it to Hulset then turned around," he confessed sheepishly. "I wanted to talk to you about something."

"Okay," she said, somewhat awkwardly, "what's up?"

Charlie proceeded with questions regarding Ava and

Corey's relationship, her plans for herself, and how she was doing in general. She enjoyed the conversation, but still sensed that something was waiting to surface. After visiting for about ten minutes, Charlie had finally worked up the courage to ask the question he feared the answer to.

"Are you ever guna go out with me?" He blurted, surprising himself with the bluntness of the question, and immediately feeling a pang of embarrassment.

"Not if you don't ask," she replied without thinking.

Immediately, she regretted her response, wondering where her conviction to be on her own had suddenly gone. She had not had any trouble declining date and relationship invitations from the other men who had recently approached her, but as soon as Charlie asked his first question, it was as if she had not ever been hurt before.

"Ok then," he said with a surprised smile. "Will you go out on a date with me?"

"Sure," she said, returning a sweet smile. "Gimme a call sometime."

"Do you still have the same number?" He inquired excitedly.

"Yep," she replied. "I've had the same number since I first got a cell phone in 1995."

He immediately, and a little clumsily, took out his phone and found her name. He read the number he had to her and she confirmed it was correct.

"Okay!" He said, clearly very excited. "I'll call you!"

"Sounds good," she said. "I need to get goin'. I'll talk to ya later."

"Okay, yup," he responded as he flipped the kickstand of the motorcycle up.

She stepped past him and opened the door of her vehicle. After putting all of her purchases in the back seat, she got in and pulled the door closed. Looking out the window, she saw Charlie raise his hand in a wave, as he prepared to drive away. She returned the wave and turned the key in the ignition. Charlie gracefully steered the motorcycle toward the exit of the parking lot, and in a few seconds, disappeared out of her view. She tilted her head back against the headrest of her seat, closed her eyes, and let out a confused and apprehensive sigh. After only a few seconds, she reached for her cigarette pack and lit one, then shifted the truck into drive and creeped forward. Her mind was reeling.

"What the hell are you thinking?" She asked herself out loud. "You don't want to date anyone, remember? This guy could fuckin' break you in half if he decides to beat you!" She continued, still scolding herself aloud for not following to her own directives.

Everything about the impending date made her feel uneasy, but at the same time energized and hopeful. She felt weak for accepting the date, as if somehow she knew she would not be strong enough to make it on her own. At the same time, she also felt a tinge of hope, as if something beyond herself was guiding the events which had just taken place. Everything in her mind screamed at her to protect herself, and preserve her new-found safety, away from anyone who could hurt her. Her own rationale seemed to be battling with something far beyond her own understanding, as it relentlessly convinced her to avoid changing her mind about the date. As she made her way to the four-lane highway, she shook her head slightly, and felt as if she were a failure who had just made a mistake. Various trivial thoughts filled her mind as she drove to Carlisle, regularly returning to the interaction she had with Charlie. Once she had closed up the garage and gotten in the house, she locked the door, and proceeded with her planned tasks. After finishing everything, she got comfortable on the couch, and enjoyed some relaxation time watching television. As time passed, she finally fell asleep, with no worries about having to be awake at any certain time the next day. Little did she know, she would be awakened a short time later, to a call that would proved to be a turning point in her life.

He could not believe it! She said yes! Charlie felt so much excitement and anticipation about the date he would be making with Ava. He felt as if he were on top of the world, as he drove away from where he had been parked, next to her truck. The ride to Leahwill seemed to take place in the blink of an eye and before he knew it, he had arrived at the park where his friends, Beth and Wesley, had invited him to meet them. He parked the motorcycle in one of the spaces designated for the festivities taking place and looked impatiently around for his friends. As he searched the crowd of people bustling about their own activities, he felt as if he were not really there, as if he were nowhere. His mind spun and he felt happier than he had in a very long time. The plans to call Ava to set up a date were all he could think of, and as he sat on the motorcycle looking for his friends, he was oblivious to everything around him. His half-hearted search for familiar faces was proving to be difficult, but he did not care. All he could concentrate on was Ava. Finally, he heard his name, and turned toward the sound of the familiar voice.

"Charlie!" Beth called.

Immediately, he spotted Beth standing next to Wesley, and waved to them. Dismounting the motorcycle, he quickly secured his belongings and made his way to where they stood.

"Didn't know if you were guna make it, buddy!" Wesley joked, as he shook Charlie's hand with a smile.

"Yeah," Charlie replied, "I got held up talking to this woman I've been wanting to go out with for a long time."

Beth's smile remained on her face a she quickly glanced toward her friend, Diane, who stood next to Wesley. Diane was the woman to whom Beth and Wesley wanted to introduce Charlie. Nervously, Diane stepped forward, extending her hand, in a greeting to Charlie.

"I'm Diane," she said with a sweet smile.

"Oh, hi," he replied, clearly absent from the introduction. He politely shook her hand, then resumed his conversation with Wesley.

"I wasn't guna ask her out but I thought it might be my only chance so, once I got to Hulset, I turned around and went back to Ropschon to talk to her!" Charlie continued excitedly.

"Well!" Wesley said with a grin. "I'm glad ya got to talk to her! When ya goin' out?"

"I'm guna call her." He replied. "We haven't made any plans yet."

"That is wonderful," Beth said, with a genuine smile still on her face.

Beth and Wesley were ultimately concerned only with Charlie's happiness, and it really didn't matter to them if he had found someone on his own, or if he wanted to get to know Diane. Either way, they were happy to see him so excited and cheerful. As the evening wore on, the foursome enjoyed the various happenings of the festival, conversing and relaxing together. Charlie paid virtually no attention to Diane, only able to speak of Ava, and other general things with Wesley and Beth. Though it seemed to everyone he was really enjoying himself at the festival, in reality Charlie was unconscious to virtually everything, and everyone around him. He did not want to be spending time with his friends, though he cared for them very much, he only wanted to be with Ava.

The time finally came for the group to go their separate ways and Charlie was glad for it. He just wanted to go home and call Ava to set up their date. He bid farewell to Beth, Wesley, and Diane then swiftly made his way toward his motorcycle. Climbing onto the bike, he fired the engine, and was quickly on his way. The ride home was a blur, and he could not really recall anything from the miles he had traveled. Reaching Hulset once again, he pulled the bike into the small truck stop, unable to wait any longer before he made the call. After parking the motorcycle, he pulled his phone from his pocket, and found her number. As the numbers appeared on the screen, he suddenly realized how nervous he was. He was terrified to press the call button, imagining Ava would have changed her mind before he could contact her. He had made no plans regarding the date, believing it would be best for her to choose where they would go, and when they could get together. He was afraid she would only begin to get to know him before she decided she did not like him. Though these fears were significant in his mind, his ultimate fear rested in the age difference between the two of them. Ava was only thirty-two and he would be turning fifty-three in about another month. This detail made him very nervous, unaware of what she would think of his age, or if she would even be interested in developing a relationship. Abruptly shoving his thoughts and fears to the back of his mind he pressed the call button.

"Hello?" Ava answered in a groggy voice.

"Hi!" He said excitedly.

"Hi," she replied, clearly trying to find her way out of sleep.

"Did I wake you up?" He asked apologetically.

"Yeah," she said, "but it's okay. I fell asleep on the couch."

"I was wondering if ya had any ideas about when and where ya wana get together?" He inquired.

"Um," she stumbled, "we could meet in Wayfield at that little restaurant on Main Street."

"Okay," he answered, immediately familiar with the place. "When?"

"Monday?" She asked sleepily.

"I have to go to Warford Monday," he replied as his hopes began to waver.

"Oh, okay," she said, now sounding a little wider awake. "Do ya wana wait 'til next weekend, or…"

"I'd rather do it before I go," he said, trying hard not to sound demanding.

"Okay," she said, "how about tomorrow then? I need to be in bed kinda early for work on Tuesday, but we could meet in the afternoon if ya want."

"Okay," he said, regaining all of the excitement he had felt earlier. "How 'bout two o'clock?"

"Sure," she agreed. "Sounds good. I'll meet you on Main in Wayfield at two tomorrow."

"Sounds good," he said happily. "See ya then!"

"Okay," she said. "Talk to ya tomorrow."

"Yup, bye," he said, and ended the call.

Charlie was elated. Finally, a definitive plan had been set. He put his phone in his pocket and started the motorcycle. Making his way back to the highway, he followed it until he came to his exit, where he turned onto the road that would lead him to his house. He could not believe he had finally made a date with Ava! His elation kept him from recalling anything from the rest of the ride home, and he was barely able to sleep, once he had retired to bed. His mind raced, thinking of things that might go well, things that may go wrong, and everything in between. Finally sleep overtook him, and he drifted off, happily and peacefully. Ava was also able to fall back to sleep quickly, feeling relaxed, with no thoughts of fear whatsoever.

As the early morning sun crept across the sky, Ava remained asleep, resting better than she had in a long time. The television had been on all night, but it had not interrupted her restful slumber. The sunlight leaked through the blinds of the kitchen window, casting a pool of brilliant illumination upon the floor, seemingly deep enough to lose one's self in. The light seemed to infect the entire house, leaving no room for shadows, and touching Ava warmly. Her eyes fluttered as she awoke, and she stretched and yawned. As her eyes focused, she felt the need to rise, unable to deny nature's call. As she walked through the kitchen, on her way back to the living room, she stopped at the refrigerator to get a soda. Cracking the top on the can, she returned to the couch and sat back down, as she lit a cigarette and tried to find her thoughts.

"What time is it?" She thought to herself as she looked at the clock on the wall.

It was only ten, so she picked up the remote, and flipped through the channels. After only about an hour, she decided to get up and shower to ready herself for the date she had made with Charlie. After going through her routine, she climbed the stairs to her bedroom, to find something to wear. After choosing a light outfit, she found a pair of sandals, and went back downstairs. Starting a load of laundry, she was confident she would be able to finish it before she needed to leave the house, in order to make it Wayfield on time. As she closed the lid of the washing machine, her phone rang, so she went to answer it. The call was from the school in which she had decided to attend to earn her psychology degree, the admissions counselor checking in to see if she had any questions, or needed anything. She was scheduled to start classes in September, only about a month away. The conversation wafted through various topics, including online classroom navigation, ordering books, and preparing for the new experience. The call was ended after some time, and she felt completely ready to begin her education, her heart full of excitement, trepidation, and joyful anticipation all at once. Things really seemed to be moving in a positive direction for her and she felt so confident and alive. She decided to get on her computer, looking at the school's website, and familiarizing herself with the various aspects within. Time seemed to slip away quickly, and before she knew it, it was time to leave for Wayfield.

After making the twelve mile drive to Wayfield, it was clear not much was happening in the town. It was Sunday afternoon, and she had expected the small restaurant to be open, but it looked as if it were abandoned. She pulled her truck into one of the parallel parking spaces in front of the building, and in only a few seconds, saw Charlie's car turn from a side street toward her. He stopped in the middle of the deserted street, with his window down, to talk to her.

"It's closed," he said, offering an apologetic smile. "Is there anywhere else ya wana go?"

Ava thought for a moment, and decided to suggest a sports bar back in Carlisle.

"How about The Spur in Carlisle?" She suggested.

"Is that the one on the north side of town?" He asked, attempting to pinpoint the location.

"Yeah," she answered. "You can just follow me if ya want."

"Okay," he said happily. "Lead the way!"

She pulled out of the parking space, and headed back toward Carlisle, the same way she had just come. Charlie had simply made a U-turn in the middle of Main Street, and was directly behind her within seconds. As the miles disappeared under her wheels, she began to wonder about Charlie, and whether or not the rumors she had heard about him were true. At the factory, she had heard he had beat his ex-wife, prompting her to leave him. She had also heard he was into drugs, something she had decided she would never tolerate again, after Alex. From somewhere deep within her heart, she decided to simply be direct, and ask him about the rumors, once they had reached The Spur. She then realized he did not yet know where she lived, and she thought it best to keep it that way.

Making her way through the small town, she finally reached the gravel driveway of The Spur. Slowing down, she turned the truck into the driveway, and found a parking space. There were several vehicles in the parking lot, given it was a Sunday afternoon, and it was a sports bar. She wished she had suggested it to begin with, instead of wasting Charlie's time finding the restaurant was closed. He parked next to her, and they both exited their vehicles. Walking to the side entrance, he opened the door for her, something she had not been used to. Offering a polite smile, she stepped past him, and led the way to a table in the corner of the bar. Several people greeted her happily, as many of them played pool on the same leagues she did, and they all knew her. She felt welcome there, and did not find herself at all uncomfortable. She took the seat against the wall, her preferred position in any public place, and Charlie sat across from her.

"Do you want anything?" He asked sweetly.

"Maybe just a sweet tea," she answered graciously.

He immediately rose from his chair and made his way to

the bar. She studied him as he walked, and found herself quite physically attracted to him. He was tall, slender, and muscular and carried himself with a commanding yet respectful air. His head was shaved but he wore a dark, neatly trimmed mustache and beard style goatee. She had always loved the way that style of goatee looked on a man, at it was clearly one of the things that physically attracted her to him. Continuing to watch him, as he ordered their drinks and interacted with a few people, she tried to build up the courage to ask him about the rumors once he returned to the table. Only a few minutes later, he had returned, setting her tea in front of her carefully. He had ordered a sweet tea for himself as well, thinking it a happy coincidence they both liked tea.

"So," Ava began. "How was your night?"

"Good," he answered. "Went to Leahwill to hang out with some friends."

She smiled, feeling an awkward pause building.

"I have to be honest," she blurted. "I really need to ask you a few things."

Charlie looked inquisitive, clearly caught off guard by her statement.

"Okay," he said with a smile, "what do you want to know?"

"I heard some things about you, and I just wanted to ask if they were true," she said.

"Okay," he said again, looking down at his glass of tea, and wondering if this would be the way she would tell him she wasn't interested.

"I heard you beat your ex-wife and that's why she left you," she began. "Is that true?"

Charlie shook his head slightly, giving Ava a glimpse of an inner sadness she had never seen from a man.

"No," he answered somberly. "That is the furthest thing from the truth."

She waited before speaking again, sensing he had more to say.

"I loved my wife very much," he began. "But she didn't love me, I guess. I came home from work one night to find an empty house. The kids were gone and so was she. I had never raised a hand to her. My dad always taught me to never hit a woman, no matter what, and I never have."

She noticed a change in his face, the sadness in his eyes immediately telling her his words were true. The remanence of the pain he had felt the day he walked into the empty house, seemed to quickly spread throughout his entire body, as if he were feeling it all over again. She seemed to feel a connection with him in that moment, as if he may understand her pain, at least to some degree.

"I also heard you're into drugs," she continued, simply wanted to get through her inquiries.

He chuckled slightly, seemingly understanding why such a rumor may have made its way to her.

"Also not true," he said. "Before my wife left, I had loaned a tractor to a neighbor. It broke down and I had been over there a few times to fix it. They got busted for drugs and, since I had been there off and on, the cops thought I was involved."

Again, Ava felt as if his explanation was completely true, as she watched the slight indications of his eyes, face, and body language.

"Anything else?" He asked as he kindly met her gaze.

"No," she answered sorrowfully. "That's all I heard. I just wanted to ask *you* about it instead of assuming the rumors were true."

"I'm glad ya did," he said. "People say things and other people add to it. It gets outa hand and people can get hurt in the process."

She nodded in response, understanding all too well how

rumors can grow with no basis in reality. She felt Charlie had told her the truth regarding the questions she had posed. She had asked questions such as these, of others in the past, deciding the degree of honesty in her own mind based on her limited life experiences. She had always wanted everyone to be honest and had naïvely accepted the lies as truth. This time, however, it seemed something on another level was confirming Charlie's honesty, something far beyond her own understanding. As the afternoon date progressed, the two of them conversed, laughed, and enjoyed each others' company. Though she liked him very much, and seemed to trust him quickly, the turmoil she had endured at the hands of those in her past kept her from opening herself completely to him. She still did not want to share the location of her home with him, though that would prove to change in less than a week, as she came to understand the love that already existed in his heart for her.

As the days passed, Charlie and Ava became closer to one another, and the relationship flourished. Though she still struggled with many things, the new relationship seemed to promise a world she had never experienced. He seemed to be supportive of whatever she aspired to do and wanted to be a part of everything in her life. He spent every free moment with her and they quickly began to talk about a possible future together. He had always felt something remarkable in his heart, each time he was with her, even before their first date. It was different for him than it had been with any other woman, as if God himself were fostering the relationship. It was different for Ava too. In every relationship before, she had always felt the typical initial feelings of beginning a relationship. She felt those feelings with Charlie also, however, she felt other things that had never before been present. She realized this reality immediately, and given the mystery of the unfamiliar aspects, the allure was even stronger for her.

Ava moved in with Charlie after only three months of dating, they were engaged on Christmas Eve of 2009, and married in October of 2010. The couple was destined for a life long love, one full of happiness, mystery, surprises, sadness, faith, and growth. But that… is another story.

Chapter Seventeen

A note from Ava...

Though my life is far from perfect, I feel that I am blessed, none the less. I am just as much of a real person as anyone else and prone to make mistakes. Though I strive to make the right choices, I am human, and that is an endeavor I will not always succeed in. Ultimately, however, I know that I am doing the best I can and I am proud to be me. No longer am I a prisoner of the maze within my mind. No longer do I think about ending my own life. I look to the future and welcome whatever it brings.

No matter who you are, no matter what you have been through, <u>you do not have to be a product of your past</u>. Even though life is hard and no one is perfect, life <u>is</u> worth living, and <u>everyone</u> is valuable. Do not let suicide win. The maze in my mind still exists. There is a maze in the mind of every person and all our mazes are different. My maze is now lighted by self worth, confidence, optimism, and faith – this combination of lighting elements took time *to gather, and continue to take ambition to fuel. Even though the lights in my maze still dim from time to time, sometimes considerably, the multiple elements burn individually so it is no longer pitch black. For at least one of the flames are always there to lead the way, helping me find the momentum to relight any that may have been extinguished, as I go through life and find my way through my once pitch black maze. Even if your lights are different from mine, find them, light them, and keep them burning. Help me to light the beacons around the world that will help others understand <u>there is always hope</u>.*

So many things have been revealed about my life in this book. I have to apologize for ending the story where I did, but if I had continued, it would have never ended. I was taught in a creative writing class, in the sixth grade, that good writers tend to leave their readers hanging, wanting more. Hopefully, I have done that. Another book is already in the works. It will be another based on a true story novel. I hope your interest endures.

If you have stuck with the story, and read it all the way through, thank you. At this point, I will reveal to you that I, Charlotte Roberts, am Ava. I'll also reveal another truth. Charlotte Roberts is a pseudo name I chose to hide my true identity, at least while my mother is alive. I did not write this book in an attempt to seek revenge on her, or anyone else, which is why all of the names of people and places are fictional.

Eventually, I will reveal to the entire world, my true identity. If you happen to be one of the many individuals who already know my true identity, let's keep it a secret for a while, okay? ☺

Writing this manuscript has proven to be a life changing experience for me on so many different levels. First, it has helped me to face many things I had so far unconsciously avoided. Many of the things within these pages were recalled during the process of writing, and had to be emotionally, as well as intellectually worked out. There were many instances where I simply had to walk away from the creation of the story, in order to regain my own perspective, and emotional stability. Recalling all of the struggles, pain, turmoil, and upset was, at times, more than I could handle. Those delays, along with needing to concentrate on school, were the two most significant delays in the completion of the manuscript. Secondly, revealing the disturbing details of my life, even under a veil of pseudo identity, has been very liberating. It has helped me to come to terms with the things in my life that have scarred me, and helped me to find new meaning in life, which is that I ultimately exist to help others. That's the reason *we all* exist.

Charlie and I are still happily married, and in a few months, we will be celebrating our seventh wedding anniversary. I truly believe, with everything I am, that it was part of God's plan for us to be together. I say that, not because life with him has been without struggles, but because he has proven he loves me unconditionally. We've already been through some very difficult things together, and no matter what has happened, he has never given up on me. He's taught me so many things about life, love, faith, and understanding. I have been introduced, through Charlie, to a new reality in which I am not subjected to abuse and cruelty. Some of the difficulties we have been through involve health problems, relationship doubts, and others who seek to destroy a love they do not understand. The storms have come and gone, and I'm quite sure there will be more, but we have continued to grow together and love each other no matter what has transpired. One of the most truthful adages in existence comes from an unknown source, but speaks volumes:

"A perfect marriage is just two, imperfect people refusing to give up on one another" - Unknown

Indeed. Throughout the challenges Charlie and I have faced, we have faced them together, and prevailed. I am not at all professing that you can not make it in life unless you find your true love. On the contrary. What I am attempting to convey is that, regardless of where you come from, where you are in your life, or whether or not you are in a relationship, you are absolutely capable of growing and becoming a better person for yourself and those you love. You have only to be willing.

For those of you wondering about the relationships between myself and my family members, as well as some of the other significant characters in the book, I offer elucidation. I still have not met my father, Lars, though I attempted contact by letter about a year ago. After no response, I am left to wonder if he is even still alive. As mentioned earlier, my mother is still alive. She is now coping with dementia, as well as other health problems, and I do my best to stay in contact with her. I make this effort not because I condone the things she has done in her life, but because I have forgiven her. I have learned that forgiveness is not a gift to be given to those whom have hurt you, but rather, a gift you give to yourself to be free of the painful prison choosing not to forgive creates. To this day, my mother will not admit her wrongs. Though I find it difficult to talk with her after so much pain and sorrow, I will not condemn her, as only God holds the authority to do that. After all, God will not forgive you if you do not forgive others.

I seldom speak with Able, the last time being about three years ago. He has maintained the attitude of superiority toward others and I find I am unable to accept it. This is a struggle I must figure out within myself, as I know I should not be critical toward him and the man he has become. He seems to be doing well for himself, and for that, I am grateful. Lilly and I have become very close and I have come to find she has been one of the most influential people in my life. I have always looked up to her, and I continue to do so, each and every day. She is an amazing, loving, and wonderful person I am so very blessed to call my sister. Emma passed away only four short months ago, having had a massive heart attack. We had also become very close, and I will hold her in my heart forever. She was, and always will be, a very significant part of my life. Though we had our differences at times, she was an extraordinary woman and I am blessed to call her my sister as well.

From what I understand, Alex remarried several years ago and had a child. I see him periodically around Ropschon and I simply look away. Mark remarried several years ago, and passed away in 2011, from a massive heart attack. Upon learning of his death, I felt nothing. Leo is now in a relationship and things seem to be going well for him. He and I, as well as Charlie, are friends and we even get together periodically. No animosity exists and we do what we can to support one another as friends. Corey is also in a relationship, and I wish him the best. I no longer hold any bitterness toward him and I hope he is able to find happiness.

Sophie, Payton, Cheryl, and I have remained the best of friends throughout the years. Cheryl moved to another state a few years ago, but we do our best to stay in contact with one another. Sophie, Payton, and I still play pool together, and have even recruited new friends who will likely remain in our lives as extended family. Sylvia and I are still close, and I consider her the mother I never had. We do our best to meet often and visit, in order to stay current with each other.

Ultimately, I think the most important thing I've learned in life, is that escape from the black maze is not at all what I should have been trying to accomplish. In reality, we all exist in our own black mazes, indicative of life itself. With that metaphor in mind, escape from our black mazes is ultimately the equivalent of suicide. Instead of *escaping* our black mazes, we must *seek to light our paths* with the illumination of experience, faith, love, forgiveness, and an inextinguishable fire inside our hearts to live life to the fullest.

...And so ends the story of Ava's past.

Printed in the United States
By Bookmasters